BAD IDEAS & HORRIBLE PEOPLE
OF OLD OREGON

BAD IDEAS & HORRIBLE PEOPLE
OF OLD OREGON

OFFBEAT OREGON HISTORY VOL. III

By FINN J.D. JOHN

Copyright ©2024 by Finn J.D. John

All rights reserved. However, please note that most stories in this book are edited, revised, and augmented versions of stories that initially ran in the Offbeat Oregon History syndicated newspaper column under a Creative Commons Attribution-Share Alike license. Those earlier versions are still covered under the license, and can be easily found with a Google search.

For information about permission to reproduce selections from this book, write to Ouragan House Publishers, Post Office Box 77, Corvallis, OR 97339, or e-mail permissions@ouragan-house.com.

Hardcover Edition
ISBN: 978-1-63591-131-2

Other edition ISBNs:

Softcover:	978-1-63591-132-9
EPUB E-book:	978-1-63591-133-6
Kindle E-book:	978-1-63591-134-3
PDF:	978-1-63591-138-1

Dust jacket design and cover art
by Natalie Conaway and J.J. Davitt

Ouragan House Publishers
An imprint of
Pulp-Lit Productions
Corvallis, Oregon

http://ouragan-house.com
http://pulp-lit.com

A complimentary copy of the e-book version of this book is included with your purchase, regardless of whether you obtained it new or secondhand. Available formats include PDF and EPUB.
  To obtain it, go to https://ouragan-house.com/131.

TABLE OF CONTENTS.

Part I: Bad Ideas. 1

Blow up a beached whale with dynamite. 3
    #ExplodingWhale   *#SmashedCar*

Start a "free-love" cult in Honduras. 9
    #HarmonialBrotherhood   *#ApplesToOregon*

Start a shooting riot over a Vaudeville actress. 21
    #SusieRobinson   *#GoldRush*

Build a high-speed highway on a scenic beach. 27
    #NestuccaSpit   *#GovernorTomMcCall*

Move your airplane's wings to see what happens. 33
    #FlyingFlivvers   *#TedBarber*

Build a town on beach sand. 39
    #Bayocean   *#WashedAway*

Build a riverboat powered by cows 45
    #HayBurner   *#Sternwheeler*

Open a Disneyland-type park someplace rainy 51
    #Pixieland   *#AmusementPark*

Replace Timberline Lodge with a skyscraper. 59
    #MountHood   *#SkiResort*

Use a city bus as a cable-car gondola 65
    #Skiway   *#AerialTram*

Open an amusement park and make it creepy 69
    #LotusIsle   *#JantzenBeach*

Buy a ten-ton, ill-tempered ex-circus elephant. 75
    #TuskoTheTerrible   #LotusIsle
Let A.C. Edmunds work for your social-justice cause. 81
    #OwnGoalKing   #TemperanceMovement
Try to climb Haystack Rock. 91
    #DeadBabyBirds   #HelicopterRescue
Try to win a labor strike with acts of terrorism. 97
    #PublicRelationsDynamite   #NewspaperStrike
Demolish a historic hotel to build a parking lot. 105
    #PortlandHotel   #MeierAndFrank
Build luxury condos during the Great Depression. 111
    #DelakeRodAndGunClub   #OlympicGoldMedalist
Try to force the U.S. Mint to build in your city. 115
    #TheDallesMint   #GoldRush
Spend millions to make a really bad movie 121
    #TheWayWest   #BoxOfficeBomb
Strip the bride of her U.S. citizenship at the altar. 127
    #EnemyAliens   #FirstWorldWar
Try to exclude Black people from your new state 133
    #RaceExclusion   #LashLaw
Sell milk out of the same cans you slop hogs with. 139
    #PureMilkCrusade   #MilkWasMurder
Introduce super-flammable invasive plants to your town. . 145
    #Bandon   #Gorse
Burgle the county treasurer's office looking for treasure. . 149
    #Dynamite   #Pawnshops
Convict murder suspects on a majority vote. 155
    #Unconstitutional   #SixthAmendment

Try to take a skunk pelt with your bare hands. 161
    #Trapper   #Sprayed

Bring an unexploded bomb home in the glovebox. 167
    #SecondWorldWar   #JapaneseBombing

Trade Celilo Falls for some cheap hydro power. 171
    #ScenicWonder   #DrownedWaterfall

Part II: Horrible People Part One: Shanghaiers. 177

Jim Turk, O.G. shanghaier of old Portland 181
    #ShanghaiMillionaire   #RemittanceMan

Larry Sullivan, godfather of Oregon shanghaiers 185
    #PoliticalOperative   #GoldMineStockSwindler

"Mysterious" Billy Smith, world champion shanghaier . . . 203
    #Prizefighter   #Barfighter

The Jost Brothers, wannabe shanghaiers 213
    #TheLastShanghaiers   #BoardinghouseCommission

Shanghaiers of Astoria 219
    #ManpowerShortage   #TheShanghaiedMinister

L.G. Carpenter, shanghaiing lawyer and land thief 223
    #DariusNorris   #ShanghaiedForHisLand

Bridget Grant, shanghaiing boardinghouse keeper. 229
    #Carroll Beebe   #VisitingRube

"Mr. Smith" and his shanghaiing riverboat party. 233
    #AquillaErnestClark   #StewartHolbrook

The U.S. Supreme Court in 1897. 239
    #AragoFour   #RelegalizedSlavery

Portland's Shanghai Tunnels: Are they real?. 247
    #MichaelJones   #ShanghaiingHoboes

Part III: More Horrible People 255

    Greenberry Smith, homestead-land thief. 257
        #LetitiaCarson   #SoapCreekValley
    M. Ryan, gun-fighting pro-slavery college president. 263
        #ColumbiaCollege   #CivilWar
    W.F. Woodward, vindictive Libary Board member. 269
        #TraitorLibrarian   #FirstWorldWarBonds
    Maj. Gen. Charles H. Martin, fascist ex-governor. 275
        #SupervillainGovernor   #BonnevilleDam
    J.C. Gardiner, entrepreneurial-minded prison warden. 293
        #OregonBoot   #OregonStatePen
    Othniel Charles Marsh, dinosaur-bone hunter 299
        #BoneWars   #ThomasCondon
    W.C. Conner, eugenics enthusiast and chicken fancier. ..305
        #CottageGroveLeader   #BigChicken

Part IV: All of the Above. 315

    Stealing the wreck of the Peter Iredale. 317
        #SalvageClaim   #Shipwreck
    A mugging gone horribly wrong. 323
        #DaltonAndWade   #Murderers
    Jungle Juice, naturally flavored with dead lizards 331
        #JohnTownsend   #LaboratorySpecimens
    Ku Klux Klan: The Multilevel Marketing version. 335
        #KlanInOregon   #GraftAndKorruption
    The plan to forcibly sterilize Oregonians. 349
        #Eugenics   #SpayAndNeuter
    Dumb but deadly train robbers. 357
        #DeAutremontBrothers   #ForensicDetective

A monument honoring a known mass murderer?........369
    #ChineseMassacreCove   #BruceEvans

The scheme for West Coast secession. 375
    #CivilWar   #JosephLane

The inland-whale poachers.......................387
    #StrandedOrca   #Ethelbert

When a newspaper baron burgled a candidate's home. ...391
    #PortlandOregonian   #WillDaly

Roseburg's newspaper editors and their gunfight........397
    #Shootout   #BudThompson

The racists who snubbed Billie Holiday. 403
    #Jumptown   #DudeRanch

Debating school-board issues with dynamite. 407
    #MohawkValley   #PingYangSchool

The slave "owners" who ignored the Civil War. 411
    #OregonTrail   #Ame

The 100-year land grab 417
    #KaNeeTaResort   #McQuinnStrip

The world's dumbest pirates......................421
    #FrenchWest   #SSBuckman

When the "Sex Guru" came to Oregon.................429
    #SheelaSilverman   #BhagwanOsho

PROLOGUE.

"Whew. Boy. That escalated quickly."

— Will Ferrell as Ron Burgundy

This volume, the third in the Offbeat Oregon series and by far the largest so far, has been a long time coming. Initial plans were to release it in the summer of 2021. Now here it is, more than two years later, and what's the excuse for such tardiness?

Pretty simple, really: More and more Bad Ideas kept coming to my attention, clamoring for inclusion in this collection.

Bad Ideas and Horrible People of Old Oregon is a collection of stories from over the years that showcase ... well ... bad ideas and horrible people. It's pretty self-explanatory.

What's not so self-evident is why these two topics go so well together, and why they're so appealing.

In the case of the Bad Ideas, it's probably the same impulse that leads us to sometimes watch America's Funniest Home Videos on ABC, or, for the more jaded viewer, foreign-country dashcam footage on YouTube.

Take, for instance, the most famous Bad Idea in Oregon history — the decision to dispose of the carcass of a beached whale just south of Florence with half a ton of dynamite. (The full story is in the next chapter, starting on Page 3.)

The thing is, most of us have never been in a position to bodge up anything as large as an eight-ton whale, but we have all been in the position that highway engineer George Thornton found himself in on that unseasonably sunny November day: Going forward with a Cunning Plan, having convinced ourselves that it will work, ignoring the increasingly desperate efforts of others to stop us, and then learning the hard way that they were right.

We can relate!

As for Horrible People, we tend to find them interesting for pattern-recognition purposes, so we can be sure and stay well away from anyone like them. Also, when they finally do get their long-delayed comeuppance (as they usually do) it often yields a spectacle that rivals that of any Bad Idea story.

After all, being a Horrible Person is by definition a Bad Idea, right?

We'll be meeting some lulus in this book, and they run the gamut.

Some of them are merely arrogant and misguided, like the progressive activists who pushed for forced sterilization of Oregonians they considered genetically inferior (see Page 349).

Some of them made the decisions to do Horrible People things when their Bad Idea went off the rails, like the DeAutremont brothers murdering all the witnesses after their badly botched train robbery (see Page 357).

And some of them — not many, fortunately, but some — were just straight-up evil people, like Bruce "Blue" Evans, the leader of the gang of horse thieves who murdered 34 Chinese gold miners in Hells Canyon in 1887 (see Page 369).

So, with apologies to the great Bette Davis, fasten your seat belts ... it's going to get bumpy.

PART I:

BAD IDEAS.

"Hold my beer and watch this!"

— Jeff Foxworthy

Sometimes it's hard to believe; but, every truly Bad Idea started out in someone's mind as a brilliant plan.

And in many cases, they really *were* brilliant plans; they just weren't very well thought through, and executed.

For instance, the anonymous naval architect who created the "Hay Burner," the cow-powered riverboat (see Page 45), could have spent a little more time testing his idea to figure out how many cows he'd need to make headway against the Willamette River current. He didn't do that ... Bad Idea.

Likewise, the idea of using off-the-shelf skyline logging equipment to make a cable-car tram service on the cheap (see Page 65) *was* actually kind of brilliant. If only the inventor had spent a little more time thinking about the ride quality ....

And, of course, who among us has not admired the beautiful, fluffy fur on the back of a big skunk? It must have seemed a great idea to Clarence the fur-trapping logger to go ahead and take that pelt with his bare hands (see Page 161). But, of course ...

OK, so that last one was a bit of a stretch. Sometimes Bad Ideas really are bad, through and through — like the Expatriation Act of 1907, under which American women were literally stripped of their citizenship at the altar when they married non-American citizens (see Page 127).

In that last example, of course, there were some certifiably Horrible People involved as well. One of them may even have been President of the United States at the time ....

In this, the first part of Bad Ideas and Horrible People, we'll mostly be focusing on the first half of the title; but, as that last example demonstrates, sometimes Bad Ideas and Horrible People go together like ice-cold milk and an Oreo cookie.

Read on!

THE EXPLODING WHALE.

THE BAD IDEA:
- *Disposing of a dead whale, washed up on the beach near town, by blowing it up with half a ton of dynamite.*

November 12, 1970: It's an unseasonably sunny day on the beach near Florence, and Oregon Highway Department project manager George Thornton is standing near a very large, very dead whale, talking to a TV news crew. He's explaining the department's plan for getting rid of the big, stinky thing.

"Well, I'm confident that it'll work," he remarks, in the mild, competent drawl of a West Coast engineer. "The only thing is, we're not sure just exactly how much explosives it'll take to disintegrate this thing so the scavengers, seagulls and crabs and what-not, can clean it up."

Years later, the reporter, Paul Linnman, remembered this response well.

"As the young producers on our staff today like to say, OH-MY-GOD!" he wrote in his 1996 book, *The Exploding Whale and Other Remarkable Stories from the Evening News*. "The engineer in charge of blowing up something that weighs eight tons doesn't know how much dynamite to use? That should have been my reaction."

But, perhaps baffled by the very incongruity of the response, Linnman simply rolled with it. "Any chance it could be more than a one-day job?" he asked.

"Uh, if there's any large chunks left," said Thornton.

Not to get too far ahead of ourselves here, but . . . there would indeed be some large chunks left.

The morning of November 12 had dawned bright and clear on the Florence beach — clear and stinky. Up on the beach near the town, the rotting carcass of a 45-foot, 16,000-pound whale slumped on the sand. It had lain there for three days, its black surface soaking up the unseasonable winter sunshine, pouring forth putrid gases that oozed out over the beach and nearby sand dunes.

At that time, the beaches in Oregon were the responsibility of the Oregon Highway Department — as most Oregonians will know, it was by getting the beaches declared state highways that Governor Oswald West preserved them for public access, back in 1913. So the chore of disposing of the carcass fell to the highway engineers, for the same reason it would have been their problem if a king-size waterspout had picked the whale up out of the sea "Sharknado"-style and dropped it in the middle of Highway 101.

Whale disposal was not a common problem for highway engineers, of course, so there was no textbook to look it up in. So the engineers spent some time evaluating possible solutions. The carcass could be simply buried in the sand, true; but it was winter, and storms often removed large amounts of sand. The fear was that the carcass would resurface in a month or two, even more putrid than ever. Or, worse, it could work its way up to just a few inches below the surface of the sand, and a strolling beachcomber could fall through into it and drown in liquefied whale guts.

An alternative might have been to drag it up high on the sand dunes and bury it there. But by its third day cooking in the unseasonably warm winter sun, that option was no longer viable. Any attempt to drag the thing anywhere would simply pull it apart.

So, after some conversations with the U.S. Navy, the highway department decided to handle it as it would handle a boulder of similar size: with dynamite.

There was a difference, though. Boulders were big and crunchy; dead whales were soft and, well, blubbery. A couple sticks of dynamite would probably have sufficed to knock a boulder into the ocean. Thornton would have known exactly how much dynamite to use on a boulder. But a dead whale?

And another thing. A boulder, blasted into the sea, would sink. A whale would float along for a day or two and then be delivered back on shore by

BAD IDEAS.

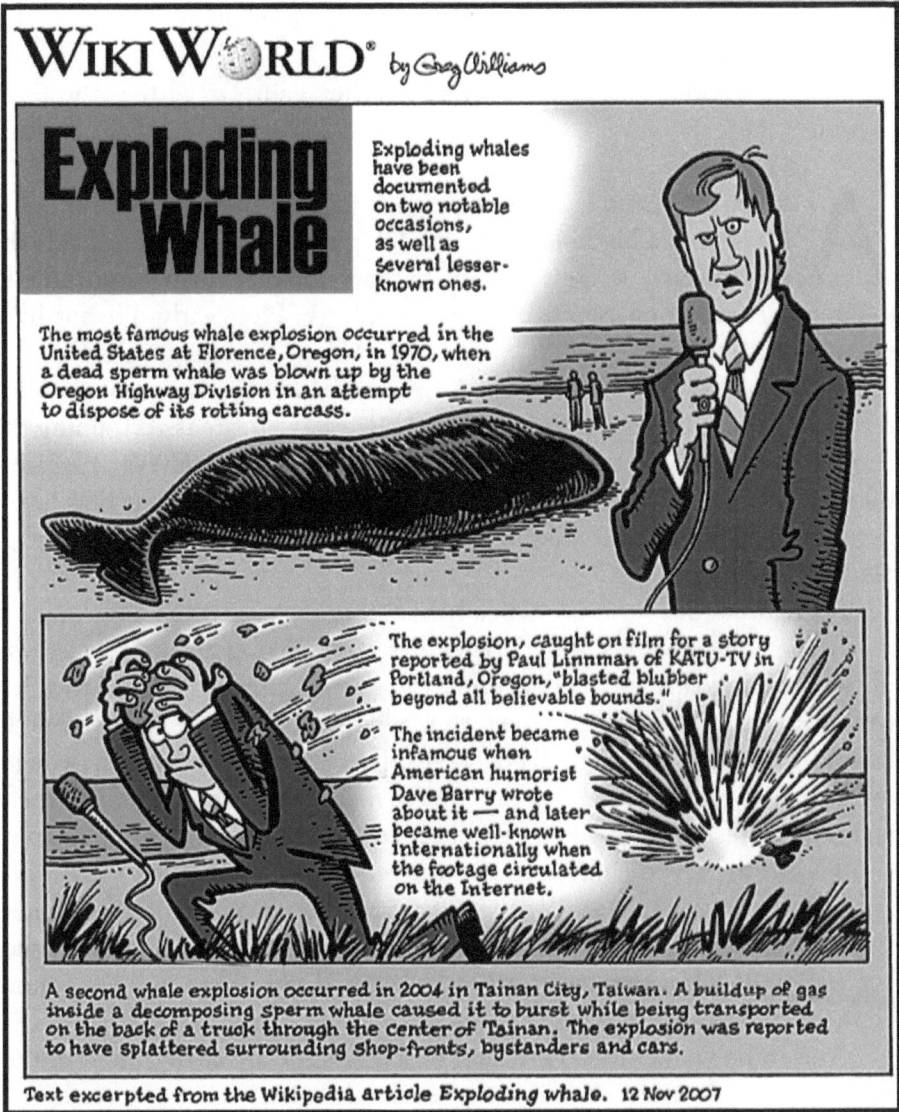

An episode from Greg Williams' Web comic "Wiki World" on the subject of the blowing-up of the Florence whale. (Image: Wikimedia Commons | CC-by-SA)

prevailing currents, stinkier and more unmanageable than ever. No, the whale would have to be disintegrated — torn into ribbons of blubber and bone.

District head highway engineer Dale Allen had left on vacation shortly after the whale appeared on the beach, so the job fell to assistant engineer George Thornton, and there was considerable local pressure to solve the problem fast. Had the whale not smelled quite so bad, Thornton might have spent a little more time in researching his project. But everyone was eager to get the whale off the beach. Thornton didn't see why he shouldn't get after it immediately. He figured if the amount he used wasn't enough to do the job, he could just set another charge.

This would not turn out to be the case. But again, I'm getting ahead of myself.

As Thornton and his crew were packing case after case of DuPont's finest into a big hole in the sand dug under the shoreward side of the carcass, a crew-cutted military-looking man approached, looking the operation over with a practiced eye. He clearly did not like what he was seeing.

This was Walter Uemenhoefer, a Springfield business executive with the Kingsford Charcoal company who had received extensive training in explosives handling in the military during the Second World War. He later told reporter Ben Raymond Lode of *The Springfield News* that he'd been in town on an undercover mission to scout a possible location for a charcoal plant in Florence.

He had no idea how dramatically his cover was about to be blown.

Right now, though, Uemenhoefer was not thinking about his mission. He was trying to explain to Thornton why twenty cases (half a ton) was the wrong amount of dynamite to use for a job like this. What was really needed, he told Thornton, was a small charge, like twenty *sticks*, to push the whale off the beach and into the sea; or a much, much bigger one. Twenty cases, he said, was just enough to make a big mess, and maybe hurt some people.

Thornton blew the know-it-all stranger off.

"The guy says, 'Anyway, I'm gonna have everybody on top of those dunes far away,'" Uemenhoefer told reporter Wayne Freedman of San Francisco TV station KGO in an interview 25 years later. "I says, 'Yeah, and I'm gonna be the furtherest SOB down that way!'"

And so he would. But if Uemenhoefer thought his involvement in the exploding-whale project was over, he was sadly mistaken.

Finally, after moving all the spectators about a quarter-mile down the beach and away from the blast site, Thornton and his crew took cover, pushed the plunger, and filled the winter sky with smoke, sand, and bits of dead whale.

If you search for "exploding whale" on YouTube, you'll easily find the KATU-TV story that reporter Paul Linnman and cameraman Doug Brazil filed that night. It does a spectacular job of showing the whole event: the massive explosion ("like a mighty burst of tomato juice," Linnman recalls in the book); the yells of delight from nearby onlookers turning to quavering shrieks of fear; the tiny specks visible above the crowd growing

BAD IDEAS.

This is South Jetty Beach, near where the whale washed ashore. The beach looks very remote, but downtown Florence is just over the dunes to the right, across the Siuslaw River, close enough to be affected by a "whale of a smell" on the beach here. (Image: F.J.D. John)

larger and resolving themselves into slabs of rotting meat, ranging in size from pinhead-size bits to truck-tire-sized chunks, falling out of the sky, splashing into the ocean, thudding into the sand.

You'll hear possibly the most unintentionally comic part of the whole clip: A woman's motherly voice behind the camera saying, "All right, Fred, you can take your hands out of your ears now . . . here come pieces of . . . oh my—"

You'll also see what happened to Walt Uemenhoefer's brand-new 1971 Oldsmobile Ninety-Eight Regency. Remember Walt? The know-it-all stranger who was trying to tell engineer George Thornton how to do his job? He'd taken himself well away from the explosion before the plunger was pushed, but when he got back to the parking lot afterward, he found an unpleasant surprise awaiting him there. A chunk of flying whale meat the size of a coffee-table top had dropped out of the sky directly onto the roof of his big new luxury car, blowing glass out in all directions and leaving its top flatter than its owner's military haircut.

"My insurance company is not gonna believe this," Uemenhoefer remarked ruefully when he saw what had happened. But he had to chuckle later on, when he remembered the sales promotion that had been going on at Dunham Oldsmobile in Eugene when he'd bought the car just a short time before. It was taglined, "GET A WHALE OF A DEAL ON A NEW OLDSMOBILE."

"Fortunately, no human was hurt as badly as the car," Linnman said in his newscast. "However, everyone on the scene was covered with small particles of dead whale."

Uemenhoefer, by the way, was later the titular "Baron" of The Baron's Den, a gun store and indoor shooting range just south of Eugene in Goshen, visible from Interstate 5 (usually sporting a big blue banner reading "SHOOT A REAL TOMMY GUN"). He died at the age of 84 in the early 2010s, after which The Baron's Den was renamed Northwest Arsenal. You can still rent a Thompson M1928 "Tommy Gun" to shoot on the range there, as well as a large list of other fully-automatic guns ranging from Uzi submachine guns to M-16 rifles.

In the aftermath of this debacle, Thornton was spinning hard — or trying to. "It went just exactly right," he told Larry Bacon of the *Eugene Register-Guard*. "Except the blast funneled a hole in the sand under the whale" (thereby causing some of the whale chunks to be blown back toward the parking lot, he went on to say).

Decades later, Thornton was still defiantly sanguine about the whole affair. Contacted by Linnman in the mid-1990s, he refused to be interviewed on camera, and seemed to feel that news coverage of the event had converted a successful operation into a public-relations disaster. The conversation ended on a sour note when Linnman asked Thornton if he didn't want to tell the public about it — about what had gone wrong that day.

"What do you mean, 'what went wrong?'" he asked Linnman tersely — apparently by way of implying that nothing had.

Sources and Works Cited:
- The Exploding Whale and Other Remarkable Stories from the Evening News, *a book by Paul Linnman published in 2003 by West Winds Press;*
- *Archives of* The Springfield News *and* The Eugene Register-Guard.

THE VEGAN (-ISH) FREE LOVE CULT.

THE BAD IDEA:
- *Sell your fabulously successful business, found a cult, buy a schooner, and sail off to Central America with your fellow cult members to start a commune.*

Among most cherry aficionados, the deep-red Bing is the gold standard. Rich and sweet, almost like chocolate in its intensity of flavor, this cherry utterly dominates the supermarket and is most people's favorite variety.

But few people realize that this variety of cherry would not exist today if a Quaker nurseryman named Henderson Luelling had not brought its progenitors all the way to Oregon, from Iowa, along the old Oregon Trail in 1847.

Other important events sprang from Luelling's Oregon Trail adventure as well. Fellow Quaker John Minthorn's Oregon Land Company, 40 years later, made a specialty of developing orchards to sell — a business plan obviously dependent on the tradition Luelling imported. Had Luelling not made his journey, there likely would have been no Oregon Land Company; and no Oregon Land Company likely would have meant that Minthorn's teenage nephew, Bert Hoover, would not have gotten the early training in sound business practices that was to be so important in his later careers, first as an engineer, then as United States Secretary of Commerce — and then, of course, as President of the United States.

So a lot of good things happened as a result of Luelling's journey, and perhaps you are even now saying to yourself, "Well, self — Henderson doesn't seem to have been a Horrible Person, and none of this sounds like a Bad Idea. Why is he in this book? And what's with this chapter's clickbait-y title, anyway?"

You are correct: Henderson was not a Horrible Person. He was, however, pretty clearly nuts — or maybe "eccentric" is a better word. Excessive eccentricity often leads people to Bad Ideas. Bad Ideas such as leaving the Quaker church, co-founding a "free love" cult, and sneaking off to Central America in the dark of the night to found your own Utopia, leaving your wife and children behind and penniless.

Come to think of it, that's — well, it's not exactly an un-Horrible thing to do, is it?

Henderson Luelling and his brother John were partners in a nursery business in Indiana, starting in the mid-1830s. They were Quakers, and all of them were dedicated abolitionists; in fact, when Henderson moved to Salem, Iowa, a few years later, he built a house with secret rooms in it so that runaway slaves could be hidden there, as part of the Underground Railway.

Luelling must have been extraordinarily zealous, because his abolitionist activities were so vigorous that he was read out of meeting (basically, excommunicated) from the Salem church. This was unusual; Quakers were some of the most dedicated abolitionists. A Quaker getting disfellowshipped for being too serious about abolition would be like Yogi Bear getting eighty-sixed from Jellystone Park for pooping in the woods too often.

In any case, this trouble with the home church may have been part of the reason Luelling decided to head for Oregon.

The Luellings' overland journey was actually a joint venture with another Iowa nurseryman, William Meek. Meek, hoping to found a nursery in the Willamette Valley, also made the journey with trees in his wagon . . . but not nearly as many trees as the Luellings did.

In fact, when the Luellings left Iowa in 1847, they brought with them a specially constructed wagon full of fruit trees — seven hundred of them in all, ranging from tiny slips to four-foot-tall saplings. Essentially this was a wagon full of dirt with trees sticking out of the top, looking like a giant Chia Pet on wheels, with Old Man Henderson perched up on the driver's box. If you've ever hauled dirt or gravel with a standard half-ton pickup truck, you'll have some sense of how heavy this thing must have been.

BAD IDEAS.

This political cartoon, by Thomas Nast, ran in Harper's Weekly in 1871. It nicely illustrates society's attitude toward those who advocated "free love" — in this case, Victoria Woodhull. The woman is shown struggling under the heavy burden of a drunken husband and several children, but saying, "Get thee behind me, Mrs. Satan; I'd rather travel the hardest path of matrimony than follow your footsteps."

The family — Henderson; his pregnant wife, Elizabeth; and eight children — traveled with two other Quaker families, the Hockettes and the Fishers, along with the Meeks. In all, they made up a train of seven wagons, counting the one full of trees.

Along the way, they tried to travel with other emigrants for safety, but friction developed because of the trees. Because the tree wagon was so heavy, it slowed everyone down. It also attracted noticeable attention from Indians, which made everyone who wasn't a Quaker (and probably some of them too) very nervous. So the other emigrants forged ahead.

This was likely a mistake on their part. Luelling was later told that many Native Americans saw trees as sacred, and considered that a wagon train carrying trees over the mountains was under the protection of "the Great Spirit." Whether for this or other reasons, not only did the Luellings have no "Indian trouble," but when the pregnant Elizabeth went into labor during the Columbia River part of the journey, they offered to help, loading her into a canoe for a quick paddle to The Dalles for medical attention. She gave birth to the family's ninth child — a girl named Oregon Columbia Luelling — in the canoe on the way there.

After Elizabeth and Oregon Columbia had recovered from this, the voyagers had to face the powerful and dangerous Columbia Cascades — trees and all. Again, Native Americans helped, retrieving a runaway flatboat that had missed the take-out point and was headed into more danger.

By the time Henderson and Elizabeth got to their destination in Milwaukie, they had lost only half their trees. But they'd gained a child and a large cohort of Native friends along the way. They also gained the opportunity to start what would become one of Oregon's most important industries, especially early on. Besides the Bing cherry, the Luelling family went on to develop the Black Republican, Lincoln and Willamette cherries, the Golden prune, the Sweet Alice apple, and several fruits bearing the Luelling name.

By the way, the story of the Luellings' overland journey is the basis for Deborah Hopkinson's children's book, *Apples to Oregon*, one of the Oregon Reads book selections for the 2009 sesquicentennial celebration. The book springboards off the story to generate a "tall tale" about the journey.

The other part of Henderson Luelling's story, though, is rather less suitable as reading material for children. That, of course, would be Henderson's free-love cult, which he called "The Harmonial Brotherhood."

The Harmonial Brotherhood was founded in 1858, a good 15 very lucrative and productive years after Henderson arrived in Oregon. By this time, he had moved to Oakland, California, leaving the nursery operation in Milwaukie to his brother Seth. He was also on his fourth wife — he'd outlived his first three wives, including Elizabeth.

Historical information about Harmonial Brotherhood is very scant. I have only been able to track down one newspaper article about the venture, in an 1860 article in the *San Francisco Times*. But, luckily, it's a long one.

The sect was formed when Henderson met a onetime circus performer turned preacher and spiritualist, whom the newspaper identifies only as "Dr. T." This "doctor" had developed a communistic philosophy that was a veritable bouquet of Bad Ideas. It made free love the centerpiece of a strict regimen of self-denial that included an all-vegetarian, stimulant-free diet, water-cure "hydropathy" for any medical need, and a Utopian all-property-in-common social structure.

Now, you may think "free love" meant something different in 1860 than what it means today. And in at least one important way, it does: The term today conjures visions of swingers, "swappers" and dreadful paperback books with titles like "The Lust Lords" and "Bedroom Bingo"; people who practice or recommend it today are openly and unabashedly interested in the sexy parts of the doctrine.

That wasn't the case with the Harmonial Brotherhood, or indeed most of the "Free Love" advocates of the 1800s. Most of these — including, as we shall shortly see, the Harmonial Brotherhood — still cherished most of the classic Victorian sexual mores and "hangups." But the core concept of "Free Love" wasn't too far away from "Bedroom Bingo," for younger and friskier members at least. It was basically the abolition of marriage or any other tradition of sexual and familial exclusivity.

This idea was far from new even in 1858. It probably wasn't even a new idea when Plato proposed it in *The Republic* three thousand years ago. Over the centuries, and especially in the American West, at least half a dozen generations have produced at least one "daring" philosopher who calls for a throwing-off of the age-old yoke of marriage and family and urges his (or her, but let's be real here — it's pretty much always a man recommending this) followers to revert to the mythic "noble savage" life of naked and unashamed people gathering freely and openly, men and women, living and eating and sleeping together with no rules, no judgment and no squabbles over paternity.

Such appears to have been the vision that Dr. T successfully sold to Henderson in Oakland. It was quite a score for Dr. T, roping Henderson in, because Henderson had enough money to think very, very big. And that was good, because the Harmonial Brotherhood congregants really wanted out of Oakland. The problem was, California society just wasn't hospitable to their vision of the world — especially all that "free love" stuff.

So Luelling and Dr. T decided it was time to pick up the flock and fare forth into the wilderness somewhere, where they might create a whole new society — a society founded on their own principles. In such a place, the Brotherhood could demonstrate the soundness of its philosophy without interference and judgment from the squares.

So Luelling sold his beautiful farm and, taking all the money, invested it in a schooner — the *Santiago*. Its destination: Honduras.

Realizing belatedly what he was up to, Luelling's wife rushed to court to swear out a "writ de lunatico inquirendo." What the old man had in mind would leave her and the children — all but the two boys who were going with him — homeless, penniless, and dependent on charity.

The courts were very sympathetic, and soon there were cops on the prowl looking for Luelling. He quickly went into hiding, waiting until the *Santiago* had sailed out to the Golden Gate, and then stealthily paddled out into the bay under cover of darkness to join his fellow travelers aboard ship.

Those fellow travelers, according to the *San Francisco Times*, were quite a group. Luelling wasn't the only one of them who had to board the ship by stealth and by night. One fellow passenger had skipped on some bills and was running from the law; another couple was delayed trying (unsuccessfully) to force their teenage daughter to come on the trip. Still others just didn't want to undertake the walk of shame up the gangplank of the *Santiago* in broad daylight. After all, what would the neighbors think?

Once on board, the Free Lovers immediately got busy creating great merriment for the professional crew of sailors aboard the schooner — who, upon their return, became the cult's rather merciless biographers with the help of the reporter from the *Times*.

The journey appears to have been dogged with several major issues. The first was a question of leadership. Luelling having financed the whole enterprise, he naturally thought he would be the leader of the expedition. However, this was not to Dr. T's taste at all. As the intellectual father of Harmonial Brotherhoodism, Dr. T thought he himself ought to be the alpha. Out of this misunderstanding grew a remarkably unharmonial and non-brotherly feud over who would be top banana.

Speaking of bananas, the second issue, and the one that generated the most drama aboard ship, was a matter of nutrition. The problem was, they were all starving. Their diet plan — the "Harmonial Diet," which Dr. T apparently crafted arbitrarily out of then-prevalent faddish nutritional theories, liberally mixed with hot air and invested with the full power of religious belief — was a nutritional train-wreck. Members ate almost nothing but coarse-ground whole-wheat flour. Anything that might actually be fun to eat — sugar, coffee, tea, all animal foods — was strictly forbidden. So, naturally, they had brought none of that sort of stuff on board.

The power of belief is a force that can move mountains, but many of those mountains are imaginary, and when that power fetches up against a more grounded force, things can get interesting. In this case, the cult members' firm belief in the goodness and healthfulness of their "harmonial diet" was now slowly being ground down by the animal cravings of their starving bodies, which they were trying to force to subsist on almost nothing but wheat berries and cold water. Consequently, there was, according to the article, "much secret eating of salt pork, and drinking of coffee and tea which were also forbidden." And when that sort of dietary cheating was discovered, there were accusations and recriminations, salted liberally with that particular viciousness that springs from secret envy.

HENDERSON LUELLING
Founder of Fruit Business

The ship made landfall in Zihuatanejo a few weeks later, and the passengers hurried ashore to bathe in a stream. This they did in fine Noble Savage style, stripping and plunging in buck naked, the ladies moving about 50 yards upstream from the gents. Unfortunately, this Edenic party was interrupted at its upstream end by a group of local men, who immediately rose to the occasion, rushing to disrobe and join the skinny-dipping damsels frolicking in the water. A cry of alarm from one of the ladies brought one of the Harmonial Brotherhood

This portrait of Henderson Luelling was published in 1911, but probably was made much earlier — most likely five or ten years after his undertaking of the ill-starred journey to create a free-love Utopia in Honduras in 1860.

Patients at the Battle Creek Sanitarium engage in group breathing exercises in 1900. The nutritional and medicinal doctrines of the Sanitarium, guided by John Harvey Kellogg, developed from the same American frontier movement that earlier had inspired the Harmonial Brotherhood group — although Kellogg's practices were far better developed and devoid of the "free love" part. (Image: Postcard)

men rushing up, and he drove the local interlopers off — and that might have brought an end to it had not "Dr. T" then belatedly arrived on the scene. Apparently forgetting that he was supposed to be rejecting such bourgeois hang-ups, Dr. T took offense at the rescuer's having seen his wife naked, and threatened to "break every bone in his body" in defense of her honor. (Presumably it was OK for Dr. T. to see the other naked ladies, though. Alpha-male privilege, perhaps?)

It wasn't a great start. And things would not get better.

A few weeks later, the *Santiago* arrived at its next port: La Ventosa, Oaxaca, Mexico. There it disgorged its cargo of pilgrims.

Those pilgrims were a different bunch, though, from the starry-eyed *naïfs* that had boarded the *Santiago* in San Francisco. Back then, they had been in the full bloom of their innocent belief in the doctrines of the Harmonial Brotherhood sect and its leaders. Now, after a hungry and grueling month at sea, the faith of the strongest among them was at least a little bit bruised.

But now they were almost there. Their destination was a place called Tiger Island. La Ventosa was quite close to Tiger Island.

The biggest problem was, they were all still starving. They had cheated on their diet as much as they could while under way, but they hadn't brought anything worth eating on board the schooner, and the sailors certainly were not willing to share *their* rations.

By the time they got to La Ventosa, the pilgrims were ravenous. So they poured into town in a great wave of hungry, unwashed bodies with money in their hands, looking for meat.

Amid this tumult came the event that would split the Harmonial Brotherhood into warring camps, and earn for it the nickname "Discordant Devils" among the *Santiago's* crew: The Egg War.

It seems Luelling, having found a vendor selling about eight dozen eggs, bought them all and then went off to fetch a suitable container to carry them away in. While he was doing that, his rival, Dr. T, spotted the eggs and hastened to purchase them, not knowing they'd already been sold. The vendor, quite sensibly, accepted his money (doubling his profits) and quit the scene before the mistake could be discovered. Then, as Dr. T was gathering the eggs up, Luelling arrived to collect them, and . . . .

Neither of the two Harmonial Brothers would accept the other's claim on the eggs. Each intended to have every one of the eggs he had paid for, and other claimants be damned.

From this pathetic display of truculence at the highest levels of Harmonial Brotherhood leadership sprang an epic civil conflict among the ranks, with different Brothers taking sides against each other and battling most un-Harmonially with words and perhaps with fists as well — the newspaper article hints at physical violence, although it doesn't specifically say.

Luelling called a meeting of the faithful and made a passionate speech on his own behalf, hinting that his claim on the eggs had the backing of divine authority. Dr. T accused him of abusing his authority and vowed revenge. The other Harmonial Brothers and Sisters took sides, and (this is a direct quote from the newspaper article) — "the women, also, who called each other liars and no ladies."

Eventually, though, the rebellion was quelled and the *Santiago*, with most of its cargo of lapsed vegetarians still aboard, was on its way to Tiger Island.

Tiger Island sounds a lot more interesting than it is — or, at least, than it was in 1859. It was a big pyramid-shaped island with not much foliage, in the middle of the Gulf of Fonseca, where the borders of El Salvador, Honduras and Nicaragua meet the Pacific Ocean. It wasn't suitable as a place to found a colony, but it made a fine jumping-off point from which to scout for one on the mainland.

So upon arrival there, the pilgrims made excursions to various nearby places where they thought they might establish their home.

Finding nothing suitable by the sea, they explored up the Como River on the mainland, and finally found a spot about 60 miles inland that they thought would do.

They thought wrong. Honduras is deep in the tropics, and the spot they staked out was subject to all the tropical diseases to which the residents of northerly climes are so susceptible. Almost immediately the pilgrims started getting deathly ill with what was probably malaria or yellow fever.

Now, Harmonial Brotherhood doctrine held that the unusual healthfulness of their "harmonial diet" of ground-up wheat berries and cold water would ward off all sickness. But that was turning out to be yet another hopeful fantasy; folks got sick anyway. So they turned to the practices of hydropathy to treat the sick.

Hydropathy, a.k.a. "Water Cure," is mostly a discredited practice today, but in 1859 it was almost mainstream. It advocated the use of water — usually cold water, but sometimes hot, taken internally or used externally — to cure disease. Extremist hydropathy, such as the kind espoused by the Harmonial Brotherhood, eschews all other medicines. Now, with many pilgrims desperately ill, it was time for the Brotherhood's medical dogma to be tested, just as its nutritional dogma had been tested on the journey from San Francisco. Would it fare as poorly?

It would.

"They took Mrs. C., while raging with the fever, wrapped her in a wet blanket till she perspired profusely, and then threw cold water over her," recounts the newspaper article. "The speedy result was her death."

Most of the stricken fared better, in spite of the Harmonial hydropathic interventions. But several others also died, either from the fever or from the treatment.

By this time, things had gotten really bad for the pilgrims. Dr. T and his wife had seceded from the group. Several others had abandoned the whole affair and were making their way back to "civilization" as best they could. Finally, the Harmonial Brotherhood disbanded entirely and, the *Santiago* once again under their grateful feet, proceeded to slink back to San Francisco.

Luelling survived the jungle fever and returned on the *Santiago*, living for a time in San Jose with friends, possibly under a pseudonym. In 1878, while clearing land to plant a new orchard there, he died of a heart attack.

Sources and Works Cited:
- Portland: A Food Biography, *a book by Heather Arndt Anderson published in 2014 by Rowman;*
- A Garden of the Lord: A History of the Oregon Yearly Meeting of Friends Church, *a book by Ralph Beebe published in 1968 by Barclay Press;*
- *"Early Days and Ways in and around Milwaukie," a report written in 1939 by Sara B. Wrenn of the WPA Federal Writers' Project for its Oregon Folklore Studies collection;*
- *Archives of* San Francisco Times, *19 May 1860.*

VAUDEVILLE SUSIE'S RIOT.

THE BAD IDEA:
- *Trying to calm a belligerent, pistol-waving mob of Civil War soldiers and Rebel sympathizers by singing to them.*

In the winter of 1860, the little riverside frontier town of Corvallis was home to a young singer named Susie Robinson.

Susie was the star attraction of the Robinson Troupe of Vaudevillians, led by her father. And "star" was the word for Susie: Virtually the entire male population of the mid-Willamette Valley was in dopey, hopeless love with her.

"Her form and voice were praised by all, and her virtue extolled, while her father gathered at the door of his theater willing tributes enough, each day, to have made her a golden crown," recalls pioneer George A. Waggoner in his 1905 memoir. "Was ever a queen so fortunately situated?"

Waggoner opines that, although Susie's talents would not have carried her far on Broadway or even in San Francisco, she was by far the best thing anyone in Corvallis had ever seen.

"We know now that she was not a great actress or singer," Waggoner remarks, rather ungallantly; "and my roving eyes have since discovered that she was not a remarkable beauty, but at that time many Oregon boys had never seen the gay tinsels of a stage costume; never been thrilled by the rich tones of a cultivated voice, or seen a beautiful woman poised on one toe, and she took the frontier heart by storm."

Had Susie Robinson and her father stayed in Corvallis, she probably would have had a long and rewarding career in the up-valley stock-theater scene, such as it was. But in the autumn of that year, something very exciting happened near a little creek way out in what is today the state of Idaho: Gold — lots of gold — was found in Orofino Creek, a little way east of Lewiston. Then, the following spring, a little party of prospectors struck gold even closer to home — on the banks of Griffin Creek, just a few miles from Baker City in Eastern Oregon.

Torrents of eager miners departed from Corvallis and other valley towns that year, headed for the gold fields of the east. Ramshackle, lawless towns sprang up, with names like Auburn and Granite. Eager young swains poured eastward hoping for a lucky strike — closely followed by the usual crowd of gamblers, swindlers, robbers and other hard characters looking for easy marks.

And, of course, as towns sprang up in the gold fields with populations in the thousands composed entirely of young bachelors, it was clear that the demand for good Vaudeville would be nearly unlimited.

How could the Robinson Troupe stay in boring, depopulated Corvallis when such a literal golden opportunity beckoned?

And so the Corvallis Family Robinson packed up its things and followed the eager miners over the mountains, and re-established itself just across the Columbia River in Walla Walla, in what was then Washington Territory.

Now, as you may recall, 1861 also saw the outbreak of the American Civil War. There was a frontier fort in Walla Walla, and a couple of companies of Army regulars had been stationed there. And when the Robinson Theater set up shop in town, word of Susie's talents and charms spread through the ranks of the boys in blue like a bugle call. Soon entire companies were pouring into the theater, seating themselves by platoons before the stage, filling the entire joint.

The local Walla Walla miners resented this a great deal. They, too, were thoroughly smitten with Susie, and did not intend to be kept from her shows by these out-of-town interlopers. These feelings were especially strong among residents who were in sympathy with the South — which was, at that time, the majority of the town.

Tensions grew, but not much; frontier miners weren't big on impulse control. Instead, they simply showed up in force and drove the soldiers out of the theater one day, ordering them not to return.

Now, these soldiers were men who had enlisted to fight the Southern

BAD IDEAS.

An illustration showing a Vaudeville theater scene in around 1899, from Schribner's Magazine, by William J. Glackens. The theater in which a riot broke out over frontier Oregon beauty Susie Robinson was, of course, considerably less refined than this one. (Image: Library of Congress)

rebels. And yet now, instead of doing that, they found themselves parked in a crappy fort in the middle of nowhere, where their sole purpose was to discourage the area's Native American tribes from getting "uppity." They were already a little sensitive about being left out, especially as word came in of battles and conquests back east. They were in no humor to let the humiliation heaped upon them by these rowdy Rebel sympathizers go unchallenged.

Accordingly, on the next performance at the Robinson Theater, the soldiers came prepared.

"They came fully armed, and determined to insist upon their rights," recalls Waggoner — who was in the crowd that day. "We all knew a fight was coming, and divided our sympathies according to our political opinions."

Members of both camps were able to get into the theater before capacity was reached, and harsh words started being exchanged. Susie, obviously hoping to defuse the brewing blow-up, came out on stage and started to sing. This made things better at first ... but then suddenly it made it all much, much worse:

"A hearty round of applause greeted her, and she acknowledged it as a favorite can, and commenced to sing," Waggoner recalls. "One of the soldiers, who had been drinking, continued to cheer, and the marshal attempted to take him from the room."

The drunken soldier wheeled on the marshal, whipped out his heavy Colt Dragoon revolver and pistol-whipped the officer with it.

And then the fight was on.

"Instantly the house was in an uproar," Waggoner recalled. "Susie screamed and ran from the stage. Navy Colts leaped from their scabbards and bellowed like the roar of artillery."

A local outlaw named "Cherokee Bob" jumped up and started shooting, picking soldiers off like bowling pins at a shooting gallery. Return fire knocked him off his chair, but it later turned out he'd been wearing armor, Ned Kelly style, under his shirt.

"The firing continued from all parts of the room, and a terrible stampede ensued, everyone but those engaged trying to get out of the house," Waggoner writes. "More than fifty shots were fired, and the room was filled with smoke, out of which pistols blazed, fired at supposed enemies, although several times friends fired upon each other."

Waggoner, unfortunately, gives us no hint of what his role in the fracas was — whether he was among those shooting, or those running for the exits. But he was there in the aftermath, carrying a man shot directly in the breast to a surgeon for a desperate attempt to save his life. The man, who had given himself up for a goner, turned out not to even need the surgeon; a bag of coins in his pocket had turned the bullet away from his vitals, leaving him with a minor flesh wound.

Others weren't so lucky. However, considering the number of shots fired and the size of the crowd packed into the theater, the death toll was astonishingly light: Just three men died. Dozens more were wounded, however.

In classic gold-field boomtown style, this deadly riot was accepted as just part of life on the frontier; the wounded dressed their injuries as best they could and got back to work, the dead were buried with appropriate ceremony, and everyone else made plans to sit closer to the exits next time Susie took the stage.

"No one was arrested, and the theater went on as usual," Waggoner writes. "But Susie never seemed quite the same afterward. A slight commotion in the audience would attract her attention in the midst of her best song, and in her best play she always looked as though she was afraid someone was going to shoot."

This sort of shell-shock on Susie's part is certainly understandable. Still, as Waggoner points out, it's not every Vaudeville actress who can honestly say that men have fought and killed and died for the right to hear her sing.

Sources and Works Cited:
- Stories of Old Oregon, *a book by George A. Waggoner published in 1905 by the* Oregon Statesman;
- *"Frontier Humor: Plain and Fancy," an article by Erik Bromberg published in the September 1960 issue of* Oregon Historical Quarterly.

THE NESTUCCA SPIT WAR.

THE BAD IDEA:
- *Re-route Oregon Coast Highway 101 onto a colossal concrete causeway running directly over a scenic beach, on pilings drilled into the sand below.*

Tom McCall was a smart, articulate man, and not easy to swindle. But Glenn "Mr. Oregon" Jackson was, by all accounts, even smarter — and he had something he wanted from McCall.

Which was fair enough, because McCall also wanted something from Jackson — wanted it badly: An endorsement of his candidacy for governor.

It was 1966. McCall, having clinched the Republican nomination, was going up against the smart, tough-minded state treasurer, Democrat Bob Straub. McCall and Straub were very similar in many respects, and although Oregon voters tended to favor Republicans at that time, the outcome was by no means a sure thing.

And Jackson, the state highway commissioner and owner of ten Oregon newspapers, was the most powerful behind-the-scenes player in the state. People answering to him built the Interstate freeway system and made Oregon's secondary highways the envy of the West.

So for McCall, a lot depended on this endorsement interview. Put starkly,

Jackson was in a position to choose the next governor; neither McCall nor Straub could win without his influence.

On that day, McCall found Jackson in a genial and friendly mood. And the meeting seemed to go very well. After the preliminaries, the commissioner made a proposal: There was a project he was working on, he explained. A highway improvement over at the coast. It would bring huge economic benefits to the communities there; it would open up the north coast to motor tourism from surrounding states; it would give Oregonians access to a part of the coast that few would otherwise see. All the engineering work was done; it was ready to go. But Jackson was running into some trouble with the usual ragtag band of local obstructionists, and this particular group was proving especially troublesome.

Now, if McCall would commit to taking a strong position in favor of this project, and promise to help Jackson get the job done, and promise not to be influenced by the local band of would-be Progress-stoppers, why, yes, Jackson would endorse McCall. And he'd do it full-throatedly, with all the influence he and his ten community newspapers and network of well-connected friends could provide.

McCall, lulled into complacency by the friendly and laid-back character of the conversation, accepted immediately. One pictures him walking on air as he left the building. With Jackson's endorsement, he *would* be elected

An aerial photograph of Nestucca Bay as it appeared in 2009. Nestucca Spit is the large tapering land mass at the bottom right. (Image: US Fish & Wildlife Service)

governor; it was almost guaranteed.

But it couldn't have taken McCall more than a day or two to find out he'd been played. The fact was — as McCall would have quickly learned if he'd done a little homework before saying yes — the fact was, he already had Glenn Jackson's support, simply because he was running against Bob Straub. Jackson would sooner have cut off his left foot than endorse Bob Straub. Bob Straub was Glenn Jackson's number-one political enemy.

And there was a good reason for that. Rememember that ragtag band of local obstructionists whom Jackson had casually mentioned? In reality, it was neither ragtag, nor exclusively local.

It was, in fact, Bob Straub and his friends.

State Treasurer Bob Straub looks out over Nestucca Spit as a construction worker in a tractor works on some preliminary road construction, circa 1966. (Image: Western Oregon University)

The project over which Straub and Jackson were locking horns that year was a doozie — and a strong candidate for Bad Idea of the Decade. It was a plan to move and straighten Highway 101 between Neskowin and Tillamook. If you've ever driven up that way, you'll doubtless have noticed that the highway leaves the coast behind and plunges inland for 35 miles — routing around sandy estuaries at Nestucca Bay, Sandlake and Netarts Bay, and impassable granite promontories at Cape Kiwanda, Porter Point and Cape Lookout.

That was a lot of grand ocean scenery that was inaccessible to anyone not willing to drive miles out of the way on little bumpy back roads and maybe even get out of the car and walk. And this was the era of Sunday drives; dependable and comfortable cars were, in the mid-1960s, a relatively new thing for most people of modest means.

So in 1964, Jackson's highway department worked up a plan to, as it were, bring the mountain to Mohammed: He'd bring all that grand ocean scenery to those Sunday drivers by re-routing the Oregon Coast Highway right through the middle of it.

There were actually three possible plans for the new highway, but the cheapest one, and the one the department wanted, was to have the new highway route start just north of Neskowin and go straight to the beach. From there the roadbuilders would blast through Porter Point, cross the Nestucca River with a 90-foot-high bridge, then traverse the length of Nestucca Spit State Park on a causeway built on pilings drilled into the sand. It would then go through Cape Kiwanda with the aid of more dynamite, across McPhillips Beach and through the Sandlake Estuary on a roadbed made with acres of trucked-in fill, before finally rejoining the current highway route just south of Tillamook.

This was a Bad Idea on so many levels, it's almost hard today to understand how a smart man like Glenn Jackson could have believed it would work. It was, of course, a different time, and there was a lot less focus on the damage, both scenic and environmental, that a raised causeway literally hovering over the beach and howling with traffic 24 hours a day would do.

But also, by the mid-1960s the town of Bayocean, just to the north of Nestucca Spit, had fallen entirely into the sea, providing a fantastic real-world demonstration of the dangers of building heavy infrastructure on beach sand. (See Page 39 for that story.)

But, Jackson clearly felt his department could handle it.

Public response to the plan was mixed, but mostly favorable. The local year-round residents were mostly in favor of the plan, but the weekenders — Willamette Valley residents who owned cabins at the beach — were less enthusiastic. Where the real trouble arose was with residents who particularly enjoyed natural features that the plan was about to completely ruin. These now started to form groups to oppose the plan — notably one focused on Nestucca Spit. This group called itself "SOS," which stood for "Save Our Spit." This, as you may have guessed, was the "ragtag band of local obstructionists" who were so much on Glenn Jackson's mind during Tom McCall's endorsement interview.

No problem. The department was used to this sort of thing. A few public hearings so folks would feel "listened to," and then construction would start whether they liked it or not. You couldn't stop progress — not in 1965 you couldn't.

What the department was *not* used to was powerful politicians getting involved. And that's what happened now. Because among that ragtag band of locals who enjoyed natural features that the plan was about to ruin was one Robert W. Straub, the state treasurer — and a regular visitor to Nestucca Spit.

Straub took one look at the plans and instantly became Jackson's worst-case scenario. He wrote hundreds of letters and memos, carried a petition with 12,000 signatures around with him much of the time, organized marches and protests — all the while continuing to do his job as state treasurer and, in 1965, launching the bid for the governorship that brought Tom McCall to Jackson with cap in hand. If only McCall had done a little research before he showed up for that meeting ... if he had, he probably could have saved himself the trouble of even bothering to show up for it.

A color snapshot of Bob Straub relaxing at Nestucca Spit in 1966. (Image: Western Oregon University)

So time marched on, and McCall was elected. He kept his word to Jackson and pushed for the highway, albeit with far less enthusiasm than Jackson might have wished for; ironically, he was doing this at the same time as his far-more-well-known fight to preserve public beach access.

The optics of the whole thing were terrible, and people were already starting to ask uncomfortable questions about it.

Luckily, the matter was taken out of McCall's hands before it could go much farther. Bob Straub had been in contact with Interior Secretary Stewart Udall after learning that most of Nestucca Spit had carried a deed restriction when the federal government handed the land over to the state back in 1961: it had to be used for a park.

Jackson, of course, had figured this was no problem. The spit was already a state park; the highway would simply provide better access to it. But Straub thought Udall might not consider that to be in keeping with the spirit of the deed restriction, and brought it to his attention.

It took a while for Udall to get around to looking into the matter. But when he did, he was unambiguous about it. No, the state of Oregon could not build a highway through the middle of the park. If it did, the Bureau of Land Management would take action to retroactively cancel the land transfer.

And just like that, the fight was over. The highway department prepared and presented a new plan — a much costlier one, involving running the highway around the former BLM land on a raised causeway over miles and miles of open water in Nestucca Bay. It seems likely this plan was offered as a face-saving move, because it quietly died a few months later, and Nestucca Spit has been a peaceful, highway-free park ever since. In 1987 its name was changed to Bob Straub State Park.

As for Straub, he was finally elected governor of Oregon in 1974 after McCall's second term ended. He lived long enough to see his beloved Nestucca Spit State Park renamed in his honor; he died in 2002 at his home in Springfield.

Sources and Works Cited:
- *"Epilogue," an article by Matt Love published in* Citadel of the Spirit: Oregon's Sesquicentennial Anthology, *an anthology edited by Matt Love and published in 2009 by Nestucca Spit Press;*
- Fire at Eden's Gate: Tom McCall and the Oregon Story, *a book by Brent Walth published in 1994 by Oregon Historical Society Press.*

THE FLIVVER FLYERS.

THE BAD IDEAS:
- *Install a 20-horsepower engine that weighs 500 pounds and has a famously inadequate cooling system in a home-built airplane and then attempt to fly it.*

- *Remove the wings from your airplane, move them to a different part of the plane, and take off in it.*

Part of the problem with owning and operating the only flight school in town in the 1920s and 1930s was, every time one of your students slapped together some home-built piece of kit, you'd be expected to help get it in the air.

At least, that seems to have been how it worked for Ted Barber, owner of Bend Flying Service and Central Oregon's first commercial aviator.

"I was never one to back away from adventure in an airplane," Barber wrote in his autobiography, *The Barnstorming Mustanger*. "I always figured airplanes were made to fly, and I was made to fly them."

This was a nice general principle, but it's easy to see how applying it too generously could shorten a fellow's life a bit. Having this for a personal philosophy was not necessarily a Bad Idea, but it probably wasn't a good one either.

Luckily for Ted, building a home-built in the inter-war years was not easy to do. The problem wasn't with engineering — there were plenty of good workable plans for home-built airplanes, and lots of people could and did put them together in barns and sheds. The problem was with power. It was hard to find an engine lightweight enough to get off the ground with an airplane attached to it. Especially in the thin air of the Central Oregon high desert, 3,500 feet above sea level.

Every now and then, though, someone would come up with something; and Ted would have to choose between telling the student "no" and helping him fly the thing.

And in at least this one case, "helping him fly it" meant "go first."

Ted's personal philosophy came close to cooking his goose one day in the early 1930s when the Stevens brothers called him over to check out their new homebuilt: a super-light parasol-wing monoplane with a super-heavy Ford Model T engine bolted to the firewall up front. The brothers hoped that the lightness of the airframe would make up for the fact that the old flathead flivver mill weighed close to 500 pounds, while putting out less than 20 horsepower.

Ted walked around the airplane, inspecting it carefully. Other than that cast-iron hunk of dead weight hanging off the front firewall, it was a beautifully done piece of equipment, and he told them so.

Then, foolishly, he told them he'd fly it for them.

Or maybe not so foolishly. Because here's the thing — Model T motors were everywhere. They were probably the easiest and cheapest kind of power plant you could find in the 1930s. If the Stevens brothers had really done what they'd set out to do — created a new airplane design that could actually be powered in flight by a Model T engine — it could actually make them some money. Nobody had been able to do that before, and what Ted was looking at now seems to have convinced him that maybe, just maybe, they had.

Ted climbed in and started the motor up. The familiar putt-putt of a Model T greeted his ears. He taxied to the edge of the field and paused, letting the motor warm up.

Then he opened the throttle wide, and the little homebuilt started gathering speed down the field.

About halfway down, Ted pulled back on the stick. The little plane lifted off, hung a second, and dropped back onto the field. He tried again. Same result.

The engine was literally about two horsepower short of what it would take to get the plane off the ground.

But Ted liked what little he had seen of the plane's handling. He taxied back over to where the Stevens boys were waiting, looking crestfallen, beside the field.

Pioneer Central Oregon aviator Ted Barber in the pilot's seat of his trusty Waco 9. (Image: Ted Barber)

"Let's wait until we get a little wind, boys," he said. "We'll give 'er a try again."

Several days later, with a gentle steady breeze blowing along the airfield, the three of them returned to Knotts Field for a second run.

This time, it worked. Ted pulled back on the stick, and the little flathead-four motor roared valiantly, and the tiny plane lifted off and went into a very, very slow climb as it neared the end of the field.

The Stevens boys cheered as they watched it rise to about 300 feet ... and then they stopped cheering as it leveled off and started slowly sinking.

Meanwhile, in the cockpit, Ted was nervously scanning the ground in front of him. The Model T engine was making just barely enough power to keep the plane in the air, at full throttle. He hoped it wouldn't quit from the strain. He didn't have enough power to try any turns; he'd have to go straight ahead and hope for the best. Scanning his memory of the local geography, he remembered that there was a field a couple miles ahead — but it was strewn with lava rocks. He'd for sure hit one, and break the plane. Maybe break his neck too.

But five miles beyond that was a big open field. Could he make it?

He glanced over his shoulder to see how much ground he'd covered since leaving the airfield — and that's when he really became nervous.

Because hanging in the air behind the little airplane was a great billowy contrail of steam. He was two miles into a seven-mile flight and the engine was already overheating.

Would it make it? Would *he* make it if *it* didn't?

Ted focused on the task. The little airplane droned on, its engine belching steam like a half-quenched dragon. Sooner or later the radiator water would all boil away, and it would seize up ….

Then the field was in front of him, and he was touching down, and bouncing to a stop. The steam poured out and surrounded him like a fog bank as he climbed gratefully down from the plane. He probably felt like kissing the ground.

As a side note, it's interesting to speculate on what the Stevens plane could have done on an airfield in the Willamette Valley. It's pretty likely that if he'd been taking off from, say, the Eugene airport — elevation 374 feet, more than 3,000 feet lower than Bend — he would have been able to do a lot more with the little plane.

With another homebuilt that Ted was supposed to try out, he was saved from having to risk his neck by the builder's impatience. Eddie Campbell of Prineville had, in 1930, got hold of the plans for a homebuilt design called "The Storms Flying Flivver," a tiny high-wing monoplane powered by a Ford Model A engine.

The Model A engine was roughly the same size and weight as the Model T, but made twice as much power. And Eddie worked at a Ford dealership's

A Model T engine photographed at a car show at Prins Bertil Memorial in Stockholm, Sweden. This engine put out only 20 horsepower and weighed almost 500 pounds, making it a very unlikely airplane engine; but in the early 1930s they were cheap and plentiful. (Image: Liftarn/ Wikimedia Commons | CC-by-SA)

Images from 1930s magazine ads show the "Storms Flying Flivver" in fully-built form. This was the kit-built plane Eddie Campbell of Prineville crashed in, and it probably wasn't dissimilar from the Model T-powered one Ted Barber test-flew for the Stevens brothers — which was also a tiny, lightweight parasol-winged plane. (Image: aerofiles.com)

repair facility, so he had access to the equipment necessary to soup it up a bit.

Ted was out of town for when Eddie finished his project, and not expected back for another four days. Eddie, already a fairly experienced glider pilot, grew impatient. Plus, it was his plane; he wanted to be the first to fly it. So, he pulled it out and fired it up and pointed it down the field.

It would not take off. He tried it several times; at the proper speed, it simply would not leave the ground.

Eddie looked it over, scratched his head, and decided the problem was that it was "nose heavy." Getting his tools out, he took the wing loose and moved it a little bit forward. Then he climbed back in to try again.

Bad Idea.

This time, the plane came off the ground, all right. It went straight into a steep climb, completely ignoring Eddie's attempts to control it. It stood on its tail, trying to hang from the prop like a helicopter, about a hundred feet in the air; then it stalled and pitched forward and slammed down into the ground, nose first, ending up in a tangled heap.

Eddie's friends gaped at the wreckage. Nothing moved in it. "Eddie's killed!" they shouted in horror, then raced to the scene.

They found Eddie slumped motionless amid the wreckage. Fearful of a fire breaking out, they each seized one of his shoulders and started trying to drag him out.

This, of course, is always a Bad Idea at a crash scene. But, luckily for everyone involved, Eddie hadn't suffered any spinal injuries.

Eddie regained consciousness while they were tugging on him. "Hey, you guys!" he called out. "Take it easy, will you? . . . My feet are stuck right through the firewall. You've got to get a saw and cut me out."

They did so, then hustled him to the doctor's to get checked out. His skull was cracked, and he later learned that one of his leg bones also had been cracked; but overall, he came out of the experience not much worse for wear.

The same couldn't be said of the Storms Flying Flivver, though.

Sources and Works Cited:
- The Barnstorming Mustanger, *a book by Ted Barber published in 1987 by Barber Industries;*
- *"Pioneer Pilots of the Sagebrush Country," an article in* Little Known Tales from Oregon History, Vol. 1, *an anthology edited by Geoff Hill and published in 1988 by Sun Publishing.*

THE WASHED-AWAY TOWN.

THE BAD IDEA:
- *Build your dream resort town on a big deposit of beach sand, then ignore the advice of the Army Corps of Engineers when it tells you what kind of jetty you need to protect it from washing away.*

Just off Highway 131, near the town of Tillamook, there's a scenic overlook from which you can gaze out over a long, mostly barren peninsula, slender and low-lying and sandy, dotted with beach grass and Scotch broom.

The name of the peninsula is Bayocean Spit. It's named after the posh resort town that once adorned it — a town that, over a 35-year-period, dropped house by house into the ocean. Today, nothing remains but beach sand, memories, and whatever's left of an old Pacific Northwest Bell telephone cable, which as of 1989 at least was still in place.

Bayocean had its start in 1906 when a real-estate mogul named Thomas Benton Potter learned of the spit from his son, who had just returned from Tillamook. The younger Potter told of a great waterfront headland, shaped like a club, its head towering 140 feet high and half a mile wide between the bay and the ocean, covered with pine trees, salal bushes, and Oregon Grape vines. And it was available for purchase ... and development.

The elder Potter soon visited the site and the possibilities enchanted him. It looked to him as if, with the proper promotion and investment, the site could become the Atlantic City of the West Coast. There was plenty of room for it to grow, a full 600 acres; and the lovely, broad, flat beach seemed to stretch on forever, from the mouth of Tillamook Bay all the way down south to Cape Meares — nearly five miles.

It was the perfect opportunity to steal a march on the competing developers who were at that very moment, Potter knew, drawing up plans for a resort at Seaside. And so he purchased the land and got to work.

The plan was for a world-class resort community. Potter envisioned a majestic hotel — the concept drawings look very similar to the old Portland Hotel, which once stood where Pioneer Courthouse Square is today (see Page 105 for that story). There would be a massive natatorium right on the beach full of heated seawater and equipped with a wave generator, so that guests could choose between warm and cold surf; a movie theater; a dance hall; and many other resort amenities. The town would have telephone

A pile of concrete rubble on the rapidly shrinking beach was all that remained of the grand surfside natatorium, once the crown jewel of Bayocean, in 1947. (Image: Image: Ben Maxwell/Salem Public Library)

service, indoor plumbing utilities, electric lights, and concrete roads.

Potter built most of these things immediately, then got busy selling lots in the new and growing town. Getting people to the town was a challenge which he met by having a 150-foot motor yacht built, the largest yacht on the Pacific Coast at the time, suitable for accommodating a hundred guests. On this he led excursions out to Bayocean via the open sea. This was phenomenally expensive, of course, and the trip took three days; Potter always took his guests on a sort of "scenic route" to Bayocean, going far out to sea, ostensibly so that he could show guests the Columbia River Lightship and Tillamook Rock lighthouse; but his real motive was to prevent anyone from catching a glimpse of the hated rivals at Seaside.

A soon-to-be ex-homeowner tries to prevent his Bayocean home from falling into the sea with a row of sandbags in 1947. (Image: Ben Maxwell/Salem Public Library)

Upon arrival, the "marks" would be wined and dined and sales-pitched in the classic time-honored fashion before being ferried back again to Portland. Potter was a top-shelf salesman and the townsite really was striking; many of them bought in on the spot.

When the railroad line came through close by, these excursions became far more economical for Potter, and faster to boot. Sales continued very briskly.

Following the grand opening in 1912, the town grew quickly for a couple years. But by then Potter's health had started to fail, and he handed things over to his son — who had other interests and didn't fancy a life of promoting Bayocean like his father had. By 1915, neither Potter was really involved any more.

The Potters left Bayocean, essentially, half built. Its growth had been mostly financed by lot sales, and lot sales hadn't yielded enough cash to fully realize their dreams. The grand hotel was yet unbuilt — they'd built an "annex" hotel, which they hoped would one day be used as housing for resort workers, but now it looked as if that would be it. The roads were very nice, and poured in concrete; but there was no connection to the outside world, so the only cars on the streets were brought in by ship. The telephone exchange worked fine for local calls, but until much later it lacked a connection to the outside world. And the water supply lacked a booster pump to send water service up the side of that 140-foot-tall bluff, on which all the nicest homes were built.

Speaking of that bluff, though — it wouldn't be 140 feet tall for much longer. Not after 1917, it wouldn't.

That was the year that the U.S. Army Corps of Engineers built the North Jetty, extending out from the north side of the entrance to Tillamook Bay. The Corps had wanted to build two jetties — the configuration that's there today — but the residents of Tillamook, Bay City, Garibaldi and Bayocean would have had to pay a quarter of the cost of such a jetty, and none of them wanted to do that. And now that the railroad gave them alternatives for shipping out produce, so that everyone didn't have to brave the rough, frightening passage over the unprotected bar to get in and out

The dike road across what was left of Bayocean Spit as seen in 1963, covered with driftwood and the fallen trunks and debris of the trees that had fallen into the sea as the peninsula was worn away. (Image: Image: Ben Maxwell/Salem Public Library)

of Tillamook County, it didn't seem nearly as important to them. So, over the Corps' warnings that a single jetty would be at best a temporary solution, it agreed to put one in.

Bad Idea.

The results were obvious almost immediately. That broad sandy beach at Bayocean started getting less broad. During winters, the storm-driven waves started getting higher and higher.

Then, in 1932, a particularly vicious storm

One of the abandoned homes at Bayocean as seen in 1960. Note the driftwood piled up around it by the winter's storm-driven waves. (Image: Image: Ben Maxwell/Salem Public Library)

drove waves ashore that washed the footings out from under the gorgeous seaside natatorium with the heated saltwater swimming pool and wave generator.

The waves, surging over what used to be the beach, started to undermine the 140-foot bluff. Great flakes of the sandy hillside started falling into the sea, carrying with them trees and bushes and, eventually, houses. The hotel "annex" started falling into the sea, room by room, until it was gone. By 1938, 59 homes were also gone.

The winter storms started driving waves all the way over the thin part of the peninsula, filling the bay with saltwater — much to the dismay of the oyster farmers who, since 1928, had been growing oysters there.

It all culminated in a disastrous winter of 1952, when a big storm actually washed out a mile-wide gap in the waist of the spit, turning Bayocean into an island and drenching the bay with beach sand. The oyster farms were buried beneath it, a multi-million dollar local industry wiped out in an instant. The other estuary fisheries started to collapse, too, as the salinity of the bay surged to levels the local fish couldn't tolerate.

The federal government now sprang into action, building a riprap seawall across the gap to stop further damage.

By this time, there were just a handful of residents left on Bayocean. The last to leave were Francis and Ida Mitchell, who kept the little store there and were, throughout their time in Bayocean, the town's biggest boosters. Francis died in 1965 at the age of 95; Ida died some years before that, after having had a stroke.

By 1970, Bayocean Spit was a thin line of riprap trailed by a low bar of sand. By then not even Francis Mitchell would have been able to hang on there. The formerly big, solid, 140-foot-high head now more resembled the ghost of a sand dune rising feebly from the sea. The only thing maintaining most of the spit was the line of riprap across the seaward edge.

But by 1970, crews were working on putting another jetty in — the south jetty.

Today, nearly 50 years after the south jetty was completed, visitors to Bayocean Spit can look out on a much more substantial place. Today one can almost visualize the large and bustling town that was platted there a century ago — a town that could, if its founder's dreams had been fully realized, have been home to some 3,000 people. The foliage is coming back, although the dominant species is the invasive and suppressive Scotch broom; but at least the spit is green once again.

As for the town — well, technically, it still exists. Several dozen people still own lots there. Some of those lots are still underwater. None of the lots can be built on, and because of waste disposal issues, it's even illegal for owners to park a motorhome on them.

But that's all that's left. All physical traces of the town of Bayocean are long gone.

Sources and Works Cited:
- Bayocean: The Oregon Town that Fell Into the Sea, *a book by Bert and Margie Webber published in 1989 by Webb Research;*
- "Bayocean," *an article by Ulrich H. Hardt in* The Oregon Encyclopedia, *online at oregonencyclopedia.org.*

THE "HAY BURNER."

THE BAD IDEA:
- *Build a riverboat powered by four hungry cows, without checking to make sure you didn't actually need six or eight.*

It's probably fair to say, with studied understatement, that the mid-Willamette Valley town of Corvallis is into alternative transportation.

Corvallis is one of the most bike-friendly towns in the state. There are probably more electric vehicles per capita there than any other Oregon town. And, of course, engineering students at Oregon State University regularly work on projects such as solar-powered racing cars.

It's a town tradition that goes way back; Corvallis has always had a funny relationship with transportation. That may be because, its name to the contrary, it's not really in the heart of the valley, but rather fetched up tight against its western wall; so as soon as the river stopped being the main inter-city arterial, the town's importance started to fade relative to other, more centrally located cities like Albany and Salem. Transportation on the river built Corvallis; and the town probably would have faded with the riverboat industry had its status as a transportation hub not been rekindled by T. Edgenton Hogg's making Corvallis the head of the Corvallis and

Yaquina Railroad link to Newport and the sea, in the 1870s. (That story is in Volume One of this collection, *Heroes and Rascals of Old Oregon*.)

None of that had gotten started, though, in 1860, when a Corvallis entrepreneur got the town's alternative-transportation tradition started with his invention of a new kind of riverboat — one that he no doubt hoped would be the first of a mighty inland fleet, and powered by something far easier to come by in the antebellum Willamette Valley than steam engines:

Cows. Or, more specifically, oxen.

This inventor's name, as far as I have been able to learn, has been lost in the mists of time; historian Howard Corning, in his 1947 book, just refers to him sarcastically as a "genius." This is either a very un-clever jab or an impressively witty reference to the *Genius of Georgia*, a horse-powered riverboat that tried and failed to do the same thing on the Savannah River in 1820 using earlier and less efficient drive technology.

The *Genius of Georgia*, which the "Genius of Corvallis" surely knew all about, was a massive thing, an 85-foot-long catamaran 55 feet wide, dominated by a massive 40-foot-wide capstan — a great wheel which horses rotated around, like a merry-go-round with two dozen real horses and no riders. The horses plodded in circles all day around the wheel, which drove a pair of side-mounted paddlewheels.

The *Genius of Georgia* successfully made at least two 200-mile round trips between Savannah and Augusta, but after the second trip it disappears from the historical record; presumably it didn't turn out to be cost-effective.

An ancient Roman drawing of a cattle-powered sidewheel war galley. (Image: Smithsonian Press)

BAD IDEAS.

Willamette Falls as it appeared around the turn of the 20th century. In 1860, when the Hay Burner was allowed to go over it, the falls would have looked much like this, although the land in the background would have been covered with old-growth timber. (Image: Postcard)

Two dozen is a large number of horses; the "fuel bill" for a team that big would have been close to half a ton of hay per day, plus more than 200 pounds of grain to supplement it. Not to mention, of course, the waste disposal challenges.

The Corvallis "genius's" new undertaking, though, 40 years later and on the opposite side of the continent, would be different — or so its inventor surely hoped.

There were a few key differences that should have made it so.

For one thing, it was powered by oxen rather than horses. Oxen were in plentiful supply in the Willamette Valley in 1860, because they were the draft animal of choice on the Oregon Trail, which was then still in use. Oxen were not as fast as horses, but they had more endurance and more power at slow speeds; they were to horses what diesel engines are to gasoline ones. Plus, with their four stomachs, they could get their nourishment entirely from hay rather than needing to be supplemented with grain.

Also, by 1860 the treadmill had been invented. Treadmills solved a number of the problems the *Genius of Georgia* had been plagued with, including the need for the boat to be almost as wide as it was long (which reduced its hull speed) and the fact that it's very hard on livestock to spend all day walking in circles.

So our anonymous inventor built a broad, flat hull; mounted a wide treadmill near the stern; and mechanically linked its output shaft to a pair of side-mounted paddlewheels. With fine and self-deprecating humor, he christened the vessel the *Hay Burner*. He purchased four head of oxen to drive it. Then, presumably with a load of grain for the Portland markets, the "Genius of Corvallis" embarked on the *Hay Burner's* maiden voyage, heading for Canemah — the little waterfront town, now a neighborhood of Oregon City, that faces the river just above the falls.

The spectacle of this strange new vessel lumbering down the Willamette River turned plenty of heads. The hull was low in the water, and from far away it looked like a team of oxen nonchalantly plodding down the middle of the river.

Things went well for a while. Then, near the then-thriving town of Wheatland near Salem, the cattle drove the boat onto a gravel bar — or, as Golding wisecracks, "walked ashore" — at McGoogin's Slough. Hours of hard and fruitless work followed as the crew tried unsuccessfully to pull the boat off the bar against the brisk river current.

Meanwhile, with nothing to do but eat, the oxen ramped up their "fuel consumption" considerably. It was definitely a drawback of cow power that even while idle, the Hay Burner's "engines" had to eat.

By the time a passing steamer had come to the rescue and pulled them off the bar, the "engines" had wolfed down most of the "fuel" on board.

The rest of the trip to Oregon City was uneventful. The *Hay Burner* arrived, discharged its cargo, and took on a big load of baled "fuel" for the homeward journey.

It was then that the boat's owner made an awful discovery: The *Hay Burner* was vastly underpowered for an upper-Willamette boat. The bovine "engines" simply could not generate enough horsepower — or, rather, cowpower — to drive the boat back upstream against the brisk river current.

And thus ended the maritime careers of the oxen, and Corvallis's fledgling reputation as a hotspot for innovative naval architecture. The oxen were auctioned off; the *Hay Burner* was pushed off the dock at Canemah and allowed to go over the falls; and the "Genius of Corvallis" and his crew took passage on a regular steamship for the long, slow, humiliating ride home.

A few animal-powered ferryboats soldiered on in Oregon waters into the early 20th century — probably the best example was Jehu Switzler's horse-powered ferry, which crossed the Columbia River at Umatilla regularly for a dozen years or so after 1896. But as far as I've been able to learn, no one else ever tried to use animal power for long-distance marine transport; and I have never found any reference to any other boat in Oregon powered by cows — ever.

Sources and Works Cited:
- When Horses Walked on Water, *a book by Kevin J. Crisman & al., published in 1988 by Smithsonian Press;*
- Willamette Landings: Ghost Towns of the River, *a book by Howard M. Corning published in 1947 by Oregon Historial Society Press.*

LIKE DISNEYLAND, ONLY MORE COLD AND RAINY.

THE BAD IDEA:
- *Build a Disneyland-style amusement park in a place that only gets a few dozen dependably sunny days per year.*

It goes without saying that Oregon has changed in the half century that's gone by since the Tom McCall era.

People who remember Oregon in 1967 or so look back on a sort of Edenic place, comfortably conservative in some ways and thrillingly progressive in others; a place with plentiful good-paying jobs and high levels of public services and low taxes and excellent roads, all paid for by a booming timber industry.

It went away, of course, when the mills started mechanizing and the available logging projects dwindled, starting in the late 1970s. But while it lasted, it was a real and distinctive regional culture.

To get a sense of that culture (or, for those of us who have been here long enough, to remember it), there's really no better refresher than the story of Pixieland.

That's especially true because the shift in Oregon's culture is at least partly responsible for the demise of Pixieland.

Pixieland no longer exists; it was open for just four years, fifty years ago. But those four years captured the essence of that postwar Oregon culture that was celebrated in the state's Centennial bash in 1959: a culture, really, of endless progress and proud commercialism and innocence ... topped off with the occasional Bad Idea.

The Pixieland story starts back in 1953, when Jerry and Lu Parks bought a little restaurant called the Pixie Pot Pie in Lincoln City.

The Parkses renamed the restaurant Pixie Kitchen, and over the subsequent decade or so built on the pixie theme until the place almost had a mythology of its own. The décor was themed around a community of pixies, depicted in a distinctive artistic style with little green pointed caps. There was a set of funhouse mirrors in the foyer for kids to entertain themselves with while their families waited to be seated (there was *always* a wait at the Pixie). The restaurant focused heavily on kids, providing paper placemats that could be folded into pixie hats. The tables along the back wall looked out through huge plate-glass windows on a courtyard with a motorized diorama of three pixies running a little train.

The Pixie Kitchen as it appeared in the early 1960s, shortly after Jerry and Lu Parks bought it. (Image: pdxhistory.com)

And, of course, the food was excellent, and there was lots of it. The Pixie specialized in big appetites — for most menu items, if you finished your meal and were still hungry, they would bring you more. It was all-you-can-eat.

By the late 1960s, the Pixie Kitchen was a destination restaurant, and a meal there was an integral part of thousands of Oregon families' regular beach-trip plans. In an age when waiting for a table was almost unheard-of at a diner, the Pixie Kitchen sometimes had so many people waiting that they had to line up outside.

So Jerry and Lu decided they would build on that popularity by giving the kids more of what they loved so much about the Pixie Kitchen: A 57-acre amusement park centered around those pixies.

It would be more than a collection of thrill rides, though, this amusement park. No, Pixieland would be a cultural artifact, a teaching tool for young

Oregonians to learn about their state and its history and culture. It would be, as Jerry Parks put it, "a fairy-tale story of Oregon."

There would be a frontier town, *a la* "Little House on the Prairie"; there would also be an Indian village and canoe docks. Vaudeville shows would be performed in a frontier-style opera house, and there would be an old-fashioned penny arcade. A petting zoo would feature the important animals of Oregon history. And the logging industry would be represented by an old 1890s-vintage narrow-gauge steam logging locomotive (dubbed "Little Toot") and by the *pièce de résistance* of the

A plaque commemorating the dedication of Pixieland by Gov. Tom McCall stands on the park's main street, with the buildings behind. The rocky lump at the far left, next to the Darigold Barn, is the Darigold Cheese Cave. (Image: OSU Libraries)

park: A log-flume ride, like Disneyland's Splash Mountain, in which kids would sit in fiberglass boats shaped like hollowed-out logs and ride a sort of water powered roller-coaster track through the park.

If none of this sounds like any kind of a Bad Idea, just keep in mind what the weather is usually like at the Oregon Coast, and ask yourself: Would you enjoy a ride on something like Disneyland's Splash Mountain if it was 45 degrees and drizzling rain outside? Or even just foggy?

But hindsight is always nice and clear, and everyone at the time thought Pixieland was a fantastic plan. Jerry and Lu unveiled their plans in 1967, and the response was uniformly enthusiastic. The two of them put up $300,000 as seed money; made the rounds of businesses for sponsorships; held a public stock offering to raise another half-million; and got to work on the project.

They hired two former Disneyland executives to help them design the place. It would be built on a 57-acre swampy tidal flat on the edge of the Salmon River estuary; they built a dike around it and drained it to get the requisite firmness underfoot.

Oregon businesses loved the idea, and hurried to get into the act with sponsorships of rides and exhibits. Their participation gave the place a delightfully shameless kitchy quality, probably best illustrated with the Franz Bread Rest Hut — a structure shaped like a great hollow log with a huge fiberglass loaf of balloon bread jutting incongruously out of its top.

BAD IDEAS *and* HORRIBLE PEOPLE *of* OLD OREGON.

Pixieland opened for business on June 28, 1969, with Gov. Tom McCall officially dedicating it. Shiny and new, it featured a frontier Main Street lined with Western-style shops — a print shop, gift store, a penny arcade. There was the Darigold Barn, serving milkshakes and chocolate milk and other dairy treats; and, slumped improbably against it and looking a bit like a colossal drop of drywall mud with a hole in the front, the Darigold Cheese Cave, in which visitors could sample every kind of cheese then known to pre-hipster-cheese-bar-era Oregon.

Other business sponsorships included the Fisher Scone concession building, its roof made of a colossal plaid-painted fiberglass replica of a Scottish tam, and of course the Franz Bread Rest Hut. Inside this, guests could watch their kids enjoy the park's only real thrill ride: the log flume.

Then too, there was the Blue Bell Potato Chips Opera House, a big two-story structure built like a 1910s Grange hall, in which live Vaudeville melodramas ran daily — with noble, manly heroes saving virtuous young maidens from mustache-twirling villains, and other fondly-remembered nineteenth-century theatrical tropes.

And everywhere there were murals and sculptures and plywood cut-outs of those ubiquitous pixies, flashing winning smiles with a hint of mischief behind them.

There were hints of trouble from the start. Plans fell through; costs ran high; the Parkses had to scale back the planned exhibits and rides. They also seem to have had to cut back on their landscaping budget. As a result, even in the postcard views of Pixieland, it looks a little bit unfinished — like the playground at a rural elementary school. The paths and walkways are asphalt, at the side of which the well-groomed grass starts up without the formality of a curb or border. And there's a good deal of unused space.

Children ride the Pixieland log flume ride into the splash pool at the end. Behind it, to the right of the flume, the Blue Bell Opera House can be seen. (Image: OSU Libraries)

That slight air of seediness may have contributed to the park's demise. But it was far from the only factor conspiring against Pixieland.

One of those factors was the U.S. Forest Service. The Forest Service was trying to buy up property around nearby Cascade Head, to preserve its scenic beauty and prevent gated communities and housing developments from covering it. As part of that, they were looking to lock up the Salmon River Estuary so that it could be restored as wildlife habitat and natural land. Pixieland was built on reclaimed estuary ground. As far as the Forest Service was concerned, it should never have been allowed to build where it was, and the sooner it went away, the better. Their aggressiveness in pursuing the goal of getting Pixieland closed down became the source of some hard feelings at the park.

A second factor was the 1973 gas crisis. Motorhomes and travel trailers were a relatively recent trend in the late 1960s, and Pixieland was designed to cater to them. The sudden spike in gas prices made it much harder for motorhome campers to finance trips to the coast. And it also cut down on Willamette Valley familes making day trips to the beach.

Siuslaw National Forest crews dig up concrete footings and other artifacts of Pixieland during the habitat restoration process. The little gray hut was the only remaining building on the site. (Image: Siuslaw National Forest)

But the biggest challenge, by far, was the short operating season. There is a reason Disneyland is located in a place that gets 15 inches of rain a year. Almost all of Pixieland was outdoors, and even in the summertime things can get drizzly and chilly in Lincoln City. How many families chose a different destination for their beach vacation out of fear that the weather would ruin it? It's impossible to say.

And just in case the damp, chilly weather was not enough to qualify Pixieland as a certifiable Bad Idea in and of itself — again, it has to be said that of all the different kinds of thrill rides Pixieland could have chosen as its flagship attractor to draw in the children on those chilly, misty summer days, the log flume ride was probably the worst choice they could have made. A huge part of the fun of any log flume ride is getting soaked with spray. When it's sunny and warm, that's delightful. When it's 53 degrees and the park is shrouded in a light misty drizzle, it's . . . not.

In any case, by 1974 Pixieland was no more. The log flume ride and Little Toot were sold to the Lagoon Amusement Park in Utah, where as of the mid-2010s they were still in service. And by the late 1970s, the park was essentially a 57-acre blackberry bramble.

The Pixie Kitchen soldiered on for another dozen or two years, but it seemed as if the magic had been drawn out of it and infused into the failure of Pixieland. It changed hands several times, and finished its run as a nightclub. Sometime in the 1990s, a fire damaged the structure, and although the best part of the building was still OK, there apparently was no reason to keep it going. It was demolished, and today a Motel 6 occupies the spot that once was home to the best and most popular restaurant in Lincoln City.

Today, the site that once held Pixieland has been restored as part of the Salmon River estuary. The tides have been allowed to flow freely back in and mix with river water, providing cover for all sorts of wildlife — especially salmon smolts. As late as 2005 there was still a building on the grounds — a little tide-gate shack, built in the classic cartoon-pixie style. But by now, even that is gone. A mere 50 years later, Nature has reclaimed its own.

So, could Pixieland have been saved? Likely not. It was other factors that killed it, but by 1974 the culture of Oregon was changing as well, as the demoralization of the Watergate scandal and the growing legitimacy of the anti-war counterculture, plus environmental objections to full-throttle logging, started undermining the shared vision of progress and egalitarian libertarianism that had knitted postwar Oregon together as a community. With its brazen commercialism and proud kitschiness, Pixieland was old-fashioned almost before it was opened for business. If the weather hadn't done Pixieland in, the changing Oregon culture likely would have killed it within a few more years.

And there's another point, which *Portland Oregonian* writer Inara Verzemnieks makes in her 2008 article about the place: "It's hard not to wonder whether if by disappearing, Pixieland became an even better place in the end," she wrote. "If Pixieland had stuck around, we might have been forced to see those things that photos reveal and memories don't: Children bundled up against the bracing cold in Nordic sweaters and wool shirts; the pathetic descent of the log flume ride; the way the pixies in the background actually look kind of menacing. The Pixieland we see now in our minds is more fantastical and impossible than the one that actually existed, which seems right somehow."

By the way, Peter Dibble's documentary film on Pixieland is excellent. If you're interested in more details, and maybe seeing some original footage from the North Lincoln County Historical Museum's collection, you should definitely look it up on YouTube.

Sources and Works Cited:

- *"Pixieland,"* a detailed blog post by Mark Moore posted on his personal Website, *pdxhistory.com;*
- *"Invisible Cities: Pixieland, the Mythical Amusement Park,"* an article by Inara Verzemnieks published in the Jan. 22, 2008, issue of the Portland Oregonian;
- *"Pixieland Restored,"* an episode of Oregon Field Guide produced by Steve Amen for Oregon Public Broadcasting on Feb. 3, 2011;
- *"The Forgotten Story of Pixieland,"* a one-hour documentary film by Peter Dibble released on YouTube on Aug. 12, 2022.

TIMBERLINE LODGE AS A SKYSCRAPER.

THE BAD IDEA:
- *Build Timberline Lodge as a nine-story tower in concrete and glass, instead of as a cozy mountain chalet.*

High up on the side of Mount Hood, Timberline Lodge has, over the years, become an Oregon icon. Its rustic, WPA-financed design and construction strike most visitors as a good fit for the state's general reputation for woodsy civility.

But had it not been for a particularly persnickety U.S. Forest Service manager, Timberline might have looked a lot different.

How different? Think "Bauhaus school of architectural design." With nine stories of concrete and glass, and a cable-car tramway.

The cable car wasn't such a bad idea, although that sort of thing depends a lot on how it's implemented. A cable tramway of sorts was actually installed at Mount Hood in 1950, but it was objectively awful and closed for good a few years later. (More on that in the next chapter.)

But however fun it might be to ride in a gondola up the side of Mount Hood, the idea of scabbing a Manhattan-style skyscraper onto the side of Oregon's tallest mountain seems likely to qualify as a Bad Idea in anyone's book.

The whole scheme had its roots in the early 1920s after the Good Roads movement started resulting in … well, good roads. Once the roads were no longer terrible, and getting stuck in the mud in the middle of nowhere was no longer a real danger, people started venturing out in their Ford Model Ts, Nash Tourings, and Chevrolet Superiors to explore the state. And lots of them explored their way out to the mountain, driving on the freshly built Mount Hood Scenic Loop.

Once there, they started looking for a place to stay so that they wouldn't have to drive all the way home in the dark.

And on that score, most of them were out of luck. There was a hotel on the mountain — the Cloud Cap Inn, built in 1889 as a sort of permanent base camp for mountain climbers — but at 3,500 square feet, and with just a few guest rooms, it was woefully inadequate to this new surge of demand.

(The Cloud Cap Inn, by the way, is still there. The Forest Service acquired it in 1942, and it was probably destined for demolition in the 1950s when the Crag Rats, the oldest search-and-rescue organization in the U.S., pitched a deal whereby they would take responsibility for restoring and maintaining it in exchange for permission to use it as a permanent base from which to launch rescue missions on the mountain. It's not available for public use, but occasionally it's open for public tours.)

Meanwhile, business people in Portland weren't slow to see the

This postcard image, from a note mailed in 1909, shows the tiny Cloud Cap Inn on Mount Hood, with the peak behind. Built in 1889, the Cloud Cap was the only hotel on the mountain until Timberline was built, and after guests started arriving in cars rather than on horses, it proved woefully inadequate to serve the demand for lodgings there. (Image: Postcard)

BAD IDEAS.

The Cloud Cap Inn as it appeared in the early 1890s.. (Image: Frances Fuller Victor)

commercial potential in having a mountain so close, now that anyone could just drive on out and visit it. By developing some destination features there, they could generate a bunch of money from tourism, not just for the owners of the development, but for everyone else along the way. So they started thinking about ways to make Mount Hood a more desirable place to spend vacation time ... and, of course, money.

But to a group of locals who had the requisite magic combination of money, health and leisure, this was not a welcome development. These lucky souls preferred to keep the mountain just as it was — a quiet, magical place of solitude and wildness. They worried that it would be turned into a sort of alpine Coney Island, a wasteland clogged with hamburger stands and tacky roadside attractions, full of noisy children and irresponsible teenagers and other non-Walden-Pond-ish features.

Hah, the businessmen retorted. You just want to keep it as your own personal rich-person playground. (Which, let's be honest here — was a fair comeback.)

This debate got more heated as the 1920s wore on. But it was all just so much talk until a businessman named L.L. Wyler — as part of a committee — came forward with an $800,000 plan to develop the mountain with a flashy, modern high-rise hotel and resort, with gas station and cable tram car.

The Mazama Club — the local mountaineers' organization, which was open only to those who had been on Mount Hood's summit — geared up for battle. But it was over before they knew it. To the surprise of most people on both sides, Forest Service District Forester W.B. Greeley turned the project down flat, calling it a "profit-making eyesore."

Wyler's outfit pressed on, making changes to the plan to try to win the Forest Service over. They refined the plan into that nine-story skyscraper mentioned above, still involving a tram, and went over Greeley's head with it.

Perhaps they thought the glitz factor of such a modern design would win approval. This would be logical, since the administration of Calvin Coolidge (the President who famously said, "The business of America is business") was in charge in D.C. at the time.

They thought wrong. Coolidge's Forest Service planners turned the plan down flat. They didn't go so far as to call it a Bad Idea, but they did say they thought the design looked inappropriate for the scenery.

Much scrambling ensued as various parties tried to come up with something that would look more appropriate. At length they came up with a more rustic-looking lodge plan, one very much on the lines of Timberline Lodge as it appears today. It worked: the Forest Service green-lighted it. All was clear for the developers . . . well, sort of clear.

The problem was that by the time all this wrangling was done, it was 1929; the country was sliding into the Depression, and the Portland businessmen were suddenly unwilling or unable to take on the financial obligation.

This image is from a postcard showing one of the rustic but comfortable rooms at Timberline Lodge; it dates from roughly 1950. (Image: Postcard)

BAD IDEAS.

This image is from a photo postcard made just after World War II. It shows the view of the mountain from the highway at Timberline Lodge. (Image: Postcard)

So, nothing happened.

But some important issues had been settled: Yes, development on the mountain could go forward. But it would have to respect the mountain.

There matters stood for about five years, as the country plunged into the Depression and started trying to claw its way back to normalcy. Part of that process, of course, was the Works Progress Administration, which was offering government grants for infrastructure projects.

Of course the proponents of Timberline Lodge were not slow in getting their application in. They formed the Mount Hood Development Association and drew up plans for a 300-bed hotel, costing $275,513 and following the general outlines of the plan that had been approved in 1929.

Their plan was approved (or re-approved) in 1935, and construction on Timberline Lodge got started the following year.

When the place was finished, the government invited the king of Norway to come demonstrate a wild new sport called "alpine skiing." They needn't have bothered. Plenty of Oregonians of Scandinavian and Swiss descent were able and eager to show the way.

The lodge opened for its first overnight guests in 1938, and the following year Oregon's first chairlift, the Magic Mile Chairlift, was established there.

Perhaps the most enduring symbol of Timberline is the 750-pound

BAD IDEAS *and* HORRIBLE PEOPLE *of* OLD OREGON.

Architect Gilbert Stanley Underwood's design for Timberline Lodge, shown in this 1936 elevation drawing from his firm. (Image: Timberline Lodge)

bronze weathervane, crafted in a sort of abstract primitive design suggesting a bird. Most people assume it's a Native American design, and perhaps it is — but the workers who built it actually cribbed the design from a Camp Fire Girls handbook.

So, this all sounds like great news, doesn't it? A Bad Idea was proposed, and cooler heads prevailed. A good outcome, all around.

That would not be the case with the next big Bad Idea proposed for Mount Hood, though. We'll get into that story in the next chapter.

Sources and Works Cited:
- Timberline Lodge: A Love Story, *a book by Judith Rose published by Graphic Arts Center Publishing in 1986;*
- Hiking Oregon's History, *a book by William L. Sullivan published by Navillus Press in 2006.*
- *"A Weekend at Cloud Cap Inn," an article by Lindy Callahan published on the Travel Oregon Website on Dec. 7, 2016.*
- *"The History of Timberline Lodge," a page on the lodge's Website at timberlinelodge.com/about-us/history*

THE 20-TON BUS IN THE SKY.

THE BAD IDEA:
- *Modify a noisy, uncomfortable city bus to operate as a massive, terrifying aerial cable car, and use it to bring skiers to Timberline Lodge.*

If, while you were reading the last chapter, the idea of cable car service to Timberline Lodge struck you as a not particularly bad one, you're not alone. Over the years since the Wyler group proposed its glass-and-steel mountaintop skyscraper, several proposals have been floated for cable-car service up the mountain.

So far, only one has been built, and it was an immediate failure: The Skiway Tram project.

The Skiway was the brainchild of Dr. J. Otto George, who came up with the idea just after the Second World War, as the popularity of skiing started to explode nationwide. George hit on an idea that would, he hoped, make it possible to build an aerial tramway at a very low relative cost. With a group of other investors, he formed the Mount Hood Aerial Transportation Co. to implement his plan.

The usual process for creating a new cable tram line was, and still is, to engineer it with a lightweight six- to ten-passenger gondola which is pulled up and down the mountain by means of a ground-mounted engine or electric motor. All of this, of course, is extremely expensive. One can't just buy

The Skiway aerial trolley works its way along with the mountains in the background. The buses were of the double-ender type, with one running on each of two sets of cables. (Image: portland-history.net)

cable-car gondolas out of the Grainger catalog; they have to be custom built for each project, as do the power systems and cable handling mechanisms.

But Otto George had another idea that he thought could get the job done on the cheap: He'd use skyline-logging equipment to do it.

Skyline logging setups are built strong enough to carry loads of logs weighing hundreds of tons through the air, up the side of a hill and to a log landing. George figured wrangling a trolley full of skiers up the side of Mount Hood would be a doddle for a skyline setup. And the components could be bought, in most cases, off the shelf; the development and engineering had already been done.

Since a skyline setup could handle almost any amount of weight a passenger service might require, George picked a double-end city bus to serve as the gondola. Again, he'd save plenty of money by using equipment that was already in service; and being able to carry more than a few passengers at a time would enable him to charge a more competitive fare.

This would also save the cost of a ground-based power plant, because the buses, of course, had their own engines. Each bus — there were two of them — was modified somewhat crudely to transfer the power from its drive wheels up to a 1.5-inch overhead traction cable, which it would claw its way along up and down the mountain.

Most truly Bad Ideas are good ideas gone awry through some key detail being overlooked. Not this one. The Skiway was a Bad Idea through and through, from the very start. It was slow, loud, and terrifying. Enormous amounts of force had to be applied to the traction cable just to move the buses up the side of the mountain, so the trolleys made the uphill run with their engines running flat out. The engines weren't diesels, so they could have been louder; but nonetheless they were plenty noisy, too loud for passengers to carry on a conversation during the trip.

Nor was the Skiway at all suitable for the faint of heart. Skyline logging setups are not designed with passenger comfort in mind; they just have to get the logs to the landing to be trucked away, and if the ride is rough and unpleasant, well, the logs don't care.

A city bus full of passengers weighs 15 to 20 tons, which is a lot of weight to have dangling from a cable in the air. The weight dragging down the cable would make it sag deeply as the bus moved from one piling to the next, so that the trip up the mountain became a roller-coaster-like cycle of the tram clawing its way up to one of the towers and then almost free-falling down the other side (nose down, of course) before starting the climb to the next.

"I've ridden the tramway," board member George Rauch said, at one of the later company meetings, as the failure of the venture was becoming obvious. "I've listened to the shrieks and I've taken the jolts over those, what you call them — the saddles, and I've heard what people say."

The Skiway aerial trolley emerges from its "hangar" in Government Camp for a run up to Timberline Lodge. (Image: Oregon Historical Society/ Al Monner)

All these issues might have been OK, because when the Skiway was planned, there was no other convenient way to get up to Timberline for a day of skiing. But at just about the same time the Skiway opened for passengers, improvements to the highway to Timberline eliminated this advantage. One could now drive to Timberline, or take a ground-based shuttle bus, and get there ten minutes quicker (and, in the case of the bus, for 25 cents less; the tram was 75 cents one-way, and the buses were 50).

When the Skiway flying-bus service opened in 1951, there was considerable nationwide fanfare, and lots of people lined up to ride it. But for most of them, one ride was enough. Activity quickly dropped off to the point where the sky-buses were idle for months on end. By 1956, the run was shut down, and the Mount Hood Aerial Transportation Co. board was faced with some hard decisions.

Should they pull the buses and replace them with smaller cars? What about investing in a ground-traction system, like ski lifts use, to reduce the weight and noise?

But all these options cost money, and the board had no stomach for risking further sums. A liquidation committee was formed, and by the early 1960s the sky-bus line was no more.

Sources and Works Cited:
- *" 'Most Extraordinary of Buses': Documenting the Rise and Fall of the Mt. Hood Aerial Skiway with OHS Collections," an article by Lindsey Benjamin published Jan. 7, 2020, on the Oregon Historical Society blog at ohs.org/blog;*
- *"Skiway Tram," an article by Cheryl Hill published Jan. 5, 2016, on portlandhistory.net.*

WORLD'S WEIRDEST AMUSEMENT PARK.

THE BAD IDEA:
- *After the amusement park owners you're trying to shake down call your bluff, go ahead and build your competing park after all — and do it in a way that will remind folks of a David Lynch movie.*

For a small group of Portland-area businessmen in 1929, opportunity was knocking — or so they thought.

Jantzen Beach, the legendary swim-and-play amusement park on Hayden Island in the Columbia River, had opened in 1928 to vast sell-out crowds, and was doing very well there. It was backed by some deep pockets, and was a showplace for the Jantzen brand of swimwear.

Well, these businessmen happened to own a large piece of real estate on the other side of the island — the easternmost tip of it, in fact. So ... why not announce plans to develop a huge amusement park there, and get the rich backers of Jantzen Beach to buy them out? Easy money, right?

The businessmen got busy working on Operation Shakedown. They called it "Lotus Isle."

The trouble was, they had to spend some money to make the Jantzen Beach people think they were serious. So they did, confident in their assumption that they'd get it all back when Jantzen Beach bought them out.

Bad Idea.

In mid-1929, Jantzen Beach called their bluff, saying jovially that there was plenty of room for all and the competition was welcome.

So the would-be bilkers were more or less forced to open their park up after all.

And thus was born a theme park that seems, today, remarkably like a setting for a David Lynch movie.

As it turned out, the Jantzen Beach people were right — at least, at first. There really was business enough for both parks. When the plan to get bought out by Jantzen Beach failed, an investor named Edwin Platt stepped up with enough money to do it right; this wouldn't be a "good enough" park, like what would happen four decades later with Pixieland when construction costs overran (see Page 51 for the details on that, if you haven't already).

When it was finished, Lotus Isle had a sort of Arabian Nights theme, with Moorish-inspired architecture, and more than 40 rides spread out over 128 acres. The grand ballroom was the centerpiece of the place, and it was enormous — approved for 6,400 people. There was a 5,000-car parking lot, and space for 15,000 picnickers. It was Oregon's biggest theme park by a considerable margin, and when it opened for the first time in June 1930, Lotus Isle was an instant hit.

And for two months it looked like a real winner. The folks at Jantzen Beach have to have had a few bad moments when they saw the sheer scale and quality of the thing.

A vintage 1940s postcard image of the swimming pool at Jantzen Beach. (Image: Postcard)

But Lotus Isle was also, hands down, the most surreal amusement park in Oregon history. The roof of the bumper cars ride was shaped like a giant hairless bulldog, complete with fangs protruding from a menacing frown, crouched down as if preparing to pounce on a small child. At the park's entrance was a hundred-foot tall neon sign in the shape of the Eiffel Tower in Paris; this massive, random piece of commercial art could be seen from miles away, on both sides of the river, and was used to guide visitors in. The windows of its mammoth Moorish-style dance hall, the Peacock Ballroom, were screened with chicken wire hooked to an electric-fence charger; this was apparently to keep non-paying guests from getting in, but it's not hard to imagine where a good horror-film screenwriter might go with this little detail.

The roof over the bumper-cars ride at Lotus Isle, seemingly crafted for maximum scariness to small children. (Image: pdxhistory.com)

Even the name seemed like an obscure joke dreamed up by an opium smoker with a master's degree in classics. Who wants to go play on the Island of the Lotus Eaters, really?

None of these oddities and inconsistencies hurt attendance at Lotus Isle, though. What did hurt attendance would actually have been pretty on-brand for a David Lynch movie: Death.

It happened late in August — almost exactly two months after the place opened. An 11-year-old boy, clambering around under the diving board where nobody could see him, fell into the Columbia River and drowned.

The next day, Edwin Platt was found dead — shot through the heart, with a suicide note close at hand.

This, naturally, cast an awful pall over Lotus Isle for the rest of the 1930 season.

Over that fall and winter, new management came in and tried to reorganize the place to give it a go in 1931.

As part of that plan, Al Painter, a colorful promoter with a checkered past and sketchy business associations, came to Lotus Isle. Al was rumored to have been running from some creditors when he came to Portland. He certainly was running from some when he left.

One of the first things Painter did was to bring Portland what might have been its first "dance marathon" event — the "Dance-a-thon," held in the cavernous Peacock Ballroom. It was well received, and for most of the season all was well and Lotus Isle was thriving again.

Dance marathons were a sort of weird 1920s and 1930s fad that came along just about the same time the Great Depression did, and stuck around longer than they probably would have if people weren't desperate for some way to make money. The idea was, a promoter sold tickets to a bunch of dancers, and part of the ticket price went into a pot. The couples would then take to the floor and dance for literally days on end — dance until they dropped or were too exhausted to continue. One by one, they'd quit or collapse. The last couple standing (by the end, they were mostly just leaning against each other and trying not to fall over while swaying side to side; if they stopped moving, they lost) won the pot.

Sounds like great fun, doesn't it? And it's probably safe to say that nobody much enjoyed it. But with dozens or even hundreds of couples pitching into the pot, the last couple standing stood to take home a pretty hefty wad at the end of their 72 to 84 hours of romantic torture, and plenty of people were desperate for cash in 1931; so the events were very popular, both for the dancers themselves and for spectators.

Lotus Isle also sponsored "Walk-a-thons," which at that time meant something like a dance marathon without the dancing. Individual participants would basically walk until they dropped, and the last walker still on his or her feet and in forward motion won the pot. Local radio stations kept

A very early aerial photo of the Highway 99 bridge over Hayden Island, with Jantzen Beach in the very center of the image. Lotus Isle was a mile or so beyond the right-hand side of this picture. (Postcard image)

The marina and the old streetcar-trestle pilings from Lotus Isle, the amusement park, as seen from Lotus Isle City Park today. (Image: brx0 photography | CC-by-SA)

listeners updated with who was still in competition, who'd dropped out, and so forth.

For a time, once again, things were looking pretty good for Lotus Isle.

But late August seemed to hold a special jinx for Lotus Isle. On August 24, 1931, the Peacock Ballroom caught fire and burned to the ground in one of the more spectacular structure fires of Portland history. Folks in Vancouver at the time could feel the heat of the blaze, from 700 feet away on the other side of the river.

The word on the street was that the fire was arson — and that it was intended to hurt Al Painter.

If so, it certainly did. The timing was pretty lousy. Al had, three months before, purchased an elephant — the biggest elephant in captivity, a 12-foot-tall, 20,000-pound circus veteran with the burly stage name "Tusko." Tusko had acquired a reputation as the bad boy of ten-ton elephants a few years earlier by going on a rampage through downtown Sedro-Wooley, Washington. (There's more about Tusko, including details of his Sedro-Wooley rampage, in the next chapter.)

Painter first tried to give Tusko to the Portland zoo, but, mindful of the elephant's reputation for testiness, the city demurred, and Tusko ended up becoming part of the exhibit at Lotus Isle.

After the fire, Painter brought Tusko down to Salem for the Oregon State Fair and then disappeared, leaving the state with the ten-ton elephant to feed. Nothing was heard from him until December, when someone spotted an article in a New Orleans newspaper, which reported that he'd launched his Dance-A-Thon promotion there, run up large debts (including the prizes for the winning couple in a Dance-A-Thon which was still ongoing), and skipped town. It must have sounded pretty familiar to the Portlanders who heard about it.

After Painter's midnight slinking-off, there wasn't much left of Lotus Isle. It hung on through the 1932 season, but early in 1933 everything was liquidated in a bankruptcy proceeding.

Today, all that's left is Lotus Isle City Park, on the south side of the island, and a row of rotting pilings heading out across the Columbia River where the streetcar trestle used to be.

By the way, Mark Moore goes into a lot more detail about Lotus Isle on his blog, with tons of historic photos. It's well worth the 30 minutes or so that it takes to see and read everything he's collected and curated at pdxhistory.org.

Sources and Works Cited:
- Round the Roses, *a book by Karl Klooster published in 1987 by Klooster Promotions;*
- *"Lotus Isle Amusement Park," a detailed blog post by Mark Moore published Oct. 22, 2017, on pdxhistory.org;*
- Great and Minor Moments in Oregon History, *a book by Dick Pintarich published in 2009 by New Oregon Press;*
- Portland Morning Oregonian *archives, 1929-1931.*

POOR OLD TUSKO.

THE BAD IDEA:
- *Buy a ten-ton, famously ill-tempered bull elephant that eats two tons of hay per week for an amusement-park mascot.*

Under the light of a single bulb, in a big storage room at the University of Oregon's Museum of Natural and Cultural History in Eugene, are the bones of a famous onetime Oregonian named Ned.

Ned had other names. On stage, he was billed as "Tusko the Magnificent," "Tusko the Terrible," or just plain "Tusko." Toward the end of his short life, he was known in the newspapers as "Tusko the Unwanted."

But he always answered to Ned, and toward the end he started getting angry when people called him Tusko ... and Ned had this much in common with David Banner: you definitely did not want to be around when he got angry.

Ned was, of course, an elephant. Specifically, he was the biggest elephant in captivity in the 1930s, when he came to Oregon to join the cast and crew of history's most surreal amusement park, Lotus Isle.

Ned had started out his career in show business at the age of six, when he was just five feet tall. He'd been shipped to America from the lumber camps of Siam in 1898, and spent the following quarter-century on the road with various circuses and traveling shows. Along the way, Ned ate and ate, and grew and grew. Unfortunately, the bigger he got, the more nervous he made people.

The beginning of the end for Ned's show-business career came in 1922. He'd been acquired by the Al G. Barnes Circus, and was being promoted as "Tusko the Terrible." On May 17, 1922, Ned and his circus were in Sedro-Wooley, Washington, when "Tusko" went on a rampage.

Why he did this is unclear. One source suggests he was drunk at the time, and that was possible — Tusko's later reaction to being presented with a tub of moonshine (to fight a cold) suggested a long familiarity with strong drink. Another source says Tusko was responding to an unusually vigorous beating, which, unfortunately, wouldn't be unusual for a circus elephant in the 1920s.

In any case, Ned tossed his handler aside (breaking several of the man's ribs in the process) and lit out for the wide open spaces. He overturned a number of cars, knocked a few buildings off their foundations, and caused a mass panic in a Sedro-Wooley dance hall. By the time the circus crew caught up with him, he'd carved a 30-mile trail of destruction through the northern Washington countryside, demolishing a chicken coop and trashing a lumber camp. His handlers found him stuck between two angled boxcars, so he was easily recaptured.

Circus people then followed his trail of destruction through the countryside with a suitcase full of money, indemnifying anyone and everyone they thought might sue them.

The rampage seems to have changed Ned somehow, though. While before this incident he'd been known for a mellow disposition, he now started getting increasingly testy, and circus customers were starting to notice. Finally, Barnes pulled him off the circuit for a rest at the circus's winter headquarters in southern California.

What was supposed to be a short break turned into a two-year sentence after Ned lashed out at his manicurist, breaking both tusks against the bars of his prison-cell-like home.

While he was serving this time, another bull elephant was touring the country as "Tusko the Magnificent." This impostor elephant, at a show in Texas, went on a deadly rampage, killing a spectator, and was promptly shot and killed. But after that many circus visitors assumed Ned was a killer — which, it must be noted, he never was.

That bad reputation, coupled with his famous appetite — two tons of hay each week, plus supplements of apples and carrots — made Ned a net

BAD IDEAS.

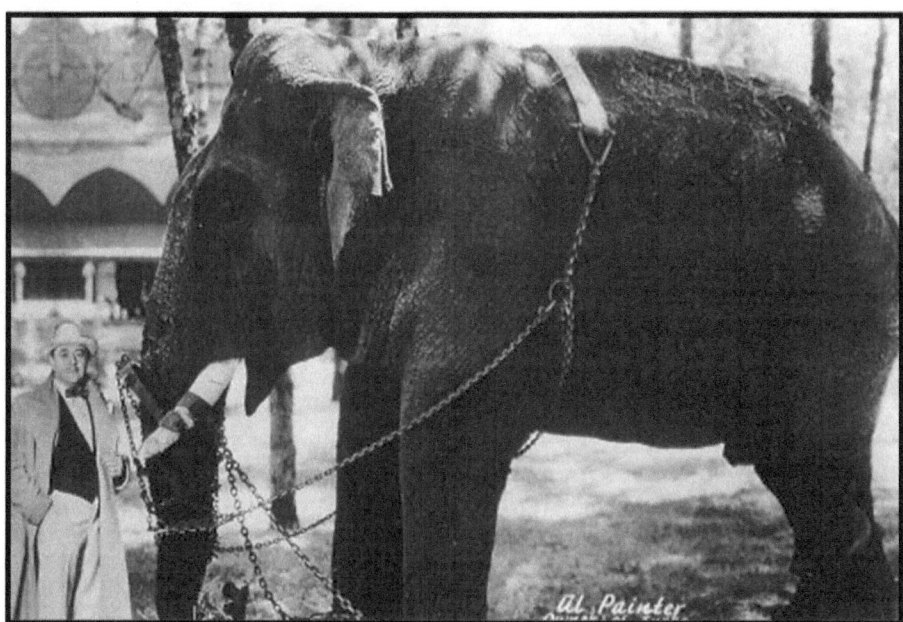

Promoter Al Painter stands with Ned ("Tusko") at Lotus Isle during the 1931 season.

liability for the circus. So it sold him off in 1931 for $2,800 to a dapper, stocky showman from Portland's Lotus Isle: Our old friend from the last chapter, Al Painter.

And that's how Ned came to Oregon.

As mentioned, Painter first offered Ned to the city zoo, hoping apparently to score some goodwill points for Lotus Isle. But, mindful of what happened to the city of Sedro-Wooley, the Portland Zoo declined the gift. So Ned spent the summer as a prime attraction at Lotus Isle.

This probably didn't seem like a true Bad Idea at first. It made a certain amount of sense for an amusement park where everything was styled after Arabian Nights, in a commercialized Moorish style, to have an elephant for a mascot. But his handlers soon had reason to think otherwise. Tusko was noticeably crotchety most of the time, and when early aviator Tex Rankin flew low over Lotus Isle in his biplane one day, Tusko spooked, breaking his chains and going on a short but panicky rampage that destroyed several of Lotus Isle's remaining buildings.

At the end of the 1931 season, Painter could see that Tusko was not working out. He wasn't bringing in enough business to justify his staggering food bill, let alone the damage from his rampage.

So Painter asked fellow show-biz man T.H. Eslick (known to friends and enemies alike as "The Slick") to bring Tusko to Salem for the Oregon State Fair, and while Eslick and Ned were down there, Painter disappeared like a puff of smoke on the wind.

Eslick, at the end of the state fair, left Ned behind and slipped off home to Portland, and Fair Director Max Gehlar found himself stuck with the baby. Eslick claimed Ned was Painter's responsibility, and Painter could not be found. It was about this time that newspapers started referring to Ned ruefully as "Tusko the Unwanted."

A couple months of expensive hay munching later, the state finally managed to auction Ned off for $200. His new owners chained him to a flatbed truck and hauled him north to Portland — a trip that took four hours in those pre-freeway days, and surely came near to killing Ned from the cold; by then it was October already.

In Portland, he was lodged in a ramshackle tin building near the waterfront, at East Main and Water streets, where people could pay a dime to look at him. Here he spent a miserable, cold, hungry winter.

At one point, he caught a cold and it got bad enough to put him off his feed; everyone knew what a legendary trencherman Ned was, and for him to stop eating he had to be really sick, so his handler brought him a ten-gallon keg of moonshine, cut it with five gallons of water and poured it into a trough for the visibly excited Ned. Three giant gulps later, Ned was happily and drunkenly frolicking with a hay bale, then soon fell asleep. *The Morning*

This photo of Tusko is from Salem and probably was made after he was abandoned there at the Oregon State Fair. This episode, and the state's subsequent complaints about his food consumption, led the Portland Morning Oregonian to sympathetically dub him "Tusko the Unwanted."

Oregonian covered both his "ten-gallon spree" and the ensuing hangover on its front page.

The good times were rare for Ned, though, that winter. In his cold tin shed, unable to move around much, Ned was mostly miserable. That winter he went on another rampage, this time on Christmas Eve. This one didn't do much damage, other than to the shed he was living in; Ned seemed mostly to just want to run away. Shivering cold in the winter weather, he was soon recaptured.

The following spring, the elephant left Portland as his new owners took him on the road. All the press coverage of Ned's troubles at the state fair and his Christmas Eve bustout had raised his profile, and tens of thousands of Northwesterners were eager to see him. But still he lost money. He simply ate too much. His handlers decided he needed to retire to a nice city zoo, and they picked Seattle.

Then they launched an elaborate con: They were going to "execute" him. They even advertised in the *Seattle Post-Intelligencer* for a big-game hunter to be their trigger man.

It worked. The city rallied; schoolchildren broke open piggy banks; the mayor made a speech. A few weeks later, Tusko moved into his new digs at the Woodland Park Zoo.

He died about a year later at the youthful (for an elephant) age of 42. The official cause of death was a blood clot in his heart, but one of his old handlers later told the *Oregonian* he'd developed debilitating arthritis from standing on concrete all his life, and he'd had to be euthanized with "the black bottle" — that is, poison.

Even in death, poor Ned could get no respect. He was skinned immediately; one of his owners planned to stuff his hide and mount it outside a motel to attract business. The hide was ruined by vermin before he could get this done, in one of history's very few examples of rats making the world better instead of worse.

The bones were cleaned by boiling in a huge pot, and the skeleton spent a summer on tour as a circus sideshow attraction. It ate a lot less, of course, but people were less willing to pay to see it. Finally its owners gave up and put it away, and eventually donated it to the University of Oregon.

Maybe someday soon Oregonians will be able to come to Eugene to visit old Ned ... and, maybe, mutter a little apology to the giant animal's long-suffering bones.

Sources and Works Cited:
- "Lotus Isle Amusement Park," a detailed blog post by Mark Moore published Oct. 22, 2017, on pdxhistory.org;
- Great and Minor Moments in Oregon History, *a book by Dick Pintarich published in 2009 by New Oregon Press;*
- Portland Morning Oregonian *archives, 1931.*

THE OWN-GOAL KING.

THE BAD IDEA:
- *Very nearly every social-justice project undertaken by A.C. Edmunds, a social reformer for whom the perfect was always the enemy of the good.*

One of the most dramatic things that can happen in a soccer game is an "own-goal." Not the kind where a player on offense bounces a shot off a defender and into the net, but the full-on kind in which a defender gets excited and confused and blasts a barn-burner straight past his own team's goalie, scoring a point for the other team.

If Oregon history were a soccer club, and kept stats on such things, there is one particular player who would stand head and shoulders above all the others in the "own-goals" category: A.C. Edmunds.

A.C. Edmunds, throughout his several careers in Oregon and California, was almost like a cartoon — a larger-than-life loser in the vein of Wile E. Coyote, with a little Carrie Nation mixed in along with a whole lot of Don Quixote.

Nor were his "own-goals" minor affairs. A.C. Edmunds was almost singlehandedly responsible for the demise of the early Universalist Church in California, the temporary collapse of the Universalist congregation in Portland, and for the sudden death of the temperance and women's suffrage movements in Oregon in 1874. Before he got involved, Oregon was on track to become the first state in which women could vote. His efforts to help make that happen set the process back a good 40 years.

All in all, A.C. Edmunds was an especially important historical character — but for all the wrong reasons.

"His impact was in fact sometimes significant," historian George Belknap writes, in his 1983 *Oregon Historical Quarterly* article about Edmunds. "But his impact was usually the ruin of sometimes worthy and promising causes through his unfailing skill in antagonizing his publics."

In other words, A.C. Edmunds wasn't so much a man full of Bad Ideas, although he did have some, so much as he himself *was* a Bad Idea.

Abraham Coryell Edmunds was born in 1827 in the Toronto area, and grew up in the Northeast — New York and later Ohio. In 1846 he joined the Army to fight in the Mexican-American war, but apparently by the time his Ohio regiment got to the scene, the war was over. On his return, he later recalled, he and his comrades collected an assortment of well-shaped sticks from along the banks of the Mississippi, which they sold to new recruits as walking canes captured from Mexican officers.

When the Gold Rush broke out, Edmunds headed for California to join the throng, but didn't get there until 1850. This may be because he walked the entire way, on foot, from his then-home in Michigan. This would become something A.C. would be known for, in his youth: he walked everywhere. He later claimed to have logged 34,000 miles on foot.

What Edmunds did upon arriving in California is unknown. He probably started out, as so many did, mining for gold. Whatever it was, it left him with a nice cash balance that he seems to have been very good at stewarding — because he would spend much of the rest of his life starting and abandoning money-losing ventures of various sorts.

Whatever it was, he was done with it by 1857, because we know that year Edmunds was working as an itinerant preacher spreading the gospel of Universalism among the mining camps of the West.

Universalism, in the 1840s, was a strain of evangelical Protestantism that argued that every human soul would be saved — that there was no "elect," and that Hell was a temporary posting to which souls were sent to square their accounts before admission to Heaven.

Edmunds would set out in the early morning, walk 20 or 25 miles to a mining camp, preach a harsh but rousing sermon, and do it again the next day; he composed and refined his sermons as he walked.

BAD IDEAS.

Edmunds' combination of boundless energy and enthusiasm, plus his passion for righteousness, smoothed his climb into prominence in the growing Universalist church. He moved to Marysville, founded a Universalist Society, and launched the first of what would become a long string of short-lived publications: The *Star of the Pacific*.

It was in this magazine that the reading public got its first taste of Edmunds' rhetorical style. It was cocky, self-righteous, savage, and Manichean — there were no shades of gray in it. One was either in full agreement with Edmunds and right, or entirely wrong and irredeemably evil. As a personal style, it was an odd fit for a Universalist.

Nor did he reserve such invective only for important topics. A.C. Edmunds seemed ready, willing, and able to die upon every hill, however insignificant. For example, a pious newspaper

A portrait of A.C. Edmunds which appeared in Western Life-Boat, *one of the mug-books he published back east just before his return to Portland, in early 1873. The portrait is accompanied by a phrenological reading (phrenology is the "science" of extrapolating human type and character based on the shape of one's head). (Image: Oregon Historical Society)*

writer's reference to a group of ladies who claimed they'd been saved from a tornado by the power of prayer drew this little gem:

"We are surprised that a man, claiming a decent respect for intelligence ... should send forth, before an enlightened world, such nonsensical trash .... If prayer had such a magical, miraculous influence over the elements, it would be wisdom in our city fathers to employ their services, thereby saving the enormous expense of organized fire companies ... If our gill of brains could not father a more noble sentiment, we would blow them out, and fill the vaccum with cabbage seeds."

This kind of style, of course, had the effect of turning every potential ally into an enemy. And this was especially true as he started increasingly mixing religion and politics in the runup to the Civil War — taking up the hatchet against the pro-slavery "Copperheads" with a ferocity and savagery that made most of his readers uncomfortable, whatever their political leanings were.

Still, it was a rough era, and Edmunds' style worked well enough in the mining and logging camps where he continued to travel and preach. Historian Belknap suggests that his constant motion was actually a mechanism he employed to cope with the inevitable eventual failure of his enterprises — that before the pigeons could come home to roost, he'd have moved on to greener pastures — and there may be something in that; but, anyone with more than a smattering of the cognitive style known as "Attention Deficit/Hyperactivity Disorder" will understand that the "outrunning failure" theory isn't the only possibility here.

In 1860, while still down in California, Edmunds organized the first statewide Universalist convention. He drew up an ambitious and exciting plan for the event, including the establishment of a Universalist college. Edmunds was, it seemed, on the cusp of becoming a very important person indeed.

But before the convention members could meet to get things started, the American Civil War broke out. Edmunds dropped everything, ran to the recruiting office, enlisted in the California militia, learned that his company wasn't going to go and fight, quit in disgust, and moved to Portland.

The Universalist Convention, abruptly deprived of its leader, vanished.

Meanwhile, that leader was diving headlong into the rhetorical battle over slavery and the secession of the South. Edmunds plugged back into the Universalist circle, of course; but by mid-1962, barely nine months after his arrival, the Portland Universalists were already wishing he would go away. He leaped back into journalism by founding the *Portland Daily Plaindealer* as a stridently pro-Union paper,

This drawing, from an 1874 issue of Frank Leslie's Weekly, shows the Ohio ladies who were the Portland temperance workers' primary inspiration, singing and praying before a saloon. This scene, drawn by S.B. Morton, is set in Logan, Ohio. (Image: Library of Congress)

and for a while it looked like a winner; but Edmunds eventually got around to insulting enough people that his investors pulled out, and he was forced to close up shop.

He then moved to Eugene and did it all over again, launching the *Herald of Reform*, renaming it the *Union Crusader*, and then — in case anyone thought that was too subtle — subtitling it "Copperhead Killer."

This was very inconvenient for the Eugene Republicans, who really wanted to reach out the olive branch to the less strident faction among the "Copperheads," the Douglas Democrats (those who had supported Stephen Douglas in the 1860 election). The Douglas Democrats opposed slavery and were pro-Union; but they were not ideologically pure enough for Edmunds, who seems to have felt that an ally who disagreed on one or two minor points was a threat to doctrinal purity, and therefore more dangerous than the bitterest enemy.

Well, having a literal death threat printed at the top of a newspaper does not do much for that newspaper's ability to win the hearts and minds of those on the fence about such things. So the city fathers in Eugene got together with Edmunds' print-shop foreman, Harrison Kincaid, and bought Edmunds out, renaming the paper the *Oregon State Journal*.

The *Journal* went on to a prosperous 50-year run in Eugene, and was on at least one occasion "borrowed" by Edmunds as a success story (he called himself a "co-founder").

But by now it was 1864, and Edmunds decided it was time to volunteer for war service for real. He went back east to do it, and finished the war as an Army hospital administrator.

Edmunds stayed back east for a few years after that, settling in Iowa and Nebraska and engaging in more publishing ventures. He attempted to revolutionize the business of publishing mug-books — which are, basically, collections of fawning articles about important community members illustrated with pictures of their subjects, usually paid for by the subjects. Edmunds' mug-books, though, mixed fawning articles about paying subjects with not-so-fawning articles about people who not only hadn't bought profiles, but probably wouldn't have if paid to. These "freebies," of course, came with the full A.C. Edmunds style of personal savagery. Paying customers soon grew loath to be associated with this enterprise, and it collapsed.

By the early 1870s, he was back to seeking out unburned turf where he might yet have another go ... and that's what brought him back to Portland, where his biggest and most history-shaping own-goal waited to be scored.

A.C. Edmunds' experience in Portland before the Civil War had been so short, and by his personal standards so uneventful, that the turf there was for all practical purposes unburned.

And when he arrived, late in 1873, his timing could not have been better. The city was alive with the fervent spirit of reform — just the sort of environment in which Edmunds most thrived. Plus, the topic of reform was one of his regular hobby-horses: Temperance.

If you've read *Heroes and Rascals of Old Oregon*, the first volume of this collection, you'll know this story. The society ladies of Portland, inspired by reports of the great temperance movements back east, had organized themselves through the main downtown Protestant churches into the Women's Temperance Prayer League. The plan: Members of the League would fare forth into the city each day and visit a saloon. There, they would hold a prayer service, plead the cause of temperance to its owner and patrons, circulate a pledge to abstain from alcohol consumption in future, and move on.

It took a little while for the ladies to get their program dialed in just right, but by the spring of 1874 it was hitting nicely on all twelve cylinders and sending ripples of fear through Portland saloon owners.

Their intervention led at least two saloon owners to quit the business. But it enraged one particular saloon owner — Walter Moffett, owner of the

Webfoot Saloon. Moffett's scandalously ungentlemanly behavior on the frequent occasions when the ladies came to see him not only inspired the ladies' determination to wear him down, but also galvanized public opinion in Portland against the saloons, and in favor of the ladies — and, by extension, temperance.

The ladies were still riding that wave of popular support and esteem as the election day for Portland City Council positions drew near.

There were at least two slates of candidates for the Council seats: a reform-oriented Republican one, and a "People's Ticket" that was generally stocked with liquor-business-friendly candidates. (The Democratic party did not put forth a ticket.)

Several sources claim there was a Temperance ticket as well. That's not technically correct; the temperance crusaders, according to historian Belknap, made the practical decision to work with the reform-minded Republicans rather than trying to field their own slate of vote-splitting Temperance candidates. None of them were happy with this decision, of course; they would much rather have had a slate of pure-hearted teetotalers to vote for; but they knew if they found and put one forward, the liquor ticket would ride to easy victory over a divided opposition.

But this was exactly the sort of practical political

Voters' Book of Remembrance.

Voters of Portland, The Book of Remembrance is this day opened, and you are called upon to choose "whom ye will serve." On one hand are found prostitutes, gamblers, rumsellers, whiskey topers, beer guzzlers, wine bibbers, rum suckers, hoodlums, loafers and ungodly men. On the other hand are found Christian wives, mothers, sisters and daughters of the good people of Portland. You cannot serve two masters. You must be numbered with one or the other. Whom will ye choose?

Remember the Temperance ticket. Vote for it early and work for it earnestly all day. It is the safe side.

Remember that this is a struggle between virtue and vice. May you be found on the side of virtue.

Remember that the success of either of the other tickets is the success of whiskey—supported by bad men and polluted women.

Remember that the whiskey advocates employ prostitutes to insult Christian women while praying and reading the Holy Bible.

Remember that the police of Portland arrest, fine and imprison the Christian women of Portland for reading the Bible and praying.

Remember that the police of Portland are devoted to the protection of prostitution, drunkenness and debauchery and the persecution and punishment of virtue.

Remember that persons are known by the company they keep. Birds of a feather flock together.

Remember that R. R. Thompson, one of the whiskey candidates on one of the whiskey tickets, served on the jury that fined and imprisoned Christian women in Portland for reading the Bible and praying.

The first page of the "Voters' Book of Remembrance," A.C. Edmunds' double-sided election's-eve flyer, which insulted Portland voters badly enough to turn them off both temperance and women's suffrage for nearly 40 years. (Image: University of Oregon Libraries) compromise that always seemed to bring out the worst in A.C. "Copperhead Killer" Edmunds. And it seems to have, in this situation, done just that.

Shortly before the election, Edmunds stepped forward with a small essay that he proposed to have printed and circulated on Election Day, which he assured the ladies would tip the balance and assure them the win. The circular was titled "The Voter's Book of Remembrance," and it was a simple half-sheet flyer.

"Voters of Portland, the Book of Remembrance is this day opened, and you are called upon to choose 'whom ye will serve,'" it starts out. "On one hand are found prostitutes, gamblers, rumsellers, whiskey topers, beer guzzlers, wine bibbers, rum suckers, hoodlums, loafers and ungodly men. On the other hand are found Christian wives, mothers, sisters and daughters of the good people of Portland. You cannot serve two masters. You must be numbered with one or the other. Whom will ye choose?"

It actually gets worse as it goes on, blatantly accusing Portland's police of being "devoted to the protection of prostitution, drunkenness and debauchery, and the persecution and punishment of virtue" and claiming that "whiskey advocates employ prostitutes to insult Christian women while praying and reading the Holy Bible."

By modern standards of campaign polemics, it's not that far out of line. But when it was released, it put the entire city — the male half, at least, the half that was legally allowed to vote — into a cold fury.

The result was an electoral pounding for the ages. The least temperance-friendly slate of candidates was swept into office by a landslide. And the hostility was so bad that the Women's Temperance Prayer League actually dissolved.

Unfortunately, while it had existed, the Prayer League had done a yeoman's job of hitching its wagon to the women's-suffrage star. The events of 1874 left most male voters with the clear belief that if women ever did get the right to vote, they'd use it to cram Prohibition down everyone's throats. That's why several historians, including Belknap, have suggested that the "Temperance Riots" set the cause of women's suffrage in Oregon back a whole generation, or maybe even two.

Edmunds was, of course, *persona non grata* in temperance and suffragist circles after this. Not only had his tactic backfired, but some fairly credible rumors started to circulate that he had done it deliberately to punish his allies for having been willing to work with the ideologically impure Republican reformers.

So, back on the lecture circuit he went. By this time, he had turned against religion entirely, and now he brought the same savagery and self-righteous fury to the cause of atheism that he had once rallied to the standard of "Black Republicanism" and Universalism.

In 1877 he took up the cause of trade-unionism, assumed the pen-name "Portland Mechanic" (although as far as I've been able to learn he never worked in any mechanical trade) and set about leading the foundation of what would become The Workingmen's Club of Portland. The organization, though, once formed, ejected him from membership within six months. I have not been able to learn the specifics of why they did this, but it was almost certainly a wise decision.

Finally, in 1879, during a lecture tour in California where he was speaking on labor issues, A.C. Edmunds suffered a paralytic stroke and died. He was just 51 years old.

He left behind a remarkable record of negative achievement. Like the stormy petrel of marine mythology, he brought trouble with him everywhere he went, and his record of own-goals has yet to be topped. His heart may have been in the right place, but plenty of his fellow activists and co-religionists in Oregon, California, and back East must have wondered, "With friends like him, who needs enemies?"

Sources and Works Cited:
- *"He Was a Starter but Got No Further: Careers of A.C. Edmunds," an article by George Belknap published in the June 1983 issue of* Oregon Historical Quarterly;
- *"The War on the Webfoot Saloon," an article by Malcolm Clark Jr. published in the March 1957 issue of* Oregon Historical Quarterly;
- The Women's War with Whiskey; or, Crusading In Portland, *a book by Frances Fuller Victor published in 1874 by Himes the Printer.*

THE BABY-BIRD MASSACRE.

THE BAD IDEA:
- *Claw your way to the top of a 200-foot-tall rock and get stuck on its top, requiring a rescue that results in the death of thousands of baby birds.*

In Cannon Beach, one could think of June and July 1968 as the Summer of the Dead Baby Birds.

The disaster started on June 28, when, at the height of the nesting season, a 23-year-old man from Portland scrambled up the side of Haystack Rock, the iconic intertidal sometimes-island that towers nearly 200 feet over the beach and sea by Cannon Beach, and found himself stuck at the top.

It wasn't common for people to climb the rock, but it wasn't exactly unheard-of either. The problem was, it was a very difficult and dangerous climb, especially on the descent. So, only two kinds of climbers attempted it: Highly skilled mountaineers, who were up to its challenges; and rank amateurs, who were too ignorant and inexperienced to recognize what a Bad Idea it was going to be to scramble up the thing because of how much more difficult it was going to be to get down than it would be to go up. Everyone else, noticing what a bag of snakes the descent would be, turned around at the base.

The result was that a significant percentage of climbers who tackled

Haystack Rock ended up stuck at the top like a young housecat stuck on a tall tree branch, waiting to be rescued.

For Kitty, of course, that would entail someone's dad getting out an extension ladder, or maybe the local fire department doing the job with a rescue truck as the neighborhood children stand around and watch admiringly. For the amateur rock climber, though, it involved a helicopter. And the process of rescuing a stranded climber from the top of Haystack Rock with a helicopter was, to put it mildly, hard on the local wildlife.

The first climbers to tackle the rock, so far as is known, were three experienced German Alpine climbers in 1929. As one would expect, they had no particular difficulty in getting back down.

In the mid-1930s, local lifeguard Earl Hardy took to climbing it somewhat regularly, actually going so far as to cut handholds in the rock with a hammer and cold chisel.

Others tried. Some failed. People got hurt. For the most part, locals figured it wasn't a big deal. Most of them felt that if some daredevil idiot tried to climb the rock and got hurt, that was unfortunate; but society is not a nursery school, and government should not be in the business of deciding what people are allowed to do based on whether it thinks they are competent enough to not hurt themselves.

So the shows went on, and nothing much changed.

That is, until 1953, when a number of aspirants took it on, and for the

An aerial view of Haystack Rock at Cannon Beach, as seen from the north. (Image: Postcard)

first time their failures started causing substantial problems for others.

A trio of Portland climbers were the first to tackle it that season, apparently successfully.

But then two other young men, Portlander Sherwood Willits and Iowan Jim Curtis, took the rock on with considerably less success. They got to the top and back down, all right, but on the descent found themselves stuck at the seaward end of the big rock, and it was high tide, and would be until the following morning.

Curtis solved this problem by jumping into the sea, intending to swim ashore through the breakers. He ended up stranded on one of The Needles, just south of the rock, and had to be rescued by a squad of three Navy "frogmen," who managed to get the poor fellow back to dry land; but by the time they got back to shore, rescuers and rescuee alike were badly bruised and cut by being dashed against the rocks.

Willits, rather sensibly, opted to resign himself to a miserable night on the rock and wait for the next morning's low tide; but, luckily for him, someone had noticed all the nesting birds he'd disturbed, and the Coast Guard spotted him and rescued him with a helicopter.

Ah, the helicopter. Here we come to the core of the problem with climbing the rock, and the immediate cause of all the dead baby birds.

Helicopters, invented in the form we know today just before the Second World War and popularized just afterward, were still very new in 1953. Just five years before, this elevator-in-the-sky method of rescue had not been available to idiots who climbed dangerous rocks and didn't think they could make it down. So, any idiots who did so ended up having to do the best they could, since there was no alternative.

Well, now there was. But the 1953 season made it clear that this wasn't an unmitigated miracle.

Helicopters, of course, basically fly by hanging on a giant propeller. They have to continually push their weight in air, plus a little more, downward to stay aloft. In 1953, when the little bubble-canopy Bell 47 was the most common "copter," that was already a good bit of air; but apparently, not more than the local wildlife could handle, as Sherwood Willits' rescue doesn't seem to have, er, ruffled too many feathers (sorry about that).

But by 1968, when the Coast Guard was flying full-sized jet-turbine-powered Sikorsky HH-60s as its ambulances in the sky, the rotor wash was several orders of magnitude more powerful.

So when young Richard O. Willis, standing atop Haystack Rock at the height of the nesting season in 1968, signaled his distress to the watching Beach Patrol, he was essentially summoning a hurricane to his rescue.

That hurricane soon arrived, in the form of U.S. Coast Guard Lt. Alexander Klimshuk's rescue chopper.

"I went down slowly so the birds could get out of the way, but I wasn't going to hover a hundred feet above the rock just to save a stinking cormorant," Klimshuk told *Portland Oregonian* reporter Jim Kadera. "We are in sympathy with birds, or else we wouldn't fly. We don't like to disturb birds, but we aren't going to tell a guy to climb off a rock by himself just to save birds. One human life is worth more to us than all the birds on the coast."

And so Willis got his ride back to dry land ... and all over Haystack Rock and the surrounding sea and sand, hundreds of hatchling cormorants, tufted puffins, gulls, and other seabirds rained down out of the sky, blown from their nests by the rotor wash. Local resident Jack Bentley told reporter Kadera more than a hundred dead baby birds washed ashore the next day — and that's just the ones that were found.

By the time this happened, Haystack Rock had, the previous year, been designated a bird sanctuary. There had been a certain amount of controversy over this, locally, because it happened in the context of a noticeable clamping-down by authorities on what you might call freedom of beach use. There was a small but growing movement to exclude cars from the beach, for one thing (until 1985 it was legal to drive on the beach at Cannon Beach). Governor Tom McCall's Beach Bill, passed the previous year (in 1967), enjoyed widespread support, but those who opposed it mostly saw it in the context of a rolling-back of property rights.

The Department of the Interior hadn't specified that nobody was allowed to enter the bird sanctuary — after all, birdwatchers were a big part of why there *were* bird sanctuaries, and if the birdwatchers couldn't come watch birds, they might withdraw their support.

But there was definitely a sense that when the visitors' activities disturbed the birds, that was crossing a line. And when the visitors caused an entire generation of baby chicks to wash up dead on the beach, that was more than most local residents were willing to tolerate for the sake of personal liberty. Fine, they thought; be an idiot, get yourself killed; but if in the process you make every other beach user miserable for several days and damage the local wildlife population, your idiocy is no longer just your problem.

Reading the local newspaper coverage of this cataclysmic rescue, it's very clear that letting Willis go free without so much as a traffic ticket really stuck in the craw of the local authorities. After picking

BAD IDEAS.

Haystack Rock and The Needles, as seen from the beach south of the rock. Right around the middle of the rock, in this view, is the spot where a convenient little shelf of land once stood, which provided climbers with an easy place to start from; it was blasted away in October 1968 to discourage climbers. (Image: Postcard)

him up from the top of the rock, Klimshuk basically took him straight to jail, where the authorities pondered whether they could charge him with anything. The conclusion was that they could not — he'd invaded a bird sanctuary, but that wasn't against the law.

Not yet, it wasn't.

So one week after the rescue, Haystack Rock was sporting a brand-new "Do Not Enter" sign. And when, less than a month after that, a Portland teenager scrambled to the top of the rock on a dare, he was greeted at the bottom upon his return with a nice big ticket, which the local cops were no doubt very pleased to present to him. The kid told the police he'd seen the sign — he'd practically had to step on it to climb the rock — but claimed not to have realized that "do not enter" also meant "do not enter and climb the rock."

And a month or two after that, in October 1968, Oregon State University professor of pyrotechnics Ralph Reed was asked to blast away the ledge from which climbers started their attempts. This was done — although it took two tries. And the rock has been almost entirely unmolested since.

(As a side note, "Professor of Pyrotechnics" has to be the ultimate dream job title. But, one has to wonder why Dr. Reed didn't get a phone call from the highway department two years later, when engineers were pondering whether dynamite was a suitable means of disposing of a dead whale in Florence, in the incident we went over on Page 3 of this book.)

BAD IDEAS *and* HORRIBLE PEOPLE *of* OLD OREGON.

Today, Haystack Rock is part of the Oregon Islands Wildlife Sanctuary — as are all the rocks and islands off the Oregon Coast, except for Tillamook Rock, site of the Tillamook Rock Lighthouse — and it's illegal to set foot on them, or even to fly a drone within 2,000 feet of them.

Sources and Works Cited:
- *"Blasting of Haystack Rock Brings Men Chilly Interval," an article by Emma Edwards published in the Oct. 10, 1968, issue of the* Seaside Signal*;*
- *facebook.com/cannonbeachmuseum;*
- Portland Oregonian *archives, June to October 1968.*

PUBLIC-RELATIONS DYNAMITE.

THE BAD IDEA:
- *Try to win popular support of your union strike by committing acts of domestic terrorism.*

It may be true that the movement of a butterfly's wings can seed a hurricane thousands of miles away, or it may be an exaggeration. But minor events sure can lead to big things — as was the case with a Portland man who, back in the early 1960s, got into a little affair with a married woman.

Stepping out with someone you met on ashleymadison.com is always a Class-A Bad Idea, of course. But in this case, it was even worse.

This fellow's infidelity, it seems, led directly to a shooting that shortened an innocent man's life, and that shooting in turn led to the complete takeover of Portland's metro newspaper market by the New York mogul whose company still owns the *Portland Oregonian* today.

An amateurish duo of car bombers with a box of dynamite also played a key role in the outcome, so there's another Bad Idea to add to our list — and it could never have happened at all had not several hundred Portlanders had their inheritance stolen from them, a few years before that, by the crafty attorneys in charge of a deceased widow's estate, who kindly furnish us with some genuine Horrible People for this story as well.

All in all, it was a bad few years for Portland, but pretty much a red-letter decade in the history of Bad Ideas.

Now, before we get into the story, it has to be said that the "unfaithful husband" narrative is a theory, not a proven fact. Despite a generous reward offered for his arrest, the man who shot Donald Newhouse in the crotch through his basement window on Oct. 16, 1960, with a shotgun, as he stood at his workbench, has never been identified, so the shooter's motives can't really be known.

What is known that Newhouse had just moved into the house; the previous resident had a reputation as a womanizer; and the gunman, from the position the shot was fired from, would not have been able to see (or shoot) Newhouse's face and head. Hence, the theory goes, he took the shot thinking he was blasting the philandering former owner of the house, not realizing he had the wrong man.

But Donald Newhouse wasn't just any innocent bystander. He was the production manager at the *Portland Oregonian*, and the nephew of the New York mogul who owned it. He was the man in charge of defeating the various newspaper unions which had been on strike there for nearly a year. That union had already shown itself willing to get heavy — one member had threatened to shoot Newhouse as he crossed a picket line, and another had been caught bombing company vehicles (more on that in a bit).

So the competing theory — that the shooter was a thug sent by the union — is far more often heard today. It's certainly what Newhouse and his wife believed, and when Newhouse died in surgery 12 years later — from complications he might have survived if not for the damage the gunman inflicted — his widow publicly blamed the union for his death.

The fact that Newhouse's injuries came from a shotgun blast to the pelvic area — not the usual target for an assassin, but a very popular one among vengeful cuckolded husbands — suggests she may have been mistaken. But it scarcely mattered. In the minds of most Portlanders, the union now had the moral taint of attempted murder upon it. It would take several more years to play out, but for the union, the battle was already lost — and with it, through various ripple effects, the local ownership of the *Oregon Journal*, Portland's only remaining independent daily, and the city's status as a true two-newspaper town.

The events that led up to this fateful shooting were complicated and controversial, and involved some of Oregon's most powerful people; this is most likely why the story has been so little told or studied.

A stereotyper makes a mold at a printer's shop in Leipzig, Germany, in 1953. (Image: Deutsche Fotothek)

Until recently (with the work of historians like Caleb Diehl), information about it came generally from two sources: The newspaper itself, and its former union members. Obviously, both these sources are at pains to present themselves in the best possible light at all times, so the real story can be hard to pick out. What follows is my best shot at doing just that:

Late in 1959, the Stereotypers Union No. 49 at the *Oregonian* voted to walk off the job, thereby — according to union historians' interpretation — taking the bait in a cunningly laid trap. They most likely are right about that, but it has to be said that stupidity on the part of the union played a huge supporting role in their falling into that trap. From a public-relations standpoint, their position was terrible: Samuel I. Newhouse, the owner, had installed new technology that would automate the expensive, labor-intensive stereotyping process, eliminating their positions. To the public, it looked like they were going on strike to try to force the company to stick with inferior technology just so they could keep their jobs.

Union sources said it was more complicated than that — that they'd been willing to work with Newhouse, but Newhouse had wanted a fight and liked how it would look to have the strike break out over this particular issue.

Union sources also claimed it was all part of a complicated and cunning plot to take over the competing newspaper, the locally owned *Oregon Journal* — thereby establishing a local newspaper monopoly — and to break all the newspaper unions, all in one fell swoop. The level of prescience Newhouse would have had to show for this accusation to be true makes it seem pretty unlikely. But everyone agrees that, whether that was the plan or not, it's basically what happened.

It didn't look like it was going that way at first, though. After the stereotypers walked out, they threw a picket line up around the building, and a picket line was not something one lightly crosses even today, in an era in which unions are generally pretty weak; to cross a picket line back in '59, in the heyday of strong unions, was an even bigger deal. It generally was just not done. Hundreds of other employees stayed away from work, effectively swelling the number of strikers. In response, Newhouse brought in a cadre of out-of-state strikebreakers — some of whom turned out to be thugs with sawed-off shotguns and prison records — to keep the paper going. These "scabs" turned out to be better at making trouble than they were at making a newspaper, and the *Oregonian's* quality suffered shockingly, which made the union organizers' door-to-door efforts to get locals to cancel their subscriptions that much easier.

Meanwhile, over at the *Oregon Journal* — the competing Portland daily newspaper, which was still locally owned — one might have expected things to be going rather better. In fact, they were going much worse. The *Journal* and the *Oregonian* had made a deal for both newspapers to bargain together with the unions; this meant that even though the *Journal* had no dog in the *Oregonian* stereotypers' fight, it was forced into it, essentially, by treaty obligations. And unlike the *Oregonian*, the *Journal* was not financially prepared for it.

The *Journal* was no longer being run by the family that had founded it back in 1902. Fearsome newsman Sam Jackson, and later his son Philip, had built it from nothing into Portland's leading newspaper. But by the late 1950s all members of the family were dead. And the last surviving Jackson, Sam's widow Maria, had left specific instructions in her will that the paper was under no circumstances to be sold to Newhouse.

But it was no secret that Newhouse wanted very much to buy it, so that he could enjoy an effective local monopoly; and the trustees were quite willing to sell it to him, if they could just figure out how to get around Maria Jackson's clearly expressed command.

They'd already defeated one such command. In her will, Maria had instructed that all the family's stock in the company was to be distributed to the employees. But the trustees had challenged the bequest, and got a judge to rule that she had made it in "wishful" language, and that it was therefore null and void; so, the trustees got to keep control, effectively stealing the newspaper from its rightful owners under color of law. Needless to say,

Newhouse found these trustees far easier to work with than would have been the case had the *Journal* been owned by its employees — especially during the strike.

So the year 1960 found the *Journal* hard-pressed, and *The Oregonian* not much better. They'd teamed up to produce a single edition, the *Oregonian-Oregon Journal*, which was delivered to all their dwindling subscribers; but delivery was suddenly very uneven, and the quality of the newspaper was terrible. And cancelations were pouring in. Most Portlanders were pro-union. Union members were going door to door asking everyone to cancel their subscriptions, and tens of thousands of them were doing it.

The unions realized it was asking a lot of residents to give up their daily newspaper, so they pooled their resources and expertise and launched a third newspaper in Portland — at first a weekly, and then, as it became clear that this would not suffice, a daily. It was called *The Portland Reporter;* it was excellent, if a bit thin; and, until its closure for financial reasons in 1964, it helped a great deal.

The Oregon Journal *building as it appeared in the late 1950s. Although the* Journal *had no problem with the stereotypers' union, it was drawn into The* Oregonian's *battle through a deal the two newspapers had made to negotiate labor contracts together; this made it possible for* The Oregonian *to indirectly break the* Journal *by picking a fight the* Journal *couldn't afford, which is essentially what happened in 1959. (Image: Bud Holland/ Vintage Portland)*

Would that have been enough? We'll never know. Because one of the stereotypers — the obsolete workers whose walkout over equipment upgrades had started the whole thing — apparently got impatient.

And so it was that, at midnight on Jan. 31, 1960, a series of ten colossal dynamite blasts shook sleepers awake in Oregon City. Stereotyper Levi McDonald had hired some young fellows, given them dynamite and fuses, and sent them out into the night to apply a little direct pressure to some of the trucking companies that had had the temerity to continue doing business with the *Oregonian*. Ten trucks had been blown up; luckily, no one had been hurt.

Now, it's important to understand that in 1960, the vast majority of people in Portland had lived through or participated in the Second World War. The way to win the hearts and minds of people who have experienced total war is not to show oneself as the side most willing to resort to brownshirt terrorist tactics like dynamite attacks. Furthermore, the recklessness of the action was appalling: What if someone had been in one of those trucks, or working nearby? Unlikely, yes, but unlikely things do happen sometimes.

The next day, the sun came up on a completely new world. Now, when union reps knocked on a Portlander's door and asked him or her to cancel his or her subscription, the Portlander's perception of the whole affair would be different. It wasn't "local guys getting stiffed by a New York mogul"; it was "bomb-throwing union thugs squabbling with a New York mogul."

It's not hard to understand what that change did to the union canvassers' success rate.

It is entirely possible that McDonald, the stereotyper with the dynamite, was discreetly ratted out by fellow union members who, realizing that he'd probably just lost them the war, figured their only hope was to show the world that the bombings had been a rogue member's freelance action, not an official union operation. It's also possible — as union members immediately afterward claimed — that the whole thing was a false-flag operation, and that McDonald had been put up to it by the *Oregonian*.

But the more likely explanation is that McDonald did it on his own initiative, probably inspired by stories of the famously dynamite-happy ironworkers' union that bombed the *Los Angeles Times* building and dozens of others in the 1910s; and the newspaper, recognizing public-relations salvation when it saw it, grabbed onto it with both hands.

And, of course, when someone shot Donald Newhouse in the groin a few months later, everyone was already primed to assume this was more "direct pressure" from the union.

The unions decried the bombings immediately after they happened, and even contributed $1,000 to the reward offered for the perpetrator's capture. But it wasn't enough. Essentially, the bombings turned a strike that had been on a relatively fast track toward a successful (for the union) resolution, into a losing stalemate that would drag on for five years.

For Sam Newhouse, a five-year fight was tolerable. He owned a big string of other newspapers, and revenue from them could prop up the temporarily-money-losing *Oregonian* nicely. Plus, he had, with remarkable prescience, bought a very expensive strike-insurance policy before the whole mess broke out.

But for the *Oregon Journal*, times were tough indeed. Remember, this was just a few years after the last member of the founding Jackson family, Maria, had died. As mentioned earlier, Maria had tried to pass her stock in the newspaper on to the employees, but the three trustees in charge of her estate challenged the bequest in court and won, thereby essentially robbing the employees of their inheritance — and, more importantly, leaving the trustees in control of the newspaper. It was the trustees who had made the deal to jointly negotiate labor contracts with *The Oregonian*. And it was soon very clear that the trustees — who were charged with caring for the entire Jackson estate, not just the newspaper — were far more likely than the employees would have been to regard the newspaper as a financial asset rather than a public trust.

Now, having made and stuck with a labor-negotiating deal that had brought the *Journal* to the brink of insolvency, the trustees moved to subvert the other major command in Maria's will: the part that specifically prohibited them from selling it to Newhouse.

With the *Journal* facing bankruptcy and a union strike that they could blame for the situation, the trustees could now plausibly claim that they were faced with a choice of either honoring Maria's wishes and allowing the paper to fold, or selling to Newhouse. Surely no reasonable person would fault them for saving Maria's paper, even though it were necessary to flout her express wishes to do so ... right?

And so, in 1961, the trustees accepted an $8 million offer from Newhouse ... and Portland became, effectively, a one-newspaper town.

As for the strike, it petered out over the following several years. In 1963 the National Labor Relations Board ruled it illegal. Finally, in the spring of 1965, the pickets called it quits, and both papers became open shops.

Sources and Works Cited:
- *"The Newspaper Wars," an article by Caleb Diehl published in the December 2015 issue of* Portland Monthly;
- *"Let Me Say This about That," a column by Gene Klare published in the Jan. 1, 2002, issue of* Northwest Labor Press;
- *"The Portland Reporter," an article by Caleb Diehl in* The Oregon Encyclopedia *(oregonencyclopedia.org).*

DEMOLISHING HISTORY.

THE BAD IDEA:
- *Demolish one of the most interesting and historical buildings in the state to replace it with a two-story parking garage.*

Next time you're in the neighborhood of Portland's Pioneer Courthouse Square, take a minute to look at the wrought-iron fence and archway at its south end. Looks a little out of place, doesn't it?

That ironwork is all that's left of what may have been the grandest hotel in Oregon history.

The Portland Hotel started as a railroad baron's scheme in the mid-1880s, and was opened in 1890 — a colorful yet stolidly tasteful stone palace of hospitality, at the dawn of some of the most colorful and memorable decades of the city's history.

And then, in the early 1950s, the hotel — aging, but by no means gone to seed — was gone, pounded into powder and rubble to make way for a parking garage.

The Portland Hotel got its start in 1882, in anticipation of the coming of the transcontinental railroad to Portland the following year. Railroad mogul Henry Villard wanted a nice hotel at the

Portland end of the line. So he bought the property to do so — a city block, across from the courthouse on Sixth Street, in the center of town.

With uncharacteristic overeagerness, though, he failed to read the fine print. He soon learned that his new property contained a deed restriction: The hotel he planned to build there would have to be made of brick or stone.

This was not what Villard had in mind. But at the time he was feeling flush with cash, so he got started on it.

Bad idea. Business in the 1880s was a fickle goddess, and in the winter of 1883 she turned on Henry Villard. Construction on his grand hotel stopped. Then, early the next year, chastened and bankrupted, Villard slunk out of town.

The weed-infested foundation and roofless stone walls of his palatial hotel lay there for several years after that. The place soon acquired a sinister reputation as a dangerous place, the kind of reputation an outlaw gang's hideout picks up. It was, as the *Morning Oregonian* seemed never to tire of pointing out, an eyesore. (Of course, the *Oregonian* had plenty of reason to think about the ruins; they were only a block or so away from the paper's offices.)

So, there it sat. The problem was, having been half built as a stone structure, "Villard's Folly" would have to be either completed as one or demolished and built afresh with cheaper wood. None of the

A hand-tinted postcard from the 1910s showing a streetfront view of the Portland Hotel, with the Portland Oregonian building (the one with the clocktower) in the background.

A hand-tinted postcard of the Hotel Portland in the early 1910s. The wrought-iron railing across the courtyard is all that remains.

other Portland bigwigs were inclined to spend the money required to do either one of those things.

Finally, a newcomer to town named George Markle realized that completing that hotel was his ticket to the inner circle of the Portland Establishment, and took the project on. He went into action, soliciting subscriptions from the cream of Portland's social crop to add to his own investment, and work got started once again.

While clearing the brush to restart construction, crews found out the evil reputation of "Villard's Ruins" was well deserved. The bodies of two murder victims — a drifter and a prostitute — were concealed in the weeds there.

By the spring of 1890, the new hotel was complete. It had cost more than $1 million to build — the equivalent of $29 million today. It also may have been the first hotel on the West Coast with electric lights; Markle's father was an associate of Thomas Edison, and Portland had power coming up from Oregon City, so the builders were able to wire the place.

That May it had its debut with a massive high-society party that raged on into the small hours of the morning. And for decades after that, it stood as a sort of monument to the sophistication and refinement of Portland's social elite. This elite, in the early 1890s, had already started getting a little sensitive about the rough-hewn frontier reputation of their city, still commonly called "Stumptown." In the Portland Hotel, they sought to build a facility just as refined and sophisticated and elegant as anything in St. Louis, or Chicago, or even New York. And they got it.

Throughout the 1890s this hotel set the high-water mark for West Coast high-class hospitality with gorgeous rooms and spectacular food and drink. The hotel bar's signature cocktail, the "Peach Blow," was served to everyone from shanghaied sailors all the way up to Presidents of the United States; although it's not known if any of the 11 Presidents who stayed in the hotel over the years actually ever tried a Peach Blow, it's likely at least one of them did. And as for shanghaied sailors, well, more on *them* a little later in this book (specifically, on Page 233).

Legendary *Oregonian* editor Harvey Scott, who had contributed to the fund-raising effort and was a stockholder there (and who vividly remembered the place when it was "Villard's Ruins"), walked the block or so from *The Oregonian's* offices to the hotel for lunch each day. The Arlington Club was close at hand as well — as was Madame Fanshaw's establishment, the praises of which Stewart Holbrook sings as the "*ne plus ultra* of Portland

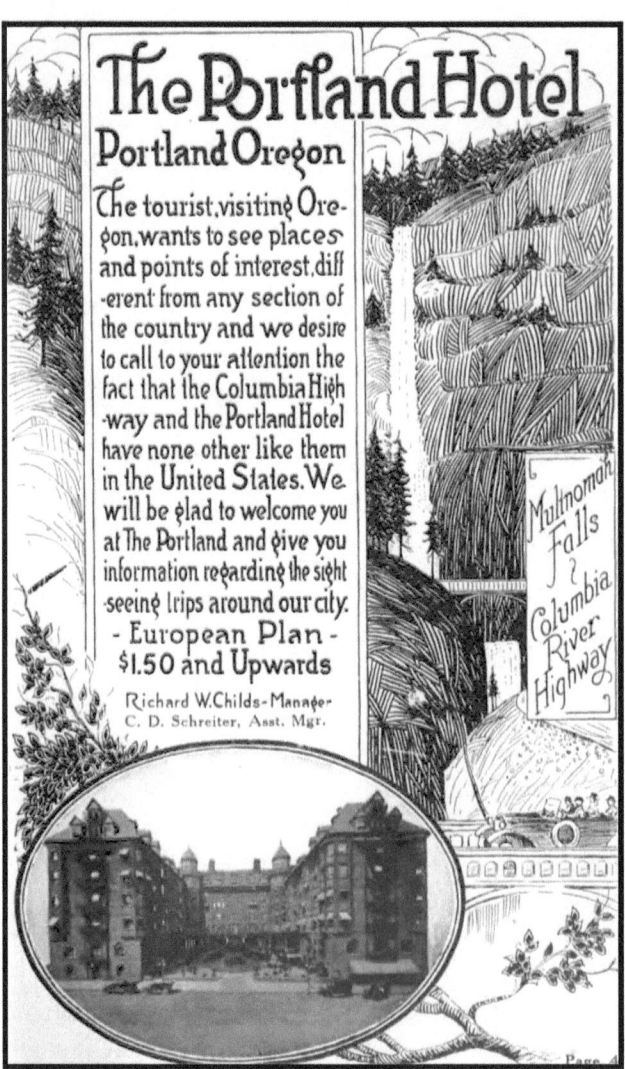

An advertisement from the 1919 Automobile Blue Book, offering European tourists first-class accommodations during their hoped-for visits to see the Columbia River Gorge.

BAD IDEAS.

A scene from a postcard postmarked 1909, showing the Portland Hotel as seen from the lawn of the Pioneer Courthouse, with streetcars and pedestrians.

parlor houses."

("Parlor house," of course, was a euphemism for "upscale bordello.")

Over the decades as the twentieth century wore on, though, the old hotel increasingly showed its age.

A chill must have gone through the staff at the storied old hotel in 1944, though, when it was learned that Julius Meier and Aaron Frank — owners of the neighboring Meier & Frank Department Store — had bought the place. By now automobiles were common in Portland, and it didn't take a champion chess player to figure out what the department store's next move was going to be.

They made that move in 1951. The last day of operations was August 15, and two weeks later all the hotel's fixtures and dishes and furnishings were auctioned off — including furnishings and sets of china used to serve Presidents of the United States.

Then the wrecking balls were deployed, and the rubble cleared away, and a two-story parking garage arose where once the finest hotel on the West Coast had stood.

The parking garage lasted only a few dozen years. By the early 1980s it was gone, and Meier & Frank happily sold the land to the city — which now wanted to make it into public space.

In planning what became Pioneer Courthouse Square, the city launched a nationwide design competition, and more than 150 submissions came in. There followed a short squabble over the vision for the place — soon-to-be Mayor Frank Ivancie and some other downtown businessmen wanted to build it as an enclosed atrium with an admission charge (to keep "hippies and sex bums" out, as Ivancie memorably put it) which would have meant tossing all the design submissions into the bin and starting over.

Ivancie's faction backed down, though, in the face of near-universal resistance, and construction began on the site. It was completed in 1984.

There are a few bits of the Portland Hotel still at the square today. Of course, there is the ironwork along the south side, looking very Edwardian and out of place surrounded by the square's more modern features.

But if you took up a few of the bricks that make up the floor of the square, you'd likely find a giant block or two of cut stone — cut 135 years ago to make the foundation of what may have been the finest and most luxurious hotel in Oregon history.

Sources and Works Cited:
- Merchants, Money and Power, *a book by E. Kimbark MacColl published in 1988 by Georgian Press;*
- Great and Minor Moments in Oregon History, *a book by Dick Pintarich published in 2003 by New Oregon Press.*

THE ROD AND GUN CLUB.

THE BAD IDEA:
- *Start construction on an elaborate resort-condominium at the beach, in the middle of the Great Depression.*

In late May, 1978, the wreckers went to work on Lincoln City's most eligible Haunted Mansion: the sprawling, Timberline Lodge-shaped husk of what was to have been the Delake Rod and Gun Club, on the shore of Devils Lake.

It couldn't have really been haunted, of course. To be haunted (if you believe in that sort of thing), a house needs to have been occupied at some point, and this one never was. No, the only ghosts in this sportsman's palace were the dreams of a fellow named Robin Reed — former shipyard worker, newspaper editor, real-estate agent and Olympic gold medalist, and quite possibly the best amateur wrestler of any weight in American history.

Reed was an Arkansas native, but his wrestling story started after his family moved to Portland — and it was almost an accident.

"I needed gymnasium credits to graduate from high school, but I didn't want any gym because I was already getting all the exercise I needed operating an air hammer at the shipyards," Reed explained in an interview. "I was only 125 pounds and could barely hold onto that hammer, so that was all the gym I needed."

So he went for wrestling instead — and quickly found he was a natural.

By 1921, he was already a legend, attending college at Oregon Agricultural College (now Oregon State University) and winning wrestling matches at the collegiate level. By 1924 he had three National Freestyle Wrestling championships under his belt and had earned a berth on the U.S. Olympic team — and had still never once been pinned.

The entire U.S. Olympic wrestling team traveled to Paris for the games on the same ship. En route, of course, they did what they did best — and Reed did it better than any of them. Reed pinned every member of the team but one, whom he battled to either a draw or a pinless victory, depending on who you asked. One of the men he pinned would go on to take the gold in the heavyweight class in Paris.

So, in the 134.5-pound class, would Reed. And there are those who believe if he'd been allowed to wrestle in every weight class, the U.S. would have swept the gold medals that year.

"He had a genius for knowing how to handle the human body in wrestling," one of his former coaches told authors Jeff Welsch and George Edmonston. "He was tremendously flexible and quick. He had great balance, was a keen competitor, and his ingenuity was so remarkable that he would figure out a way to beat you."

But he was definitely not someone you wrestled with for fun. He was notoriously nasty on the mat.

"He is generally regarded as the most feared and punishing wrestler of all time," Mike Chapman writes, "a man who would break an opponent's arm if the mood struck him to do so."

On his return from the Olympics, Reed coached the Beavers for a couple years, bringing them to a national championship in 1926. But in that same year, he was accused of cheating at a tournament, and OAC dropped the wrestling program entirely in response.

Reed spent some time as a professional wrestler, but was never very happy with the flashy show-biz image of the pros — no Macho Man Randy Savage, he. So in the mid-1930s, he quit for good ... and got into real estate.

Reed had a plan that was not so much a genuine Bad Idea — rather, it was maybe a few dozen years ahead of its time. He wanted to build a mammoth lodge on the shore of Devil's Lake. It would be like a hotel — complete with lobby, lounge, swimming pool and casino — but the living quarters would be condominiums, not guest rooms. He called it the Delake Rod and Gun Club.

It took Reed a couple years to get the project under way. The Depression took a large divot out of his timeline. Finally, in 1938, ground was broken

The vacant Delake Rod and Gun Club building as it appeared in January 1960. (Salem Public Library, Ben Maxwell collection)

on the huge building.

Reed styled his creation after Timberline Lodge, built just a few years earlier and already something of an icon for the state. It featured three giant stone fireplaces built with stone blocks salvaged from the ruins of the Polk County courthouse, which had burned earlier.

But the following year, Hitler invaded Poland. The U.S. started gearing up for the war its leaders knew was coming, and the markets started to tremble a bit. Reed also found he was having trouble selling the concept of a condo-resort. Progress slowed to a crawl.

Then World War II broke out, and Reed's project was dead in the water as resources and workers were concentrated on the fight. By 1942 he was facing legal hassles over the whole thing, and after the war ended construction never resumed. Reed moved on.

So there the Rod and Gun Club sat, vacant, gaping and full of nothing but echoes, the salty air turning its cedar siding grayer every year as the decades rolled by.

Finally, in 1978, wrecking and salvage crews moved in and started taking the massive structure apart. Within a few months, it was all gone.

1978 was also the year Reed was inducted into the National Wrestling Hall of Fame — and also the year in which, on Dec. 20, he died.

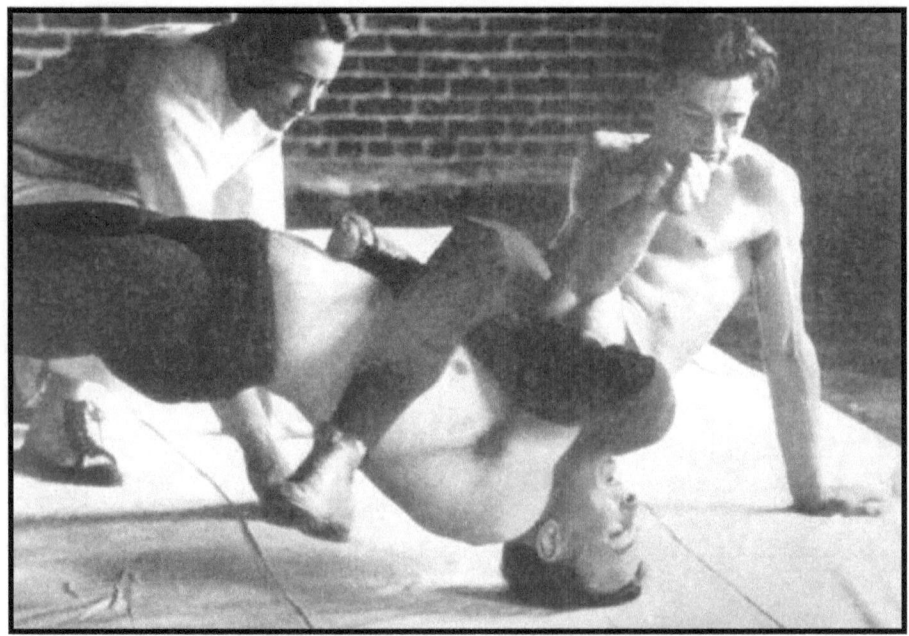

Looking cool and professional, Robin Reed pins an opponent at Oregon State University, then known as Oregon Agricultural College, in the 1920s. (Image: OSU Athletics)

Throughout his wrestling career, Reed was famous for his willingness to wrestle opponents of any weight, up to and including heavyweights. He was also known for winning. Not once in his entire 19-year career did Robin Reed lose a wrestling match. This is a record that only one other Olympic wrestler — Japan's Osamu Watanabe — has ever matched, and Watanabe's career was much shorter.

But in the arena of condominium development, well, Reed did get himself pinned once . . . by a super-heavyweight real-estate dream.

Sources and Works Cited:
- Tales from Oregon State Sports, *a book by Jeff Welsch and George Edmonston Jr. published in 2003 by Sports Publishing LLC;*
- Encyclopedia of American Wrestling, *a book by Mike Chapman published in 1991 by Leisure Press;*
- "Robin Reed: The Case of the Vanishing Mansion," *an article posted on oregonbiographies.com;*
- *Personal correspondence with Peter Bellant.*

HOW TO LOSE A MINT.

THE BAD IDEA:
- *Hold up progress on a new federal facility to try to force them to move it to your town, until the feds lose interest completely.*

When hardcore coin collectors examine a promising piece of numismatic history, the first place their eyes often go is to the bottom right side of the front, looking for a tiny letter known as a "mint mark."

Usually the mint mark is a P or a D — representing the main mint at Philadelphia or the branch mint at Denver, respectively. Less commonly, you'll see an S, representing the branch mint at San Francisco, or a W, representing the mint's newest facility at West Point, N.Y.

Mint marks of "O" (New Orleans), "C" (Charlotte, N.C.), or "CC" (Carson City, Nevada) are very rare, and in most cases signify a considerably higher value for the coins they're stamped on. (Offers of 1880s Morgan Silver Dollar coins mint-marked "P" are averaging about $40 in eBay right now, as of 2022; an "S" mint mark raises that to about $100; and a "CC" doubles it again, to about $200. These figures are very rough, of course, and are just asking prices, not the amounts of actual sales.)

That list of rare mint marks came close to including another, which probably would have been "DC" — for Dalles City, as the The Dalles was once called. In fact, it probably would have, had it not been for some jealous business leaders in Portland — whose enthusiasm and municipal boosterism led them to try to force the feds to build it in their own town instead.

Bad idea.

The plan for a branch mint in Oregon was hatched in 1862, and for the same reason that one had been built in San Francisco eight years before: There was a full-on gold rush going on, and the area was flooded with raw gold nuggets and dust; hauling raw gold thousands of miles to a far-distant mint before it was fully assayed and properly measured was both expensive and risky.

San Francisco, of course, had been the main city center of the great California (and southern Oregon) Gold Rush of 1848, and after the branch mint was built there in 1854 it stayed busy striking coins from California gold and Nevada silver for most of the rest of the 1800s.

The Dalles was the main city center of the smaller gold rush that had broken out in 1861 in Griffin Gulch, near Baker City. More gold was found the following year in Whiskey Gulch near Canyon City, and by the end of that year, eastern Oregon and western Idaho Territory were flooded with prospectors digging out tons of raw gold.

The Dalles, rather than Portland, became the center of all this activity, because there was a mountain range between Portland and the gold fields; the best and safest way to get to the gold fields, in those pre-railroad days, was to get on a Columbia River steamboat to The Dalles and travel overland from there. Riverboat passage was expensive and there really wasn't anything in Portland that The Dalles didn't have, albeit at inflated prices.

So The Dalles became the San Francisco of the new gold rush, and Portland became a downstream port that supplied it — and helped get the raw gold from The Dalles to the federal mint in San Francisco to be refined and stamped into coins.

This wasn't as cumbrous a process as the one that had inspired the San Francisco branch — hauling raw gold over 10,000 miles around the horn of South America and back to Philadelphia — but it was plenty cumbrous for all that. The raw gold would be shipped down the river on a riverboat, portaged around the rapids at Cascade Locks, re-loaded to finish the passage to Portland, transferred to a coastwise sailing ship or steamer in Portland or Astoria, and sent down the West Coast to the branch mint at San Francisco — a risky, expensive, and complicated journey of more than 900 miles.

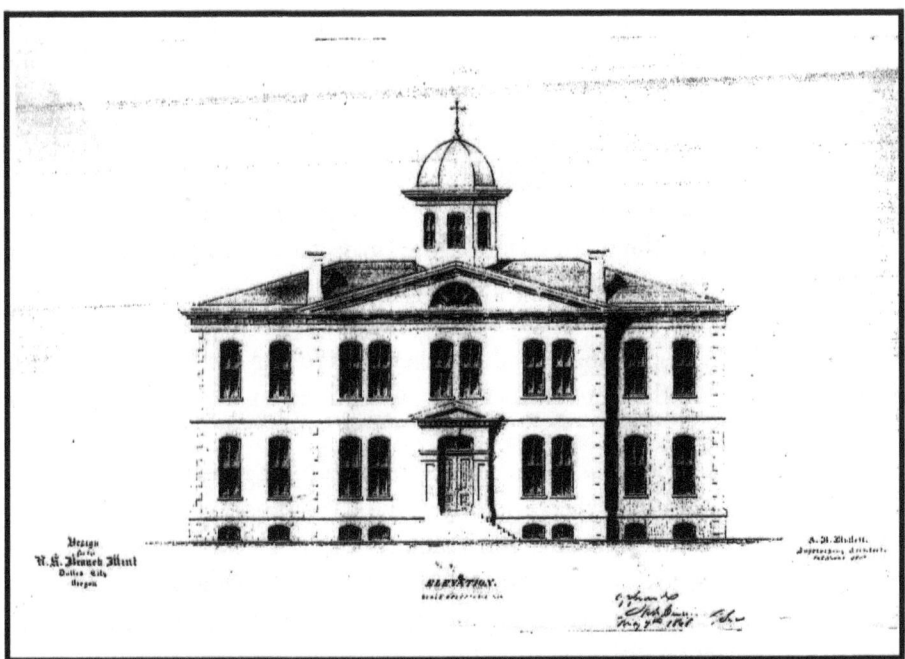

The elevation drawing from the original blueprints for the Dalles City Mint show what the building would have looked like had it been finished. The project was abandoned before the roof was finalized, so the outline of the building looks different today. (Image: Wikimedia Commons)

So in December of 1862, Sen. James Nesmith introduced a bill to build a Portland branch mint to handle it.

This was early in the Civil War, though, and legislators had yet to feel the full financial pinch that an Oregon mint branch would help them solve; they'd be scrambling to find hard currency to finance the war effort within a few years, but that hadn't happened yet. Plus, putting a mint in Portland only solved half of the problem; the gold would still have to be brought down the Columbia from The Dalles. Congress passed, and time went on.

A year and a half later, though, wartime financial circumstances inspired Congress to abruptly bring it back up and pass it — but the location, quite sensibly, was changed to The Dalles.

Oregon politicians — few of whom represented The Dalles, but many of whom represented Portland — did not take this well. The next year, 1865, they introduced a bill that would change the location back to Portland. It was defeated, but all of the wrangling took time and the mint couldn't start on its facility until it knew where to build it. So, nothing happened before the end of the Civil War. And with the end of the war, the federal government lost its sense of urgency.

The project got under way nonetheless, and William Logan was appointed superintendent of the new mint. All appeared to be on track; but then Logan and his wife died in the wreck of the steamer *Brother Jonathan* on their way home from San Francisco.

Three years went by without a new superintendent being named. Then, finally, construction started on the building.

That construction was well on track to being done when, in summer of 1870, the crews got the word to stop. The project was being abandoned.

What had happened?

First of all, the West Coast states' transportation infrastructure had changed radically since 1862; suitable stagecoach routes had been developed, and everyone could see that there would soon be railroad lines everywhere.

Secondly, The Dalles wasn't the only branch mint the government had started construction on, when the late-Civil-War pinch started to be felt. Down in Carson City, Nevada, construction had started on a branch mint to serve the Comstock Lode silver mines; and the Nevada politicians had quite sensibly not held the project up by trying to steer it to a less-appropriate location for purely political reasons.

The Carson City mint opened in 1870, the same year The Dalles crews got their stop-work orders. The overland route from the gold fields and silver mines to Carson City was much less arduous than the journey to San Francisco had been. It was no longer necessary to load the gold and silver on and off of three different boats and ships and sail across the Columbia River Bar on a 900-mile journey through storms and fog to get to the mint. A single stagecoach trip would do.

But probably the biggest factor was the fact that by the end of the 1860s it was clear that the Eastern Oregon gold rush was petering out. It might be re-energized, everyone knew, if another big strike opened up a new set of gold fields somewhere else in the area; but it had been seven years since the Whiskey Gulch strike near Canyon City, and since then, basically nothing. The party appeared to be winding down, and the federal government was not keen to have a big facility in the middle of nowhere servicing a tiny and dwindling trickle of local gold — which they were increasingly convinced would be the situation by about 1875.

And, well, they turned out to be right.

The half-built mint building in The Dalles remained; there was no reason to demolish it, and it would have been pretty expensive to do so. It was built like a city-block-sized bank vault with windows, with thick walls made out of cut stone blocks and storage vaults beneath capable of shrugging off both dynamite attacks from above and tunneling

BAD IDEAS.

The Mint building in The Dalles as it appears today, the home of Freebridge Brewing. In front (above) it looks modern and unremarkable, but the view from the back of the building (below) reveals the building's antiquity and solid construction. (Image: F.J.D. John)

efforts from below by any would-be burglars. Its heavy construction enabled it to function as a one-building fire line when the town caught fire in 1871; the flames leaped from building to building, gobbling up about six dozen homes and buildings before slamming into the fireproof stone walls of the mint building. The break slowed the fire down enough for the fire department to get a handle on it, saving the other half of the town from a similar fate.

A later fire damaged the inside of the building heavily in 1943, but stone doesn't burn, and it was repaired.

Today the old mint building houses Freebridge Brewing. Its catacomb-like vaults, full of archways built with bricks, lend themselves very nicely to the atmosphere of a brewery and wine shop.

Sources and Works Cited:
- *"Mint that Never Was Makes Interesting Tale," an article by Brent Zimmerman published in the July 23, 2009, issue of* Numismatic News*;*
- *freebridgebrewing.com.*

"WORST WESTERN EVER."

THE BAD IDEA:
- *Make a big-budget Western full of bad Western clichés and unlikable characters, then renege on your promise to let a local charity group host the world premiere.*

If you've never heard *Harold Hecht's "The Way West"* referenced as a legendary box-office bomb, that's probably because of Michael Cimino. Cimino's epic testament to directorship run amok, a baroque five-and-a-half-hour Western picture titled *Michael Cimino's "Heaven's Gate,"* is famous as the most colossal box-office bomb of all time. As of the time of this writing, nothing else has ever come close — not even *Ishtar*. It earned only 8 percent of its $44 million budget back (equivalent to $132 million today). It lost so much money it drove its studio, United Artists, out of business.

Maybe if United Artists had taken a closer look at one of its earlier box-office flops, it would have handled *Heaven's Gate* differently. Because the similarities between it and *The Way West* are kind of striking.

Both were big-budget Westerns that aspired to get beyond the Golden West mythology and show the gritty reality of life of the old West. Both are branded ostentatiously with the names of their "auteurs."

Of course, only one of those movies was over five hours long and included

BAD IDEAS *and* HORRIBLE PEOPLE *of* OLD OREGON.

a six-minute-long shot of a guy playing a fiddle while roller-skating around a massive frontier cowboy skating rink. So, yeah, maybe not. There are bad ideas and there are Bad Ideas.

The movie poster for "The Way West," when it was released in 1967. (Image: United Artists)

BAD IDEAS.

he Way West was part of the wave of big-budget shot-on-scene Westerns that came out in the mid-1960s in response to the popularity of the "Spaghetti Westerns" shot in Italy by directors like Sergio Leone. Leone and his colleagues brought a darker, more chaotic feel to a genre that many Americans had grown bored with after decades of little houses on the prairie, singin' cowboys in big white hats, and wholesome Western maidens in gingham.

So American moviemakers started looking for darker, edgier stories to tell, and authentic places in which to shoot them.

Places like Eastern Oregon.

Director Andrew McLagen was familiar with the terrain. The previous year, he'd directed *Shenandoah*, much of which was shot in Lane County. So when doing location scouting for this new Western, he had a good sense of where to look.

McLagen had a policy that all the actors had to be in costume and in character on the set at all times, which meant that when they weren't performing for the camera they were more or less performing for each other and for any visitors on the set; some of them found this exhausting, but it made for a movie-making spectacle that local residents would remember for the rest of their lives.

Shooting started out in 1966 near Eugene, where a set had been constructed to stand in for Independence, Mo., and a spectacular scene of a wagon train crossing the McKenzie River was filmed.

After spending about a million bucks shooting in Lane County, the company moved east, where they landed in southern Deschutes and northern Lake counties to drop a million and a half more. Oregon's Fort Rock stood in for Independence Rock in Wyoming, much to the amusement of local raconteur Reub Long ("the Sage of Fort Rock"); and the Christmas Valley sand dunes stood in for the Western desert, much to the delight of real-estate hustler M. Penn Phillips, who was at this very time working to turn Christmas Valley into a cowboy paradise.

Then the whole huge caravan of cast and crew moved on, filming on Crooked River Ranch (which was, at the time, a working ranch; the TV commercials with Crooked River Bob and his cowboy-hat trick were about a decade in the future) and finishing up near Burns with a scene involving a buffalo stampede.

Then the crews headed back to Hollywood to put the film together.

As release day approached, the Eugene Jaycees were working with United Artists to host the world premiere screening of the movie in Eugene, slated for June 13. They'd hired a public-relations firm to get the word out, and were well into the project when to their dismay, the movie was released early. It screened in 21 theaters in New York City on May 24.

"To add to the Jaycees' woes, the New York reviews of the film were all bad," noted the writer of an AP article about the kerfuffle in *The Oregonian* the following Wednesday. "The only thing anyone liked was the Oregon scenery."

Indeed, bad they were, those reviews — and generally contemptuous as well.

"It's all very promising material, but Hecht and ... McLaglen bury it in a panorama of scenery and stock Western clichés," wrote Roger Ebert, whose two-and-a-half-star review was probably the gentlest one of the lot.

The main issue for most critics was that the film tries to tell too many stories. The plot of the movie is, basically, a wagon train full of flawed characters of various types making their way across the country, experiencing lots of interpersonal dramas and physical hardships along the way. It's hard for viewers to emotionally invest in all of them at the same time, and the film doesn't make a particularly strong case for why they should; and the tendency among critics watching it for the first time seems to have been to shrug their shoulders, look at their watches and count down the minutes until they could be safely back in the office writing a scathing takedown, probably including the words "worst," "Western," "movie" and "ever."

Of course, once the first few of these ferocious reviews came out, the general negativity started to influence others, in a classic "information cascade." Today, in the cold light of history many years later, the movie actually holds up pretty well. In 1967, in the hot blood of the moment, with the sheer momentum of the bad press feeding back into the coverage to influence more bad press, well ... United Artists was in for a bumpy ride.

At the end of May, the Eugene Jaycees were gamely trying to put the best face they could on the "world premiere" debacle.

"What we've got is a Pacific Northwest premiere, call it what you want to — but we have the first showing in this area," Jaycees spokesman Jim Cisler told reporters.

But United Artists was not making things any easier for its erstwhile partners. In a press conference, studio representative Murry Lafayette emphatically declared that he was "in no way, shape or manner prepared to make a statement" about the studio's plans for the regional premiere showing — which was, of course, the stated topic for the press conference he'd just called — and added, less than helpfully, "As far as I'm concerned, the less I know about it, the better I feel."

He did, however, mention that Michael Witney, one of the supporting-role actors in the flick (he played the philandering newlywed Johnny Mack), would be there; and the three male leads would be "represented" by Troy Donahue — who wasn't actually in the movie at all. (Troy, as our younger readers may not recall, was a tall, handsome blond actor who had been one of the hottest sex symbols in the business about ten years before this, but whose career had cooled considerably as a result of an ill-considered feud with studio mogul Jack Warner.)

Lafayette said producer Harold Hecht would be there, though — "which," the reporter adds, "may be considered an act of bravery. Critics who have seen the film thus far have universally panned it."

Bravery, or . . . or not. As the days passed, the brutality of the criticism of the movie mounted to the point that the United Artists people simply canceled the "premiere," leaving the Jaycees holding the bag, and slunk back to Hollywood to hide under their desks.

Sources and Works Cited:
- *"The Way West (film)," an article published by Gregory P. Shine on April 9, 2018, in The Oregon Encyclopedia, oregonencyclopedia.org;*
- *Archives of the Portland Oregonian, May and June 1967.*

THE "ENEMY ALIEN" BRIDES.

THE BAD IDEA:
- *Strip American women of their citizenship at the altar if they get married to men who are not American citizens.*

Nobody remembers it today, because it was so long ago. But the outbreak of the First World War changed Oregon — and the rest of the United States — a great deal.

News of America's entry into the fight was greeted with excitement, eagerness and dread. But there was one particular group of Oregonians for whom the dread was especially pronounced: The German-American community.

The German-born cohort of Oregon residents was bigger than any other foreign-born group, totaling 18,000 in the 1910 census, with another 22,000 children of German-born parents — roughly 6 percent of the state's total population. Before the war broke out, society's leaders had considered them among the most desirable immigrants by the lights of the day — Northern European, mostly Protestant, hard-working, clean-living, solid.

Now, all of a sudden, they were "huns."

J. Henry Albers, one of Portland's most prominent citizens and the president of the Albers Brothers grain-milling company, found out the hard way how much things had changed, shortly after the U.S. entered the war. On his way home from a business trip to San Francisco, he had a few too many drinks and started singing ... in German.

Upon arrival in Portland, Albers was arrested and charged with "Seditious Conduct by a German Alien." He was convicted and sentenced to three years in prison — for singing!

Over the following four years, Albers appealed his conviction all the way to the Supreme Court. The federal government fought him every step of the way, even years after the war had ended, only to drop its case on the day the Supreme Court was to hear it in 1921 — claiming that it had made a technical error. It's impossible to read that in any way other than as a malicious prosecutorial move to make sure Albers didn't get a chance to be vindicated. (There certainly were some Horrible People involved with that one.)

For Albers, the shame of it all was devastating. The final blow came when he was expelled from his Elks Lodge, and ten days later he suffered a stroke and died.

Most of the German-born Oregonians didn't suffer as dramatically as Albers did, of course. But many of them did have their lives turned upside down. President Woodrow Wilson had issued an executive order barring them from coming within a hundred yards of the waterfront or a half-mile of the armory, which was a huge problem for non-naturalized Germans who worked as longshoremen (or even as owners of saloons on Front Street). This obstacle could sometimes be overcome, but not always, and it involved lots of red tape and hassle — hearings, paperwork, permits and so on.

A far more disturbing problem, though, involved the American women who'd married one of those German citizens.

Back in 1907, while the battle for women's suffrage was heating up, a little-noticed law had been passed stipulating that women who marry foreigners would be stripped of their citizenship. The idea, following the now-thoroughly-discredited eugenic theories of the day, was to discourage American women from participating in "race suicide" by marrying men from "inferior races" (Italians, Hungarians, Russians, etc.) and to encourage them to leave the country if they did. Stripped of her citizenship at the altar, the now-stateless bride on her wedding day was expected to acquire citizenship in whatever country her husband was from, and she was not eligible for the naturalization process to become an American again.

That meant that a native-born Oregon woman who had fallen in love with and married one of the thousands of non-naturalized foreign citizens in Oregon — be he British, Irish, Italian, Japanese or German — was now officially a foreigner in her own country, with no rights to vote (after 1919) or hold elective office or travel with an American passport.

Of course, under ordinary circumstances, the average woman in 1907 didn't typically do anything with her citizenship. If she didn't travel to countries that required a passport, she might live her entire life never knowing she was stateless.

For some women, though, that changed drastically in 1917. But not for all of them: just for the ones who had married a German man.

1917 was, of course, the year the U.S. entered the European war. When that happened, those American girls who'd married a German boy suddenly started receiving letters ordering them to report to their local police station and register themselves as "enemy aliens."

An example of the anti-German war propaganda posters depicting Germans as bloodthirsty "huns" in order to whip up popular support of American participation in the First World War. (Image: UC Davis)

Hattie Burbank was one such "enemy alien." Born and raised in Sherwood, she was a second-generation Oregonian who had fallen in love with a German-born logger named Adolph Dahrens. Adolph had, in 1916, started the process of applying for naturalization, and in June 1917 — two months after America entered the war — he registered for the draft, offering his services to the American army for purposes of fighting against his "fellow Germans."

Hattie's parents strongly objected to her marriage — probably as a result of the anti-German sentiment with which the non-German citizens of

BAD IDEAS *and* HORRIBLE PEOPLE *of* OLD OREGON.

The enemy-alien registration form for newlywed Hattie Burbank Dahrens. Hattie was stripped of her American citizenship when she married logger Adolph Dahrens in 1918. (Image: Oregon Historical Society)

Oregon were then saturated. What their motivations might have been, we can't know, but two weeks after the marriage they reported her to authorities as an enemy alien.

Hattie at first refused to register. Her position — not an unreasonable one — was that as a native-born American who had never been to Germany and didn't speak German, she was not an enemy alien, no matter what President Wilson's opinion on the matter was.

Finally, offered the choice of registering as an enemy alien or going to prison, Hattie relented and submitted to the indignity of having the postmaster of Sandy describe her nose as "large and fleshy" on her registration paperwork.

And then there was Grace Reimers, who really *was* in a pickle. She'd married German citizen Paul Reimers a year or two before Germany went to war in 1914. Early in August of 1914, Paul left Portland to join the German army, leaving Grace and the baby to fend for themselves. In 1918, when she found out she'd have to register as an "enemy alien," she promptly filed for divorce.

Luckily, courts and authorities were sympathetic to her story; after all, it played perfectly into the narrative of the cruel "hun," abandoning his wife and baby in his zeal to crush democracy. After the divorce was granted, she was quietly restored to citizenship.

Once the war was over, and America started its quest to get "back to normal," things quickly got better for most German-American Oregonians — particularly after the realization started to dawn on their neighbors that they had been snookered by a carefully crafted anti-German propaganda machine designed to manipulate them into supporting Wilson's war.

But although they were no longer "enemy aliens," women who had married foreign men remained stateless and legally dependent on their husbands' citizenship for years after the war ended. The Cable Act of 1922 restored the citizenship of most, but women who'd married Chinese or Japanese men were still being stripped of their citizenship at the altar until well into the 1930s.

Sources and Works Cited:
- *"From Citizens to Enemy Aliens," an article by Kimberly Jensen published in the Winter 2013 issue of* Oregon Historical Quarterly;
- The Growth of a City, *a book by E. Kimbark MacColl published in 1979 by Georgian Press.*

THE LASH-LAW SCHEME.

THE BAD IDEA:
- *Ban Black people from living in your state, be they slave or free, on pain of regular public floggings.*

In middle-school history classes, most Oregonians learned that Oregon was a "free" state in the runup to the civil war.

The familiar map of slave states and free states was a source of some pride, since everyone today sees the ludicrous injustice and inhumanity of the slavery system.

But the map was wrong.

The new state of Oregon was, in fact, unique in the country. Black people in Oregon in 1859 were neither slaves nor free; they were simply illegal.

Oregon is the only state that was admitted to the union with a racial exclusion law baked right into its constitution. No African-Americans could legally come to or live in the state — no slaves, no freemen, nobody.

And although the restriction was apparently never actually enforced, it wasn't removed from the state's law books until 1926.

As if that weren't enough, after the Civil War, the state legislature actually rescinded its ratification of the 14th Amendment (equal protection). As for the 15th Amendment (voting rights for Blacks), that was left unratified for 90 years — until 1959, on the eve of the state's Centennial Celebration.

So, what gives? Most Oregonians today consider themselves among the more enlightened citizens of the country when it comes to matters of race. And yet the popular attitudes of just a few dozen years ago seem like those of another place entirely.

The answer is that Oregon *was*, in essence, another place entirely. Specifically, it was Missouri — which was very much a slave state.

The Oregon Trail started in Missouri, and although plenty of emigrants came from other places, the trail's draw was strongest in the Show-Me State. Consequently, most of the torrent of settlers coming out west in the wagon trains of the 1850s were frontier southerners. Moreover, they were poorish frontier southerners — with enough money to outfit a wagon and leave town, but not wealthy enough for it to make financial sense to stay. That gave them a particular outlook on race matters, and it's that outlook that Oregon ended up stuck with.

First, the emigrants were near the bottom of the social pecking order, with free Blacks just below them. That meant they felt the pressure of social and economic competition from Blacks more than their wealthier peers would have.

And secondly, the emigrants were leaving an environment in which the deck was stacked against them because their wealthier competitors were benefiting from free labor.

Emigrant Wilson Morrison, who left Missouri in 1844, phrased it succinctly: "Unless a man keeps [slaves] . . . he has no even chance; he cannot compete with the man who does . . . . I'm going to Oregon, where there'll be no slaves, and start over."

So for these guys, it came down to competition. Free Blacks would compete with them for social standing and for available resources; and slaves would make it impossible for them to compete with their slaveholding neighbors.

And there was another aspect to this as well: The Native Americans. Though many tribes were wiped out by exotic diseases, other Native Americans in Oregon were actively resisting the settlement process in those days — especially in the southern and eastern parts of the state. What might happen if a population of free Blacks were to move to Oregon and make common cause with the Native Americans there?

Something hinting at that sort of thing had already happened, involving a free Black man named James Saules, back in 1844. Saules had married a Native American woman; in a subsequent dispute with a man named Cockstock over ownership of a horse, he threatened to raise an army of his

Former slave Louis Southworth sits by the fireplace. Southworth, a gifted violinist, was brought to Oregon in 1853, while one of the exclusion laws was still in effect. He earned and saved enough money playing fiddle for dance schools to buy his freedom, and eventually homesteaded a claim near the Alsea River west of Monroe. (Image: oregonencyclopedia.org)

wife's relatives and start a race war. This, of course, was utter balderdash, but it got taken seriously at the time.

The Saules incident touched off the first of several territorial laws excluding Blacks from Oregon, later that year. That first law was known as the "Lash Law" — because it stipulated that any African-American caught in the territory would get "not less than 20, nor more than 39" stripes laid across his or her back with a whip. Then, if he or she did not leave within six months, the punishment would be repeated.

The brutality of this penalty proved shocking even to the hardened Southern settlers of the day, and its author, Peter Burnett, was later embarrassed by it. It was modified to exclude the whipping before it went into effect; but the name stuck, and the sentiment behind it could not have been more clear.

What made Oregon different from Missouri, though, was the presence of another cohort of settlers clustered around the trading port cities of the lower Willamette — such as Oregon City, Portland and Astoria. Of the elites of these towns, very few had come over the Oregon Trail from Missouri. They were, by and large, from New England states like Massachusetts, and they had come by sea, "around the horn." Most of them were traders and businessmen.

These New Englanders were not particularly worried about Blacks one way or another. They were mercantile libertarians, wanting primarily to be free to pursue business success and personal happiness free of distractions such as the Civil War. From their standpoint, the presence in Oregon of free Blacks and slaves alike held only the potential for trouble; it would get the passions of those Southerners all inflamed. These Yankee traders saw the Civil War as a massive destruction of wealth and resources, and wanted no part of it. So they were just fine with keeping Blacks out.

After the Civil War, though, worries of getting sucked into the war were gone, and the Yankees lost all enthusiasm for exclusion. Furthermore, Portland was a very Republican town in the 1800s, while the rest of the state was predominantly Democratic. And after the Civil War, the Republican Party was far less hostile to free Blacks.

So the African-Americans who did move to Oregon tended to settle in Portland, where they formed the nucleus of a friendly colony and could look after one another — rather like the Chinese did.

The cultural legacies of Missouri and Massachusetts, and their disparate attitudes toward Black people, were still very influential in Oregon right through the end of World War II — when thousands of Black families came to work in the shipyards, and returning servicemen brought back a more cosmopolitan, combat-forged attitude on race. The fruits of those influences are Oregon's attitudes today, which most people agree are pretty modern.

But when you walk down a street in downtown Portland at rush hour and see only one or two non-white faces, it's a reminder that Oregon is a latecomer to egalitarian enlightenment.

Sources and Works Cited:
- Breaking Chains: Slavery on Trial in the Oregon Territory, *a book by R. Gregory Nokes published in 2013 by Oregon State University Press;*
- A Peculiar Paradise: A History of Blacks in Oregon, *a book by Elizabeth McLagan published in 1980 by Georgian Press;*
- "Black Exclusion Laws in Oregon," an article by R. Gregory Nokes published in The Oregon Encyclopedia *(last update: July 6, 2020) at oregonencyclopedia.org.*

WHEN MILK WAS MURDER.

THE BAD IDEA:
- *Transport milk to market in the same cans you use to transport slop home to feed your pigs.*

In the late summer of 1909, a dairy farmer near Portland started getting worried. His barn cats kept dying, and after a few days he'd figured out what was killing them: The milk from his cows.

This whole time, of course, he'd been shipping gallons of the same milk off to Portland to be fed to babies and young children.

So he went to the state dairy and food commissioner, J.W. Bailey, and asked what he should do.

It was a natural worry for a dairy farmer in 1909. Concerns about bad milk in Portland had been building for some time. Two years before, after finding disgusting conditions at several area dairies, Portland city health commissioner Dr. Esther Pohl (better known today by her name from after her second marriage, Esther Pohl Lovejoy) lobbied for and got a city ordinance passed requiring that dairies be inspected by an actual health inspector, not just a food commissioner.

The ordinance didn't include enough enforcement provisions, though,

A lantern slide from around the turn of the last century, depicting an unidentified "modern dairy farm." (Image: Oregon State University archives)

and the dairy farmers were able to simply ignore it. Nothing had really changed.

Most likely, the farmer was a little afraid of Dr. Pohl and her staff. Anyone would be; for Pohl, the matter had become deeply personal a year earlier, in 1908, when her six-year-old son, Freddie, died of septic peritonitis caused by drinking contaminated milk.

So the farmer instead turned to a friendlier official face — the food and dairy commissioner who basically approved every dairy as long as the milk didn't taste watered down. Maybe Commissioner Bailey could give him some good advice about what to do.

The commissioner's advice, in essence, was, "It's just tuberculosis; don't worry about it."

"Tuberculosis milk may kill cats," Bailey reassured the worried farmer, "but it will fatten babies."

That didn't sit right with the dairy man, so he stopped by the offices of the *Portland Journal* on his way home. And that was how the great Portland "pure milk crusade" was launched.

Two *Journal* reporters immediately set out for the offices of the dairy commissioner to learn the truth. When they got there, the older of the two, John Wilson, set the tone for the interview by calling Bailey a "baby killer."

Bailey backpedaled, explained, denied, and finally demanded to know what business of the newspaper's it was, anyway.

"You're a liar," Wilson shot back, and somebody threw a punch, and the fight was on. The other reporter — Marshall Dana, who was at the time brand-new on the job — had to physically separate the two before somebody got hurt.

The next day, Wilson quit his job at the newspaper. It's not clear whether this was prompted by the scene in the commissioner's office; getting into a fistfight with an interviewee would get a reporter canned in a heartbeat today, but a hundred years ago the life of a newspaper guy was much less circumscribed.

In any case, editor Jack Travis told Marshall Dana to get on the story — and get on it he did. The result was a days-long parade of Bad Ideas and Horrible People marching across the front page of the *Journal* in 72-point type.

The reporter started his investigation with a tour of the dairy farms of

A Hillcrest Jersey Stock Farm delivery truck parked on the side of a street in a residential neighborhood in the early 1920s, some time after Portland's milk supply had become among the cleanest and safest in the world.

FLIES SWARM ON FILTH IN DAIRIES THAT SUPPLY CITY OF PORTLAND WITH MILK

REVOLTING IN EXTREME ARE CONDITIONS

Secretary of State Board of Health and City Milk Inspector Take a Look at Some of Sources of Supply on Columbia Slough.

Conditions incredibly vile were found when Dr. R. C. Yenney, secretary of the state board of health; Dr. D. W. Mack, city milk inspector, and a representative of The Journal inspected a few of the dairies supplying Portland with milk this morning.

The tour was originally planned at the suggestion of J. W. Bailey, state dairy and food commissioner, and he had arranged to be leader of the party, but at the time of starting he withdrew, giving as reason that the milk situation had been taken in charge by the city health authorities and he would not need to concern himself with it longer.

Flies, billions of them, swarmed over the dairy equipment of Mike Tannler on the Columbia Slough road, which was the first place visited. Filth was everywhere. Swill barrels were side by side with unwashed and foul smelling vessels. The closet used by the family was only a few feet distant.

From sour milk, fetid water, heaps of accumulated manure, arose an odor indescribably sickening. Long rows of stanchions stretched the length of the barn, so close together that the cows enclosed would have touched side and side the entire distance. There was absolutely no arrangement for ventilation.

Cow Will Soon Die.

Four cows were discovered in the vicinity of the barnyard. All gave evidence of having been recently milked. The udder of one cow was swelled to abnormal proportions. "She is badly diseased," said Dr. Mack, briefly, after examining her. "Unattended as she is now gangrene will develop, the cow will ultimately die horribly, but before she dies the pus from the diseased udder can affect the cows, and their milk, of all the rest of the herd. The other three cows here are injured in various ways."

Yet there was no evidence apparent that these cows were kept from contact with the rest. In fact, there was no evidence that any care for sanitation was taken at all. In addition to the conditions already described, the milk cooler was found exposed to the millions of infesting flies, the water used beside the barn was drawn from a well dug beside the barn. No gutter was arranged to catch the liquid manure from the animals and there was every evidence

(Continued on Page Six.)

A MOTHER'S PATHETIC STORY

A few days ago Alfred F. Howe, a fine boy just a little more than 4 months old, died, and Dr. Carrico, attending physician, assigned bad milk as the chief contributing cause. Last night Mrs. Howe, at her home, 452 Mississippi avenue, told The Journal how she lost her boy. In the mother's mind memory of her grief was still very fresh, and the sobs broke into her voice continually as she talked.

"Alfred never had a sick day until he drank the milk the night before he was taken sick," Mrs. Howe said. "We had been living in South Portland; then my husband, who is an engineer, found it better for him to be on the east side, so we came over here.

"We got a new dairyman, the milk looked all right and we gave it to Alfred. That same night he was taken sick. Poor little fellow, how he suffered! Somehow I knew he was going to die, yet nearly worn out taking care of my little girl who had died a short time ago, I was scarcely able to watch over him.

"How was I to know that the milk was bad. I had no one to tell me. I hear that in other towns the man who sells milk has to have a certificate that it is pure and won't hurt babies. But I didn't have any such defense. Some way to let people have milk they can't find out about and to let it kill our babies seems almost like murder. But I am a mother. My boy is dead. Perhaps that is why I feel as I do."

Indignation made Mrs. Howe's eyes flash before she had finished speaking. Her concluding sentence was: "Because I am a mother, because my boy is dead, I want to warn other mothers that they will have to take care. You don't know the sorrow death brings until death comes. I am going to help The Journal in this crusade, all I can."

Mrs. Howe's experience is that of half a hundred mothers in Portland during the month. Dr. Robert E. Yenney, secretary of the state board of health, points out the economic aspect of the situation.

"Pure milk, even if it costs more, is worth getting, when you think of the doctors bills saved, the funeral expenses, the grief that comes with death," he declared. "This fight would be worth while if only one life was to be saved. It looks now as though we under value human life."

BAILEY CLASHED WITH JUSTICE OF PEACE IN TRYING MILK CASES

Court records kept by the clerk of Fred L. Olson, justice of the peace, show peculiar methods of prosecution inaugurated by J. W. Bailey, state dairy and food commissioner, against offending dairymen. Instead of bringing offenders against the pure milk laws into open court, Commissioner Bailey made the custom of trying them in his own office, assessing the fine and turning in the fine to the justice of the peace, whose duty it thereupon became to send the money to the state treasurer.

Fine money was deposited by the treasurer in the pure food fund, and Commissioner Bailey says he drew it out again to aid in the maintenance of office expenses.

M. Tannler, a dairyman living outside the city, was found to be a case in point. Commissioner Bailey complained that Tannler was selling watered milk. The records show that Bailey offered to bring Tannler into court, saving the services of the constable, and the other usual court procedure. Within a few days he announced that he had given Tannler a hearing, had decided that his fine should be $25, and was on his way to deposit the money.

Judge Olson stated to the commissioner that as an officer of the law he did not conduct business that way, and that Tannler would have to be brought into court and answer for himself before the public the charges against him. After considerable delay Tannler was brought into court. It was found that at the innocent suggestion of a customer, he had thrown a quart of water into a 26-gallon can of milk to keep the contents cool until he made his deliveries. Evidence showed that Tannler had no intention of diluting or adulterating the milk which he sold and he was dismissed with a warning.

The records go on to relate that Commissioner Bailey was highly incensed that he was not allowed to try his own cases in private, and at the time stated that such, had always been his custom. Justice Olson, replying that such procedure would not obtain at any time in his office, the commissioner took his cases before another magistrate.

TUBERCULAR COWS CANNOT PRODUCE GOOD MILK--LYTLE

Unlicensed dairies supply Portland with unfortified milk. The menace of the unclean hangs over the city. Few customers know the names of their dairymen. Much less do they know whether the milk comes from tubercular cows, kept in filthy stables with unwashed help attendant.

The problem resultant is an equation in human life. In demanding that J. W. Bailey, state dairy and food commissioner, center of authority and sworn officer, note the excessive infant mortality of Portland and heed the pleadings of the mothers, The Journal has but one object—to save the lives of the babies.

In the open court of public opinion the case of the people versus the dairies is being tried. The dairies will be sentenced to self improvement. The officials who have condoned filth and denied the menace of disease will not be allowed to remain obstructionists to progress and purification. Old fashioned negligence in modern times is deadly. Congested life makes pure food vital. Milk must be good food, not breeding ground for disease. The question is put to the people of Portland. They will decide and, backed by their cooperation and aid, The Journal will not rest until Portland's milk supply is clean.

Dr. W. H. Lytle, state veterinarian, said to The Journal:

"Tubercular cows have not sufficient vitality to produce milk up to the 3 per cent standard in butter fat. Sterilizing milk precipitates the minerals; its use gives children rickets. There is no use beating around the bush, cows known to be sound by test, kept in clean dairies, must produce the milk children and adults drink. An expert in the office of the dairy and food commissioner would insure just such gratifying conditions."

Coverage of the Pure Milk Crusade on Page 1 of the Oregon Journal, Sept. 2, 1909.

northwest Oregon, and it was quite an eye-opener.

"Out on the Columbia Slough road there was a dairy operated by a dairyman named Mike," Dana wrote, 40 years later, in his book. "The door of the dairy barn stood open. When (we) got a little closer the disturbed flies flew up in a cloud. In front of the barn lay a dead calf. Evidently it had been there quite a while."

The condition of the cows at the farm left little doubt in Dana's mind as to why the calf had died. There was filth everywhere. One of the dairy cows, he could see, had an open sore on its udder.

The farmer, Mike Tannler, freely admitted he had a bad reputation with the state regulators — but that wasn't because of the filth.

"I get arrested for puttin' water in the milk," he told Dana cheerfully. "I pay a fine. Then I put enough more water in the milk to pay the fine."

But then, given the apparent quality of this farmer's milk, watering it down might have saved someone's life!

Dana found another dairy on Canyon Road at which the owner made a practice of bringing his milk to town in big cans and then, after delivering the milk, using the empty cans to transport restaurant garbage back to his farm, where he fed it to pigs. After emptying the garbage out of his milk cans, he'd rinse them out, fill them back up with milk and repeat the process. Dana learned that one of this fellow's customers over in east Portland had given some of this milk to a child, who subsequently died in convulsions — an event that may have been entirely unrelated to the garbage-milk, but probably wasn't.

Dana soon learned that Portland had one of the highest rates of baby deaths from gastrointestinal complaints in the nation — a statistic that was clearly related to its cavalier attitude toward its milk supply.

Dana filed story after story, and they ran under banner headlines that shouted from the top of Page One. The paper kicked off the campaign with a massive banner headline, in red type, that read, "BAD MILK KILLS PORTLAND BABIES," and while they didn't all rise to that level of drama and impact, they remained on Page One for weeks and they had a considerable impact. Meanwhile, editorial writers fulminated and denounced the various players who were, as they saw it, conspiring to kill babies for a fatter profit.

The public exploded with outrage.

Civic and social clubs adopted resolutions. The Chamber of Commerce weighed in on the issue, pointing out that bad milk was bad for business — nobody wants to make a home and grow a business in a town where babies die.

City and state officials responded to the pressure immediately, too. In fact, support came from every quarter save the dairy farmers — who, naturally, felt a bit singled out.

Although he had a job to do, Dana was sympathetic. "There was so much censure and condemnation that it was no longer respectable to be a dairyman," he wrote. "The Page-One stories and the big headlines hit the good dairymen as well as the bad."

Among the dairy farmers, there was a good deal of resentment at the prospect of government interference with their business — at first. They came around quickly, though, when they realized what was really going on: The government was stepping in to protect the good farmers from the bad ones — to keep them from having to compete with men who undercut their prices by taking dangerous shortcuts.

By the following year, the statistical situation was completely turned around, and Portland's milk supply was among the safest in the country.

That still didn't do reporter Marshall Dana much good, though. It would be years before he could touch a drop of milk without retching.

Sources and Works Cited:
- Portland: A Food Biography, *a book by Heather Arndt Anderson published in 2015 by Rowman and Littlefield;*
- Newspaper Story: Fifty Years of the Oregon Journal, *a book by Marshall Dana published in 1951 by Binford and Mort;*
- Round the Roses II: More Portland Past Perspectives, *a book by Karl Klooster published in 1992 by Klooster Promotions.*

THE ARSON SHRUB.

THE BAD IDEA:
- *Introduce a non-native species of shrub that burns like diesel fuel, and let it take over an entire town.*

When Lord George Bennett founded the little town of Bandon on the very western rim of Oregon in 1873, he must have been pining for his native Ireland. It was from Ireland that Bennett imported both the name of his new home town — and a certain ornamental shrub that reminded him of home.

Which turned out to be a very Bad Idea.

The shrub is called gorse. If you've driven much along the southern Oregon Coast you'll have noticed it; it's increasingly dominant as you approach Bandon from the north or south, displacing the native salal plants with their waxy dark-green leaves and bland-tasting purple berries. It's usually in the form of a chest-high gray-green mass, sometimes speckled with little yellow flowers like those of Scotch broom. Its leaves are protected by a tangle of low-grade prickles, like those on a thistle.

But it's not for its prickles that the stuff is feared in Oregon. It's for its love of fire.

Gorse is a plant that's made to burn. It's happiest in an environment that burns fiercely every few decades. When a good hot fire sweeps a hillside clean, gorse's specialty is being the first green thing to return to the scene.

Cars driven to the beach by Bandon residents hoping to save them from the flames ended up ruined, like virtually everything else, by the intense heat. (Image: Oregon Department of Forestry))

Its charred-off roots start sprouting new growth as soon as things are cool again, and its seed pods, lying on the ground, are cracked open by the fire and soon get busy sprouting.

To encourage these periodic fires and to help them get hot enough to kill competing plants, gorse secretes oils in its leaves that burn like diesel fuel. Sometimes in hot weather oil actually drips from them.

In other words, gorse is a phoenix plant that yearns for its own destruction so that it can rise from the ashes and take over.

Which appears to have been its plan for the town of Bandon, if a plant can be said to have a plan, on Sept. 26, 1936.

In the 63 years that had passed since Bennett brought gorse to Bandon, the stuff had spread everywhere. Gorse seemed to really like Bandon. Gorse hedges and thickets were all over the town, and vacant lots were stuffed with it — four feet high and too thick to walk through.

On this particular day, a couple slash burns from nearby logging operations had got out of control, and a small forest fire had resulted. Although the day was uncommonly dry and warm, the fire would ordinarily not have been that big a deal. It might have claimed a house or two on the edge of town, but Bandon had — as was about to become clear — a crack fire department; it should have been OK.

But once the forest fire got into the gorse thickets at the edge of town, there was no stopping it.

Writer Stewart Holbrook, who happened to be on the scene when it happened, describes how this worked: "A stray spark would fall in a green clump of gorse near a house. An instant later the gorse was flaming higher than the house. In another instant the house was wholly on fire. Time and again it happened."

The firefighters found that large patches of burning gorse behaved differently than did the smaller fires they were used to. Squirting water on it was like throwing water on a grease fire in the kitchen — all it did was spread flaming, oily branches everywhere.

Many of the townspeople were at first reluctant to leave; they were having trouble believing they were in real danger. When the fire came over the hill and started advancing on them, though, they jammed themselves into the streets and headed for the beach. The Coast Guard ferried hundreds across the Coquille River to the dunes on the other side. The firefighters covered their retreat until the tires of the fire truck melted, effectively immobilizing it; at that point, they too fled to the beach, where townspeople with their backs to the sea knelt behind driftwood logs charred and smoking from the heat, heaping sand over them in an effort to keep them from catching fire.

In the end, ten people died, several of them in the act of trying to retrieve treasured objects from their homes. And out of some 500 buildings and homes in Bandon, just 16 remained in salvageable condition.

Today, Bandon has rebuilt itself, and enough years have passed since 1936 for the town to have reacquired an old-seaside-town charm. The majority of the visitors strolling through during the summer season have no idea they're walking on land that their grandparents would have experienced as a charred wasteland.

And yes, there's still gorse in Bandon, although the city code now includes

A postcard view of the cliffs near Bandon, covered with gorse bushes in bloom, from a photo by Ted Rosin. (Image: Postcard)

strict regulations on it. It's simply become too common to eradicate. But most Bandon residents will never look at it the same way again, and they'll never feel quite the same way about their founder, Bennett — who gave the town life and nearly brought it death.

By the way, the story of the Bandon fire was widely covered in the press worldwide. In 1942 when Imperial Japan was making plans to strike the American homeland in reprisal for the Doolittle bombing raids on Tokyo, planners remembered the story, and decided to try to induce a similar forest fire with firebombs. The result was the only wartime airstrike in U.S. history, when, on Sept. 9, the submarine I-25 launched a tiny seaplane which flew over the nearby town of Brookings, dropped a couple firebombs on Mount Emily, and returned. (More on that attempt on Page 167.)

The resulting fires were small and easily extinguished in the early-morning damp. But if the aviators had found a patch of gorse to drop the bomb in, the result might have been different.

Sources and Works Cited:
- Wildmen, Wobblies and Whistle Punks, *a collection of Stewart Holbrook's stories edited by Brian Booth, published in 1992 by Oregon State University Press;*
- *"Memories of the Bandon Fire," an article by Bob Howard published in the Sept. 30, 2008, issue of the* Bandon Western World.

THE BUNGLING BURGLARS.

THE BAD IDEA:
- *Break into the county treasurer's office, assuming there will be treasure there.*

The robbers and burglars who have made Oregon history have not always been the smartest guys on the block. Perhaps that's just because the smart ones never made history — that is, got caught. But there does seem to be a special thickness about Oregon's pioneer criminals.

Take, for instance, the D'Autremont brothers, who in 1923 pulled off history's last great train robbery, but then left a dry-cleaner's claim check with a name on it at the scene (more about them on Page 357 of this book).

And then there was Harry Tracy, the last of the Wild West-era outlaws — famously described by Stewart Holbrook as a "garden-variety idiot" — who was known for breaking out of jails. To get good at breaking out of jails, of course, one has to be pretty bad at avoiding getting thrown into them in the first place.

Also, let's not forget French West and George Wise, the would-be pirates whose brilliant scheme was to get drunk, hijack an ocean liner, force the pilot to run it aground, and disappear into the night with three tons of gold. That story appears on Page 421 of this book.

But one of the more amusing stories of early-Oregon "morons in the news" (with a tip of the hat to the Bob and Sheri radio show) came out of Corvallis, the seat of Benton County.

It all started out on the evening of April 4, 1909. Frank Clayton and George Davis, two local fellows in their late 30s, had big plans for the night.

A week or two earlier, Clayton and Davis had successfully burgled a jewelry store in the town of Peoria, just up the river, and gotten away with some very nice things. A journey to a few pawnshops in Portland had turned many of those things into a pocketful of lovely money, although of course hitting a pawn shop with an entire jewelry store's worth of stuff was bound to raise suspicions; so most of the loot was still squirreled away. The robbers had a nice hiding spot underneath a nearby church — the newspaper report says "Oak Grove Church," which might have referred to the Oakville Presbyterian Church, which is just two miles away from Peoria in a particularly quiet part of the valley.

Clayton kept one particularly nice watch for himself, though, as his personal timepiece. He would soon come to regret doing that.

But that stolen watch was no doubt in his pocket on the night of April 4, as he and Davis got ready for their big heist. They were going to break into the Benton County courthouse, blow the door off the treasurer's vault and help themselves to the treasure. Of course there would be treasure — else why would Benton County need a treasurer?

So sometime after midnight, the two brazenly entered the courthouse through the front door, breaking the lock to get in, and then hustled straight to the treasurer's office.

In the treasurer's office they arrived at the vault, a large and promising-looking walk-in safe. This was something the boys knew what to do with. They drilled a hole in the door above the combination lock, stuck a stick of dynamite in, lit the fuse and (one assumes) plugged their ears. A couple seconds later, they were in the vault.

As a side note, it's amazing how much life in Oregon has changed in a little over 100 years. If someone lit off a stick of dynamite in the middle of the night downtown in any Oregon city today, the 911 call center would be flooded with calls from anxious neighbors. But according to the *Corvallis Gazette* the next day, "no special significance was then attached to the noise."

Deep in the heart of the courthouse, Clayton and Davis were discovering

BAD IDEAS.

The Benton County Courthouse in Corvallis, Oregon, as seen on a clear winter day in 2009. The courthouse's appearance is barely changed from how it looked in 1909, when the burglars struck; however, ironically enough, in 1909 the county jail was in the courthouse basement, almost directly under the treasurer's vault. (Photo: Greg Keene/Wikimedia CC-by-SA)

that there wasn't much special significance attached to the vault in the treasurer's office, either. They were ransacking the place, throwing ledgers and papers around in a quest for the treasure that had to be there but, somehow, wasn't. No chests of doubloons, no sacks of jewels . . . nothing.

Well, not exactly nothing. They did find a little cash money. The treasurer was holding some smallish amounts for safekeeping — the lion's share of which was a $200 stash belonging to the Woodmen of the World. The two disappointed burglars hastily appropriated these little sums, hustled back out the door, and headed for the banks of the Willamette.

At the river, they climbed into a small skiff which they had stolen earlier that night from one of the local waterfront mills and set off on a star-lit paddle down the rain-swollen Willamette River — destination Albany and points north.

A couple weeks went by. A reward was announced: Two hundred dollars for information leading to the thieves.

Then the reward was claimed — by the local chief of police, who had journeyed to Portland and, following some detective action in the distant big city, arrested Clayton and Davis.

Today, of course, this could never happen. If it's your job to catch crooks, typically you don't get cash bonuses from grateful citizens for doing it. You also don't get to keep your job as a police chief for long if you neglect it to go gallivanting around a distant city playing bounty hunter.

But perhaps Chief Wells was a special case. The *Gazette* gushed about the job he'd done:

"When the burglary was committed it was thought that no trace had been left by the robbers, but Chief Wells ... found a slight clue and this he followed like a born sleuth," the paper raved. "Chief Wells deserves the highest praise for the really capable manner in which he handled this case .... With only the faintest possible clue he traced the thieves from the scene of the crime."

What was this "faintest possible clue"? The *Gazette* doesn't say. Luckily, its competitor, the *Benton County Republican*, does: Wells found claim stubs from those Portland pawnshops lying around the burglars' abandoned campsite. Since, of course, they had no intention of going back to Portland and redeeming their stolen property from the hock shops, Clayton and Davis had thrown the claim stubs away before leaving camp the night after their getaway.

Bad idea.

Wells arrested the two men on the streets of Portland — most likely, they had journeyed back to "the metrop" to hock some more stuff — and hauled them home to Corvallis in chains. The watch in Clayton's pocket was a nice bonus, because it was easily identified as coming from the Peoria jewelry store. Taxed with that, the two confessed and led the cops to the rest of their stash at the church. They drew sentences of five years each.

As for Wells, he duly filed his claim for the $200 and was granted the cash.

But what's especially interesting about this is, there was another claimant too — none other than Nate Solomon, the sketchy businessman from Portland — the same guy who bought Larry Sullivan's gambling house, The Portland Club, when Larry left town in 1904 to move to Goldfield, Nevada. (for more details on Larry, see Page 185).

Businessmen who run gambling clubs can probably be expected to also own pawnshops. Is it possible that Mr. Solomon did? Was he the guy who whispered to Wells, "Those are the guys, right there," perhaps as they were walking into his shop to pawn more stolen goods? Maybe he was cooperating with Wells as pawnshop owners cooperate with law enforcement officers, never dreaming that this particular one was moonlighting as a bounty hunter, leaving the city he'd sworn to protect in pursuit of a personal cash windfall.

BAD IDEAS.

And if Solomon was the shop owner, was he left holding the bag when all that stolen jewelry was returned to its rightful owner in Peoria?

We'll probably never know.

Sources and Works Cited:
- *Archives of the* Corvallis Gazette *and* Benton County Republican, *March and April 1909*
- *Conversation with Benton County historian Bill McCash*

"TWELVE ANGRY MEN" CAN'T HAPPEN HERE.

THE BAD IDEA:
- *Change the state law so that even if one or two jury members think a defendant is innocent, they can be ignored.*

It's ironic that Norman Rockwell's famous painting "The Holdout" appeared on the front cover of the *Saturday Evening Post* on, of all days, Feb. 14, 1959. That date was Oregon's centennial — the 100th anniversary of the founding of our state — and "The Holdout" depicted a scene that, for more than half the state's history and right up until a few years ago, couldn't happen here.

That's because in Oregon, unlike every other state in the U.S., a unanimous verdict was not necessary in jury trials. Up to two of the 12 jurors on any jury trial could be overruled or ignored. From 1933 clear up until 2020, when the Supreme Court of the United States finally got around to certifying the obvious unconstitutionality of the scheme, you could get sent up the river in Oregon for a life stretch even if two jury members were absolutely convinced of your innocence. (An exception was made for first-degree murder charges, but not for less serious forms of homicide.)

And Oregon's law was changed specifically to prevent the exact scene shown in "The Holdout" — although in the case that inspired it, instead of the lone *woman* on the jury holding out against a "guilty" verdict, it was the lone Jew.

No doubt this didn't seem like such a Bad Idea at the time, years before the Second World War ... but it certainly hasn't aged well since.

The law was changed in the aftermath of the 1933 trial of a local small-time gangster named Jake Silverman, who happened to be Jewish.

Silverman's crime was covered in full detail in Volume Two of this collection, *Love, Sex and Murder in Old Oregon;* but here's the story in a nutshell: A fresh-from-the-pen crook named Jimmy Walker had checked into small-time gang leader "Shy Frank" Kodat's boardinghouse-speakeasy and promptly moved in on Shy Frank's girlfriend, Edith McClain. One thing had led to another, and angry words had been exchanged, and Shy Frank had turned his back on Jimmy and left the room, and then Jimmy's gun had gone off and the bullet had gone through the wall and hit Shy Frank in the back. It was an accident, and it wasn't fatal to Shy Frank; but Shy Frank intended that it should be fatal to Jimmy, and Jake Silverman was tasked with the job of "taking Jimmy for a ride" and making it so.

So Jake borrowed his wife's maroon 1929 Studebaker President limousine and, posing as a getaway driver who would take Jimmy out of town so he could go into hiding, picked up Jimmy at the cheap hotel where he was hiding out. Edith accompanied Jimmy on what they both thought would be a ride into exile.

They learned different when Jake stopped the car in the middle of nowhere near Scappoose, marched them out of the car at gunpoint, made them stand over the ditch so that they would fall into it, and gave each of them two in the back of the head with Shy Frank's .38.

That, at least, was the story on which Jake Silverman was convicted.

But he was not convicted of murder. One of the jurors was not convinced — or claimed not to be.

The evidence had been copious, but circumstantial. Most damning was the car, which several neighbors had seen driving out toward Scappoose and parking by the road just before the gunshots were heard. Very few people could afford maroon Studebaker limousines in 1933, so the chances that it wasn't Silverman were very slim. The standard for conviction is "beyond a reasonable doubt," so those slim chances might be enough to get him off; but basically, almost everyone in the courtroom was convinced he'd done it.

Then, too, a rogues' gallery of seedy underworld characters worthy of a Silver Age Batman comic had been dragged into the trial to testify for and against him, and the overall impression was that he'd almost certainly done the job and that if he hadn't, it wasn't because he wouldn't have jumped at the chance to. And Silverman's gallingly insouciant behavior in court made it even more unbearable.

But one juror just didn't find it all convincing enough to send Jake to the gallows for it. Or even to send him up for a life sentence on a second-degree murder rap. So, finally, a compromise was reached: Jake would be found guilty of manslaughter instead. Manslaughter was good for a three-year sentence, which was something at least.

The public, when it heard the verdict, howled with outrage, led by the Portland *Morning Oregonian*.

"Obviously, Silverman was not guilty of manslaughter," the newspaper opined. "Either he murdered Walker or he was not involved."

The front cover of the Feb. 14, 1959, issue of The Saturday Evening Post was this famous painting by Normal Rockwell (who, incidentally, appears in this painting; he's the second juror from the right). It depicts a scene that, at the time, could only have happened in Oregon if the defendant was on trial for first-degree murder. (Image: Saturday Evening Post)

Unspoken, but understood by most, was the assumption that the lone holdout had been a fellow Jew, and he or she had held out not based on the evidence, but based on tribal loyalties.

And so the Oregonian led the charge to "reform the jury system" by making it possible to disregard one or two dissenting votes when necessary.

Now, to be fair, the paper wasn't overtly advocating for the right to suppress minorities. The case they were making was that many fresh immigrants from countries with authoritarian traditions didn't have the right mindset to fully function as an autonomous person in a democracy, and that it needed to be possible to overrule one or two my-compatriot-right-or-wrong types lest millions of dollars be wasted on multiple jury trials.

They were also mindful of the fact that gangsters sometimes try to get to jurors and, through bribes or threats, get them to vote to acquit — like Alec Baldwin's character did with Demi Moore's in the 1996 movie "The Juror."

But, as a practical matter, abandoning the unanimous jury requirement radically altered the distribution of justice for minority defendants in Oregon courts. For instance, if a Chinese person was on trial for a serious felony, and the jury was composed of 10 non-Chinese Oregonians and two of Chinese descent — how much more likely would the defendant be to get convicted if the two Chinese jurors could simply be outvoted by the others? And would that be a bad thing, or a good thing? (People in the 1930s would likely have said it was good, because the Chinese jurors would, they'd claim, vote to acquit no matter what. People today would, one hopes, disagree.)

The entire problem, of course, is nicely illustrated in Normal Rockwell's painting — or in the 1957 film "Twelve Angry Men" starring Henry Fonda, in which 11 of 12 jurors are eager to convict a vaguely-ethnic inner-city teen accused of a stabbing, and the lone holdout turns out to be right.

The law changed shortly after the trial. Responding to the pressure, the state Legislature drafted a bill and passed it on for public vote using the Oregon referendum system: Except for capital murder cases, conviction could be secured on a 10-2 vote. The measure passed comfortably.

Over the years since 1933, there have periodically been challenges to the rule from defendants who were convicted by non-unanimous juries. Concerns about the law are especially noticeable in cases where the one or two dissenting votes were the only jurors who shared the ethnicity or national origin of the defendant.

When the law was passed, only one other state allowed non-unanimous jury verdicts: Louisiana, which at the time used its law more or less openly to expedite convictions of Black defendants.

Following an exposee in the *Baton Rouge Advocate*, the citizens of Louisiana voted to stop allowing non-unanimous convictions in 2018, leaving Oregon as the only state in the country with such a law.

Oregon's last chance to save itself the embarrassment of a public, nationwide shaming at the hands of the U.S. Supreme Court came early in that same year, when the state's prosecuting attorneys proposed ditching the law as part of a deal that would have repealed defendants' right to opt for a jury trial rather than just a hearing before a judge. From civil-libertarians' perspective, that looked like a poison pill, and the effort collapsed when it became clear that they would oppose it.

So finally, in 2020, the Supreme Court delivered the verdict that brought Oregon kicking and screaming back into compliance with the Sixth Amendment of the United States Constitution.

As of the time of this writing, the state's prosecutorial establishment is busily battling to prevent convicts currently serving sentences on charges they were unconstitutionally convicted of by a non-unanimous jury from being allowed to challenge their verdicts. This position may sound harsh or even indefensible, but their justification makes a certain amount of sense: It will be hard on the victims of crimes to have to reappear in court and go through the process of remembering and re-experiencing the trauma all over again because of circumstances they had nothing to do with. It's a tough call, and someone will be unfairly hurt no matter which way it goes.

Sources and Works Cited:
- "*Non-Unanimous Jury Law in Oregon,*" *an article by Aliza Kaplan published in March 17, 2018, in the* Oregon Encyclopedia, *oregonencyclopedia.org;*
- "*Oregon prosecutors back off plan to do away with non-unanimous juries,*" *an article by Conrad Wilson published on Jan. 30, 2018, on the* Oregon Public Broadcasting *Website, opb.org;*
- "*Bill addressing old non-unanimous convictions stalls,*" *an article by Max Egner published in March 3, 2022, on the* Oregon Capital Insider Website;
- "*'Dirty secret' of Oregon jury system could go before U.S. Supreme Court,*" *an article by Shane D. Kavanaugh published in the Sept. 21, 2017, issue of the* Portland Oregonian.

THE SKUNK SKINNER.

THE BAD IDEAS:
- *Try to kill a skunk with your bare hands so that you can take its pelt.*
- *Drop a full can of kerosene on a bear cub's paw while its mother looks wrathfully on.*

One of the most appealing things about life in rural Western Oregon, around the middle of the last century, was the wildlife. Loggers and mill workers in places like Valsetz and Wendling might not have gotten paid particularly well, but they worked and lived in a real "sportsman's paradise"; the fishing, hunting, boating, and wilderness trekking opportunities were like a second paycheck. Sometimes, as in the case of loggers who ran trap lines on the side, it was a literal second paycheck.

Sometimes, though, folks would get a little too much of a good thing, and all that wildlife would get just a little too wild for comfort.

Dr. E.R. Huckleberry, writing his memoirs at the end of a half-decade in family practice in Garibaldi, tells several particularly juicy anecdotes about this. Huckleberry was, from the 1920s through the 1960s, the M.D. who was called when accidents happened at nearby Tillamook County logging shows. So he got to be quite familiar with logging operations and loggers, and he was the physician many loggers and millworkers looked to when they needed medical attention.

Sometime in the 1930s — probably before the Tillamook Burn, but Dr. Huckleberry does not say — a logger he identifies only as Clarence came to see him one day with a somewhat unusual medical request. Actually, his problem wasn't very medical at all, but the logger was desperate and thought maybe the good doctor would know something he didn't about how to address it. He was, as Huckleberry puts it, "redolent of *eau de skunk*."

This logger, it seems, had been working at the White Star logging camp for several months, deep in the woods of Tillamook County, and noticed there was an abundance of fur-bearing animals around. So he'd started running a trapline as a side hustle: Getting up every morning before daylight, he'd run around and check his traps, collect any animals caught in them, set new traps, and be back in time for breakfast.

Pretty soon, Clarence was doing very well. By the time he came to see Dr. Huckleberry, he'd gotten to where he was making almost as much money running that trapline as he was cutting timber.

But on that particular day, as he had been coming back to camp following a narrow game trail — with dense brush on both sides, like a tunnel barely wide enough to admit him; if you've spent much time at the Oregon Coast, you know the type of trail — he had seen, by the early pre-dawn light, strolling leisurely toward him on that trail, a great fluffy skunk.

"No person or animal will dispute the right-of-way with a skunk, so Clarence pushed off the trail into the bushes far enough to let Mr. Skunk get by," Dr. Huckleberry writes. "It was a beautiful pelt, one of the finest he had ever seen, and to have it walk past, touching his feet, was more than he could stand. It suddenly occurred to him that if he grabbed that animal by the tail, held it at arm's length ahead of him, and ran so fast the skunk could not get turned around to train its artillery on him, when he came to a more open place he could give a big swing and bang its head against a tree."

Without thinking his plan through much more than that, Clarence impulsively reached down and implemented Phase One on the spot.

As you will surely not be surprised to hear, things did not go strictly according to Clarence's plan. The main thing he didn't take into account was where he was, in that dense tunnel of underbrush. It was so far to any open space that long before he got anywhere near a tree big enough to safely bounce the skunk off of, he was stumbling and gasping

BAD IDEAS.

A pair of skunks in the wild. (Image: Tom Friedel/www.birdphotos.com CC-by-SA)

for breath. The skunk, at that point still fresh as a daisy and presumably somewhat put out by all the rough handling, then managed to get itself turned around, and, as Dr. Huckleberry puts it, "gave him both barrels at close range."

"By the time Clarence could get his eyes open and begin to breathe again, of course the skunk was gone," he continues. "But there remained conclusive evidence that it had been there."

Clarence stripped off his clothes, dug a hole with his hunting knife, and buried them. Then he snuck into the bathhouse to take a shower. This, of course, did not help much.

When he tried to get into the bunkhouse to get more clothes, the other loggers chased him out; then one of them, taking pity on the poor stinky wretch, got a set of clothes from his bedroll and threw it to him from as far upwind as possible.

When he tried to go into the mess shack for breakfast, the cook chased him out, telling him to wait fifteen minutes and then he'd find his breakfast on a stump at the edge of camp.

When he tried to go to work, the boys wouldn't let him on the mulligan, and his logging partner told him not to bother walking up to the job, as he wouldn't work with him again until he smelled better.

Clarence decided to take the hint, and caught the next lokey (logging locomotive) back to civilization; to get on board, he had to promise to get on the very last train car and stay there the whole way.

In desperation, he walked to Dr. Huckleberry's office to inquire if medical science had yet doped out a deodorization technology potent enough to meet this challenge.

If Clarence had thought things through, he probably would have sought out a veterinarian instead. Very few humans are dumb enough to tangle with a skunk, but plenty of dogs are; a good country vet would have had several pretty solid deodorization strategies to recommend.

Dr. Huckleberry, though, didn't have much experience deodorizing loggers, and told the poor stinky fellow as much. He suggested, though, that Clarence might try a series of Clorox baths. The young logger had a sister who lived in town, and she agreed to let him use her bathtub to do them, provided he entered and exited by the window, left the window open after he left, and never opened the bathroom door. Her family trooped across the street to the neighbor's house for bathroom business for a week or so while Clarence tried this.

It didn't help much, if at all. But, of course, time passed and the smell faded, and a few days later Clarence was able to go back to work.

"He said running that trap line was no fun anymore," Dr. Huckleberry added. "However, he felt he had to keep on with it to make up for the time and the clothes that skunk had cost him."

Another local who had some trouble with wildlife, according to Dr. Huckleberry's recollections, was local dairy farmer and midnight bootlegger Alec Swenson. Alec's bootlegging operations — tucked away in the hilly and heavily overgrown "back 40" of his dairy farm — were far more lucrative than his farm ever had been.

Most bootleggers caught by Prohibition agents in Tillamook County were busted after someone smelled the distinctive aroma of fermentation, or noticed a smoke trail rising from the same remote spot day after day. But dairy farms, of course, have a powerful smell associated with them, and part of that smell is silage — which is fermented feedstock. It doesn't smell that much different from fermented sour mash. So, Alec had the smell part covered. Anyone who caught a whiff of his mash tun drifting on the wind would just think it was silage.

That left the smoke issue as his only worry. To avoid getting found out that way, he powered his still with a kerosene stove. This worked great, but it required him to sneak up to the still with cans of kerosene to fuel it.

One fine summer day, he was doing this, when he rounded a clump of blackberry bushes and found himself in the middle of a family of bears. One of the cubs was right in the trail, and Alec almost stepped on him.

Alec immediately made things even worse by dropping the can of

A postcard photo of a tableau of a moonshine still surrounded by happy dwarves, on display at Rock City Gardens in Lookout Mountain, Georgia. (Image: Postcard)

kerosene on the cub's paw. The little critter bawled like a baby, his mother roared with wrath — and the chase was on.

"The nearest tree was a little alder, but it looked better than nothing, and that bear was gaining on me," Alec told Dr. Huckleberry. "So up I went, as high as I could get. But that wasn't very high. Mama Bear was on her hind legs, clawing and slashing at my boots, and missing them by inches only. This went on for some time, and she showed no signs of getting tired of the game ... At last I thought of my snoose can. It was nearly full."

Snoose, as you probably know, is a tobacco product that was very popular with Scandinavians and loggers. It's similar to moist snuff like Copenhagen, but mixed with salt and other flavoring agents. It has an extremely potent flavor, and, to the uninitiated, not a particularly pleasant one.

The desperate Alec Swenson now pulled his snoose can out of his back pocket, got the lid off, and, when the moment was ripe and those gnashing fangs were out and reaching for him, dumped its entire contents down that slavering hatch.

"She looked surprised, dropped on all fours, started coughing and clawing at her face, then headed for the creek, making noises that sounded like 'Ulp! Ulp! Ulp!'" Alec told Dr. Huckleberry. "She didn't even wait to call the cubs, but they followed. I climbed down, retrieved my can of oil, and tended to my still."

If that last line makes you a bit suspicious of this story, it should. It's pretty hard to imagine anyone coming off an encounter like this not turning around and running for the house. Who could have known how long Mother Bear would be at the creek washing her mouth out? Or how long her memory would be afterward?

So, most likely this story should be filed as folklore, rather than documented history. It, or something like it, probably did happen; but chances are pretty good that it's been added to, at least a little bit ….

Sources and Works Cited:
- The Adventures of Dr. Huckleberry, *a book by E.R. Huckleberry published in 1970 by Oregon Historical Society Press.*

THE GLOVEBOX BOMB.

THE BAD IDEA:
- *Sent to investigate a failed attempt to start a forest fire with an incendiary bomb, upon finding the bomb unexploded, just pop it into your glovebox and drive blissfully back to camp.*

In September 1942, a tiny Japanese seaplane launched from a submarine conducted the only air raid on the mainland U.S. in history.

And but for the intervention of some good luck, it might have succeeded in killing three Oregonians.

Pilot Nobuo Fujita hadn't planned to kill anybody directly, although there was a war on and he would have been happy to do so if he could have. But he was flying a tiny, rickety seaplane that a kid with a .22 rifle could have shot down. His goal was to set the great Oregon forests alight and get back to the submarine alive.

In fact, the whole attempt had been Fujita's idea. He'd heard about the disastrous gorse-powered fire that had destroyed Bandon a few years earlier, which had been reported on in the international press; and he thought maybe if that history could be induced to repeat itself, it would be good for the Imperial Japanese war effort.

Which, from the Japanese perspective, was not exactly a Bad Idea. It would have been a better idea, though, if the weather had been a bit dryer.

In any case, very early on the morning of Sept. 9, avoiding human eyes as much as possible, Fujita's tiny plane buzzed over Brookings, found a nice woodsy spot around nearby Mount Emily, dropped a pair of 170-pound incendiaries on it, and scurried back to the sub. A few days later he came back on a second run near Cape Blanco.

Fortunately for nearby residents, the fire season had largely ended by that time, and the fires Fujita lit were quickly stamped out. The fact that everything was still soaked with morning dew helped as well — every Oregon logger knows you're a lot less likely to have trouble with fire at 6:24 a.m. than at, say, 4 p.m.

But it was in the process of cleaning up after the second bombing run that the Japanese came closest to claiming a trio of victims.

An Oregon Department of Forestry engineer named Louis Amort happened to be in the area with two co-workers when he heard the report of the bombing, and they hurried to the scene — presumably in a "crummy" — to help.

One of the bombs had failed to explode. Bits of the other were scattered all over the place.

The three of them immediately got busy picking up bits of bomb to turn over to the Army. Speaking 48 years later to *Salem Statesman Journal* reporter Hank Arends, Amort said they "picked them up and put them in a paper sack or wrapped them in a blanket and put them in the glove box."

Amort told local historian and Brookings bombing expert Bill McCash

Two Yokosuka E14Y Type Zero reconnaissance seaplanes -- the type was known to Allied air crews as "Glen" -- in flight. This is the aircraft type that dropped the bombs on Oregon, after being launched from the Japanese submarine I-25, with Nobuo Fujita at the controls. (Image: Government of Japan)

BAD IDEAS.

A prototype of the E14Y in flight, before the war broke out. This early version had a different rudder configuration. (Image: Government of Japan)

that this included bits of unexploded bomb three inches in diameter and 10 to 12 inches long. (Whatever Amort and his colleagues were driving must have had an unusually large glovebox.)

Then they drove through the very bumpy terrain around the bomb site back to town, where they turned the bits of unexploded TNT over to an Army liaison officer.

Presumably, the Army officer handled them with greater care than Amort and his friends, who only afterward realized what an enormous risk they'd just taken by stuffing a live firebomb in their glove compartment.

Sources and Works Cited:
- Bombs Over Brookings, *a book by Bill McCash published in 2005 by Maverick Press;*
- *"Salem Man Recalls Japanese Bombing," an article by Hank Arends published in the May 14, 1990, issue of the Salem* Statesman Journal.

THE DROWNED WATERFALL.

THE BAD IDEA:
- *Trade one of the great natural wonders of the world for some cheap hydroelectric power by putting in a dam just downstream from a world-famous waterfall.*

If you first encountered the Columbia River Gorge sometime after 1957, chances are you think of the river that runs through it as being like a big, long lake.

And that's more or less what it is today. It impresses with its bigness, but it's no Mississippi. In places its current is swift, but it's nothing you can't make good progress against in a canoe. Other than the scenery rising from each bank, it doesn't appear particularly remarkable. Just a big river, that's all.

But the Columbia River wasn't always so tame. There was a time when all the water in this, America's fourth-largest river, cascaded through stony slits and roared through a 40-foot rocky gap before it reached the quieter stretch from Portland to Astoria. It was wild, turbulent and as dangerous to boaters as Niagara Falls. Salmon swarmed upstream every year, dashing themselves against the rocks in a struggle to get upstream. Native Americans stood on platforms that hung out over the rocks — platforms that looked rickety and dangerous, but did not flex or move so much as an inch under their weight — and scooped the big fish out of the water with dipnets. They had been doing this for time out of mind.

That was the river Lewis and Clark encountered in 1806. And the central point of the river was Celilo Falls, just east of what's now The Dalles.

Celilo Falls was the epicenter of the oldest continuously inhabited human settlement in North America. Every year, millions of migrating salmon made the living easy; although dipnet fishing was fraught with hazards, starvation was not one of them.

The change in the river started in 1937, when Bonneville Dam was created in part to flood the torrential rapids by the town of Cascade Locks.

But the watershed year was 1957 — the year Celilo Falls disappeared beneath the surface of what is today officially called Celilo Lake, a reservoir backed up behind The Dalles Dam.

The decision to flood the falls was surprisingly uncontroversial by modern standards. Mostly it came down to the Native American tribes that lived and fished at the falls fighting to "stop progress."

The tribes had international law on their side — a treaty that let them fish at the falls — but it wasn't enough. Each tribe member got a lump-sum cash buyout roughly equivalent to the value of a new Cadillac, and they watched sadly as their falls disappeared under 20 feet of still water.

(The tribe did get a settlement payment from the government that they

This postcard image shows The Dalles Dam, which flooded Celilo Falls when it was built in 1957.

BAD IDEAS.

This picture postcard from the 1930s shows people, apparently Native Americans, using a fishing platform to get salmon out of the Columbia. This scene might be at the Cascades near Cascade locks, or possibly just upstream from Celilo Falls.

Another postcard image shows Celilo Falls from a more illustrative angle.

were able to use to finance the construction of Ka-Nee-Ta Resort as well, though. Still, you'd be hard pressed to find a tribe member who thought it was a good deal.)

Why was the government so keen to do this?

Well, regardless of appearances, the Columbia really is an extraordinary river. A full one-third of North America's hydroelectric power-generating potential is on the main stem Columbia River. It has an unusual combination of enormous volume — five times that of the Colorado River; rapid elevation drop; and steep banks so that the impoundments behind dams don't spread out as far.

Plus, it's relatively wild and unsettled, meaning fewer people have to be paid off through condemnation proceedings when their property is flooded.

Hydroelectric projects at Grand Coulee and Bonneville created enough electricity during World War II to have a noticeable impact on America's war effort.

After the war, the country's standard of living was rising fast, and it was all powered by electricity — generated either expensively at coal-fired plants, or cheaply by dams on America's big rivers.

Once Celilo was under water and The Dalles Dam started generating power, it put out an enormous amount — although comparison with the rate of electric-power consumption in the U.S. makes it look less impressive than it is. According to the U.S. Army Corps of Engineers, the dam's powerhouse generates enough to satisfy the power needs of two cities the size of

Portland — whose population figure is just over 575,000. So the dam produces roughly three-eighths of one percent of the electricity needs of the country.

Of course, that's power that would have to be generated in other ways — probably by burning coal — if there were no dam at The Dalles.

But Celilo Falls was unique. There was nothing like it on the face of the earth, and now it's gone.

Was it a good trade? It's at least a question worth considering.

Sources and Works Cited:
- In Search of Western Oregon, *a book by Ralph Friedman published in 1990 by Caxton Press;*
- Roadside History of Oregon, *a book by Bill Gulick published in 1991 by Mountain Press;*
- "Celilo Remembered," *an episode of Oregon Field Guide produced by Vince Patton and aired in 2008 by Oregon Public Broadcasting;*
- "Celilo Falls at the Center of Western History," *an article by Charles Wilkinson published in the Winter 2007 issue of Oregon Historical Quarterly.*

HORRIBLE PEOPLE:

PART I: THE SHANGHAIERS.

In the 1880s and 1890s, shanghaiers in port cities like Portland, Astoria, and San Francisco created real hazards for visitors who strayed into the wrong parts of town.

Shanghaiing, of course, was (is) the practice of kidnapping a person in order to broker his future services as a sailor to a friendly ship captain. And as a practice, it's basically an offshoot of the sailors'-boardinghouse business; so, most of the Horrible People we're going to meet in this special section of the book were the proprietors of sailors' boardinghouses — "boarding masters," as they called themselves, or "crimps" as everyone else called them.

(The term "Crimp," by the way, probably derives from a Dutch word, "krimp," which refers to an underwater pen for holding live lobsters to keep them fresh until cooking time.)

At the time, the sailor's boardinghouse business was one of the most disreputable occupations in society, and with good reason. It was basically a forced-indebtedness scam. The system had been perfected, if that's the word, a decade or two earlier in deepwater ports like New York and San Francisco.

Here's how it worked:

You rented the cheapest building you could find, close to the waterfront, and stocked it with crude beds and furnishings.

Then you invited single men to stay there for as long as they liked. You marketed it chiefly to sailors, but laid-off loggers and naïve farmers were welcome too. Hobos could avoid getting nicked for vagrancy by checking into your place, so you'd get some of them as well. No money changed hands; it was all done "on credit."

Then would come a day when one of the ships in the harbor would need sailors, and some of the men in your boardinghouse — who by now owed you more money than they could pay — would be required to discharge that debt by signing onto that ship. You'd present your bill for room and board to the captain of the ship, who'd pay you and deduct it from the sailor's wages, and he'd also slip you a bonus, a finder's fee of sorts, which was commonly called "blood money."

Of course, you had to be a number-one fighter to make this work, because almost nobody ever wanted to go to sea when it was time to go. They always wanted to spend just a little more time safely on land.

On those occasions when a ship needed a crew and your boardinghouse was empty, you might go out drinking, meet a new friend at the bar, and dope his drink. When Nature took its course, and the chloral hydrate or Laudanum kicked in, you'd catch your new friend before he fell to the floor, make an innocent remark about helping him get back home, and leave the bar with him. Down to the waterfront you'd go, probably with the help of a friend or two, and carry him on board the ship, tuck him into a bunk in the forecastle, and run up on deck to see the captain and collect your fee. Your erstwhile drinking buddy would wake up on ship, with his name forged on the ship's articles and sometimes with a U.S. Marshal standing guard to make sure he didn't jump overboard and swim to shore before the ship got out to sea.

This was, of course, what we know as "shanghaiing."

Now, you might think that lugging an unconscious body to the waterfront would constitute suspicious activity, and you would be right ... but in the 1890s it wasn't viewed that way. After all, sailors went out and got drunk all the time, and had to be helped back to their ships by friendly shipmates. How could a bystander tell that from a shanghaiing in progress?

By the way, popular myth to the contrary, shanghaiing victims were almost never clobbered. Knocking a man out is difficult and dangerous, and if too much force is used it can lead to murder charges. Why take a chance?

HORRIBLE PEOPLE: *The* SHANGHAIERS.

Shanghaiing had certain advantages over regular forced-indebtedness boardinghouse crimping; the up-front costs, obviously, were quite a bit lower. It's not the way most crimps liked to operate, because it was dangerous and left a trail of deadly enemies — who occasionally returned to the port years later with revenge on their minds. Also, skippers didn't much appreciate finding out that the "old salt" they'd signed on was a 19-year-old plowboy who'd never been on the water before.

But at times when there weren't very many professional sailors in town, desperate ship captains would start raising the "blood money" bonuses they offered. The higher these bonuses got, the more tempted crimps were to fill their pockets with knockout drops and go out looking for someone to shanghai.

The next few stories in this book will tell the stories of some of the certifiably Horrible People who made their living as crimps, as well as several individual men who had the misfortune to fall into the clutches of Portland and Astoria shanghaiers (as well as, briefly, one who slipped through their fingers with the help of about half a ton of dynamite).

OREGON'S O.G. SHANGHAIER.

THE HORRIBLE PEOPLE:
- *Jim Turk, shanghaier.*

The "shanghai artists" of old Portland and Astoria were all a fairly secretive lot. But none of them were more mysterious, in quite so many ways, as the man who started the whole shanghaiing scene in Oregon — a burly, hard-fisted bar fighter named Jim Turk.

Jim Turk was a slum lord who lived in his own slum, a drunken brawler who got hauled into court for battery dozens of times, an abusive husband, a shanghaiier of sailors, a whorehouse operator and a dishonest clothing salesman.

Oh, and he was also the equivalent, in 1880 dollars, of a millionaire.

Here's Jim's story, or what we know of it anyway:

Jim Turk was born in England in 1832, and *The Oregonian* reported upon his death that he was "a man of family." However, he was, by the age of 16, in America and fighting in the Spanish-American war — a very odd thing for a "man of family" to be doing, a bit like a billionaire's son joining the French Foreign Legion today.

By 1866, Turk had gotten married, to a statuesque beauty named

A drawing published in 1889 showing the intersection of Front and C streets; C street has since been renamed Couch. Jim Turk's sailor boardinghouse was located on C Street between Front and First, a half-block beyond the right-hand side of this image.

Catherine who was at least his equal as a boozer and a brawler, and the two of them had opened a boardinghouse in San Francisco. They had two children, both sons: Charles and Frank.

Then, a few years later, the Turk family suddenly quit San Francisco and moved to Oregon. Jim apparently ran a saloon in Pendleton for a while, then moved to Portland and opened Oregon's first-ever sailor's boardinghouse there.

In addition to their crimping activities at the boardinghouse, Turk and his sons ran some other scams as well; on at least two occasions they sold sailors suits of marine clothing and then secretly stole them back before the ships sailed. The customers were left having paid for clothing they didn't get, with no way to fix the issue short of diving overboard and becoming a deserter — which at least one guy actually did.

These tricks were already standard procedure in San Francisco's colorful waterfront in the 1860s and 1870s. Turk simply brought them to Portland and ran the system here, like a new McDonalds franchisee.

As the 1870s wore on, Turk became a familiar figure in the city courthouse. He loved to drink and he loved to fight, and he was hauled up on battery charges literally dozens of times. Each time,

HORRIBLE PEOPLE: *The* SHANGHAIERS.

he paid his fines and posted his bail in cash. Turk never seemed to have any trouble with money.

Then, in 1877, an odd little item appeared in the *Portland Morning Oregonian*:

"A gentleman from San Francisco, by the name of T.J. Zingsen, now stopping at the Norton House, informs us that he came expressly to bring the astonishing news to Mr. James Turk, of the Portland Sailor Boarding House, that he has inherited about 20 or 30 thousand pounds, which was left to him some years ago without his knowledge," the paper remarked.

£20,000 to £30,000 translated into $89,000 to $133,000 in 1877 dollars, which would be worth $2.5 million to $4.4 million in 2023 money.

Turk, shortly after this, suddenly started making large purchases. He started by purchasing a palatial one-stop sin center called the "Grand Central Variety Saloon," which appears to have been one of the earliest of the much-maligned "variety theaters" of Portland. These theaters played low-rent Vaudeville shows, after which the actresses would come out and vamp the customers to induce them to buy overpriced drinks. And, as historian Barney Blalock points out, the fact that the Grand Central had 17 rooms in it strongly suggests it was also a bordello.

Turk also bought some land, and a restaurant in Astoria that may or may not have been more than just a restaurant. But his lifestyle didn't change, and neither did his business practices.

But in 1890, Catherine died. Jim remarried a little later, but his heart wasn't in the crimping trade any more, and increasingly he left that to his sons. He died five years later on, in Tacoma, at the age of 63.

The *Morning Oregonian* apparently felt some pressure to say something nice about this freshly-deceased thug; but apparently this was no easy task. "While he possessed a rough exterior, he had a great many friends among his own class," the obit writer managed. "He was generous and would do a friend a good turn, when an appeal to his better nature was made."

This "generosity" comment addresses the real mystery of Jim Turk: Where did his money come from? Even before his inheritance (if that's really what it was), he always seemed to have plenty of it. Was he, perhaps, a remittance man — a scion of a wealthy family who, having embarrassed the family beyond redemption by some youthful indiscretion, was sent into exile with a monthly cash payment contingent on his never returning to the family home? Perhaps — but he was fighting in the Mexican-American War when he was 16, which means he would have had to commit his great sin at the age of 13 or 14 years; this seems very unlikely.

It also seems bizarre that Turk didn't change his lifestyle in any meaningful way after inheriting all this money. He went on brawling, swindling, shanghaiing and stealing, just like before. Moreover, I haven't found any reference yet that tells whom, specifically, Jim Turk inherited that money from.

So, is it possible that Jim Turk's money came from somewhere else? Perhaps it was the fruit of some epic swindle perpetrated overseas. Maybe it was the proceeds of a decades-long blackmail scheme that finally ended with a lump-sum payment. Or maybe he'd robbed a payroll train ... who knows?

All we can really say is that the pieces don't all seem to add up. But we can also say, with absolute confidence, that without Jim Turk, Portland would have been a far less colorful place.

Sources and Works Cited:
- Portland's Lost Waterfront, *a book by Barney Blalock published in 2012 by The History Press;*
- Shanghaiing Days, *a book by Richard Dillon published in 1961 by Coward-McCann;*
- *Archives of the* Portland Morning Oregonian, *1877-1895, and* Morning Astorian, *1882-1889.*

THE SHANGHAIING GODFATHER.

THE HORRIBLE PEOPLE:
- *Larry Sullivan, legendary high-society shanghaier.*

Sometime around 1897, complaints suddenly started pouring into the headquarters of shipping companies in Liverpool and Hamburg from the captains in charge of their ships. It seemed something new was happening in the faraway American port city of Portland.

It seemed the local sailors' boardinghouses operators — the crimps — had suddenly started playing dirty. Once a ship arrived in port there, the sailors would all vanish — and the ship wouldn't be leaving the city until its captain had paid thousands of dollars to the owner of the boardinghouse in which they were staying.

Though the skippers had always had to pay "blood money" bonuses to the crimps to get crew members, they'd never before had to pay so much, for so many men. It was costing the skippers a lot of money. And the few who protested quickly found it cost them plenty more; it seemed as if the entire city of Portland was in on the scam. Complaining to the police got a skipper, at best, nothing — and at worst, an expensive delay in port while legal matters were sorted out and possibly even a little time in the local hoosegow, usually followed by a sudden increase in the crimps' fees.

All the captains knew exactly who was to blame for this dreadful new turn of events. It was the premier boardinghouse owner in Portland: Larry Sullivan.

"You cannot believe how these fellows are working," wrote the captain of the German ship *Alsterufer*, in December 1900. "It almost seems as though they hold the whole law and authorities in their hands. Sullivan himself said to the German consul, 'I am the law in Portland!'"

Larry Sullivan was an enigmatic Portland character who was far and away the most successful of Oregon's shanghai artists — a clever con man, with friends in high places, who also happened to be an active and successful prizefighter and brawler. It was he who engineered Portland's reputation as the worst port in the world for a ship to visit, around the turn of the century. He did this by forging the city's unruly collection of crimps into an exclusive business cartel, and by establishing political connections that gave his cartel the local political cover they needed to shake those skippers down.

And when the music stopped, and the curtain came down on the Portland shanghaiing scene, he moved on to Goldfield, Nevada, where he became a central figure in one of the most egregious gold-mining swindles in the history of the American West.

Lawrence Mikola "Larry" Sullivan was born in St. Louis during the Civil War, and came out to Astoria when he was around 20 years old. It's not clear why he came to Oregon; chances are pretty good that he was running from something, since Oregon was at the time the jumping-off place of the West — the farthest corner of the country in which one could hide out without having to live in a hermit's cabin.

Larry was already an accomplished prizefighter when he arrived in Astoria, and quickly set about punching his way to the top of the local boxing scene. At that time, prizefights were big stuff in Oregon towns; they were a public spectacle that folks came around from all over to see and place bets on, and top prizefighters were like rock stars.

The problem was, it wasn't the sort of gig a fellow could plan to retire from. Most of it was done the old-fashioned way — with bare knuckles, under London Prize Ring rules, which means each round keeps going until one of the boxers hits the deck and stays there for the full count. It's a tough way to make a living.

This wasn't so much a problem for Larry in Astoria, where he was pretty much the best fighter in town and wasn't getting defeated much. But when

HORRIBLE PEOPLE: *The* SHANGHAIERS.

The seaport town of Astoria as it appeared in the 1890s. Even after he moved to Portland, Larry Sullivan maintained a sailors' boardinghouse in Astoria with his partners, the Grant brothers. (Image: Postcard)

Larry moved to the bigger city of Portland, he suffered a couple painful defeats and at least one pyrrhic victory — a bloody 75-round foul-happy marathon — that has to have left him considering other options.

So Larry changed occupations. He joined forces with some friends from Astoria — brothers Peter, Alex and Jack Grant, whose father had been a pioneering shanghaiier there — to form a solid Portland-Astoria crimping consortium. He and the Grant boys named their new partnership "Sullivan, Grant Bros. & McCarron" — a rather majesterial name, sounding more like a white-shoe law firm than a gang of shanghaiers. Then, under the company name, Larry opened his own sailors' boardinghouse in a big old warehouse, deep in the North End of old Portland.

As a "boarding master," Larry was successful almost immediately. What distinguished him from the rest was not so much his fighting ability as his political skill. Larry Sullivan was the one who figured out what a great political asset a sailors' boardinghouse is. On election day, sailors in the house are welcome to vote, sometimes over and over and over, and to go around from ballot box to ballot box and do it all again, in exchange for free drinks. The waterfront was full of transient guys with no local ties, who could vote as often as they liked without anyone ever being able to trace them.

Larry soon was a part of state Rep. Jonathan Bourne Jr.'s smoothly rolling "free-silver Republican" political machine, delivering bales of votes for Bourne and his friends at every election. (If you're unfamiliar with

A street view looking toward the waterfront from Second Street along Washington Street in downtown Portland, in 1886. Larry Sullivan's notorious boardinghouse was ten blocks to the left of the artist's viewpoint in this work, at Second and G (Glisan) streets. (Image: The West Shore magazine)

Jonathan Bourne Jr., you'll find the full story of this lovably roguish Rascal in Volume One of this collection, *Heroes and Rascals of Old Oregon*.)

Bourne was also a member of the three-man Portland Police Commission, which means this alliance gave Larry law-enforcement cover — a key component in what he was about to do next.

By about 1897, Larry was ready to make his move. Through his political connections, he had the support of pretty much the entire local law-enforcement community. The harbor master, whom he'd jumped and beaten nearly senseless back in '93, was now disinclined to give him trouble. Through his careful cultivation of the local district attorney, he had an even more vital ally there. And he had forged an alliance — a sometimes rocky alliance, but a working one — with the other powerful crimps in Portland and Astoria, and forced the smaller and newer operators out of business with his fists.

It was time to make the ship captains pay.

To understand how he was going to do that, you must first understand how the system worked before Larry disrupted it. Up through the mid-1890s at least, ship captains and sailors' boardinghouse owners were like partners in crime, both busily and happily swindling sailors out of what little money they had and were owed.

When a ship came into port, runners from the local boardinghouses would go out and meet it, breaking the law by rowing out and climbing on before it had even tied up. They'd hand out cigars and bottles to the sailors and invite them to a welcoming party at the boardinghouse.

Naturally, most of the lads didn't need much persuading. After all, they'd been at sea for weeks. So, over the side they'd go.

The captain would watch them go and smile to himself. He knew that as long as the men were ashore, he didn't have to feed them or pay them wages. But more importantly, he also knew that most of them would not be around when it was time to ship out, and he'd be able to keep all the wages that were owed to them. That's because it was standard procedure in many nations' ships, notably British ones, to not pay the sailors until the cruise was over — to discourage them from deserting along the way. When they did desert, the captain got to keep all the money they'd earned for the entire voyage up to that point; the total could run to hundreds of dollars. Able-bodied sailors were generally paid roughly $30 a month (roughly $950 in 2022 dollars). Over the course of a five- or six-month voyage, that added up to a pretty healthy sum.

So, under the old system, when it came time to sail, the sailors who couldn't be found would be replaced with new

An unidentified British grain ship at the wharf, photographed in 1904. Ships like this were the primary customers for Larry Sullivan and the shanghaiiers' syndicate he formed. (Image: Robert Reid)

hires supplied by the same boardinghouse owners who had lured the old ones away. The boardinghouse bills would be paid with an advance against the new sailors' wages, and the skipper would pony up the "blood money" bonus as the price of the boardinghouse operator's services in making the sailor available.

This would, of course, cost the skippers some money ... but not nearly as much money as it made them, because they were then allowed to keep all the deserting sailors' pay, for the entire voyage up to that point.

This system was like a quasi-criminal conspiracy to rob the sailors, and it made both parties rich. The skipper got to keep all the deserters' pay, which could add up to thousands of dollars all together, and the boardinghouse operator got to charge virtually whatever he wanted for room and board, and to collect a big blood-money bonus to boot.

What Larry figured out was that there was money to be made by double-crossing the captains — essentially, robbing the other robbers. And he worked out an arrangement for how to do it.

First, he disciplined the unruly Portland shanghaiing scene into something like an informal cartel — a sort of diabolical labor union, with himself as the director. Any local boardinghouse operator unwilling to join and play by the rules would find himself, as historian Barney Blalock wryly puts it, "in a great deal of physical discomfort" thanks to the bare-knuckle boxer's well-callused fists. This would ensure that the captains had to deal with him, whether they wanted to or not; they couldn't turn to a competitor to undercut his rates and terms.

Then he and the other boardinghouse men started coaching sailors to commit some minor offense that would land them in police court: petty theft, perhaps, or public drunkenness. Larry's friends in high places would arrange for the sailors to draw a little jail time for whatever they'd done. Then, when the time came for the ship to leave, the skipper would look for his men, and find that they'd all been picked up on silly petty charges, all at more or less the same time, and had all just started serving 30-day jail sentences. Unless he was willing to wait a whole month for them to get out of jail, the captain would have to hire a new crew.

When he went to do that, he'd find the price was unusually steep. He'd shop around a little, but every crimp in town was demanding the same price; Larry had made sure nobody was undercutting the cartel.

But that wasn't where the real money was being made. The real money was the crew's wages, the money the skippers had formerly been able to keep. The thing was, the skipper only got to keep it if the crew member had actually deserted and couldn't be found. If the crew member was ready, willing and able to report for duty, but was legally prevented from doing so

HORRIBLE PEOPLE: *The* SHANGHAIERS.

The lower Portland Harbor as it appeared around the turn of the century. (Image: Postcard)

because he was locked up in the local slammer, the skipper did not get to keep those wages, because the sailor was not a deserter. He had to either stay in port until the sailor was released from custody, or leave his wages behind for him.

So not only did this unfortunate skipper have to pony up hundreds of dollars in blood money to hire a new crew, he had to pay out thousands of dollars in other people's money that he had been expecting to, essentially, embezzle.

This was actually pretty great for the sailors. Although Larry took a healthy cut of the cash as a fee for his services, they actually were getting paid part — maybe even most — of what was legitimately owed to them.

The captains, of course, were furious, and fought back as best they could. But they soon learned that their bargaining position was not a strong one. Skippers who resisted soon found themselves entangled in a world of expensive and time-consuming problems, and every day their ships were delayed in port cost them hundreds of dollars in demurrage charges and opportunity costs.

One skipper swore out a complaint against Larry Sullivan for boarding his ship without permission. Larry was found guilty and fined $200. But when it came time for that skipper to sail out of port, he found his entire crew was staying at Larry's place, and the price for replacement sailors was $117 a head. Larry more than made up his $200 fine.

Another skipper sent one of his officers on a coastwise steamer to San Francisco to hire a crew down there. Larry got wind and sent a runner down after him, probably on a train; the runner slipped aboard the steamer and almost managed to convince the entire freshly hired crew to desert en route. When this didn't work, Larry had the captain arrested on a specious kidnapping charge, delaying sailing for weeks. By the time the frustrated captain finally got under way, he'd paid considerably more for his crew than he would have by simply swallowing his pride and paying Larry's rate.

An agent for the U.S. Department of Justice tried to help solve the problem, building a case against Larry. He found, to his dismay, that all five of the ship captains he'd lined up weren't willing to stick around Portland for the months it would take to go to court.

It was a slick operation, and it generated a chorus of international protests from the British, French and German embassies. You'll find some historians who blithely assume those protests were at the shameful treatment of sailors in Portland, and the danger of shanghaiing on its waterfront; this is, frankly, naïve. The embassies didn't care about the sailors, nor about shanghaiing. They cared about their ship captains, who considered themselves robbed because they now had to pay their sailors what they were legitimately owed.

But in spite of all the wailing and gnashing of teeth, the Portland system didn't come to an end until 1904, when Larry Sullivan quit the business.

A view of the Portland harbor as it appeared in roughly 1904, the year Larry Sullivan closed down his Portland boardinghouse operations. This postcard is postmarked 1905.

HORRIBLE PEOPLE: *The* SHANGHAIERS.

Larry quit because a new crusading and reforming spirit was in the air. The Lewis and Clark Exposition was slated for the following year, and Portlanders were a little concerned about the fact that the roughest and most unseemly part of Portland was clustered around the railroad depot. Incoming visitors would see drunks vomiting in the gutter, crooked gamblers at work in faro banks, prostitutes leaning out of little windows on cushions and cooing at them, ruffians punching each other, and who knows what else. The city's underworld was just far too much on public display for the Exposition to go well if changes were not made.

Larry Sullivan *was* the Portland underworld, and he had good enough political instincts to know when to hold 'em and when to fold 'em.

The election of 1904 hadn't seemed like a lost cause at first. Larry himself was on the ballot, seeking a City Council seat representing the old waterfront North End neighborhood (known today as Old Town). And it never seriously occurred to anyone, including himself, that he might lose.

He lost.

More importantly, Portland mayor and former U.S. Attorney General George Williams — known colloquially as "Wide Open Williams" — was replaced by determined progressive reformer Harry Lane.

Multnomah County had, the previous year, replaced its former go-along-to-get-along sheriff with Tom Word, another progressive reformer, whose attitude and zeal for the job is nicely summarized by a probably-true story told about him: One day, while being driven through town on official business in an open carriage, he caught a whiff of opium fumes. Leaping from the moving vehicle with his nose in the air and sniffing about like a beagle at the county fair, he found the scent again, followed it upwind to a nearby secret opium den, kicked in the door and started arresting people.

In the "good old days," a sheriff like that would have found himself on the outside of Portland society, cut off from all re-election support, counting down the days until his term was over and raging at the lack of enthusiasm with which the line cops implemented his policies and undertook his raids.

Not in 1904.

Sullivan, always well connected to the heartbeat of Oregon politics, knew what it all meant. The crimping business was a whisper away from human trafficking; it was only really tolerated because it preyed on the morally powerless. If reformers were coming for the blacklegs and the hookers, they were certainly coming for the shanghaiers.

There was another pigeon coming home to roost for Sullivan too. By about 1903, the skippers he'd been lording over had gotten their home national governments to take some action on their behalf, and a hefty freight differential charge had been levied on all Portland freight. Traffic had already noticeably slackened as exporters were finding it cheaper to haul their cargoes to Tacoma and ship them out from there. It wouldn't be long before running a boardinghouse in Portland would get a lot less lucrative anyway.

Sullivan made one more attempt to transition to a new line of work — taking a tip from East Coast mobsters and trying, in partnership with the chairman of the state Republican central committee, to set himself up with the exclusive franchise to haul Portland's garbage. When word of this scheme leaked out, though — a job the proudly Democratic *Oregon Journal* was happy to help with — the resulting public outcry killed the plan dead.

At that point, Sullivan folded his cards and raked in his remaining chips. He sold his share of the Portland Club — his tony but illegal gambling parlor — to fellow Portland businessman (and, if my theory holds up, pawnshop proprietor — if you're reading this book cover to cover, you'll remember his name from the story on Page 149) Nate Solomon, then pulled up his stakes and folded his tent and headed for Goldfield, Nevada. Fellow crimp Peter Grant went with him.

Sullivan and Grant arrived in Goldfield and immediately opened a gambling parlor there. The town was, at the time, awash in money, much of it in the hands of miners and prospectors who had a great deal of trouble hanging onto it even without guys like Sullivan in town. So Sullivan and the Grant boys built a proper gambling palace there — which, if it wasn't as palatial as the Portland Club had been, was certainly snazzy enough to impress the miners. They named it The Palace, and it did very well indeed.

And it was at The Palace that Larry met one of the most colorful and rascally characters in the history of American con-artistry: George Graham Rice.

George Graham Rice doesn't really qualify as a full-fledged Horrible Person, although he did come pretty close at times. But he was most definitely a rascal, and an unusually brazen and shameless one at that. His life story is strongly reminiscent of the Warren Zevon song "Mr. Bad Example."

Rice's real name was Simon Herzig, and he was born in 1870 in New York City, the son of a middle-class family; his father was a furrier.

As a young man, he was, in the slang of the day, decidedly "fast," being especially fond of gambling pursuits. His father caught him stealing from the family business and sent him to reform school. It didn't take; a few years later, when he was 25, his father caught him forging a check drawn on his account, and had him prosecuted for it. This time he was sent up the river for real, to do a four-year stretch at Sing Sing.

After his release, he changed his name and got into the newspaper business for a little while. This, as anyone who has ever gotten into the newspaper business at a level lower than "owner of a metropolitan daily" can tell you, was not a career calculated to bring in enough cash to finance the high-roller lifestyle to which Rice aspired. So he quit and returned to New York.

This portrait of Larry Sullivan shows him at age 43. It's from the program of the notorious Gans-Nelson boxing event he was promoting at the time, in Goldfield, Nevada, shortly after he left Portland. (Image: UNLV archives)

There, in early 1901, with $7.30 in his pocket, he met an old friend who had a red-hot tip on Silver Coin, an underrated horse entered for a race in New Orleans the next day. Rice's friend added that he had a friend in the business with good insider information on a number of horses, and suggested that the two of them make a few extra bucks putting the connection to good use.

Rice had a better idea. Rather than betting his last $7 on this horse and maybe clearing a $63 profit, he spent the money on a newspaper ad:

"BET YOUR LAST DOLLAR ON SILVER COIN," the ad screamed. "HE WILL WIN AT 10 TO 1." Under this headline, the ad went on to urge bettors to subscribe to his horse-racing tip sheet for $5 a copy, and signed it "Maxim & Gay" — a company name he made up on the spot.

Then Rice and his friend sat in a tiny office he'd rented on credit and waited.

Sure enough, Silver Coin won, and suddenly half the betting population of Manhattan was beating a path to their door, eager to pay $5 for an edge on the next big horse-racing upset. Even better, Rice's friend's information was good enough to keep them coming back week after week for more.

This enterprise made Rice a ton of money, most of which he promptly blew through at the gambling tables.

But, of course, all good things must come to an end, and within three years Maxim & Gay had been shut down by the U.S. Postal Service on charges of mail fraud.

Rice came out of the whole thing with very little to show for it, other than three years' experience writing advertising copy. But he'd put that experience to good use. By the end of the run he was maybe America's best writer of swindley ad copy.

Following a year or so trying to get rich betting on horses himself — he ran his poke up over $100,000 and then lost it all — Rice tried to break his gambling habits by moving to San Francisco.

There, he met up with another old friend, and tried going back into the race-track tip-sheet business. This time, though, it didn't work as well. Soon he was busted flat once again.

But meanwhile, Rice had been hearing about the gold and silver mining boom up in Nevada. And so had his partner.

"Rice," the partner said one day, "come up to Tonopah and be my press agent. We will get hold of a mining property up there, promote a company, and make a barrel of money."

Why not, Rice thought? It looked to be as good as any other racket just then.

And so, off the two of them went to Tonopah — and subsequently to Goldfield.

By the time Rice met Larry Sullivan at Sullivan and Grant's "Palace" in Goldfield, he was doing a booming business in Nevada as the owner and copywriter for an advertising agency, working with the local mine owners. He provided a full-service kind of operation — not only placing ads for investors, but also sending out hundreds of fake "human interest" stories about life in the mining camps for East Coast and West Coast newspapers to run. These articles were basically dime-novel narratives of feuds and gunfights and gold strikes and virtuous-maiden-rescuings; and, of course, they prominently featured Rice's clients in heroic roles. They were eagerly run by newspapers all over the country, and the people who read them came to feel like they knew the mines and the people who

HORRIBLE PEOPLE: *The* SHANGHAIERS.

One of the ads the Sullivan Trust Company placed in the Portland Morning Oregonian, in October 1906. (Image: UO Libraries)

ran them. Naturally, they were much more comfortable investing their money in them.

It was these stories, reprinted in the Portland newspapers, that had initially attracted Larry Sullivan to Goldfield.

Soon after setting up shop in Goldfield, Rice was once again happily gambling away large swaths of his "earnings." After Sullivan arrived and built The Palace, Rice did a lot of his gambling there. By this time, of course, he was a pretty good gambler; Larry probably had his work cut out for him keeping him from winning too much.

One day, Rice was cashing out $2,500 in winnings, and Larry came out to talk to him.

"Say, young feller, why don't you cut me in on some of your mining deals?" he said. "I'm game!"

"Are you?" Rice shot back. "Well, stack up $2,500 against that money and I'll see if you are."

Sullivan came across on the spot.

"Okay," said Rice. "Put that money in a sack, and go get that big coonskin coat of yours, and take a night ride by automobile to Tonopah ... When you get there look up the owner of the Jumping Jack Mine. He is a member of the Ancient Order of Hibernians. An Irishman can buy that property from him much cheaper than anybody else. You go and buy it."

"What will I pay?"

"He wants $85,000, but get it as cheap as you can."

"What? With this $5,000?"

"Yes. Pay him the $5,000 down and sign a contract to pay the balance in 60 or 90 days."

This was done. The two of them got the mine for $45,000, and transferred it into a corporation with a million shares; and then Rice got busy sending advertising orders out, along with breathless notifications to various brokerage houses back east.

Larry probably had a few very bad moments over the subsequent week or so. The telegraph bill came to $1,200 ("When Sullivan learned of its size he nearly collapsed," Rice wrote). Then, having dipped his toe in that far, Sullivan found Rice putting the bite on him for an additional $10,000 to cover the ads he'd placed. He must have been wondering, at that point, whether he wasn't being taken for a ride.

He found out six days later, when the ads appeared in newspapers all over the country.

"Within ten days ... Sullivan showed me telegraphic orders for 1,280,000 shares of Jumping Jack stock at 25 cents a share," Rice writes. "That week and the next, Sullivan gave me carte blanche to speculate in local mining stocks with partnership money, and within a fortnight we had made another small fortune from (Jumping Jack) securities. These were advancing in price on the San Francisco Stock Exchange by leaps and bounds."

This was the beginning, as Humphrey Bogart might have said, of a beautiful friendship.

Soon their partnership was formalized into the Sullivan Trust Company, and the two of them launched themselves upon a stunningly lucrative run. They'd buy up mines, incorporate them, boom them back East and let the money just roll on in. If the mines were productive, that was great; but it was understood by all parties that mines were speculative by nature, so they could (and did) get away with a number of promotions of properties that never came close to breaking even.

But several of the mines the Sullivan Trust Company boomed up turned out to be pretty productive. Soon Rice and Sullivan were riding a real tiger. A genuine full-fledged investment bubble was growing in mining-stock investments, and Goldfield was Ground Zero in it.

At the peak of the excitement, Larry Sullivan — who was, as you'll remember, a former professional prizefighter — was in the thick of plans to stage a "battle of the century" in Goldfield between Oscar "Battling" Nelson, the lightweight champion of the world, and former lightweight champ Joe Gans. Legendary boxing promoter "Tex" Rickard had come to town to back Nelson, and the Sullivan Trust Company was the primary backer for Gans.

Sullivan became Gans's manager, and according to Rice's memoir, he did quite a bit of advance work in preparation for the fight. Having learned through the grapevine that the referee Rickard had picked really needed the work, he lodged an objection, claiming the ref was prejudiced against Gans because Gans was Black. The referee, who had traveled to Goldfield from Chicago just to cover this fight, met with Sullivan to plead his case, promising he would never dream of favoring Nelson.

"Gans is a clean fighter," Sullivan told him, "but Nelson isn't."

"If he does any fouling in this fight I'll make him quit or declare him out," pledged the referee.

Having planted this little seed, Sullivan pronounced himself satisfied and withdrew his objection.

When the fight got started, it was soon obvious that it would run long. Twenty rounds in, the fighters were still battling it out, and Rice was getting worried.

"This doesn't look like the cinch for Gans you said it would be," Rice whispered to Sullivan.

"Wait a minute," Sullivan whispered back, and went to Gans's corner and held a long whispered conference with him.

Upon his return, he told Rice that Gans had hurt his right wrist and didn't think he could use it for a knockout punch. But not to worry: they had a plan.

During the subsequent dozen rounds or so, Gans took special pains to make it look like Nelson was fighting dirty and he (Gans) was battling squeaky-clean. By the 40th round it was clear that Gans had gained the sympathy of the crowd.

Sullivan now hurried over to Gans's corner and held another whispered conference. Apparently it was time to spring the trap.

They sprang it (according to Rice) in Round 42 — this was already the longest-running boxing match most of the crowd had ever seen. Gans, after taking a blow low on the midriff, dropped to the mat like a modern soccer player flopping — clutching his crotch and howling in agony.

Sullivan leaped into the ring. "You saw that foul, didn't you?" he shouted to the referee. "It's a foul, isn't it? Gans wins, doesn't he?"

The ref — who probably *had* seen the blow land, and likely knew very well that it wasn't a real foul — had turned white. He nodded and muttered something, and Sullivan raised both arms to the skies and hollered, "Gentlemen, the referee declares Gans the winner on a foul!"

The crowd, which by now was more than ready to believe Nelson was a foul fighter, roared its approval. Nelson's protests were drowned out.

Was there a foul? The history books say there was. Rice, in his memoir, says there was not. But Rice isn't exactly a disinterested observer, so we'll never really know.

"*I* won that fight," Sullivan boasted to Rice afterward (or so Rice writes). "I told Gans that if he lost he would be laying down on his friends, and that he had the audience with him, and it was time to take advantage of Nelson's foul tactics."

The Sullivan Trust Company, of course, couldn't last forever. The mines it promoted were sometimes profitable, but Rice and Sullivan didn't much care if they were or not; and, as the mines started petering out, their batting average started to sink. The whole thing collapsed in 1907.

The unabashed and unrepentant Rice moved on, becoming publisher of the *Nevada Mining News* and launching efforts to "boom" the town of Rawhide. Later he got involved in another mining-stock swindle, this one dedicated to manipulating the stock of Ely Central Copper Company. This time, the collapse took him down with it, temporarily; he spent a year in prison after pleading guilty to mail fraud. It was during that year in durance that Rice wrote the memoir I've been quoting so liberally from, cheekily titled *My Adventures with Your Money*. (By the way, this memoir — which is in the public domain, and you can read it on line for free — is well worth the two or three hours it'll take to read it. Like its author, it's every bit as entertaining as it is untrustworthy.)

Rice would have lots more adventures with "your money" in the years after his release from prison, booming fake mining companies and publishing sketchy periodicals, making and gambling away vast quantities of money. He spent four years in federal prison in 1928 after being caught defrauding investors in a fake copper mine, earned the moniker "The Jackal of Wall Street," and finally died in 1943.

As for Larry Sullivan, he moved on to Mexico and tried to pull a George Graham Rice-type swindle down there, but was stymied by the fact that the mine he bought was an utter dud; and he lacked the magic touch that Rice had with press releases and public relations. Later he landed a job in Los Angeles, supposedly as a private detective working with Clarence Darrow for the defense of the McNamara brothers — the men who dynamited the *Los Angeles Times* building, killing 21 people, as part of a labor strike. He was suspected of trying to bribe the jury, but nothing was ever proved.

Sullivan then got involved in Mexican lotteries in southern California for a while, until authorities clamped down on that.

By the time he got back to Portland, Oregon had enacted statewide Prohibition, and all the things he knew how to do — run gambling houses, fix fights, and serve liquor — were illegal. He tried anyway, bouncing around in and out of trouble with the law and calling in old markers to stay out of jail.

Finally, when the First World War broke out, he ended up as a security man at a shipyard — quite possibly the first legitimate employment he'd entered into in his whole wild and colorful life.

But by then his health wasn't good enough to support a life of crime any more. He died in 1918 of Bright's Disease — nephritis of the kidneys — at the age of 55.

Sources and works cited:
- The Oregon Shanghaiers, *a book by Barney Blalock published in 2014 by The History Press;*
- My Adventures with Your Money, *a book by George Graham Rice published in 1911 by The Gorham Press of Boston;*
- *"Shanghai Days in the City of Roses," an article by Stewart Holbrook published in the Oct. 1, 1933, issue of the* Portland Morning Oregonian;
- Shanghaiing Days, *a book by Richard Dillon published in 1961 by Coward-McCann.*

"MYSTERIOUS BILLY" SMITH.

THE HORRIBLE PEOPLE:
- *World welterweight boxing champion by day, shanghaier by night*

It's time now to turn our attention back to Oregon, and to the Portland and Astoria shanghaiing scene around the turn of the twentieth century.

Specifically, we're going back to 1903, when Larry Sullivan was still at the height of his power in Portland. Hard-fisted and belligerent, yet socially polished and with what passed in old Portland society for refined manners, he was able to seamlessly move between the rough, hard-drinking world of the old North End waterfront, and the refined gentlemen's-club atmosphere of the Arlington Club.

As detailed in the last chapter, by 1900 or so Sullivan and his "hospitality company" — Sullivan, Grant Bros. and McCarron — had run all competitors off the Portland waterfront and had the market to themselves . . . with one especially galling exception: Mysterious Billy Smith.

Amos "Mysterious Billy" Smith was originally from Canada, but settled in Portland around 1893 or 1894. When he arrived in Stumptown, he was boxing's official Welterweight Champion of the World — a title he earned in 1892 and held, on and off, until 1900. (Welterweight is the middle weight class, for boxers 140 to 147 pounds; heavier than Lightweight and lighter than Middleweight.)

"Mysterious Billy" Smith as seen in a promotional photograph in the mid-1890s, when he was Welterweight Champion of the World. (Image: Wikimedia)

How he got the nickname "Mysterious Billy" is somewhat, er, mysterious. One of the more appealing theories is that it referred to his opponents in the ring never knowing what hit them. He was, everyone agrees, a fantastic boxer.

However, boxing was a side hustle for Mysterious Billy; apparently it didn't make enough money to live on, even for a world champion (or, more likely, managers and promoters were raking off all his winnings).

His day job was as a crimp.

Mysterious Billy started his crimping career circa 1895, working as a boardinghouse runner for Sullivan. The two of them, as professional boxers and very rowdy men, hit it off right away. A hilarious news article from 1896 tells of the courtroom drama that followed a massive knock-down-drag-out bar fight that Mysterious Billy started when out drinking with Larry. The two of them, with a companion named Jack Fahle, went to the Spokane Saloon near Second and Burnside, and there they encountered a trio of Swedes drinking 20-ounce "scoops" of beer. Billy, having already shipped a full cargo of intoxicating beverages before arriving at the Spokane, took offense at something one of the Swedes said, whereupon (in the words of the *Oregonian's* reporter) he "jumped on him and pounded his head till it was soft."

"About this time Powers" — the owner of the bar — "entered the room," the reporter waggishly recounts; "and, seeing that the well-known reputation of his place for a quiet and orderly house was somewhat in danger, he proceeded to restore quiet and harmony by seizing a chair and laying about him with it among the three Swedes. His night bartender also took a hand in the scuffle, which raised such a commotion that a police officer entered to see who was being killed.

"On the arrival of the officer, the three Swedes were the only ones that knew anything about any trouble, Powers, Smith, and the bartender having apparently forgotten all about the disturbance."

Billy was fined $25 for this little bit of horseplay. Larry, who'd had the good sense to cheese it before the cops came, got off scot-free.

But the peace and amity that made it possible for Billy and Larry to go out together to drink and brawl with loggers was not to last. About five years after the Spokane Saloon incident, Billy partnered up with the White Brothers — Jim and Harry, who were also working as runners for Sullivan at the time; more about them in a bit — and established a sailors' boardinghouse on the east side of the river, by the Albina grain docks.

Although Billy and the White boys saw their operation as covering the

BAD IDEAS and HORRIBLE PEOPLE of OLD OREGON

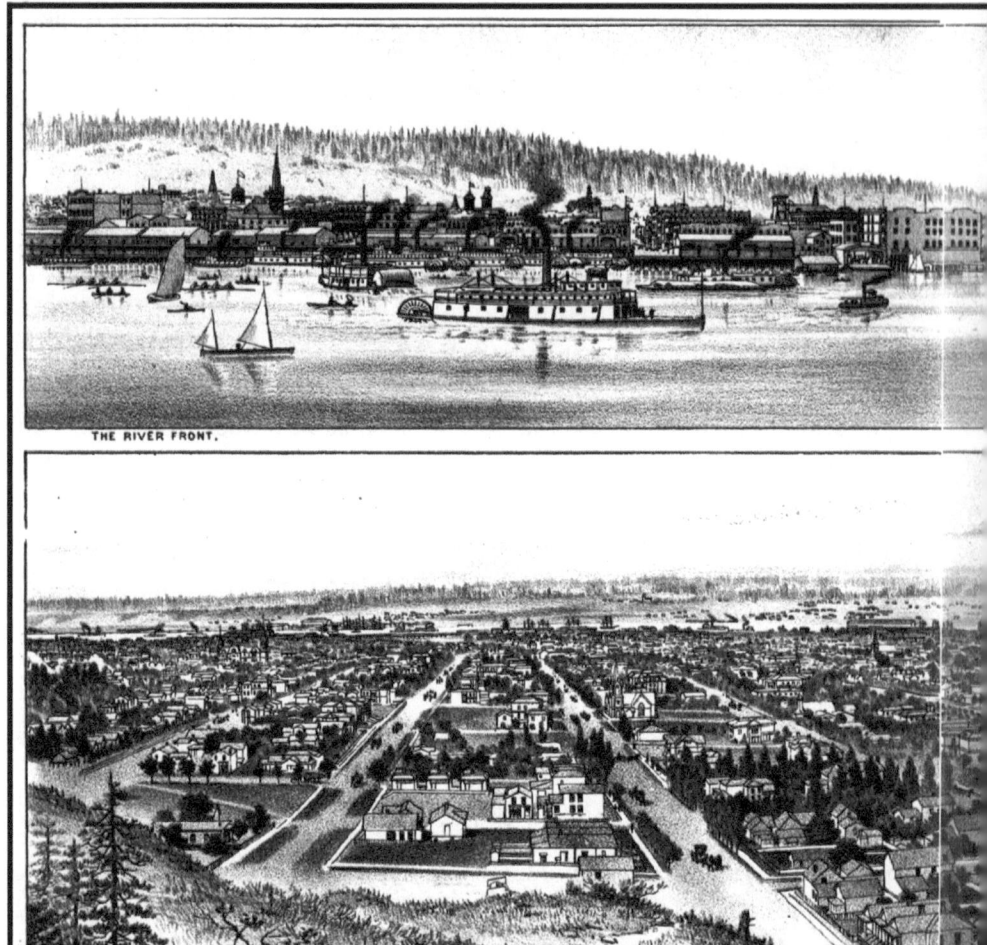

The Portland waterfront as it appeared from the shore of East Portland (above) and

east side and leaving the far-busier west side to Larry, Larry didn't see it that way. For him, competition was competition. It was to be gotten rid of as expeditiously as possible.

Of course, Larry's usual way of doing this involved "pounding heads until they were soft." He was a skilled and accomplished middleweight boxer, a talent that frequently came in handy when it came time for one of his guests to ship out and the guest was reluctant to fulfil his "obligation."

But Mysterious Billy was the welterweight champion of the world. And sure, as a middleweight Larry had a few pounds on him; but he was no world champion, and plus he was getting older.

So Larry pulled some strings in the Legislature — and got Billy's operation outlawed.

HORRIBLE PEOPLE: *The* SHANGHAIERS.

downtown Portland viewed from Council Crest (below) in 1886. (Image: The West Shore)

Now, as a responsible public historian I have to confess that I have no hard evidence that Larry pulled those strings. But, knowing how well connected he was politically, the fact that in 1903 the state Legislature created a Sailors' Boardinghouse Commission whose obvious sole purpose was to grant and enforce a monopoly for Larry Sullivan is good enough for me.

This new "state shanghaiing commission" moved immediately to declare that it was going to license only one crimping outfit: Larry's. It promptly issued a license to Larry, and a cease-and-desist letter to Mysterious Billy and his pals, the White brothers.

The commission members justified this little exercise in state-sponsored conspiracy-in-restraint-of-trade with the highly dubious claim that, by establishing a monopoly in the boardinghouse business, they were acting to reduce prices. This was, remember, at the height of Larry's consolidated control of the crimping market, and he'd used that control to run the average blood-money bonus up over $100 a head. Shipping companies had started actively avoiding the port, and exporters were starting to get used to hauling their goods to Tacoma instead; consequently the cost of shipping sailors was on everyone's mind. (Of course, Sullivan's successful scheme to shake down ship captains for their sailors' wages had a lot more to do with that than the high blood-money prices, but nobody would have admitted that.)

What Sullivan did was to boldly harness that price sensitivity and use it to make things worse, while trying to convince everyone that it would actually make things better. It was rather like a fox arguing that the solution to a chicken predation problem in the henhouse was to issue an all-the-chickens-you-can-eat license to the biggest, hungriest fox, who would then defend the henhouse from the other foxes and maybe refrain from eating them all at once, so as to preserve the resource for future meals.

The problem was, although the new commission had the law on its side, it had none of the popular respect and legitimacy that usually goes along with it. This was probably because, although it was fully empowered to revoke licenses for all violations of the state law (for instance, boarding incoming ships to entice sailors to desert, or charging $100 blood-money bonuses instead of the legally stipulated $30), it never did anything of the sort. Those practices went on unabated and unpunished. What the commission did do, at every opportunity, was to order all of Larry Sullivan's competitors to go out of business.

Those competitors, not surprisingly, challenged the commission's authority in every way they could.

Naturally, the first thing Mysterious Billy and the White brothers did was to challenge the commission's authority in court. But that sort of thing takes time; so, rather than go out of business for a year and wait, or continue doing business furtively, they adopted an attitude of open defiance.

"On that license business? What do I care about a license?" Harry White said, during an interview with an *Oregonian* reporter that ran under the headline "HE IS SHIPPING SAILORS: Harry White does Not Worry about the Law."

You may have gathered, from the subtext of that headline, that the *Oregonian* — like the rest of the Portland establishment, which got along so well with Larry Sullivan — was strongly in favor of the commission. It was not a friendly venue for Harry White.

Meanwhile, the Whites' lawsuit against the commission was making its way up through the courts. It finally made it to the Supreme Court in 1904, and the verdict was sharp and incisive: No, the state was not allowed to conspire with Sullivan in restraint of trade and award him a monopoly.

The wailing and gnashing of teeth in the issue of *The Oregonian* that followed this devastating blow comes off as almost surreal to a modern reader.

"SHORN OF POWER," screams the headline, followed by the then-customary stack of sub-headlines:

> *Boarding-House Commissioners Disgusted.*
> **PRICE OF TARS* MAY GO UP.**
> *Trouble as to High Charges May Be Renewed.*
> **THEORISTS ARE CRITICISED.**
> *Shipping Men Are Generally Satisfied*
> *with Operation of Law*
> *which the Supreme Court Declaration*
> *has Practically Invalidated.*

"When I was urged, much against my will, to serve on the board, the assurance was that we were to have full power to regulate the business for the best interests of the port," sniffed commission president E.W. Wright. "Now that the court has decided that we have no such power, it is useless to be bothered any further ... I do not feel justified in wasting any more time with it."

The Oregonian, always a reliable voice for the Portland political establishment back in those days, was sympathetic to the commission's goals. But its journalists did have the grace and professionalism to talk to some of the opposition, too — not Mysterious Billy or one of the White boys, but James Laidlaw, the British consul, whose job it was to look out for British sailors of the grain fleet and whose acerbic letters to the editor about the evils of the crimps appeared regularly in *The Oregonian*. His comment cut right to the heart of the matter.

"The commission (still) has full power to revoke licenses for enticing sailors to desert or charging unlawful exactions," he said. "If the present commissioners feel powerless, perhaps others can be appointed to enforce the law."

"One set of crimps is no better than another, (so) why grant one set a monopoly?" he continued. "If one set struts in immaculate linen and fine clothes and lends its presence to the state Legislature, that does not prove superiority. In fact, it doesn't make any difference so far as I can see."

Ah, but it made all the difference in the world, as Laidlaw surely knew

---

* *A slang term for sailors.*

well. (The reference to fine clothes and the state Legislature was an obvious shot at the always-spiffy and politically active Larry Sullivan.)

Not that it made too big a difference to Larry Sullivan. James White was convicted of kidnapping a sailor to prevent him from testifying in an upcoming hearing, and started a one-year prison sentence in February 1903, so he was out of the picture; and both Mysterious Billy and Harry White were back working for Sullivan shortly afterward. Mysterious Billy got embroiled in a bitter divorce battle with his soon-to-be ex-wife, which distracted him so much from business that Harry White was unable to depend on him. White reached out to Sullivan, who was happy to bury the hatchet and take him back as a boardinghouse runner.

Left to his own devices, Mysterious Billy followed suit after his divorce was settled, and Sullivan set him up as manager of The Atlantic Cafe, a saloon on Third Street that he owned.

By the time this whole drama was playing out, though, the crimping industry in Portland was in obvious decline. The grain fleet was switching over from sails to steam. Steamships were much more sanitary and comfortable than sailing ships, not to mention safer, and the food was much better. Crew members on them, once they'd secured a berth on one, were extremely loath to put it at risk by checking into a boardinghouse. The few who did so ran a pretty high risk of ending up back on a sailing ship with slim prospects of returning anytime soon.

Portland Harbor as it appeared on a busy day around the turn of the 20th century. The big four-masted barque in the foreground, flying a Union Jack from her mast, is typical of the mostly-British grain fleet ships that were Portland crimps' primary customers. (Image: OSU Libraries)

HORRIBLE PEOPLE: *The* SHANGHAIERS.

Longshoremen load sacks of wheat on a steamer at a Portland wharf using powered conveyer belts, around 1910. The switch from sails to steam eventually drove the shanghaiiers and crimps out of business. (Image: Postcard)

Plus, as mentioned in the last chapter, Portland was gearing up for the 1905 Lewis and Clark Centennial Exposition, and had elected a new mayor, Harry Lane, who was on a crusade against the squalor and vice that characterized the North End.

Sullivan, sensing the shift in political winds, left Portland for Goldfield, Nevada, where he promptly involved himself in what historian Barney Blalock calls "one of the greatest bunco schemes ever perpetrated — a multi-million-dollar banking and mining concern that bore the name 'Sullivan Trust Company.'" If you're reading this book from front to back, you'll already be familiar with Larry's Nevada adventures from the previous chapter.

Mysterious Billy, though, stuck around. The White brothers stuck around too, taking care of the dwindling business in tall-ship sailors clear into the 1920s. Jim White, after serving his one-year prison stretch for shanghaiing that sailor, decided the job was too rich for his blood and quit, but Harry carried on. In the 1920s, after all risk of non-homeless men actually being shanghaied was gone and it was "safe" to joke about such things, he adopted the nickname "Shanghai White" and continued serving the dwindling tall-ship fleet through at least 1928. (By the way, we'll talk more about the shanghaiing of homeless men soon, when we discuss the legend of Portland's "shanghaiing tunnels.")

By then Billy had long since quit the crimping business. But he remained a colorful Portland character. In 1910, he was in the news for socking a socialist agitator in the kisser during an argument over politics. The following year, his ex-wife's new husband emptied a five-shot revolver into him, hitting him four times and nearly killing him; he survived, though, apparently without permanent injury.

I haven't been able to learn what Mysterious Billy did during Prohibition, but all things considered it's a pretty safe bet that it involved moonshine in some way.

After Prohibition ended, he opened a new saloon, a beer joint this time, at 15th and Wheeler in Albina; he called it The Champion's Rest, and that's exactly what it was. The onetime slugger, shanghaier, and bar fighter finished his days pouring beer and reminiscing about the good old days with his customers as the host of one of pre-war Portland's favorite watering holes. He died in 1937.

Sources and works cited:
- Portland's Lost Waterfront *and* The Oregon Shanghaiers, *two books by Barney Blalock published in 2012 and 2014 respectively;*
- Portland Morning Oregonian *archives from 1896, 1902, 1903, 1904, 1910, and 1911*

THE LAST SHANGHAIERS.

THE BAD IDEA:
- *Try to resuscitate the go-go days of Portland's shanghaiing era after it's been shut down.*

When Larry Sullivan abruptly left Portland following the 1904 election, as you can imagine, he left behind him a considerably changed shanghaiing industry.

With Larry gone, and the Grant brothers with him, and his old nemesis "Mysterious Billy" Smith still too preoccupied with his divorce to step in, there was something of a power vacuum left on the Portland waterfront. Left in command of the Portland crimping scene, much to his probable surprise, was Harry "Shanghai" White — one of the White brothers formerly in partnership with Mysterious Billy, and whose feud with Sullivan a few years before had only ended when he came to Sullivan hat in hand and asked to join up with his operation.

It probably also surprised Shanghai White when he found that the state Sailors' Boardinghouse Commission, which he had feuded bitterly with when it was under Sullivan's effective control, had now became his best friend in the whole world. Although the state Supreme Court had stripped it of its power to enforce monopoly conditions, it had learned that the difference between a prohibited monopoly and an allowable one was — well, the word "monopoly." All that was necessary to accommodate the justices' conscience was to stop calling it that, and start inviting other would-be boardinghouse operators to apply, and finding an excuse to deny every serious applicant. The commission had gotten very busy doing just that, and as the last Sullivan-affiliated shanghaier standing, Shanghai White was the beneficiary of its zeal.

Time passed. The Lewis & Clark Centennial Exposition came and went. Some of Harry Lane's reforms took. The Portland Club, Sullivan's old gambling palace that he'd sold to Nate Solomon before leaving town, was raided and shut down, a month or two after the club got caught using marked decks. Ex-Portland Mayor Williams' policy of leaving the hookers and crimps and three-card-monte sharks alone as long as they stayed in the North End had given way to Mayor Lane's policy of breaking down doors and hauling people off to jail, with the result that the vast majority of underworld entrepreneurs (and entrepreneuses) had spread out all over the city to make themselves harder to find. And the North End started its long stumbling twentieth-century journey toward respectability.

Then, in 1907, a trio of interesting developments took place that probably constituted the last gasp of the go-go shanghaiing era in Portland.

First, Joseph "Bunco" Kelley was pardoned out of the state joint, into which he had been tossed in 1894 to serve a life sentence for murder in connection with the alleged attempted shanghaiing of an old saloonkeeper named George Sayres. You'll remember Bunco Kelley's story if you've read Volume One in the Offbeat Oregon book series, *Heroes and Rascals of Old Oregon* — Bunco was, of course, a number-one Rascal.

The rap that Kelley had taken had been, as almost everyone had by then figured out, a frame-up engineered by Larry Sullivan to get Kelley out of the way — although Kelley surely had accidentally killed one or two shanghaiing victims over the years, Sayres wasn't one of them.

Proclaiming his intention to live an upright, God-fearing life from now on, Kelley started wandering around the city looking for ways to earn the money to publish his book, which he had written in prison. He found that he was getting by, but only barely; when he'd gone to prison he'd been the most famous bad guy in Portland, but 13 years later nobody seemed to even recognize his name.

Meanwhile, prizefighter Charles Jost — yes, another prizefighter — was starting to realize that he wasn't ever going to make any money as a boxer. For seven years he'd been living the life, ever since 1900 when he won the

HORRIBLE PEOPLE: *The* SHANGHAIERS.

The four masted barque Arracan, one of the last of the British grain fleet in Portland, moored below the Broadway Bridge about 1913. (Image: Salem Public Library)

title of Welterweight Champion of Oregon; but by 1907 he was looking for something else to do with his life and his skills.

At the same time, Mysterious Billy Smith, of all people, was also at loose ends. He'd been running a saloon for Larry Sullivan, but Larry was gone now; and apparently Billy was doing a little pining for the good old days.

Somehow these three characters ended up at the same table at a bar, talking about the old times. They were probably in Erickson's Saloon, because "Jumbo" Riley, the 300-pound ex-boxer (heavyweight, of course) who worked there as a bouncer, was also at the table, as was Jost's brother.

The conversation soon turned to the inadequacy of Shanghai White's remaining boardinghouse operation to handle all the crimping business for the port. The problem was, in the previous few years, it had become pretty obvious that the boardinghouse commission was not friendly to the idea of anybody lending a hand in slaking that market. Which was unfortunate, because the more the five of them drank, the more they realized that they were just the fellows to slake it.

By the end of the evening, the boys had a plan: Charles Jost would apply to the boardinghouse commission for permission to enter the market, under the name "Jost Brothers" — the bunch of them having astutely guessed that everyone else at the table was so thoroughly tainted by past underworld associations that the response would be an automatic "no."

But they apparently didn't realize how much of a drag those names would be on their prospects. As mentioned in the last chapter, during the old Larry Sullivan days, the crimping and shanghaiing in Portland had gotten so bad — that is, so expensive for ship captains — that the freight companies had hit the city with a beefy freight-differential surcharge. Farmers who had the choice of sending their produce to Tacoma instead of Portland suddenly were finding it saved them big money to do so. Business in the port had suffered a great deal.

In 1907, that differential had just finally been lifted. Port authorities were in no mood to jeopardize that by letting Bunco Kelley and Mysterious Billy back into the business.

So the commission made a deal with the Jost brothers: The boys could get into the business if they'd promise none of the old ruffians would be involved, directly or indirectly; if they'd fix up their boardinghouse so that it was suitable for sailors to live in; and if they'd put up a $5,000 bond.

The boys agreed. But then, perhaps thinking it would be no big deal to jump the gun a bit, they shipped a crew of sailors on the sailing ship *Elginshire*.

As any real Portland businessman could have told them, this was a world-class Bad Idea. Hell hath no fury, as the old joke goes, like a bureaucrat scorned.

But it probably would have been survivable had not the rumor mill carried word of Bunco Kelley's involvement in the business to the ear of one of the shipping commissioners. And it didn't take much additional probing for the names of Mysterious Billy and Jumbo Riley to come to light.

"SHIPPED SAILORS WITHOUT A LICENSE," screamed the headline on Page 14 of the *Oregonian* the next day. "Jost Brothers Violate their Agreement with the State Board. BOTH TO BE ARRESTED."

"In shipping the sailors on the *Elginshire* the Jost boys have violated every article of agreement entered into between the members of this commission and themselves," board member William McMasters told the *Oregonian's* reporter. "We shall proceed against them immediately."

McMasters said the boys had presented their boardinghouse to the board, and it had been deemed inadequate. Plus, he said, board members had learned that Bunco Kelley, Mysterious Billy, and Jumbo Riley had all been involved in recruiting the sailors the Jost brothers had shipped.

Well, that was the end of that. The Jost brothers tried again in 1908, but the board simply told them no, that it didn't think it was a good idea; and the brothers seem to have had enough sense to quit at that point.

For the remaining waning years of Portland's age of sail, Shanghai White's boardinghouse would remain the only game in town.

Sources and Works Cited:
- The Oregon Shanghaiers, *a book by Barney Blalock published in 2014 by The History Press;*
- *Archives of the* Portland Morning Oregonian, *July 1907 and January 1908.*

SHANGHAIING IN ASTORIA.

THE HORRIBLE PEOPLE:
- *The usual suspects!*

In the history books when the topic of shanghaiing in Oregon comes up, the Portland waterfront tends to get most of the attention. But one of the worst ports in the world for the practice of shanghaiing — a place where almost anyone, doing almost anything, could suddenly find himself at sea — was Astoria.

The reason for that was simple: There were so many options in Astoria for a man who wanted work that did not involve signing onto a sailing ship. The lower Columbia River salmon run, one of the biggest inland fisheries in the world, was right there in town; and just outside city limits lay great forests in which a man could get a job falling timber or working in a sawmill.

All these jobs were dangerous, but certainly no more so than being a deep-water sailor, and you didn't have to live for months at a time on hardtack biscuits and lime juice under a "bucko" first mate who had the legal right to beat you if he thought you weren't working hard enough.

So maritime manpower was always in tight supply in Astoria. The sailors' boardinghouses were usually empty. This situation pushed the local crimps to adopt some desperate measures to try to fill orders for crew members.

The gunfighter.

Historian Martha McKeown recounts the experiences of one newcomer to Astoria, Mont Hawthorne, who came to the city in the early 1880s and took a job cutting timber. Hawthorne was immediately warned by a neighbor to be on his guard. It seemed another neighbor had been kidnapped in the middle of the night, out of his own cabin, and hauled down to the waterfront and shipped out on a windjammer.

Accordingly, Hawthorne took to lugging a rifle and a shotgun with him at all times when he was in the woods. He also packed a revolver on his hip when he had to go to town.

Then one night, he was awakened by a huge racket at the door of his cabin. Someone was trying to force it open.

Hawthorne bellowed a warning, which was ignored, so he put seven rifle bullets through the door. After that, he heard (or claimed he heard) a great crashing through the brush — audible, it seems, even over the ringing in his ears from all the indoor gunplay — as the crimps beat a hasty and panicky retreat. They never bothered him after that.

The minister.

However, a couple of them did make an attempt on the town's Methodist minister. Richard Dillon recounts the story in his book *Shanghaiing Days*:

The minister, George Grannis, went one Sunday to ring the bells in his church. On his way back down the stairs, someone suddenly stepped up behind him and threw an overcoat over his head, while another pinned his arms to his sides.

The would-be shanghaiers surely thought this was going to be a doddle. How hard could it possibly be to kidnap a preacher? Clergymen are the "turn-the-other-cheek" people — soft of cheek and tender of foot. After all, who ever heard of a trained, successful prizefighter deciding to quit the ring and become a Methodist minister? Preposterous, right?

Grannis kicked out at the place in space which he was pretty sure contained one of his assailants, and was rewarded with the feel of a solid hit. The other one then lost his grip enough for Grannis to get a solid head-butt in. The three of them tumbled down the stairs to the bottom, and when they got there, Grannis was on his feet and moving like a pro.

HORRIBLE PEOPLE: *The* SHANGHAIERS.

A street scene in Astoria, featuring the Odd Fellows Temple, drawn by the staff artist at The West Shore, a literary magazine based in Portland, and published in 1887. (Image: The West Shore)

A few violent, painful seconds later, his assailants decided they'd bitten off more than they could chew and ran for it.

The next day, Grannis noticed one of the local crimps was missing a few teeth. And after that day, he was left in peace to minister to his flock.

The Dynamite Kid.

This last short shanghaiing story didn't actually happen in Astoria, but the shanghaiers involved were based there. It's another story relayed by Dillon in *Shanghaiing Days*, and it concerns a young man named George Banks. George was one of those rock-solid young men, poised and confident and morally upstanding. In the mid-1890s, he had a job working on the portage railroad at Cascade Locks.

One day, George was down in Portland picking up a load of freight, and he missed his return sailing on the riverboat. So there he was, stuck on the wharf with the crates of merchandise he was supposed to bring back — probably stuck there until the next morning.

Luckily, some friendly, helpful fellows noticed George, and offered to help him out. They made a deal and soon the strangers were back with a boat of some kind (Dillon doesn't say, but it was probably a steam launch).

After the strangers had helped George load his crates onto the launch, they cast off — and started heading downstream. George was puzzled by this at first, until one of the strangers informed him — no doubt belligerently, with much flexing of muscles, to encourage him not to try to fight his way out — that he was a sailor now, and they were bringing him to Astoria to put him aboard his new ship.

"You ain't gonna shanghai me," George retorted, reaching into his pocket. "I'll blow you to hell first."

His hand came out full of blasting caps.

Presumably that's the point at which the would-be shanghaiers realized the boxes they'd helped load on board the boat were full of dynamite. They also soon thereafter learned that George's nickname among his friends was "Dynamite Kid."

Needless to say, the boat immediately turned and headed upstream to the construction site, where George unloaded his cargo, paid the men as agreed, and went about his work.

Sources and works cited:
- The Trail Led North: Mont Hawthorne's Story, *a book by Martha Ferguson McKeown published in 1948 by Macmillan;*
- Shanghaiing Days, *a book by Richard Dillon published in 1961 by Coward McCann.*

THE SHANGHAI LAND GRAB

THE HORRIBLE PEOPLE:
- *W.J. Barry, shanghaiing police chief*
- *L.G. Carpenter, larcenous attorney*

In the late 1880s, in the wilds of southwest Washington near the mouth of the Cedar River, a "stump rancher" named Peter Norris developed a more-than-professional interest in the wife of his hired hand, whose name was Browning. It wasn't long before the Brownings were aware of the fact, and things became very awkward.

Then one August day, Mr. Browning went out berry picking and never came back. His wife immediately left the area, probably worried about what Norris might do. Her husband's body was found days later; he'd been shot — but there was no evidence of who had done it. So although nearly everyone in the area figured Norris had murdered him, no charges were ever filed.

About two years after this, one of Peter Norris's neighbors, who was also named Norris — Darius Norris, no relation to Peter — was walking along the pier in Astoria when the town's chief of police, W.J. Barry, stopped him.

"Come with me," the chief said. "I have orders from Sheriff Turner of Pacific County to arrest you."

Now, Darius Norris wasn't actually a resident of Astoria. He lived with his elderly mother on a huge piece of acreage on Long Beach Peninsula — in Pacific County, in Washington state — which his father had bought years before when it was considered worthless. Now, with the steamboats bringing hordes of tourists to Long Beach all summer long, it was worth a lot of money, probably the equivalent of more than a million 2023 dollars.

Thus Norris was, on paper, a wealthy man; but he had very little cash flow. So to support his elderly mother and himself he traveled to Astoria and did work in canneries and as a longshoreman. That was why he was here, in Astoria. But he lived in Pacific County. If the sheriff of Pacific County wanted him, why would he have gone to all the trouble of waiting until he crossed the river and then asking Barry to extradite him back?

"I objected and told him to show me his warrant," Norris recalled later. "He said, 'Damn you, I don't need a warrant; you come along down to jail or I will fill you full of lead."

This mysterious arrest quickly got even more weird as Barry furtively conveyed his prisoner to the jail at gunpoint along back streets and alleys, warning him not to make any noise. Norris's request to make bail was curtly refused. The sheriff told him he would send a couple of lawyers to talk with him; Norris gave him the name of his lawyer; and the sheriff told him no, Norris would take the lawyers he sent or nothing.

"He told me a Mrs. Browning had made a confession implicating me in murdering Browning," Norris recalled, "and said that men had gone over to Pacific County to search for Browning, and that I was in a very bad fix."

Then the sheriff left his prisoner sitting there in the dark, puzzling this out.

Soon thereafter, the two attorneys arrived; C.J. Curtis and L.G. Carpenter were their names. Curtis (who may actually have been Norris's regular lawyer) promised to do what he could, and departed. Carpenter, when he arrived, rather unhelpfully reiterated what the sheriff had said, that Norris was in a very bad fix, and urged him to follow the sheriff's instructions very carefully; then he, too, took his leave.

Norris was left to rot in jail for nearly a week.

Finally Carpenter returned with some paperwork for him.

"I could only see the bottom part of the papers, and asked him to let me read the rest," said Norris. "He would not do it, and told me to sign them quickly, as he could not get me out unless I did."

Doubtless feeling a little desperate by this time, Norris signed.

A few more days passed. Then Sheriff Barry came to get him, late at night, and escorted him to the river scow on which he had been camping while working in Astoria, to get his blankets and things. The sheriff warned Norris to say nothing to anyone or he would be shot dead on the spot; and while he retrieved his things, the sheriff stood in the shadows across the road, hand on his gun butt.

Then Norris was escorted to a small boat lying close by in the shadows.

"All the way down ... Barry had been telling me my life would not be safe if I ever came back again," Norris said, "and when we reached the ladder he said, 'Damn you, get in that boat and never come back again!'"

This was probably the moment when Norris realized he was being shanghaied — by the police chief — because he knew the two men in the boat. They were Larry Sullivan and one of his boardinghouse runners.

The voyage Norris now shipped out on was a miserable one. Out of a crew that probably numbered nine or ten sailors, four — including Norris — were freshly shanghaied landlubbers who really had no idea what they were doing. To make matters worse, the ship ran out of limes very early on, so that months later when it finally arrived in Liverpool, everyone had scurvy. When he got there, Norris found that after Larry Sullivan's $140 "blood money" fee was deducted from his wages along with $40 in incidentals, he had only about $10 coming to him for wages from the trip.

He also found two letters awaiting him:

The first was from L.G. Carpenter — the lawyer. It urged him to depart forthwith to Australia and never even consider returning home, because Astoria was too dangerous for him and his life wasn't safe there.

The other letter was from the other lawyer, C.J. Curtis. Curtis wrote urging Norris to get back to Astoria as quickly as possible to settle the legal battle that had broken out over ownership of his Long Beach Peninsula land after he'd signed it over to L.G. Carpenter.

After he'd — what, now?

What apparently had happened was that several months before Norris was shanghaied, Norris's sister, Mary, had consulted Carpenter — who was, remember, a practicing attorney — about the family's property. Mary didn't like living in poverty on the 1890s equivalent of a million-dollar piece of land, and wanted to sell it; but her brother and elderly mother were both dead set against the idea. Could Mr. Carpenter help?

Well, yes, he certainly could ... help himself, that is.

> City of London, England July 29, 1891.
>
> Mr. Joplin.
> Dear Sir:-
>
> I am in this City, I was run aboard a ship, shanghaied by Chief of Police Barry, I will be back as soon as I can get back. I will go over to New York, then I will telegraph to Edgar to send me money. I will write to Edgar today. If you see him tell him I was run on a ship by them scoundrels. I will start for New York as soon as I get better. I was crippled on that ship. There was nothing given me. They shanghaied me under the name of Smith. I will come back and face the whole crowd of them that wronged me. I will telegraph as soon as I get to New York. I was wronged and disgraced by that dirty crowd and crippled. I will send a telegram to you to give to Edgar to send me money as soon as I get to New York. I hope my dear old mother is alive yet. I will write my child that Carpenter and Barry sent me off in this shape. It will be all of six or seven weeks before I get across there. The done this job to try and rob me out of my property. I will send for my money to Edgar. I left $100.00 in his care for me. They got $140 blood money on me by shanghaing me on that ship. I got nothing. The told me that I was no seaman; so I got abused and crippled and got nothing, and was left here destitute by the action of those scoundrels. I will meet them if I live. You will get a telegram as soon as I get to New York, to give to Bill Edgar, for him to send me money. I will telegraph the house I will be stopping at. At present that will not be known. You will oblige me by taking this to Bill Edgar, tell the boys how it is, from
>
> Your Friend,
> Darius Norris.
>
> This letter was addressed as follows:-
> Mr. Bill Joplin,
> United States of America,
> Astoria Oregon in care of
> Uhlenhart.

A copy of a letter Darius Norris sent home from London explaining his plight and what had happened to him. (Image: Oregon State Archives)

Carpenter got his network of business associates into gear. Either with a fat bribe or the promise of a slice of the action, he got Chief Barry to "arrest" Norris; then Sullivan shanghaied him off overseas never to return; and finally Carpenter himself set about spreading the word that Norris had fled the country after word got out that he was a murderer. The plan was for everyone to be confused by the coincidence of Norris's name with that of suspected murderer Peter Norris. It probably sounded like a great plan to the Astoria townies.

It didn't work, though. People who actually lived in Pacific County knew both Norrises well, and knew they were different men. Darius Norris also had lots of friends on the Astoria waterfront, who knew a bum rap when they saw one — and also knew how corrupt the city was at that time.

Also, although the news stories aren't specific on this topic, it appears Carpenter

The headline on the Portland Morning Oregonian's news story about Darius Norris's shanghaiing. (Image: OSU Libraries)

forgot about Norris's sister. She may have wanted advice about getting her brother to agree to sell, but having a complete stranger swindle them all out of the property was clearly not what she'd had in mind at all.

So when Norris's reply to attorney Curtis's letter arrived in Astoria, and Curtis released it to the press, things got rather hot for L.G. Carpenter. He soon found it expedient to transfer his practice to San Francisco.

Which is where he was when the state of Oregon issued a warrant for his arrest. He had hastily signed the title to the Long Beach property back over to the family before decamping, but it was pretty clear what he'd tried to do.

But he was probably never in real danger. The people he'd been working with were, essentially, the rulers of Astoria. Police Chief Barry came up for trial for kidnapping and embezzling, and was promptly acquitted; a few months later, he was back on the force, although no longer serving as chief. Larry Sullivan wasn't even charged. When the San Francisco police heard about that, they declined to bother serving the warrant, and that was the end of that.

As for Darius Norris, he finally made it home by working for his passage on the American bark *Recovery*. Upon arrival in New York, he had to hide out from the Bowery shanghaiers, who were boarding every incoming ship and asking if anyone knew about him — obviously Larry Sullivan had sent word and called in a few markers. Luckily, one of Norris's Astoria waterfront friends had journeyed to New York to meet him, and they were able to make it home safely.

Sources and Works Cited:
- The Oregon Shanghaiers, *a book by Barney Blalock published in 2014 by The History Press;*
- Portland Morning Oregonian *archives, September 1892.*

THE VISITING RUBE.

THE HORRIBLE PEOPLE:
- *Bridget Grant, shanghaiing landlady*

Sometime around 1885 or 1886, a handsome-but-diffident-looking young man named Carroll Beebe got on a westbound train in southern Minnesota, on his way to new adventures in the young frontier state of Oregon.

But the adventure he would find in the Beaver State wasn't even close to what he had in mind as he stepped aboard that train.

Carroll Beebe's story is unusual because of its very usualness. Stories like it were so common in the 1880s that newspapers didn't usually pick them up, and the people living them didn't usually bother to write them down — if they could write; Carroll's is the story of a poor boy, and in the 1880s poor folks were often illiterate.

Moreover, there was a strong bias among the new state's boosters and business interests against publishing stories like this, because it's really not the kind of story that encourages people to come to Oregon.

The only reason we know Carroll's story is through his family back home in Minnesota, courtesy of the late legendary dean of Portland waterfront historians, Barney Blalock, who shares the family's story in his book, *The Oregon Shanghaiers*.

Carroll was the oldest son of Vernon and Sarah Beebe; but he and the other kids were orphaned when he was 11, and they grew up with aunts and other relatives.

There must not have been much for him in the way of opportunities in Minnesota; or maybe he simply had an itchy foot. In any case, having heard and read about the great opportunities in the young state of Oregon, he determined to go there.

And so, off he went.

The Northern Pacific Railroad brought Carroll through the Rocky Mountains and along the Columbia River to Portland. Upon arrival there, Carroll found himself at large in a wild and rough-sawn frontier city, with many options before him. He could travel south along the Willamette and find work in one of the bucolic agricultural towns there; he could go north to Puget Sound, up in the Washington Territory; he could sign onto a logging crew and plunge into the woods. Or, of course, he could stay right there in Stumptown. Good hard workers were always in demand in frontier Portland, although it could be a dangerous place, particularly along the North End waterfront.

But instead of doing any of these things, Carroll, for some unknown reason, decided to journey to the only town in Oregon more dangerous for greenhorns than the one he was in: Astoria.

For months his family back home heard nothing from their wandering scion. Then, in the summer of 1887, a letter arrived addressed to Carroll's cousin Vernon Gilmore, sent from a faraway foreign port (probably Santa Fe, Venezuela).

"Dear Sir," it read, "I sit to inform you that your cousin, Carrel Bebby, was drowned off Cape Horn, from the American barque *Xenia*, of Boston ... Your cousin fell from the fore topgallant yard on the morning of Feb. 12, he being sent up by the second mate to loosen the sail. He missed his hold, fell overboard, and was drowned."

The letter was from a sailor named Donald McGregor, young Carroll Beebe's best (and, most likely, only) friend aboard the *Xenia*. It goes on to give a few clues as to what happened to young Carroll in Astoria to result in this abrupt change of vocation. It apparently started when he checked into the wrong boardinghouse.

"Your cousin was put aboard under false pretenses, by Mrs. Grant, who keeps a sailor's boardinghouse in Astoria," the letter continues. "She asked him if he would go aboard and answer to another man's name. She said she would send the other man aboard that night when he came down from Portland in the steamboat but she never sent him."

What appears to have happened here is, upon arrival in Astoria, Carroll Beebe checked into a boardinghouse run by a matronly woman named Bridget Grant — a onetime auburn-haired beauty still striking and charismatic in her mid-50s. A widow who kept her boardinghouse with the help of her grown sons, she certainly looked the part of a standard-issue boardinghouse landlady.

But, of course, her boardinghouse marketed itself particularly to sailors. And we've already talked about her sons — Alexander, Jack, and Peter Grant, the close associates and business partners of Larry Sullivan.

Now, in the 1800s, as you know by now, sailors' boardinghouses were different from regular boardinghouses. An ordinary boardinghouse was like a long-term no-frills bed-and-breakfast, and charged weekly or monthly rates. A sailor's boardinghouse, on the other hand, let people stay "on credit." One paid nothing for room and board, but a tab was carefully kept and when the day came when a ship captain needed a man or two, the guest was presented with a choice: Pay up, or discharge the debt by shipping out.

That's the theory, anyway. In practice, "pay up" often wasn't an option even if the guest had the resources to do it. Ship captains paid handsomely for sailors — reimbursing the room-and-board fees with no questions asked, plus that generous "blood money" service fee. So a boardinghouse operator had a powerful incentive to avoid having guests on a cash basis.

We don't know if young Carroll was staying at Bridget's place "on credit" or if he was paying weekly or monthly for room and board. It seems likely, given the nature of young footloose men, that he was on credit — but the fact that Bridget resorted to a rather dirty trick to get him to ship out suggests that perhaps he was not.

What she did was essentially to ask him, as a favor, to muster aboard the barque *Xenia* as a crew member to hold the place of a sailor she was bringing in from Portland. The sailor wasn't going to make it in time, she told him, and if he wasn't there for roll call she would lose her $60 blood-money fee (worth roughly $1,750 in 2022 dollars). Would he take his place at roll call, just long enough for her sailor to arrive?

Sure he would.

"I being going to sea for a number of years, I told your cousin what sort of woman Mrs. Grant was," Donald McGregor wrote, in his letter. "He had been what us sailors call 'shanghied' by her ... The captain refused to let him go ashore, saying he had paid Mrs. Grant $60 for him, and that he would have to make the best of it."

A drawing of the city of Astoria as it appeared when Carroll Beebe arrived, published in an 1887 issue of The West Shore magazine. (Image: UO Libraries)

There must have been some concern about potential liability, though, because immediately after the drowning the captain of the *Xenia* confiscated Carroll's sea chest and all his belongings, then took the rather eyebrow-raising step of confiscating a packet of papers that Carroll had entrusted to Donald McGregor. Donald suspected that the captain was keen to hush the whole thing up and wanted no word to get back to the young sailor's family; and he turned out to be absolutely right. Luckily, a card with cousin Vernon Gilmore's address on it had fallen out of the packet before the captain robbed Donald of it, and he was able to use the address on it to get word out.

The captain was probably lucky. Had Carroll's parents been yet alive, there likely would have been some trouble over this. But part of the reason Bridget Grant was so successful for so long as a boardinghouse operator in Astoria was her personal touch. It is extremely unlikely that she would have shanghaied Carroll without first making sure there was no one in the world who cared enough about him to make trouble from four states away.

Sources and works cited:
- *The Oregon Shanghaiers*, a book by Barney Blalock, published in 2014 by The History Press.

NO PARTY LIKE A SHANGHAIING PARTY.

THE HORRIBLE PEOPLE:
- *"Mr. Smith," a pseudonymous boardinghouse runner*
- *Larry Sullivan, Oregon's shanghai godfather (again)*

One fine day in October of 1891, a teenage boy named Aquilla Ernest Clark left the farm in Scappoose where he'd been working, headed for Portland. He was going to see the sights and maybe show himself a good time for a few days.

He wandered around the waterfront, taking drinks here and there and probably taking a hand in a card game or two.

Then, when it was getting close to evening, he met a pleasant fellow who happened to mention that he was staying at the sailors' boardinghouse at Second and Glisan streets. "It's the best place to stay in Portland," he said.

That sounded good; Aquilla needed a place to stay for the night. So he went with his new friend to the boardinghouse.

"The place was rather dimly lighted," Aquilla told author Stewart Holbrook, years later, in a 1933 interview for the *Portland Sunday Oregonian*. "A Scandinavian was playing an accordion in the big main room on the ground floor; several old-time seamen, or at least I took them to be such, were sitting in chairs around the room, smoking pipes that reeked to the skies and telling how these new-fangled steamboats would never amount to much."

It was good enough for Aquilla. He checked in.

The next morning, when Aquilla went downstairs, he was met by a jovial man who introduced himself as Mr. Smith.

Smith had gathered a group of six or eight other fellows who were obviously newcomers to the boardinghouse, and now he offered to buy them all breakfast.

Over the morning meal, Smith just happened to mention that the proprietor of the boardinghouse, a fellow named Larry Sullivan, was hosting a party.

"He has chartered a riverboat to make a trip to Astoria and back to Portland," Smith said. "Maybe you fellers would like to go along?"

"We fellers did want to go along," Aquilla told writer Holbrook dryly, decades later.

Smith had the young men wait outside the boardinghouse, and while they were there, the first of several one-horse cabs pulled up to drop off a dozen or so gorgeous and daringly-dressed young women. They, too, were there for the party. Feeling like they'd lucked onto the guest list for the hottest party in town, the boardinghouse boys tried not to stare at them too blatantly.

This picture shows young Aquilla Ernest Clark as he appeared shortly before his shanghaiing at the hands of Larry Sullivan and "Mr. Smith." (Image: Oregonian)

Then everyone trooped down to the waterfront to meet the boat.

The party boat was to be the steamboat *Iralda*, and it soon arrived at the dock, and everyone stepped aboard.

"Smith had seen to it that we all had a few snorts of hard liquor and also one each of the justly celebrated Peach Blow cocktail, which was the invention of H.C. Malcolm, manager of the Portland Hotel bar," Aquilla recalled. "Mr. Sullivan had provided an orchestra of three pieces — violin, accordion, and guitar — and the girls grabbed us and we danced."

HORRIBLE PEOPLE: *The* SHANGHAIERS.

"Mr. Sullivan stayed very much in the background on the trip to Astoria," he added. "He quietly saw to it that all of us had everything we wanted, but Mr. Smith was the life of the party, as they say nowadays."

Along about 1 p.m., still an hour or two out of Astoria, the gong rang for lunch. It was a sumptuous feast: "I have never had such food, either on salt- or fresh-water boats," Aquilla said. "There was steak if you wanted it, or there was pork, or you might order oysters, crabs, or fried salmon. Along with the mid-day dinner they served rye whiskey, rum, and three kinds of wine."

More drinking followed, and more dancing.

Finally the merry company arrived at Astoria, and just before they put into the harbor, Smith gathered the company around him and laid down some papers on the saloon table.

"We are going ashore in Astoria so all of you can see what the town looks like," he told them. "We'll have an hour ashore and then we'll go back to Portland. Just to make sure that all of you are aboard when we leave, sign your name on this passenger list. Then when we are ready to go we'll be sure that everyone is here."

Eager to get ashore, everyone signed, and then off they went for the promised one-hour town-painting spree.

On shore, Smith squired the young fellows from pub to pub, standing round after round, and after an hour or so of this hosted bar-hopping none of the boys were thinking very clearly.

Perhaps that's why not a single one of them saw anything strange about Smith's sudden suggestion that maybe they'd like to take a tour of a deep-water sailing ship before they returned to the *Iralda*.

The blue-water ship chosen for this "tour" was the *T.F. Oakes* out of New York City, a full-rigged windjammer with a steel hull loaded with 21 tons of wheat bound for the French port of Le Havre.

"We in the first boat came alongside the vessel and they let down a ladder for us," Aquilla recalled. "We climbed aboard, and one of the mates welcomed us. I forgot to say, Mr. Smith stayed in the rowboat."

Maybe if they'd had a little less to drink, one of the boys would have noticed that fact in time to do something. But there wouldn't have been much they could have done at that point. If one of them had figured out what was afoot, and dove overboard and swam ashore, a cop would have been waiting when he got there, ready to escort him back to the ship.

They didn't know it yet, but Aquilla and his colleagues were already sailors, and had been for over an hour. The "passenger list" they'd signed had actually been the *T.F. Oakes'* ship's articles; they'd been not only signing *in*, but signing *up* as well. And in the 1890s, sailors who skipped out after signing onto a ship were hunted down and dragged back to work by law enforcement the same way runaway slaves had been in the old South during the bad old ante-bellum days. It was a form of indentured servitude. (More on this practice in the next chapter.)

But, back to our story: The friendly ship's officer proceeded to give the men a tour of the *T.F. Oakes*, explaining how the steam-powered anchor winch worked, giving the names of each of the three masts, and babbling amiably about the difference between barques and barkentines and how they were different from full-riggers like the *T.F. Oakes*. He was prattling on about such things when Aquilla glanced over his shoulder and saw all the rowboats pulling for shore, leaving them behind on the ship.

That was about the time that four uniformed police officers stepped out of one of the cabins on deck. Each of them had a .45-caliber revolver in each hand — eight guns, covering ten men. They weren't taking any chances.

Then another cabin door opened and out came the captain of the T.F. Oakes, with the rest of the ship's complement of officers.

"Now, young men, you are sailors on the *T.F. Oakes* and you're going to Le Havre, France," the skipper told them. "Just to make sure you are going I'm going to sort of tie you together for a while."

Of course, the lads protested. The skipper was ready for them. One look

A view of the Portland harbor in the 1890s. The picture is hand-tinted, and the strange pink color of the steamboat in the foreground is obviously an error made while coloring the image. (Image: Postcard)

HORRIBLE PEOPLE: *The* SHANGHAIERS.

The riverboat Iralda under way. This is the boat on which the "going-away party" for Aquilla Ernest Clark and his co-shanghaiees was held. (Image: Oregonian)

at the "passenger register" they'd signed on the *Iralda*, which the skipper had in his pocket ready to show them, and the dullest among them surely knew their case was hopeless.

They had been shanghaied. It had all been a big trap — the party, the boat ride, the drinks, the friendly ladies hired to entertain them — all a trap to get the ten of them to sign that register and thus launch themselves on a new and unexpected maritime career.

As a side note, the boardinghouse runner who handled them so smoothly, "Mr. Smith," was very likely the notorious Portland underworld entrepreneur Joseph "Bunco" Kelley, whom we talked about extensively in Volume One of this series of books — *Heroes and Rascals of Old Oregon*. Several years later he and Larry Sullivan would have a very violent falling-out, and in 1894 Sullivan would railroad him into prison on a trumped-up murder rap; but in 1891 Bunco was Larry's number-one lieutenant, and a very smooth operator indeed. It's actually somewhat unlikely that Sullivan would have entrusted anyone else with a job of this magnitude. (You may be thinking this might have been "Mysterious" Billy Smith, because of the name; but the times don't line up. All this happened several years before Mysterious Billy arrived in Portland.)

The captain spent some time giving his new sailors a pep talk before sending them below. He spoke glowingly about the glories of being a sailor before the mast, and opined that all young men should go to sea for a voyage or two before settling down in life, and that an ablebodied seaman was one of the finest and noblest of God's creatures.

"I never did understand why the skipper went to all this trouble telling us how fortunate we were to go to sea and especially fortunate to go to sea on such a fine ship as the *T.F. Oakes*," Aquilla remarked to Holbrook. "He had us completely in his power, but here he was talking like a recruiting officer for the Navy."

Maybe it was because talk was so cheap. The fact was, it was very uncommon for a sailing ship to be desperate enough to accept ten total greenhorns — about two-thirds of its normal complement of sailors — on its crew. And it hadn't gotten itself into such a predicament by being a good place to work. The T.F. Oakes had a reputation as a "hell ship."

The wise sailors, the ones who had been around a while, took care to not be around the boardinghouse when ships like the T.F. Oakes were due to leave port. The captain who spoke so highly of life as a sailor was notorious — not for physically abusing sailors (he left that to his first mate, a scowling bully known as Black Johnson) but for not feeding them adequately. Sailors would put up with a lot of physical abuse, but constant gnawing hunger was something else.

Chances are, Sullivan's "party" helped the skipper out of a very tight fix, and he certainly must have paid handsomely for it.

Aquilla and his nine companions also paid handsomely. After they had passed over the Columbia River Bar (below decks, handcuffed to a stanchion) and crossed two oceans as A.B. mariners, they arrived at Le Havre to find that Sullivan had claimed $60 — two months' pay — from each of them, to cover the cost of his boat party.

It would be seven years before Aquilla Ernest Clark would see Oregon again.

Sources and works cited:
- *"I Was Shanghaied," a four-part series of articles published in the* Portland Sunday Oregonian *starting Oct. 29, 1933;*
- The Oregon Shanghaiers, *a book by Barney Blalock published in 2014 by The History Press.*

SLAVERY ON THE HIGH SEAS.

THE HORRIBLE PEOPLE:
- *Eight of the nine members of the Supreme Court of the United States, who voted to allow the literal temporary enslavement of sailors.*

In May of 1895, on the old San Francisco waterfront, four sailors signed onto the four-masted barkentine *Arago* for a voyage to Valparaiso, Chile ("and thence to such other foreign ports as the master might direct, and thence to return to the United States") via Astoria.

In the contract the four sailors signed, there was no time limitation; the cruise would be over when the captain said it was over. Such contracts were the usual thing sailors would sign (or, in the case of the shanghaied, be forced to sign) before embarking on a voyage.

By the time they got to Astoria, the four of them had had enough of the *Arago*. They stepped off the ship and essentially told the skipper, "We quit."

In doing so, they changed history — and started a drawn-out legal mprocess after which the legal status of sailors would never be the same.

The "Arago Four" were Robert Robertson, John Bradley, P.H. Olsen, and Morris Hanson. And it's possible — in fact, it's rather likely — that they signed onto the ship with the intention of deserting in Astoria. The seamen's union they were members of had been hoping for a case like this to come up, so that it could clarify in court a new law that had just been passed by Congress.

The new law had just been passed in February of that year, and it essentially decriminalized "deserting" from a merchant ship. Before, a sailor who quit a merchant ship in the middle of a voyage could be criminally prosecuted and sent to prison for several months. Now, under this new law, he couldn't.

The thing was, the law might have changed, but the practices of police and shipping masters had not. Mainly that was because sending deserters to prison had never been the focus of the old anti-desertion law. When a sailor deserted, the captain of his ship didn't want him in jail; the captain wanted that sailor back on the ship, making money for him.

But before the law changed, because desertion was a criminal offense, the captain could call the local police to go out and get the deserter. After collaring him, the cops usually preferred handing him back over to the captain rather than spending the money and resources running him through the local criminal-justice system on desertion charges; and, of course, that's what the captain preferred as well. So the police would do so. The captain would then put the deserter in irons until the ship was safely out of swimming distance from shore, then put him back to work. That's the way it had always been done, as far back as anyone could remember.

What had changed, legally, was that now the local cops didn't have a legitimate reason to be involved, because deserting the ship was no longer a criminal offense. But skippers were still calling cops, and cops were still collaring deserters and dragging them back to work at gunpoint. They were now, essentially, acting like a private enforcement squad for the ship owners.

The union felt that, regardless of whether a deserting sailor was treated as a criminal or just as a runaway worker, this practice was a direct and blatant violation of the Thirteenth Amendment — the one that had abolished slavery and indentured servitude. Which, of course, is exactly what it was.

So their plan was to get a test case sent before the Supreme Court, which would, of course, be forced to rule in their favor — since the Thirteenth Amendment specifically, and in very unambiguous language, outlaws all forms of involuntary servitude except prison labor. Then it would order police departments to stop doing this . . . right?

Well . . . so they thought.

HORRIBLE PEOPLE: *The* SHANGHAIERS.

A portrait of the "Arago Four": Robert Robertson, John Bradley, P.H. Olsen, and Morris Hanson. (Image: Sailors' Union of the Pacific)

They could not have picked a better place in which to run this play than Astoria. As we discussed a couple chapters ago, Astoria was a notoriously tough port in which to replace sailors. The town was small enough, and relatively good-paying timber jobs so close and easy to get, that crew members were hard to come by — which is, of course, why Astoria had such a reputation as a nest of shanghaiers. At any other port, the skipper of the *Arago* would have been far more likely to shrug his shoulders, hire replacement sailors out of a local boardinghouse, and be on his way.

But because there were four of them, it would cost a lot of money to replace them in Astoria, if it could even be done; and sailing all the way to Valparaiso short four men, on a modern barkentine (the *Arago* was only three years old), would be a bad and risky plan.

So the skipper "took the bait" — had the four men arrested and hauled before a justice of the peace. The J.P. promptly stuffed them in a holding cell at the local jail until the ship was ready to weigh anchor, at which time a U.S. marshal escorted them back aboard ship, like runaway slaves getting hauled back to the plantation, and ordered them to get back to work.

But the men, believing they now had a right to quit work like any other American worker, refused to "turn to."

So the captain clapped them in irons and made an unscheduled stop at San Francisco to drop them off and replace them out of a boardinghouse there.

In San Francisco, the four men were promptly arrested and thrown in the Alameda County jail to face charges of refusing their work (which, unlike desertion, was still a crime). When they got their day in court, the judge (as expected) ruled against them; so, backed by their union, they appealed to the U.S. Supreme Court.

Then everyone waited for what they thought was an inevitable verdict on the constitutionality of forcing sailors to work against their will.

They must have been astonished when, a year and a half later, the Supreme Court issued its ruling:

The Thirteenth Amendment, the court ruled, with its prohibition of slavery in all its forms, applied to all Americans, no matter what their race ... just as long as they weren't sailors.

The case was *Robertson v. Baldwin*, and it became one of the most notorious decisions in Supreme Court history. For years afterward, seamen referred to it as "the second Dred Scott decision." It essentially established the status of sailors as — well, for all practical purposes, slaves. Slaves for the duration of their open-ended contracts.

The court's ruling asserted that the Thirteenth Amendment, when it outlawed "involuntary servitude," was just talking about actual chattel slavery of the Old South plantation type. Sailors got paid, so that made it different and therefore OK. And anyway, the court added, servitude wasn't involuntary if one signed a contract to enter into it — a ruling that suggested that actual plantation-style slavery could legally come back as long as the slaves signed a contract up front agreeing to be enslaved.

The court also ruled that using law enforcement to force a worker to fulfill the terms of a labor contract he'd signed was an acceptable practice. And it actually cited a pre-Civil-War court decision over *literal runaway slaves* as a legal precedent to justify this.

The court's ruling went on to claim that the Bill of Rights — the first ten amendments to the U.S. Constitution — had only been intended to formalize an already-existing Colonial tradition of liberty, not to actually change anything from English law (an extraordinary and *very* incorrect

HORRIBLE PEOPLE: *The* SHANGHAIERS.

The four-masted barkentine Arago in the Hoquiam River in Washington in the early 1890s, being tended by the steam tug Traveler. (Image: University of Washington Libraries)

assertion); and therefore, since that tradition had allowed sailors to be treated as indentured servants at the time the Constitution was ratified, it obviously hadn't been intended to apply to them, or the Constitution would have stipulated it specifically.

The ruling went on to cite precedents for treating sailors as literal wage-slaves, including the laws of the ancient Greek mariners of Rhodes from 900 B.C. and the laws of the Hanseatic League from the Middle Ages (according to which desertion was punishable by a year's imprisonment on bread and water or by having the deserter's face branded).

Finally, the justices wrote this oft-quoted gem: "Seamen are treated by Congress, as well as by the Parliament of Great Britain, as deficient in that full and intelligent responsibility for their acts which is accredited to ordinary adults, and as needing the protection of the law in the same sense in which minors and wards are entitled to the protection of their parents and guardians."

In other words, the court ruled, sailors were a special, sub-human class of persons, unfit to be entrusted with the full rights and privileges of citizens. They were not to be expected to stand on their own two feet, to make their own choices and take the benefits or consequences like farmers and loggers and railroad workers would be. They had to be made to do as they were told, and in exchange, the government would see that they were taken care of adequately, fed sufficiently, and not abused too badly.

Every American man, the court said (almost in so many words!), was endowed with certain unalienable rights by his Creator ... so long as he was not a sailor.

Reading this decision today, it's hard to escape from the impression that the justices who wrote it were stretching as hard as they could to round up talking points, trying desperately to cover up a fundamentally wrong legal (and moral) position with every straw they could possibly grasp at.

This was an 8-1 decision by the court. Every Supreme Court justice agreed, with one exception. That one exception was Justice John Harlan, and his dissent was brutal.

"The Thirteenth Amendment of the Constitution of the United States declares that 'Neither slavery nor involuntary servitude, except as a punishment for crime whereof the party shall have been duly convicted, shall exist within the United States or any place subject to their jurisdiction,'" he wrote. "Such is the plain reading of the Constitution. A condition of enforced service, even for a limited period, in the private business of another, is a condition of involuntary servitude.... The placing of a person, by force, on a vessel about to sail is putting him in a condition of involuntary servitude if the purpose is to compel him against his will to give his personal services in the private business in which that vessel is engaged."

He goes on to almost poke fun at the majority's citing of 3,000-year-old Greek and 600-year-old Hanseatic law as precedent: "Why the reference to these enactments of ancient times, enforced by or under governments possessing arbitrary power inconsistent with a state of freedom? Does anyone suppose that a regulation of commerce authorizing seamen who quit their ship, without leave, to be imprisoned 'upon bread and water for one year,' or which required them to be 'stigmatized in the face' with the letter of the town or state to which they belonged, would now receive the sanction of any court in the United States?"

But Harlan was just warming up to the part that must have really been music to the ears of the sailors:

"The further suggestion is made that seamen have always been treated, by legislation in this country and in England, as if they needed the protection of the law in the same sense that minors and wards need the protection of parents and guardians, and hence have been often described as 'wards of admiralty,'" he wrote. "Some writers say that seamen are in need of the protection of the courts 'because peculiarly exposed to the wiles of sharpers and unable to take care of themselves.'

"In view of these principles, I am unable to understand how the necessity for the protection of seamen against those who take advantage of them can be made the basis of legislation compelling them, against their will and by force, to render personal service for others engaged in private business.... The Constitution furnishes no authority for any such distinction between classes of persons in this country."

The runaway seaman who breaks his contract, Harlan added, may be liable in damages for the nonperformance of his agreement; but "to require him, against his will, to continue in the personal service of his master is to place him and keep him in a condition of involuntary servitude."

"It will not do to say that, by 'immemorial usage,' seamen could be held in a condition of involuntary servitude without having been convicted of crime," Harlan continued. "The people of the United States, by an amendment of their fundamental law, have solemnly decreed that, 'except as a punishment for crime, whereof the party shall have been duly convicted,' involuntary servitude shall not exist in any form in this country."

By adding another exception to that blanket prohibition, Harlan said, the Supreme Court was engaging in judicial legislation — creating new law rather than sticking to its Constitutionally limited role of clarifying and interpreting existing law — and thereby usurping the power of the Legislature.

"It is a very serious matter when a judicial tribunal, by the construction of an act of Congress, defeats the expressed will of the legislative branch of the government," he concluded. "It is a still more serious matter when the clear reading of a constitutional provision relating to the liberty of man is departed from in deference to what is called 'usage,' which has existed for the most part under monarchical and despotic governments."

Zing!

Of course, in the short term, this was quite a setback. But Harlan, needless to say, turned out to be the one who was right about this. He was right about something else, too: He predicted in his dissent that this ruling would be used as a precedent for reintroducing indentured-servitude into the United States, and within a few months that was already happening as states in the defeated South started using it to defend contract-labor drag-them-back-to-work laws for the benefit of the plantations that had formerly been worked by slaves.

It wasn't a good look.

Nor was the decision popular in the press. "The American merchant marine has been disgraced in the eyes of the world," the *Oregonian* wrote in its response to the ruling, "and labeled with the iron bands of such slavery as threatened the very foundations of the country in 1860.... Immediate action is necessary to save our sailors from infamous imposition more degrading than they have suffered in the past."

The U.S. Congress was not amused, either. Harlan's caustic observation that the decision amounted to judicial activism was not overlooked by the lawmakers who had voted for the law it overturned. Within months of the decision they had replaced it with an even stronger version, the White Act, which closed several loopholes and included desertion in most foreign ports as well as domestic ones. The shipping interests, which had been happily celebrating their victory, by the end of the year surely wished they had not gotten involved.

Getting law-enforcement authorities out of the contract-enforcement-goon-squad business was a great first step for American sailors. But they wouldn't actually be free to quit their jobs without consequences for another dozen years, with the Seamen's Act of 1915.

Nonetheless, it might have taken a good while longer than it did for sailors to acquire the full rights of American citizens had it not been for the "*Arago* Four" walking ashore in Astoria and refusing to go along with the path of temporary slavery that had been marked out for them.

Sources and works cited:
- Sweatshops at Sea, *a book by Leon Fink published in 2011 by University of North Carolina Press;*
- The Sailors' Union of the Pacific, *a book by Paul Schuster Taylor published in 1923 by Ronald Press;*
- Storied & Scandalous Portland, Oregon, *a book by Joe Streckert published in 2020 by Globe Pequot;*
- "Live at the Jack London, Robertson v. Baldwin," an episode of the Weird History podcast *by Joe Streckert (Episode 89);*
- "Tying Seamen to their Jobs," an article published in The Seamen's Journal *on April 7, 1920;*
- *justia.com;*
- Portland Morning Oregonian *archives from 1897*

THE SHANGHAI TUNNELS.

THE HORRIBLE PEOPLE:
- *The staff at the Valhalla Saloon on Burnside;*
- *Everyone involved with shanghaiing homeless men in pre-war Portland.*

One of the most popular tourist attractions for visitors to Portland is a tour of the "Shanghai Tunnels" that run beneath the Portland streets.

Historians of old Portland — credentialed academics as well as pop historians like Yours Truly — tend to scoff at the whole enterprise. Doug Kenck-Crispin, resident historian of the *Kick Ass Oregon History* podcast, once memorably referred to the process by which the Shanghai Tunnels story developed as "The Bullshittening." In his books, the late Barney Blalock, Portland's dean of waterfront historians, is also extremely skeptical.

They're right ... up to a point.

The fact is that there is pretty good evidence that parts of the network *were* used to shanghai sailors. It's just that they probably weren't used in the way the Shanghai Tunnels tour guides say they were.

But then again ....

The Shanghai Tunnel tours are the fruit of the research, exploration, and imagination (in roughly equal parts) of a Portland character named Michael Jones.

In the early 1970s, Mike Jones was the manager of a financial-institution-cum-social-service organization called Transit Bank — "the world's only hobo bank" — based in Old Town. The idea was to provide a way for homeless people and "traveling" folks to keep their money safe; as any seasoned hobo will tell you (if he trusts you enough to speak frankly), getting robbed is part of the gig when you're on the road and sleeping rough or in a shelter. That's one reason why so many homeless people travel with dogs.

Obviously, this put Jones in close contact with a lot of the exact sort of people who, clear up into the 1920s, were most at risk of being shanghaied. Some of those men, in 1972, were old enough to remember those days. Others had just heard the stories from those who were. All of them were surely happy to fill Mike's ear full of wild tales of the goings-on in those dark, sinister tunnels that lay beneath the abandoned, decrepit buildings along Burnside, Couch, Davis, and other streets of Portland's Skid Row.

Jones, over the decade, collected the stories, mapped the tunnel system, and in 1979 launched the Cascade Geographic Society and went into business leading tours for the curious — regaling them along the way with the stories he'd harvested from hobos he worked with, augmented to some extent with extrapolations and interpretations of his own.

And that's the storytelling foundation on which the Shanghai Tunnels tours are based today — still through the Cascade Geographic Society.

So, what *were* the tunnels, then, if they weren't used for shanghaiing? The earliest tunnels were probably dug by Chinese merchants, to conceal and smuggle opium. Opium, in the 1890s, was perfectly legal, but heavily taxed, and smuggling it was common and lucrative.

The Chinese also had extensive illegal gambling operations that the police were constantly trying to shut down with heavy-handed raids by sledgehammer-swinging squads of bluecoats. On those occasions when a half-dozen cops suddenly showed up at one's Fan Tan parlor and started battering away at the door, having a secret hidden passage connecting the joint to a laundry shop a couple blocks away was very handy.

These tunnels were still being used for their original purpose in 1914, when Oregon instituted Prohibition, a few years earlier than the rest of the country; and suddenly there was another useful purpose for secret underground tunnels. It's not a coincidence that plenty of the "Shanghai Tunnels" connect to drinking establishments.

And it's that connection that makes the strongest case for the tunnels

HORRIBLE PEOPLE: *The* SHANGHAIERS.

A scene from Charlie Chaplin's movie "Shanghaied," which came out in 1915, several years after most historians consider the age of shanghaiing to have more or less ended. The shanghaier on the left is holding an oversized mallet, with which he has just knocked Charlie senseless; this technique was very seldom used in real-life shanghaiing, as drugging a victim's drink was much safer and easier. (Image: Postcard)

to have been used to shanghai sailors. Because by far the most common way to shanghai a man was out of a bar.

The classic vision of a shanghaiing, of course, involves a blackjack — or, in the case of scene from the old Charlie Chaplin movie shown in the postcard image on this page, a giant caulking mallet. But, as noted earlier, unless you know exactly what you're doing, clobbering a man hard enough to knock him unconscious is dangerous business. Hit him just a little too easy and you've got a bad fight on your hands; hit him just a little too hard and you can end up facing a murder rap. It's far safer, and much easier and less stressful to boot, to chat him up, buy him a couple drinks, and slip a little chloral hydrate or laudanum into his whisky while he's not looking.

"Contrary to local legend, and according to an old salt familiar with the Portland waterfront of the period, actual physical violence ... was almost never used," historian Blalock writes, in *Portland's Lost Waterfront*. "Usually it was drugged whiskey in one of the North End saloons, or some sort of trickery played on young or inexperienced newcomers. Over the years, an untold number of men woke up with a terrible hangover onboard a vessel gliding down the Columbia River to the sea."

There was a problem, though, for the aspiring shanghaier of old Portland. Shanghaied sailors are like electric current — they have to be used just as soon as they're generated — before they wake up and start yelling for a cop. So, say you're an unscrupulous bartender at, say, the Valhalla Saloon at First and Burnside, circa 1905; you've got a likely-looking prospect at the bar practically begging to be served a Mickey Finn; but the next sailing ship doesn't disembark until tomorrow night. What do you do?

That's where the "shanghai tunnels" came in.

Corvallis resident Karen Watte's family story of the adventures of her grandfather and great-uncle — two Danish ship's officers who made an unfortunate choice of places to have a drink — illustrates the system nicely.

The two of them stepped into the Valhalla for a drink, and wound up in a sort of dungeon underneath it after the bar man activated a trap door. Men lurking beneath subdued them and took them prisoner. The story doesn't specify this, but they may have escorted the prisoners far enough away from the tavern to keep them from being audible should they try shouting for help. The story does say their shoes were taken from them, and broken glass was scattered around to prevent them from trying to escape barefoot.

The two of them were held prisoner in that makeshift dungeon until the ship was ready to receive them.

When it came time to go, they were then given pills to take — probably at gunpoint — so that they would be unconscious for the transfer to the ship. The pills worked as advertised, and when the two Danes woke up, they were aboard ship.

In this case, the shanghaiing did not come off. The ship was delayed by bad bar conditions, and Karen's grandfather and great-uncle woke up while it was still anchored near Astoria waiting for things to calm down. Both dove overboard and swam to shore, to the captain's dismay; as trained officers, they were probably his first and second mates, so it was a much bigger deal to lose them than it would have been with ordinary sailors. The two of them had to hide out with a friendly fellow Dane who kept a shop there in town while the police combed the streets looking for them; but eventually they gave up.

So, this story suggests that the basements of saloons were used as a catchment system, at the very least; and for holding shanghaiing victims prisoner until the ships that had "purchased" them were ready to receive them. But, were the tunnels used to actually convey the unconscious sailors to the waterfront to be loaded aboard ships?

Almost certainly not. Why would they be? The sight of a couple of half-drunk sailors helping a passed-out shipmate back to his berth was very familiar to anyone who spent any time in the old North End. There was literally no way to tell if that unconscious sailor was being shanghaied, or just helped to bed by his trusted friends. So there was simply no reason to use the tunnels to deliver shanghaiing victims.

Furthermore, during much of the year, the ends of the tunnels close to the riverbank would have been flooded. Before the seawall was built in 1928, the river often came right up into the streets of town during spring floods.

It's that seawall that's responsible for much of the mystery surrounding the tunnels, by the way. When it was built, dozens of buildings were demolished, and any tunnels that might have run underneath them were collapsed. By that time, the Valhalla had already met a similar fate during the construction of the new Burnside Bridge two years before, in 1926. So one can't simply go into the tunnels and see if they lead to the river; if they once did, they sure don't any more.

But there is one other important thing to consider, about the shanghai tunnels. Most historians agree shanghaiing more or less ended when sailing ships were replaced with the faster, safer, more predictable steamships. That happened in a slow process between about 1900 and 1930 — the last windjammer built in Oregon was the 201-foot barque *North Bend II*, built in 1921, and it was still operating profitably in 1928 when it ran aground on Peacock Spit. Yet nearly 20 years before that, sailing-ship skippers were already having trouble finding officers and crews. The best and brightest mariners were signing onto steamers, which were much more pleasant to work on and far less dangerous. The wreck of the sailing ship *Glenesslin*, which in 1913 glided majestically under full sail straight into the rocks at the foot of Neahkahnie Mountain, was blamed on the low quality of available officers and crew for sail-powered freighters in the early years of the age of steam.

And yet, according to the conventional wisdom on the subject, by 1913 the practice of shanghaiing was virtually extinct. Ordinary loggers and farmers were more or less safe drinking and carousing in bars downtown. This in spite of the fact that seasoned sailors were leaving the tall ships as fast as they could — every able-bodied mariner who could choose between sail and steam would have to be a fool to choose sail.

So, where were the remaining tall ships getting their crews? Was shanghaiing still going on, quietly and with the tacit approval of city officials who had every incentive to support it ... so long as the shanghaiers restricted themselves to preying exclusively on the homeless?

It would not have been the least bit controversial for a politician in the 1920s to make the case that quietly encouraging shanghaiers to scoop up hoboes was the very best way to manage the homeless population, so long as the shanghaiers tacitly agreed never to shanghai a "respectable" citizen. The case they would make would be that homeless vagrants needed jobs whether they wanted them or not, and getting scooped up and forced to work on a sea voyage might turn out to be the best thing for them. They'd get a bed and meals, maybe learn the good old Work Ethic along the way, and finish the cruise with a fairly large paycheck with which to set themselves up respectably as contributing, non-homeless citizens.

To a port-city mayor 100 years ago, it must have seemed like a total win-win situation. And looking at it that way, doesn't it seem extraordinarily likely?

Mike Jones got the stories and legends he told on his tunnel tours from the hoboes. A lot goes on in the "hobo jungle" that nobody ever hears about ... of course, there's plenty of tall-tale telling being done there as well.

He's gone now, so we can't ask him — Mike Jones died unexpectedly in 2020, just before the Coronavirus pandemic broke out. But it's entirely possible, and in fact rather likely, that the truth content of Mike's storytelling was quite a bit higher than most of us would like to think.

Sources and works cited:
- Portland's Lost Waterfront, *a book by Barney Blalock published in 2021 by The History Press;*
- *"The Last Word on the Shanghai Tunnels," an article by Barney Blalock published Feb. 21, 2013, at* portlandwaterfront.blogspot.com;
- *"Shanghaiing in Portland and the Shanghai Tunnels Myth," an article by Richard Engeman published March 17, 2018, at* oregonencyclopedia.com;
- *Correspondence with Karen Watte.*

PART III.

MORE HORRIBLE PEOPLE.

So far, we've met a wide assortment of Horrible People. But, with one or two exceptions, they've all been shanghaiers. Of course you know as well as any of us that not all Horrible People are shanghaiers, right?

To be frank, shanghaiers are nowhere near the most Horrible kind of Horrible Person, and are far from the most interesting — although they are one of the most fun to read about. In this next section of this book, things are going to take a darker turn. In it, we will be meeting some characters who make any shanghaier look like the president of the local garden club.

There's a land shark who used the law to steal a homestead out from under a freshly bereaved widow, who then had to buy her own bedding back from the ensuing auction. There's a college president who was such a passionate pro-slavery man that he brought a gun to his local newspaper office to try to murder the editor. And there's a U.S. Army general who designed and led an offical program to deliberately and systematically degrade, humiliate, and break the spirit of an entire divisional cohort of

Black combat veterans after the First World War, so that they would not use their new status as war heroes as an excuse to become "uppity."

Don't worry, there will be a few rays of sunshine in this morass. For one thing, most of the time, the Horrible People we'll be talking about did not come out on top, and they got to spend the rest of their lives being judged by people like us, in books like this.

So, let's get to it!

THE LAND THIEF.

THE HORRIBLE PEOPLE:
- GREENBERRY SMITH, LAND THIEF.

Especially in the late 1800s, the Oregon frontier was no stranger to acts of judicial lynching — where the local legal system was corrupted to provide cover for murder.

What was more unusual, though, was an 1852 event that amounted to judicial cattle rustling.

Interestingly, it happened in the Marysville (Corvallis) area — the same community that, shortly before, had tried its hand at "judicial claim-jumping," supporting a local swain in his quest to steal away half of Nimrod O'Kelly's land claim and subsequently convicting him of murder when he shot the "claim jumper" in an argument over it. (That story appears in Volume Two of this book series, *Love, Sex and Murder in Old Oregon*.)

The cattle that the Benton County courts rustled belonged to a woman named Letitia Carson, and she was the widow of a recently naturalized Irishman named David Carson — or, rather, she would have been David's widow, if the two of them had been allowed to marry. But they weren't, because Letitia Carson was Black, and a former slave — born in Kentucky in the late 1810s.

The other factor that makes this episode of judicial rustling unusual is that Letitia took the thief to court — and won. Twice.

There's no documentation of Letitia Carson's transition from slave to free woman, but it seems most likely that David Carson bought her, freed her, and married her the old-school common-law way, it having been at the time illegal for a white person to marry a black person.

Perhaps hoping things would be different in the Oregon Territory, where it was considered perfectly normal and respectable for a white man to marry an Indian woman, the two of them then set out on the Oregon Trail, arriving in Soap Creek Valley (about two miles west of today's Adair Village) in 1845. There, they staked a 640-acre claim, and started building a ranch on it.

Things went well for them. Letitia's herd of cattle, which she had started on the trail to Oregon, grew and prospered. Their first child, Martha, born on the trail, was joined by a son, Adam, in 1849.

In 1850, the new territorial government took away half their land; because they weren't, and couldn't be, legally married, the Carsons were only entitled to 320 acres. There wasn't much they could do about that, so they just had to grin and bear it, and carry on with half of their land. After all,

Soap Creek Valley as it appears today, as viewed from Soap Creek Road near the former location of the Carson homestead. (Image: F.J.D. John)

320 acres of free land was still a lot of free land, and the Soap Creek Valley includes some of the most productive farmland in the world.

But it was in 1852 that the real trouble happened. That's when David, following a short illness, died. And although he'd made promises to the woman he thought of as his wife, he hadn't put anything in writing.

Neighbor Greenberry Smith now pounced. He got the county courts to appoint him executor of David Carson's estate; then he proclaimed that Letitia and the children would be handled as property, not as heirs. They were, he said, David's slaves, and they should consider themselves fortunate (as, in fact, they were, given Smith's attitude toward them) that slavery was illegal in Oregon, because if it weren't, the three of them would have been appraised and auctioned off like livestock.

A portrait of Greenberry Smith, the Snidely Whiplash of our story, as he appeared circa 1885. (Image: Oregon State Bar Bulletin)

On Jan. 4, 1853, Smith held a public auction and literally sold everything but the land and the "slaves." Onto the block and out the door went everything else — including, according to historian Bob Zybach's article in the *Oregon State Bar Bulletin*, "half-acres of potatoes, David's underwear, the family's Bible, bedding, dishes and tableware, jars, farm tools and equipment, two yokes of oxen, a wagon, a velvet vest, a watch, a clock, a gun, a thermometer, 35 cattle, 26 hogs, and a 14-year-old horse."

The sale raised $1,538.80 — including $104.87 from Letitia, who actually had to buy back her own bed, bedding, and kitchen supplies at the auction. Apparently she had managed to sequester a few dollars somewhere; in fact, it would have been surprising and out of character for Letitia Carson if she had not.

Two months later, Letitia and the kids left Soap Creek Valley, traveled

This family portrait shows Martha Carson Lavadour, David and Letitia's daughter, with her husband Narcisse and son Nelson, circa 1875. (Image: Oregon State Bar Bulletin)

south, and settled in Cow Creek Valley down in Douglas County. There, Letitia found and hired an attorney, and sued her late husband's estate.

(Historian Zybach, who is currently working on a full biography of Letitia Carson, says her attorney likely was part of a Corvallis backlash against Greenberry Smith and his pro-slavery cronies. If you think about it, anyone who believed in the humanity of Black people would have been outraged by this play — if not by the treatment of Letitia, certainly by the theft of David Carson's children's inheritance.)

Because Smith, as executor, was treating her as David's slave rather than his wife, and slavery was illegal in Oregon, her suit was basically a claim for back wages. Because she was legally prevented from marrying David, she couldn't represent herself as his heir; but she could, and did, claim they'd had an agreement and understanding that she and the children would inherit his things when he died, an agreement that he hadn't been able to put in writing before his death.

Subpoenas went out to various witnesses who could testify to something like this, and the case was placed on the docket for trial.

Greenberry Smith's response to this seems to have been outrage at the temerity of this "uppity" Black woman, who, instead of being grateful for the gentle treatment he had given her (not selling her back into slavery, not seizing the money with which she bought back her things), was resisting his pseudo-legal theft of her property.

Through his attorney, prominent local pro-slavery lawyer John Kelsay, Greenberry asserted that Letitia had been a slave up to the time of her death, as had her children, and that as such she was entitled to no compensation, and even if she were, her freedom was compensation enough. He then undermined that argument by quibbling about the dollar amounts she put on the various things she was claiming in the suit.

That incoherent pleading may have had something to do with the verdict — or maybe Smith's Snidely Whiplash coldness and intransigence rubbed his neighbors the wrong way. In any case, when it was handed down on May 7, 1855, by a jury of Smith's white male property-owning neighbors, it was a win for Letitia — sort of. They awarded Letitia just $300, which Smith, representing the estate, paid — reluctantly and only after the Oregon Territory's chief justice, George H. Williams, ordered him to accept and pay it.

As Zybach notes, not much of that $300 made it back to Letitia after the sheriff's expenses and witness fees were deducted from it — likely much less than she'd had to pay to redeem her things from that illegal auction.

But it was a moral victory, and a foot in the door, and she followed it up with a suit for compensation for the theft of her cattle.

This time, Letitia's attorney was able to get in touch with a key witness, a neighbor who had had a conversation with David Carson about the cattle just before he died. David, complimented on the size and health of his herd, had replied, "Most of those are Letitia's." He then pointed to one particular dowager cow and told the witness that 27 of the cattle in the herd were the offspring of that one cow, which she had bought on the plains in 1845 while en route to Oregon.

This was good enough for the jury and for Judge Williams, who issued a judgment for $1,200 to compensate Letitia for her rustled cattle.

As Zybach notes, one of the most interesting aspects of this whole story is the paucity of newspaper coverage. Many of the most prominent members of the community were attending the hearings and watching the outcome, and Greenberry Smith was one of the richest men in the county; but the story barely touches the newspapers. It's as if they were deliberately suppressing the story to keep it from sparking hope in the hearts of other swindled Black people, who might, if they learned about Letitia's success, lawyer up and sue instead of quietly going away.

And perhaps that's what it was all about — or maybe they were just trying to avoid a subject that had become uncomfortable for everyone involved. After all, most of the ancient Romans who stuck their knives in Julius Caesar were ashamed of themselves afterward, weren't they? And some of the most prominent members of the Benton County community had attended Smith's auction and bought Letitia's stolen property. Chances are, by the time the court had ruled that she'd been done dirty, they weren't super proud of the part they'd played in the drama.

As for Letita Carson, in 1863 she filed a Homestead Act claim on 154 acres near Myrtle Creek; this was, of course, something she'd been unable to do prior to the Emancipation Proclamation, especially after the Supreme Court's infamous 1857 Dred Scott decision proclaimed black people to be non-citizens.

She proved her claim up, of course. Finally laboring for herself and her children, with real legal protection from marauders like Greenberry Smith, she seriously overdid it. The improvements on her property included an 18x22-foot one-and-a-half-story log home, a barn, a granary, a smokehouse, an orchard with a hundred fruit trees in it ... and — of course — a big herd of cattle.

Hers was one of the first several dozen homestead claims certified, and was quite likely the first Homestead Act claim proven up by an African American in U.S. history.

Sources and works cited:
- *"Strangely Absent from History: Carson v. Smith," an article by Bob Zybach published in the October 2016 issue of* Oregon State Bar Bulletin.

COLLEGE OF ARSON AND WAR.

THE HORRIBLE PEOPLE:
- *M. Ryan, college president and attempted murderer*

The University of Oregon, as most alumni can tell you, was founded in 1876 as the flagship of Oregon's university system.

But the channels the university project flowed through, with the enthusiastic support of the Eugene community, had already been cut 20 years before by a short-lived institution called Columbia College.

Columbia College was far from a Bad Idea; in fact, if it had been founded just a few years earlier, it probably would still be around today (although it would have had to change its name along the way — the college we know today as Columbia University in New York had dibs. CU was chartered in 1754 as King's College and changed its name just after the Revolutionary War. By 1856 it had been called Columbia College for more than 70 years.)

But it never got the chance. Oregon's Columbia College was brought down by bad timing, helped along by a few certifiably Horrible People. And it happened very quickly.

The college collapsed a few months before the Civil War broke out, after the college president, a staunch pro-slavery man, tried to murder the editor of a local Abolitionist newspaper, and then jumped bail and went on the lam.

But while it lasted, the college made up a huge part of the Eugene City population — about a quarter of the town's residents were students. And it gave all the residents of old Eugene City a taste of what it was like to be an important regional center of learning — a taste that they would remember, 15 years later, when it really mattered.

Columbia College was initially chartered by an offshoot branch of the Presbyterian Church, but it was intended to be a real college, not just a training program for ministers. Part of the financing for the college was an innovative and effective plan reminiscent of the punch-cards used at Dutch Bros. coffee kiosks: Scholarships were offered at $100 each, and anyone who sold nine of them got one for free. Anyone who wanted to participate could earn one of those free scholarships by selling nine to neighbors and friends.

This marketing campaign turned out to be unusually effective not only in "putting butts in seats," but in making the new college a surprisingly diverse place. Students from all over the expansive Oregon Territory signed up, as well as a number from outside the area. By the fall of 1856, when the college was scheduled to open, 52 pupils were signed up, both men and women.

That number would rise steadily over the next few years, peaking at around 150 students — and in the process, totally dominating the town of Eugene City, whose population at the time was around 500. Columbia College would have more than its share of challenges to overcome over its short run, but lack of students was never one of them.

Speaking of those challenges, the first of them came literally less than a week after classes started. The first day of classes started two weeks late because the building wasn't ready for students yet. But on Nov. 20 — literally the very first Thursday after classes started — the freshly built college building caught fire and burned to the ground.

College president Enoch P. Henderson promptly proclaimed it the work of an arsonist. This was probably untrue, but it hinted at the real problem Columbia College would be facing throughout its run: Politics. Henderson was an abolitionist, and so were most of his associates on the board and in

The fireproof stone building which was under construction throughout the short life of the college. (Image: Oregon Historical Society)

the classroom; but many others were pro-slavery. Passions were high and mounting on both sides. By the time the school was founded, the tension between the two factions had already gotten bad enough that people were accusing one another of arson. Things would only get worse as the months wore on.

College board secretary J. Gillespie reassured the community not to worry; the show would go on. And so it did, with the loss of only one day of classes, in a rented house nearby.

Meanwhile, work continued on a new building — one intended as a temporary structure, to tide them over while a deluxe fireproof building made of sandstone was prepared. This building was ready for them when the 1857 fall semester started. It lasted longer than the first building had — but that wasn't saying a whole lot. The new building went up in smoke on Feb. 26, 1858.

Again, Henderson claimed it was arson. This time, though, he was more likely to have been right. By 1858, a lively tug-of-war was under way between the pro-slavery and abolitionist parties. The pro-slavery activists had, the previous year, launched an ongoing campaign to take over the college board. They failed twice, in 1857 and 1858, and in 1859 tried and failed to have Henderson's salary reduced; but after that he decided to take the hint and tendered his resignation. Without him there to galvanize the Abolitionist forces, the pro-slavery people easily took over, and quickly consolidated the college board to push the remaining abolitionists out.

Henderson was replaced as college president by a man named M. Ryan. Ryan was a staunch pro-slavery Southerner, and wrote several articles for the *Pacific Herald* newspaper under the pseudonym "Vindex." In these, of course, he blasted away relentlessly at the abolitionists.

Those editorial broadsides were answered in *The People's Press* by one of Ryan's own students, H.R. Kincaid — later one of Eugene's most prominent citizens — writing under the pseudonym "Anti-Vindex."

Ryan was so incensed by Kincaid's work that on the evening of June 22, 1860, he tried to kill *People's Press* editor B.J. Pengra, whipping out a pistol and firing at him with it.

"The ball was not well aimed," the *Oregon Journal's* reporter recounts, "and missed Pengra, who sprung upon Ryan, bore him to the ground, and choked him till he was black in the face, when some bystanders interfered and separated them."

Pengra immediately filed charges against Ryan for attempted murder, and Ryan had to post $1,500 bail. He then promptly jumped bail and skipped town as a fugitive from justice.

After that, Columbia College was basically done. It straggled on for a few more months; but a combination of the brewing American Civil War and a hefty judgment stemming from a lawsuit filed by former president Henderson (whom the new pro-slavery college board had attempted to stiff for a semester's pay) forced it to declare bankruptcy and dissolve.

But just before that happened, the students finally got to move into the new fireproof stone building — the permanent structure that had been under construction since the first building fire. It wasn't quite finished and ready yet, but the students were, so some classes were moved into it. And although it didn't catch fire, the college's building jinx was apparently still going strong. According to ex-President Henderson's niece Kate, "one stormy day there came a creaking and rattling overhead, and the timid ones among us were greatly frightened, supposing the whole building was about to fall upon us, but our fears were quieted as it was ascertained that it was only the tin roof loosened from its fastenings, and being rolled up in a scroll was literally thrown from the building and rolled off down the hill."

Perhaps it just wasn't meant to be.

From the first day of classes to the day the roof blew off, Columbia College was only open for four years. But during its short run, the College had a surprising impact on the intellectual development of frontier Oregon — which must have had a lot to do with the sheer number of students who came.

Among those students, the most well known name nationwide was that of Cincinnatus "Joaquin" Miller, the future "Poet of the Sierras," who attended classes there for several months. Miller would later claim Columbia College as his alma mater, writing in later years that he "graduated summa cum laude from Columbia," likely pleased to let everyone think he meant the other, more famous and prestigious Columbia College, in New York; but, as historian Perry Morrison delicately puts it, "It is very difficult to separate fact from poetic license when one deals with the career of the Poet of the Sierras."

Other important names on the student roster include J.J. Walton and J.M. Thompson, two of the primary movers in the establishment of the University of Oregon 15 years later; and future U.S. Congressman J.D.H. Henderson, the college president's brother, who came to Eugene specifically so his children could attend Columbia College, and later supplied the 20-acre parcel of land on which the U. of O. would be built.

Cincinnatus "Joaquin" Miller as he appeared in 1858, when he was a student at Columbia College. (Image: UO Libraries)

But Columbia College's influence goes beyond the names of its students. It basically gave the rough-cut backwater settlement that was pre-Civil-War Eugene City a taste of life as a Mecca of letters, and the citizens clearly liked it.

"The people here, many of whom had been its students, never forgot in the struggles of later years that this place had once been an important center of learning," writes historian Joseph Shafer in his 1901 article. "To this fact I believe may be attributed much of the ardor shown a decade and more later in the pursuit of the university project."

Fortunately, when the real university project got under way, it took care not to hire any prickly pistol-waving Southerners as its university president.

Speaking of which, ex-President Ryan was never caught, and never heard from again. A probably-true rumor claimed he'd fled back to old Dixie, and when hostilities broke out a few months later joined the Confederate army.

Sources and works cited:
- *"Columbia College 1856-1860," an article by Perry D. Morrison published in the December 1955 issue of* Oregon Historical Quarterly;
- *"Survey of Public Education in Eugene," an article by Joseph Shafer published in the March 1901 issue of* Oregon Historical Quarterly;
- *Archives of the* Oregon Statesman, *1860.*

THE WAR-BOND 'TRAITORESS'

THE HORRIBLE PEOPLE:
- *W.F. Woodward, vengeful Library Board member*

On April 12, 1918, Oregonians opened their newspapers to learn that there was a traitor in their midst. "PORTLAND LIBRARIAN RADICAL IN DECLARING LOYALTY TO KAISER!" shrieked the *Salem Statesman*. "Declaring that she would rather be ravished by a Hun than support the United States in this war, M. Louise Hunt, assistant librarian at Central Library here, brought down a storm of indignation from Portland citizens today."

"Miss Hunt's attitude is an insult to the motherhood of our nation and to their boys who are knee-deep in the muddy trenches of France fighting for liberty," fulminated Portland Mayor George Baker.

"Not only should she be dismissed (from her position), but if she continues her anti-war propaganda she should be interned during the course of the war, like any other disloyal citizen or enemy alien," proclaimed Oregon Governor James Withycombe.

So, what exactly *was* the great sin against the American people perpetrated by this quiet assistant librarian? What was this despicable act of treason that had brought upon her the censure of the most powerful men in the state?

Simply this: When offered the opportunity to lend the government money to finance participation in the First World War, she said "no thanks."

Oregon was in the grip of war fever as the late winter of 1917-1918 ripened into spring. The war was being sold to the public, very successfully, using all the techniques of propaganda and mass persuasion known to President Woodrow Wilson's Committee on Public Information.

The vast majority of Americans had caught the crusading spirit and jumped wholeheartedly aboard the Committee's bandwagon; and now the government was taking advantage of that enthusiasm, passing the hat to get buy-in from members of the public (literally!) through the Liberty Loans war bonds program.

There had been two drives for Liberty Loans, in which the government had asked citizens to dig as deep as they could to help finance the war. Besides being an expression of patriotism, Liberty Loans were actually a pretty good investment; the government was paying 4.5 percent interest on them, and there was almost no risk of default. Plus, failing to participate was tantamount to failing to "do one's bit," in the slang of the day. So the drives had been very successful.

Now, as April came, a third Liberty Loan drive had gotten under way, and Portland's civic leaders had a goal: they wanted their state to be the first in the nation to make its quota of sales.

To achieve that goal, they planned very carefully in advance. There was much advance publicity, urging Oregonians to get the cash ready so that all the drive's volunteers had to do was race around from house to house scooping up money. The kickoff day — Saturday, April 6 — was declared Liberty Day. There were parades, and open-air band concerts playing patriotic tunes, and prominent appeals published in the newspapers to all Portlanders to get their wallets out. "Over the Top in a Week" was the slogan.

It didn't take even that long. Six days later, the newspapers were able to report a resounding success. Oregon had indeed been the first state in the union to reach its quota of $18.5 million, of which Portland alone had kicked in just over $10 million.

But right next to the celebratory headline on the front page of the *Portland Evening Bulletin* announcing that success, there appeared another:

"LIBRARIAN WITH BIG PAY CHECK WILL NOT PURCHASE BONDS."

A political cartoon by the legendary Tige Reynolds, on the front page of the April 13 edition of the Portland Morning Oregonian, illustrated the response to assistant librarian M. Louise Hunt's refusal to invest in war bonds. (Image: UO Libraries)

In this other article, the *Bulletin* reported that it had come to the attention of the Liberty Loan executives that assistant librarian M. Louise Hunt of the Multnomah County Library had not purchased any Liberty Loan bonds. So the organizers had sent two representatives to the library to find out why, and to arrange for Hunt's apparent oversight to be promptly and generously remedied.

"Miss Hunt" proved a much tougher nut to crack than the representatives apparently expected. She quietly informed them that she was not buying bonds because she did not believe in war, and did not wish to financially support it.

Attempting a sort of Socratic-dialogue closing technique, the representatives asked if she was an American citizen, and, upon getting her "yes," pounced: Did she not agree that it was the duty of every American citizen to help defend their country?

She said she did not consider participation in the European war to be a defense of country.

The representatives then tried an appeal to pecuniary interest (it was, after all, a very safe investment with a guaranteed rate of return) and, when that didn't work, made an appeal to pity: Didn't she realize that the Germans were running around all over France and Belgium raping women, they asked her? The boys in France were fighting to protect *her* from the same fate. How could she deny them her financial assistance in their quest to save Belgian and Northern French Womanhood from The Fate Worse than Death? Wouldn't she want the same consideration if she were in their position?

Hunt parried that thrust by assuring them that she was prepared for any suffering (this exchange was the source of the "would rather be ravished by a Hun" line in the newspapers) and then riposted that if the government wanted her money, it could come and take it; but she would not give it voluntarily.

The representatives hurried back to make their report, and to leak it to the press; and when it appeared, in the *Bulletin*, it sparked a popular furor. The district attorney called for Hunt to be fired from her job; the mayor and the governor soon weighed in as well, as quoted above; and angry letters started pouring in to the newspapers and to the library board.

The headline stack and first few paragraphs of the Portland Morning Oregonian's coverage of the dramatic meeting at which assistant librarian M. Louise Hunt's resignation was accepted. (Image: UO Libraries)

So the library board called an emergency meeting to discuss the matter.

Aware of the mounting hostility, Hunt carefully prepared her statement for the board, in writing, and forwarded it to them before the meeting. "I am an American, and no one can more earnestly desire to see America leading in the world's progress to a higher civilization," it read. "It is increasingly a source of pride to me that in this conflict our President now stands head and shoulders above the statesmen of the other warring nations. His aims and ideals and those of other earnest people with whom I disagree are my aims and ideals. The disagreement is purely an honest difference of opinion about the methods which will best achieve those ends. At no time have I desired to be an 'obstructionist.' I merely wish to claim the Constitutional American right privately to hold a minority opinion."

The board was convinced — all but board member W.F. Woodward; and the board voted to support her right to abstain from buying bonds, even as every member disagreed with her stand.

As far as Woodward was concerned, though, this was tantamount to aiding and abetting high treason.

Woodward was soon being quoted in the newspapers as calling the decision a disgrace. Nobody, he said, who was getting a $175-a-month salary in a publicly funded position should be allowed to keep her job if she refused to support her country.

The public outrage now worked itself up to such a pitch that the library board was more or less forced to meet again three days later. Woodward clearly came to this meeting armed for bear, and was apparently surprised when it was announced that Hunt had resigned her position.

"Because I do not wish in any degree to hamper the usefulness of the Library, and because I am unwilling to place upon the Library Board the burden of a conflict to maintain its brave stand for freedom of conscience, I hereby tender my resignation," she wrote.

This was not good enough for Woodward, who promptly moved that action be deferred on the resignation until after the board had voted to dismiss her outright — in other words, a "you can't quit, you're fired" move. This failed, and the resignation was accepted. Woodward, cheated of his prey, then started pounding on the table and shouting accusations that the head librarian, Mary Frances Isom, was "disloyal" as well. Isom, enraged, leaped to her feet and shouted back at him that he was "no gentleman." Board member Jonah B. Wise jumped up as well and, addressing Woodward, said, "I am ashamed of you, sir."

All the other board members joined in the general condemnation, and

Woodword, in high dudgeon, got up and stalked out of the room without another word.

"I want to be quoted as saying that Mr. Woodward's conduct is yellow and he is yellow clear through," Board president W.B. Ayer told reporters after the meeting.

"Yellow," of course, was 1910s slang for "cowardly"; so Ayer's statement was, in effect, an ever-so-slightly-more-civil version of "Put up your dukes." The newspapers don't give any indication of whether this challenge was accepted, though.

In short order, the whole affair was forgotten — especially after dead soldiers started coming back from France and the whole jingoistic glow of propaganda-driven excitement started to drain away. Within a few months of the end of the war, most of the people who had so bitterly opposed Louise Hunt were now firmly in her camp; but by then she was gone. After resigning her job, she moved immediately back to Maine, and later finished her career as head librarian at the public library in Racine, Wisconsin.

Sources and works cited:
- *"Conscientious Objector: Oregon, 1918," an article by Annette M. Bartholomae published in the September 1970 issue of* Oregon Historical Quarterly;
- *Archives of the* Portland Morning Oregonian *and* Salem Statesman, *1918.*

AN OFFICER AND A SUPERVILLAIN.

THE HORRIBLE PEOPLE:
- *Gen. Charles H. Martin, USA (Ret.), Governor of Oregon*

Remember General Jack D. Ripper, the character from the 1964 movie *Dr. Strangelove; or, How I Learned to Stop Worrying and Love the Bomb?* Can you imagine what might have happened if General Ripper had been elected to office as a state governor?

For Oregonians, just a few years ago, it wouldn't be too much of a stretch. In 1934, voters elected a retired major general named Charles Henry Martin — known to soldiers during the First World War as "Old Iron Pants." And although Martin isn't known to have gone on any anti-fluoridation rants or spluttered about "precious bodily fluids," his political style was more than a little reminiscent of Ripper's ... and, of course, it's not a work of fiction.

"If things come to a crisis," he wrote to a sympathetic fellow military man in 1937, while discussing the likelihood of a Communist takeover in America, "there are enough strong men left in the country to handle it properly .... The Italians wouldn't submit; they organized their blackshirts.

The Germans wouldn't submit, so they had their brownshirts and Hitler. I don't believe Americans will submit."

Left unmentioned in this remark was any suggestion for who might play the role of an American "strong man" analogous to Mussolini or Hitler, but it was clear that if called upon, he felt himself to be up to the challenge.

Charles H. Martin stands athwart Oregon history like a cartoon super-villain, a larger-than-life caricature of a would-be fascist dictator. He established his own forces of secret police. His agents infiltrated every leftist organization in the state with undercover agents tasked with reporting, provoking, and occasionally soliciting perjured testimony. He responded to at least one labor strike by deploying the National Guard and State Police with orders to shoot to kill. And according to historian Gary Murrell, he gave official support to a plan to euthanize 900 inmates at the Oregon State Institution for the Feeble-Minded as a cost-saving measure.

These are just a handful of the most egregious things Martin is remembered for.

On the other hand, we have him to thank for the federal government's decision to build the Bonneville Dam and establish the Bonneville Power Administration in 1934 . . . and the existence of Bonneville Dam had a lot to do with the United States' victory in the Second World War.

Ironically, his attempts to reserve the benefits of Bonneville for his plutocrat private-power-company friends by denying connections to public electric co-ops was a significant factor in his eventual downfall.

But Oregon, and America, would have to wait a long time for that downfall, and a lot of damage would get done before it happened.

I. The Army Man.

Charles Henry Martin was born near the town of Grayville, in southern Illinois, during the American Civil War. He was the third of ten children, with two older brothers, and his father was determined that his oldest boy would pursue a military career. Charles was happily pursuing his goal of becoming a gentleman-farmer and writer when the unthinkable happened: His two older brothers drowned in the Wabash River. One of them got in trouble, the other dove in to save him, and both perished.

A titanic clash of wills ensued. But in the end, the old man had his way, and Charles reluctantly went off to West Point.

Charles had a rough time at West Point, characterized at first by extreme homesickness and misery, but he eventually graduated 19th in a class of 65.

Brigadier General Charles F. Martin at the Citizens' Military Training Camp, Camp Meade, Maryland, in 1922. (Image: Library of Congress)

He was assigned to an infantry regiment stationed in Fort Vancouver, just across the river from Portland.

During the decade in which he was stationed in Vancouver, Martin put down roots in the Portland area. In 1897, he married a Portland girl — Louise Jane Hughes, daughter of Portland attorney Ellis G. Hughes.

The very next year, when the Spanish-American war broke out, the young officer — by now a captain — was sent to the Philippines to help organize, with the Filipino rebels, resistance to the Spanish. Shortly after that, when the Boxer Rebellion broke out in China, he was dispatched to China to help with that.

These operations — especially the experience in China, where the allied European and American troops storming through the Chinese countryside looking for rebelling "boxers" adopted a sort of "kill 'em all and let God sort 'em out" attitude — seem to have crystalized Martin's attitudes toward members of other ethnic groups into frank disdain. In this he was hardly unique among imperialism-era military men. When it's one's job to kill people, thinking of them as subhuman beasts to be eradicated rather than as brother men makes that job a lot more psychologically tolerable. And that kind of reductive, dehumanizing thinking can and did become a lifelong habit for an entire generation of British, French and American military men. (Well, and German ones too, but that sort of goes without saying.)

Following the Boxer Rebellion, Martin returned to the states and served in various functions with great discipline and competence, much of it in the Portland area. In 1913, the Army lent him to the limping, ramshackle Oregon National Guard so that he might instil some proper military discipline into it. In 1916 he was deployed to reinforce General John Pershing in his operations against Pancho Villa in Mexico.

And then the U.S. entered the First World War.

Martin, by now a full-bird colonel, received a brevet (temporary) promotion to brigadier general and was put in charge of training camps. It's in this capacity that he earned the nickname "Iron pants."

His success in breaking down recruits to build them back up as soldiers led to Martin being given a particularly noteworthy assignment near the end of the war — an assignment that would arguably be the ugliest stain on his military career and probably on his entire life. It's also one of, if not the ugliest stain on the reputation of the United States Army.

The military authorities had a problem that they wanted Martin's help with. It seemed that the African-American soldiers who had signed up to go to France and fight had been treated as equals by the French, rather than as subhuman drudges and errand-boys. Despite increasingly desperate attempts by white American officers to induce the French to adopt the proper attitude of arrogance and disdain toward them, the black doughboys were enjoying an unprecedented level of social freedom and acceptance. The Army's worry was that they had gotten used to this, and would use their new status as war heroes to demand similar equality upon their return to the States.

What was needed, according to military authorities, was a re-indoctrination clinic of sorts, under the guise of "training." And who better to administer that "training" than old Iron Pants?

Martin himself had no use for Black people, opining many times that they were inferior in every way to himself and his white friends, and was thoroughly on board with the plan to "put them back in their place." He was ready, willing, and able to take on this assignment.

Thus did Charles Henry Martin, future governor of the state of Oregon, become the central figure in one of the most shameful episodes of American military history — the deliberate, systematic breaking of the spirit of an entire divisional cohort of American combat veterans and war heroes.

The Black veterans were given the most degrading duties Martin could find for them, including cleaning out toilet pits, burying rotting corpses, and the kind of meaningless rock-breaking busywork one associates with

MORE HORRIBLE PEOPLE.

Brigadier General Charles F. Martin, with an unidentified junior officer, watches from a reviewing stand as "doughboys" march past at the Citizens' Military Training Camp, Camp Meade, Maryland, in 1922. (Image: Library of Congress)

prison chain gangs. They were worked all day and given no liberty to leave the camp. Meanwhile, Martin and his staff cultivated rumors back home that they had been running amok in France, raping French girls by the dozens, and Martin openly referred to them as the "rapist division." (An investigation later revealed that for the entire war, just two charges of rape were made against members of the division.)

It is worth noting that Martin, after the war, blamed the low status of this "training" assignment for the fact that his brevet promotion to one-star general was not made permanent after the war. Perhaps lingering resentment of that belief is why, after the war, Martin filed a report that would become the core of the U.S. Army's policy on African American soldiers from the early 1920s until the early years of the Second World War. It was designed to minimize Blacks' access to the kind of combat roles in which they might distinguish themselves as heroes, to avoid having Black officers over the rank of first lieutenant, and most of all to ensure that no white soldier or officer ever had to take an order from any Black man of any rank whatever.

Martin's Army career ended with his retirement in 1927. He left the

Army a very different man than he had been when he entered it. A merciless disciplinarian with a worshipful attitude toward vested authority and a growing fear of communism, he was already starting to show signs of the Gen. Jack D. Ripper-style paranoia that his political career would reveal after his return to civilian life.

II. The Congressman.

When Charles H. Martin retired from the United States Army in 1927, he was in his mid-60s and still a vigorous and powerful man. He had no intention of retiring to the Arlington Club to sip drinks by the fireplace and swap war stories. So, after a couple years spent getting his family real-estate development business in order, he put his hat in the ring for Oregon's third Congressional district, against incumbent Franklin Korell, and won.

Martin, as a Congressman, turned out to be remarkably effective. The highlight of his one-term service there was getting the Bonneville Dam built. He and Sen. Charles McNary overcame President Roosevelt's diffidence and Interior Secretary Harold Ickes' active opposition to get the project green-lighted.

In so doing, though, Martin set in motion the forces that would lead to his downfall, and to the temporary destruction of his political party in Oregon.

At the time, there were two opposing philosophies about government power projects like Bonneville. One side saw the dam as a nice source of power for aluminum plants and other power-hungry industries and for private electric utilities such as Portland General Electric and Pacific Power, which could buy its power cheap and resell it dear to their customers.

The other side wanted the dam's power to be available to all wholesale buyers, so that they could form public electricity co-ops, buying power from Bonneville and using it to compete with the private utilities.

As for Martin, his loyalties were never in doubt. "The power that the government will develop at Bonneville is not intended to force down the rates of existing power companies," he said, in 1933. "This power is intended for the great chemical and metallurgical reduction plants whose first consideration is cheap power and an inexhaustible supply."

Martin's leading political adviser and confidant was none other than former Governor Oswald West. West is mostly remembered today for his youthful idealism as the young state governor who saved the state beaches for public access back in 1913. But by 1930 West had matured into a rather

MORE HORRIBLE PEOPLE.

Governor Charles Martin gives his speech at the opening of the new Oregon State Capitol on Oct. 1, 1938. This is the event at which Martin shouted "Get back, you bastards!" at the crowd waiting to enter the new capitol building. (Image: Salem Public Library/ Ben Maxwell)

less lovable character — a crafty and mendacious Democratic Party leader who was at the same time a lobbyist for Portland General Electric.

PGE, of course, was delighted at the prospect of buying cheap hydroelectric power from the new Bonneville Dam, but had no intention of voluntarily passing those savings on to its customers. So PGE must have been quite pleased that the congressman who got Bonneville built was virtually in the pocket of its chief lobbyist.

It would be this fight, as much as or more than his squabbles with labor leaders, that would destroy Martin's legacy as a governor.

III. THE GOVERNOR.

It was the morning of Oct. 1, 1938, at the ceremonial dedication of the new Oregon state capitol building, built to replace the old one, which had been destroyed in a spectacular fire three years earlier. Following several dedicatory speeches (including one by President Franklin D.

Roosevelt), the ribbon was cut and the crowd outside invited to come in and have a look.

But as the crowd moved forward, those at the front found themselves up against a door stuck shut. The crowd of Oregonians found itself packed tightly against the door.

Then a voice rang out, strident and harsh and full of authority. It was the governor of Oregon, Major General Charles Henry Martin, and if he'd been in his dress uniform he would probably have had his sword out whacking people with the flat of its blade.

"Get back, you bastards!" he blared.

"It was just like a blowtorch," former Oregon Senator Mark Hatfield told historian Gary Murrell. "The people fell back."

This surely wasn't the only case of a governor cursing at his constituents. But it may very well have been the only case of one doing so a month before a hotly contested election, and in the presence of a sitting President of the United States.

By 1938, though, General Martin probably felt like cursing at people. In the previous four years, the arrogance and stubbornness that had served him so well in the Army and in the U.S. House of Representatives had earned him a bevy of personal enemies working tirelessly for his downfall. His Army life had conditioned him to regard such opposition as insubordination at best (and treason at worst), and he reacted to nearly every sign of opposition as if it were an existential threat to democracy. And the gathering clouds of his paranoia were increasingly keeping him out of touch with reality. In the end, he would not win a second term as governor, and President Roosevelt himself would intervene to see to it that he did not.

Martin was elected to the state's top job in 1934, and almost immediately set about making most of the people who'd voted for him regret having done so. He'd campaigned as a New Deal Democrat, but it quickly became clear that that had been a pose struck to sucker voters into giving him power. He dropped the mask almost immediately. Throughout his term, Martin was a fierce opponent of any government policy that might result in individual citizens getting anything from the government: Social Security, welfare relief, disability relief, the works. In other words, he was the New Deal's fiercest opponent.

In 1936, the unemployment rate having fallen from roughly 20 to 18 percent in the previous year, Martin issued a gubernatorial proclamation declaring the Great Depression over — wishing it away, essentially — and told the federal government to keep its relief funds out of his state.

A family of Dust Bowl refugees along the highway near Bakersfield, Calif., most likely on their way north to the Roosevelt Transient Camp near Roseburg, in 1935. Gov. Martin was very hostile toward these "okies" and ordered the Roosevelt camp, which he called a "tramp camp," closed. (Image: Library of Congress/ Dorothea Lange)

"There is no need why anyone willing to work cannot find it in this state with crops to be harvested," he said. Oregon was supporting too many "loafers and chiselers," he added.

"I am trying to teach our people to show the courage and fortitude of good soldiers," he wrote in 1935. "Democratic nations have lost their moral force through pampering their people."

When Dust Bowl refugees tried to come to Oregon, he ordered the state relief committee to close down the Roosevelt Transient Camp in Roseburg — he called it a "tramp camp" — and hustle them on their way. He vetoed every attempt at relief for veterans, and when some of them began falling behind on their government-guaranteed home loans, called them "skunks." He even proposed, in a speech to a group of Young Democrats in

Eugene, that 900 developmentally-disabled patients at the Fairview Training Center in Salem should be "put out of their misery."

"War is the normal state of man, in spite of all the wishful thinking of pacifists," he said; and in that war, in which only the fittest will survive, society can ill afford to coddle its unfit elements.

This was a philosophy Martin shared with many other military men at that time — including the ones who had seized power in Italy and Germany. Like them, he was not opposed to public spending — just to public spending on relief programs. During his term, the National Guard and State Police never wanted for resources.

And those resources got used. The 1930s were a time of much unrest among unions and labor leaders; federal legislation had recognized unions' right to exist and to strike a few years before. Now, as they started doing so, they seemed to inspire Martin's full paranoia. Apparently thinking of a labor strike as analogous to a mutiny among soldiers, he saw the unions that called and coordinated those strikes as an existential threat to democracy and Western civilization.

"The purpose of both (the AFL and the CIO) is the same," he wrote to a sympathetic fellow military man. "To seize control of the government."

Harry Bridges testifies before Congress in 1939. (Image: Library of Congress)

To counter this threat to democracy, Martin felt that antidemocratic measures were warranted. Martin waged what amounted to a cold civil war in Oregon from 1934 until he was stripped of his power in a bitter primary fight and sent kicking and screaming into retirement in 1938. And it's time to talk in detail about that cold civil war — the spies, the bribery, the perjury, the attempts to get people fired, and even a case in which a bloodbath was barely avoided — now.

IV. The Dirty Trickster.

In August of 1937 when Stanley Doyle called on her, Gwendolyn Ramsey can't have been too happy to see him.

Doyle had been the key figure behind framing Ramsey's husband, Ernest, and two of his fellow union leaders, for the murder of a ship's officer the year before. And although Doyle had been working undercover, chances are pretty good that she knew exactly who he was, and what his role had been.

But what he wanted to see her about — that interested her a great deal. He was there to offer her a special deal: All she needed to do, he told her, was "sign a statement that Harry Bridges was a Communist and that she had seen him at Communist meetings."

"All you have to do is sign it," Doyle told her, "and your husband will be released from San Quentin."

Ramsey wasn't interested in perjuring herself to help Doyle take down Bridges, the controversial Australian-born labor-union leader whom every industrialist on the West Coast seemed to be trying to get deported. But she was very interested in how he proposed to get her husband released. Ernest Ramsey's trial and conviction might have been a corrupt fraud, but a conviction was a conviction. So she played along a little, and asked him the question: How did he have the power to overturn a conviction and get Ernest sprung?

It was because, he told her, he was "a secret service agent for the Immigration Service and the governors of California and Oregon" — and he flashed a fancy gold badge that read, "SPECIAL AGENT — STATE OF OREGON — No. 280."

Stanley Doyle was essentially a personal undercover operative answering directly to the governor of Oregon — Major General Charles H. Martin (USA-Ret.).

And although there was widespread consensus on the subject among the governors of all three West Coast states (as well as the executives of every major shipping company), it was Martin who seemed to most hate Harry Bridges. At the very least, it was he who devoted the most taxpayer resources to the decades-long fight to have him deported — a goal that would have gotten a lot easier if he could be identified as a "red."

Evidence today is pretty strong that Bridges *had* been a member of the Communist Party at one time, probably in the early 1930s. In 1937, that evidence wasn't yet known — but it was fervently wished for. And Stanley Doyle's mission was clear: Either find or fabricate that evidence.

It was a mission he went about with a clumsy unsubtlety that would have shocked anyone who didn't already know his methods. An attorney, he first came to the governor's attention in 1934 as the prosecutor in the case of a man named Dirk DeJonge, a newly enrolled Communist Party member who, a few years earlier, had been prosecuted for making an anti-police speech at a Portland rally. This, of course, was an activity protected under the First Amendment, but the judge found him guilty and sentenced him to prison for it anyway.

Along the way to that outcome, though, some rather startling things happened, all on the record and in open court. First, undercover State Police agent Laurence Milner, who had provided the key information in the case, sought to preserve his cover by testifying in court that he didn't know if DeJonge was a communist or not. Doyle, during a break in the case, tried to persuade him to change his mind and recant his testimony — basically, admitting to perjury — and when Milner refused, Doyle actually stated, in open court, that he had tried to get him to do so. So Milner had to get on the stand and perjure himself again to claim (with rather less believability this time) that he had not. Nonetheless, if any labor unionists ever trusted Milner again after that display, they surely deserved whatever they got as a result. His cover was effectively blown.

(As for DeJonge, his conviction was overturned by the Supreme Court two years later on grounds that throwing somebody into the cooler for making a speech was conduct unbecoming an American court of law.)

The following year, in his new role as "special agent," Doyle blew the lid off another laboriously constructed piece of anti-union James Bondery when he traveled to California to get heavy with a man named Charles Bancksy, a private undercover agent working for a San Francisco shipping company. Bancksy had a beach house in Carmel stocked with hidden cameras and microphones and with a secret fingerprint lab; he hosted parties in it, in which he essentially dragnetted leftists trying to find evidence against Harry Bridges and other persons of interest. Doyle essentially ordered Bancksy to expose himself as a spy by testifying against Bridges; if he didn't, Doyle would get him fired. Bancksy, quite naturally, figured he was as good

Former Oregon governors (left to right) Oswald West, Ben W. Olcott, Albin W. Norblad and Charles H. Martin pose for a photo with Gov. Charles Sprague (right) during a luncheon hosted by Gov. Sprague in 1940. (Image: Salem Public Library/Ben Maxwell)

as fired anyway if he let his cover be blown, so he declined — and, true to his word, Doyle got the governor to intervene and have him fired.

Doyle carried out other operations to suborn perjury using either cash bribes or threats throughout Gov. Martin's term. By the end of it, though, he'd forged for himself such a terrible reputation that, according to a Department of Labor investigation in 1939, he'd "taken so much money from so many people" in bribes and payments for illegal services that any testimony he might have been able to offer would be useless.

Nor was Doyle the only rogue agent Martin's administration employed. Convinced that what he faced was nothing less than a threat to the very existence of the American way of life, Martin was hiring almost anyone as a "special police" agent.

"My brother was appointed Special State Police Officer several months ago by you," wrote William Schmitz of Portland in 1937. "My brother has no right to have this power, as he is irresponsible, inclined to be rattle-headed and is just as apt as not to shoot somebody for no just reason."

Another "special agent" was stripped of his badge after he was caught using it to shake down an Italian businessman, whom he subsequently was prosecuted for pistol-whipping.

Meanwhile, Martin seemed completely oblivious to how all this was playing with the public. In 1938 he started gearing up for his re-election campaign. But by this time, most Oregonians — and not just the union members, either — had had enough, and Henry Hess had emerged as a strong opponent in the Democratic primary. The aging ex-governor Oswald West, who was still playing Karl Rove to Martin's George W. Bush, realized that getting his guy re-nominated was going to be no mean feat. He engineered a clever gambit in which he encouraged conservative Republicans to switch parties to help.

This would likely have worked, but at the last minute came some direct intervention from the very top. On May 18, two days before the election, several members of the President Roosevelt's "brain trust" released endorsements of Hess. Roosevelt himself, as was his wont at such times, remained coyly silent on the matter, other than to publicly deny Martin's campaign claim that the president had told him, during a tour of the Bonneville Dam, "You and I make a good pair."

Two days later, Martin was defeated in his primary. Bitterly and petulantly he blamed everything on malicious conspirators and envious pinko-libs: "Hess, ... that son-of-a-bitch Elton Watkins ... and Dave Beck of the International Teamsters ... hatched their conspiracy ... to buy off the candidates then running against me so as to concentrate the labor vote ... and the subversive elements in the state headed by the so-called Commonwealth Foundation, against me," he said, in a conference just after his defeat.

In the election, Hess in turn was defeated by Republican Charles Sprague. After four years of strident squabbling between Martin's furtive authoritarianism and the allegedly-communist trade-unionists, as far as most voters could see the Democratic Party was split between paranoid Fascists and wild-eyed Bolsheviks, and was best left out of power to stew in its own juice until the grown-ups could regain control. The damage would linger for decades.

V. The Guy who Saved the World?

As you have no doubt gathered by now, Charles Henry "Iron Pants" Martin was probably the most scurrilous and unlovable character in Oregon political history. Of all the characters showcased in this book, it's hard to think of a single one who is more deserving of membership in the Horrible People of Old Oregon Club.

So it's a little odd to think that Oregon, and the rest of the world, may actually owe him a debt of gratitude for saving it from a nuclear holocaust

This postcard image of Bonneville Dam, viewed from the Washington side, comes from a hand-tinted postcard dating from circa 1945. (Image: Postcard)

at the hands of the Nazis. He did that by securing the Bonneville Dam for Oregon.

I mentioned that earlier in this story, while discussing Martin's early political career. But although I didn't want to slow down the story by going into it at the time, it's an interesting enough narrative to merit spending a little time on the details now.

Here's the story of how it happened:

In 1933, when newly elected President Franklin D. Roosevelt set about showering the country with borrowed money in an attempt to stimulate the economy out of the Great Depression, one of the projects on his list was putting a hydroelectric dam on the Columbia River.

The government quickly green-lighted one. But to the dismay of Oregonians, it was set to go at Grand Coulee, up in Washington. It would do nothing for the navigability of the lower Columbia, where boats were still having to portage around the Cascade Rapids or use the Cascade Locks there. It would do nothing for flood control, either. And — probably most importantly, for the political elites of both parties in Oregon — it would not provide Oregon's well-connected private electric utilities with a pipeline to super-cheap hydroelectric power that they could buy cheap and make a killing selling at their standard residential service rates.

So Oregon's Congressional delegation swung into action. And that's where Charles Henry Martin comes into the story.

At that time, Martin was serving in the U.S. House of Representatives. Martin joined with Oregon Sen. Charles McNary, a Republican, to urge the President to spend some of the $3.3 billion appropriation on a second dam project on the Columbia — what would turn into Bonneville. McNary, who had been pushing for a dam there since the Hoover Administration, sent a letter to the President; so did Martin; and a couple months later they followed it up with a personal visit.

The President was convinced, and told the two lawmakers that if they could find a suitable place to put a dam, he'd put it on the list.

Elated, Martin and McNary went to work. But in the meantime, Interior Secretary Harold Ickes — who was in charge of all the projects — learned what was afoot. Ickes was a wholehearted opponent of the Bonneville Dam project from the start. It's not clear why; Martin felt it was personal animosity toward himself, but as we've seen, Martin had a deep and ugly streak of paranoia when it came to things like that. It may have been because of appreciation of the scenic beauty of the Columbia Gorge, some of which would be disappearing beneath a lake if the dam were built. Or it might have been simply a sense of financial responsibility; a green light for Bonneville, after all, meant a red light for some other project. $3.3 billion was a lot of money, but it's not an unlimited amount.

And Ickes surely was also aware of Oregon's private electric utilities' agenda; he may have thought a dam at Bonneville would simply be a gift to those wealthy private interests.

But the reason Ickes gave for opposing the project was very reasonable: With two dams on the river, there would be far more power coming out than the Pacific Northwest could possibly use. Much of it would be simply wasted. Why spend a bunch of money to build a second dam when the first one would slake the area's power needs and then some?

So while the two lawmakers were bustling about getting things ready, Ickes was smoothly and effectively walking the president back from the commitment he'd made.

Months went by, and Martin grew suspicious. Back in Washington, he learned what was up; but he also learned, through a fellow officer, that the Army Corps of Engineers had just finished a survey on the Bonneville site, and was recommending a $31 million facility there. Martin got a copy of this report, but kept it to himself. He recognized a good hole card when he saw one.

A few weeks later, he learned that the president had allocated $250,000 to investigate the feasibility of a dam at Bonneville. Instantly he knew that the 250 grand was kiss-off money — a little economic something attached

MORE HORRIBLE PEOPLE.

Another old postcard image, this one probably dating from before World War II, shows Bonneville Dam from the air. (Image: Postcard)

to an empty promise to buy a little time so that Roosevelt and Ickes could move on with a minimum of drama.

Calling home to Oregon, Martin told McNary the showdown was nigh and asked him to return to Washington. Martin knew that he, a mere House member, had little pull in the White House despite being from the president's own party; but McNary, as one of the 96 Senators who voted on Cabinet confirmations, would have a lot more clout. Reluctantly, McNary came, and the two of them essentially staged a sit-in in the White House until Roosevelt agreed to see them.

When, as predicted, Roosevelt purred that he'd allocated $250,000 to study the site, and if the results were favorable he'd for sure approve the dam ... Martin had him.

"Why, Mr. President," he exclaimed with well-faked surprise, pulling a folded document out of his pocket, "all that work has been done."

Roosevelt, after a moment of consternation, threw his arms up in the air and roared with laughter. He had been outplayed, and he knew it. The dam, he told the two, was a go, and congratulations.

By the time the dam was finished in 1938, it was clear that Ickes' concerns about overproduction were no longer valid. The answer for using all the surplus power, as it turned out, was aluminum. Aluminum production requires huge amounts of electricity to extract it

291

from bauxite ore. And an America tooling up for a war that everyone knew was coming wanted all the aluminum it could get.

As you likely know, as the war went on America's output of war equipment — notably airplanes, which in the 1940s were made almost entirely with aluminum — got bigger each year until the hapless Axis powers were completely overwhelmed with hostile (to them) tanks, planes, aircraft carriers and artillery. By 1945 the output was staggering, and it was topped off with a pair of war-ending nuclear bombings in Japan. The two Columbia River dams played a key role — an irreplaceable role — in all of this.

The role of the aluminum plants is fairly obvious. But equally important to the outcome of the war, if not more so, was the Manhattan Project. It's no coincidence that Hanford, where the fissile matter for the bombs used in Hiroshima and Nagasaki was made, is situated on the Columbia River near the dams — nuclear weapons research and production requires enormous amounts of electricity.

Now, perhaps all these wartime needs would have been met without McNary and Martin's "unnecessary and superfluous" Bonneville Dam.

But also, perhaps — just perhaps — our production abilities would have fallen short of the challenge that was before us, and we would have lost the race to build nuclear weapons. The Germans were chillingly close to developing a working nuclear bomb. Without all those aluminum airplanes flying over Germany and dropping bombs on factories and ore refineries, they might very well have gotten there first.

So, does that mean that the one man in Oregon politics who most resembles a cartoon supervillain actually saved the world from an early nuclear holocaust?

We'll never know for sure, but ... it's at least a possibility that he did indeed.

Sources and works cited:
- Iron Pants: Oregon's Anti-New-Deal Governor, *a book by Gary Murrell published in 2000 by WSU Press;*
- *"Hunting Reds in Oregon," an article by Gary Murrell published in the Winter 1999 issue of* Oregon Historical Quarterly.

GIVING 'EM THE BOOT.

THE HORRIBLE PEOPLE:
- *Warden J.C. Gardner, Entrepreneur.*

In 1866, Oregon State Penitentiary Warden J.C. Gardner had a problem. The state prison had just moved to its present home, in Salem. Its old home had been in Portland, but the city hadn't really wanted it there — especially after an incident in the early 1860s when the state tried to save some money by subcontracting the facility out to a private operator.

This turned out to be a Bad Idea. It solved the overcrowding problem in fine style: every single prisoner escaped from the contractor's facility.

Things would be better now that the penitentiary had a home. However, that home was just a big piece of bare land. Gardner was expected to build a prison facility on it — or, rather, to have the inmates build one.

And therein lay the problem. If the inmates were building the joint, they obviously would not be living in it; they'd be housed in construction shacks. And what was to keep them from simply walking away from those shacks?

Gardner's answer would not only solve the problem for him, it would make him a nice income over the ensuing decades — and make him one of the most hated prison wardens in the nation. It was called the "Gardner Shackle," but it was better known as the "Oregon Boot."

The Oregon Boot consisted of a heavy iron or lead band that locked around the prisoner's ankle. To this band was welded or bolted a heavy iron support strap that attached to the heel of a heavy shoe or boot. The whole contraption weighed up to 28 pounds, and it was attached to only one leg, with the result that the prisoner was perpetually off balance. The idea was kind of like how farmers deal with chickens that learn to fly the coop: clipping the wing feathers on only one side. Like barnyard birds, jailbirds found it very hard to fly the coop when asymmetrically hobbled like that.

So far, this is sounding like a very un-Horrible innovation, isn't it? If anything, the Oregon Boot seems almost like a humanitarian invention, enabling prisoners who would otherwise have to be locked down in solitary or chained to a big iron ball to walk around comparitively free.

Prisoner Wearing Metal Boot Can't Escape

DANGEROUS criminals, shackled with a metal "Oregon" boot, have little chance to escape during long railway journeys. The boot, a modern adaptation of the old-fashioned ball and chain, consists of a steel framework fitting over the shoe, with a 50-pound collar above the ankle.

The prisoner who wears it can walk slowly with a fair degree of comfort, but should he attempt to run, or move quickly, the heavy weight will break his leg.

This small article ran in the August 1922 issue of Popular Science Magazine, demonstrating that the "Oregon Boot" was still in regular use in the early 1920s. The caption claims it weighs 50 pounds, but that figure is almost certainly a typo or a mistake; the heaviest one used at the Oregon State Penitentiary was 28 pounds. (Image: Popular Science)

But it wasn't his invention that landed Warden Gardner his coveted spot on our list of Horrible People; it was what he did with it, and why.

As you can imagine, the solution took care of Gardner's prisoner-escape problem nicely, and a few years later, the prisoners were securely settled into their freshly built prison facility, behind brick walls and iron gates.

Time to take their "Oregon Boots" off, right?

Not a chance. Gardner had, over the previous months, become a believer in the boot's effectiveness under all circumstances. He now thought that, walls or no walls, the only way to control the prisoners was to keep every single one of them booted at all times.

Of course, as the holder of the patent on the boot, he was making a nice little cash royalty every time one was sold, so he was strongly

An old "Oregon Boot" shackle. The heavy iron collar is supported by the bands attached to the heel of the shoe. (Image: Richard Nicol/ Seattle Metropolitan Police Museum)

incentivized to believe in it . . . or, at least, that's the most charitable interpretation of what happened next

And what happened next was that prisoners continued to hobble around their new prison wearing superfluous shackles, which by now were starting to do serious damage to their feet, ankles, knees and hips. A brand-new Oregon Boot wasn't bad to wear around, but after not too long the heavy weight exerting constant leverage on the boot sole and heel would cause the sole to become flexible and floppy, with the result that as the boot got more and more broken-in the shackle would slam back and forth against the prisoner's ankle with more and more force as he walked.

Somebody else's problem, as far as Gardner was concerned.

A cynic might suggest that Gardner was in it for the money, like an early-day Robert K. Mericle (the juvenile-facility owner behind the 2008 "cash-for-kids" scandal in Pennsylvania).

In any case, the problems with the boots eventually became too widespread and serious to ignore. Some prisoners ended up bedridden for weeks at a time in excruciating pain. Finally, in 1878, the superintendent gave in: Thenceforth, the Oregon Boot would only be used when it was needed for disciplinary purposes or on inmates who posed a serious flight risk.

However, field law-enforcement officers loved the boot. It was far harder to escape from a county deputy while being transported to the penitentiary if the inmate was hobbled with an Oregon boot, and there was also a stockades-style public shaming aspect to being seen in public wearing one. Many inmates en route to the pen felt the humiliation of wearing an Oregon Boot more keenly than any amount of discomfort.

By the turn of the century the Gardner Shackle was one of the most

The art from a feature story in a 1922 edition of the Portland Morning Oregonian, explaining the "Oregon Boot." (Image: UO Libraries)

popular pieces of prison equipment nationwide, and everywhere it was called the "Oregon Boot." It certainly was used abusively in many places, and no doubt hundreds, if not thousands, of ex-cons limped for the rest of their lives as a result.

One of the more interesting aspects of the Oregon Boot's history comes from legendary Portland underworld character Joseph "Bunco" Kelley, who was sent to the prison for 13 years on what was almost certainly a politically motivated frame-up orchestrated by a competing shanghaiier.

Bunco was working in the prison bathhouse when the body of David Merrill was brought in. Merrill, you may remember, was the brother-in-law and partner-in-crime of Wild West outlaw Harry Tracy, and in 1902 the two of them shot their way out of the penitentiary in Oregon's bloodiest jailbreak (before or since). (The full story of Tracy and Merrill is scheduled for inclusion in Volume Seven of the Offbeat Oregon books, *Mysteries and Ghost Stories of Old Oregon*, which is, at the time of this writing, scheduled for release several years in the future.)

The official story of Tracy and Merrill's escape from the pen and two-month flight from justice includes a scene on the banks of the Columbia, after Tracy supposedly learned Merrill had offered to cooperate with authorities in return for lenient treatment. Tracy, the story goes, murdered Merrill in cold blood before crossing the river into Washington alone.

Didn't happen, Kelley says.

"I do not believe it was Merrill's body that was brought back to the penitentiary," he wrote. "Merrill was a smooth-skinned man, and he had a burned ankle from the time he wore the Oregon Boot two years before. There was a big scar on his ankle from the burn and the band of the boot wore a dent into the skin to the bone. Every day when he packed hot iron (in the prison foundry where he worked) the boot would cut into the flesh and bleed, and there was a hole in his ankle half an inch deep . . . . Merrill is alive today, or was a year ago" (meaning 1907).

Did one of the state's most notorious outlaws get away scot-free to start a new life? If we can believe Kelley (not always a smart thing to do) — yes.

The Oregon Boot was still in use after the First World War, but humanitarian concerns were always an issue, and after automobiles started being used to transport prisoners instead of passenger trains, there was no real reason to use them. The last time an Oregon Boot is known to have been used on an Oregon inmate was 1939, when one was installed on a Mill City prisoner for his trip to the state pen. Today, they're like stockades and lashes — just another memento of the bad old days.

Sources and works cited:

- Thirteen Years in the Oregon Penitentiary, *a book by Joseph "Bunco" Kelley published in 1908 by an unidentified publisher;*
- *"The Formation of Prison-Management Philosophy in Oregon," an article by Ward McAfee published in the Fall 1990 issue of* Oregon Historical Quarterly;
- *"Oregon State Penitentiary," an article by Jessica Rondema published on May 17, 2022, on https://*oregonencyclopedia.org.

THE BONEHEAD.

THE HORRIBLE PEOPLE:
- *Othniel Charles Marsh, deadbeat paleontologist*

Throughout the dinosaur-bone-fueled 20-year personal vendetta known jocosely today as "The Bone Wars," Oregon was never more than a minor theater of operations. For the most part, the two cowboy-paleontologists whose mutual grudge drove all the drama left the fieldwork and exploration in the Beaver State to teams they'd hired, so that the Great Men could concentrate on states with actual dinosaur bones to find.

One of the Bone Warriors did come to Oregon with an exploratory team, though, just a few months before Bone War hostilities broke out. And by the time he'd departed, he'd left enough of an impression on local scientists that the subsequent fireworks probably came as little surprise to them.

The Bone Warrior who came to Oregon did so on at the end of an expedition in the summer of 1871 at the head of a team of scientists from Yale University. He was Othniel Charles Marsh, a proud, taciturn man with a full beard and intense, glaring eyes, referred to reverently by the students in his party as "Prof." Marsh's increasingly bitter feud with colleague Edmund

Drinker Cope would not develop until some time after his Oregon visit, but locals did get a glimpse or two of the personality traits that would drive Marsh's contribution to that feud ... and, in part, earn him a place in the present catalog of Horrible People.

The early beginnings of the Bone Wars were already in place in 1871, and although they hadn't flowered into full hostility yet, they were well enough along. Marsh and Cope had met in Berlin in 1863. They'd gotten along reasonably well together, but each subtly looked down on the other from the start. The 1860s were the time when science was passing out of being something a gentleman of leisure did to occupy his time (as in the cases of patrician-scientists like Charles Darwin and Benjamin Franklin) to a calling one trained for professionally at a university (as did Albert Einstein, Marie Curie and pretty much every other scientist since).

The well-born Cope came from the older (and dying) tradition of "gentleman-scientists," who saw university-trained scientists like Marsh as a lesser breed — not true gentlemen, but merely technicians who didn't know their places. Marsh, in turn, represented the new university-trained cohort, which saw the older generation as ignorant, arrogant dabblers lacking the professional training to do good work.

A portrait of Professor Othniel Marsh of Yale University around the time of his 1871 visit to the John Day Fossil Beds. (Image: Library of Congress)

This mutual contempt started flowering into trouble almost immediately after they came back to the U.S. Cope had introduced Marsh to the owner of a marl pit where a particularly interesting dinosaur skeleton had been found; Marsh then went behind Cope's back and made a deal with the pit's owner to send any future fossil finds directly to him. This, of course, was something an actual gentleman would not dream of doing, so when Cope learned of it he reacted the way a gambler would react after catching an opponent cheating.

Sheep Rock towers over the John Day River in the John Day Fossil Beds. (Image: Wikimedia/ Finetooth | CC-by-SA)

Then Cope made a major error in assembling a dinosaur skeleton — he put the head on the end of the dinosaur's tail — and it was Marsh who spotted and maliciously publicized the mistake.

The really nasty part of the Bone Wars would come later. Cope and Marsh would spend the rest of their lives — some twenty years — trying to ruin each other, professionally and socially. Both strove to get each other fired from jobs; sent spies and "bone rustlers" to one another's quarries; paid lavish bribes; and — worst of all from a modern scientist's perspective — actually destroyed fossils and backfilled dig sites to keep fossils from each other. By the end of their careers, in the late 1890s, their feud would ruin both of them, professionally and socially, and for decades American paleontology was an international laughingstock as a result of their unprofessional conduct.

But that was all in the future in 1871, when a crew of Yale students crossed the border from Idaho, heading for the John Day Fossil Beds. Marsh had heard of the fossil beds, and had written to Thomas Condon — the "father of Oregon geology," who would later become one of the first professors at the University of Oregon when it was founded five years later.

Condon responded immediately and generously, sending a box of sample fossils to Marsh with an invitation to come to Oregon for more. It was that invitation that Marsh's crew was responding to now.

The Yale team spent a couple weeks in Oregon — first looking over Condon's impressive collection of fossils in The Dalles, and then doing fieldwork in the John Day Fossil Beds. A week later, they'd amassed a collection of some 11 boxes of bones of such creatures as saber-toothed cats, mastodons and primitive horses and camels.

While they were in the field, Marsh did some things that raised eyebrows among the locals. First, when word came to him that Professor George H. Collier of Pacific University in Forest Grove was on his way to a site where some fossil horse bones had been found, he became very agitated and dispatched some of his students "to head him off," like a nervous gold prospector trying to keep other miners away from his diggings.

Then a little later, two of his students, sent to secure some skulls from a local collector, played an ill-advised prank on him by sending word that they planned to abscond with the skulls and form their own fossil-collecting party. Their prank succeeded beyond their wildest imaginings, to the point of likely having a negative impact on their prospects at Yale; Marsh raged about the ostensible betrayal all evening. "If this had been at the first of the trip," he fumed, according to one student's recollections, "so help me God I would send them both home."

When the team left for Portland, Condon generously allowed Marsh to take a large assortment of specimens from his own collection back to Yale on loan. He would spend the rest of his life trying to get Marsh to return

The entrance and parking area at the John Day Fossil Beds National Monument. (Image: F.J.D. John)

them, making multiple appeals. Even Marsh's death in 1899 didn't improve things much, and it was only in 1906 — a year before Condon's own death — that they would finally be returned.

By then, though, Condon knew better than to expect Marsh to send the bones back gracefully. Everyone did. Marsh and Cope, by that time, had plunged themselves, their institutions and their entire scientific community into lasting disgrace with twenty years of unremitting competitive spitefulness.

In doing so, however, they expanded the field of paleontology tremendously. At the end of their colorful careers, Cope had discovered 56 new dinosaur species, and Marsh had discovered 80. Cope in particular wrote of his findings with a dramatic flair that encouraged his specimens to be brought to life in a thousand magazine articles and picture-books, and between the two of them they launched what's almost a tradition of fascination with dinosaurs among small American children.

Rev. Thomas Condon as he appeared in the mid-to-late 1850s, a decade or two before meeting the Yale paleontologists. (Image: Oregon Historical Society)

Dinosaurs were, of course, where the real prestige was when it came to fossils; and the John Day Fossil Beds are not quite old enough to contain those. That's probably why, after that one early expedition, neither Bone Warrior ever returned to Oregon to hunt fossils personally.

Perhaps it's just as well. As Condon demonstrated clearly while Marsh was his guest, their particular brand of hypercompetitive cowboy paleontology was never Oregon scientists' style.

Sources and works cited:
- *"The Yale Scientific Expedition of 1871: A Student's-Eye View,"* an article by Mary Faith Pankin published in the Winter 1998 issue of Oregon Historical Quarterly;
- *"Dinosaur Wars,"* Episode 2 of Season 23 of PBS's American Experience produced by Gary Murrell.

"THEM CHICKENS IS MISCEGENATED!"

THE HORRIBLE PEOPLE:
- *W.C. Conner, newspaper editor and eugenics fanatic*

October of 1913 was a triumphant time for Professor James Dryden, the poultry specialist at Oregon State University (or Oregon Agricultural College, as it was then called).

One of his experiment-station hens, the prosaically named C-521 (later renamed Lady MacDuff), had just shattered the world record for egg production with a stunning 303 eggs in a year, breaking the 300-egg barrier for the first time ever. The highest-producing non-Oregon chicken, prior to C-521's feat, was a Canadian bird that laid 281 eggs in 12 months. This was at a time when the average chicken laid 75.

After that, Dryden's name was in newspapers nationwide, in glowing tribute after glowing tribute to his success.

There was, however, one exception. That would be the weekly *Cottage Grove Leader*.

"In our opinion, Prof. Dryden is impracticable, out of harmony with the country's best and most successful poultry breeders, is discouraging the great and growing poultry industry of the state and is therefore out of place at the head of the Department of Poultry Husbandry in our great educational and experimental institution, the Oregon Agricultural College," the *Leader's* editor sniffed, in its Oct. 28 issue. "We would suggest, in conclusion, that he tender his resignation."

The editorial was not much of a surprise, though, to the *Leader's* readers. By the time it came out, the *Leader* had been waging what almost qualified as a campaign against Dr. Dryden for several years. Obviously, no one does something like call for the resignation of a world champion, in the very hour of his triumph, on the spur of the moment.

Nor does anyone do something like that as a solitary voice. The *Leader* was speaking for a small but influential Oregon industry ... an industry that we might call Big Chicken.

James Dryden was hired at OAC in 1907. He'd been a poultry specialist at Utah State, and had helped build the program there; now, he was given charge of the entire Poultry Husbandry department, such as it then was, at OAC.

At the college, Dryden very quickly set about his quest to breed a superhen. He knew that the conventional wisdom among chicken experts was that egg laying was not a genetically transmitted characteristic. Breeding experiments at other land-grant colleges had failed to change the chickens' egg production measurably.

To Dryden, this made no sense. Some chicken breeds regularly laid 75 to 150 eggs a year, whereas the original wild chicken (the jungle fowl of India) only laid a dozen or two. Something had made leghorn and barred-rock chickens start laying ten to 20 times as many eggs as their wild ancestors, and if that something wasn't genetics, what could it possibly be?

His theory, which he now set out to test, was that the reason for the failure of other experimenters to breed better layers was that they had been breeding for a broad array of other attributes at the same time: straighter tails, more symmetrical combs, prettier feathers, and so forth. He also noted that the previous experiments had been with purebred chickens, which raised the possibility that inbreeding might have caused the resulting chicks to be less robust. A less robust chicken will obviously lay fewer eggs.

While these experiments were going on, Dryden started printing regular bulletins for chicken keepers. These were geared toward ordinary farmers and the few specialized poultry ranchers then in operation, and Dryden made no secret of his focus: Eggs and meat.

"To encourage the poultry industry, hundreds of poultry shows are held each year and thousands of dollars are paid in premiums and all the premiums

The Portland Morning Oregonian's fanciful artist's impression of what it might look like for Oregon Agricultural College's world-record-holding hen to be crowned. (Image: University of Oregon)

are awarded on the basis of the American Standard of Perfection," he told a reporter on Nov. 9, 1910, according to the *Medford Mail Tribune's* story. "We think we are encouraging the poultry industry by paying premiums for feathers and other fancy points and for shape of body, and farmers go to the shows to purchase their breeding stock. They never suspect that the premiums indicate nothing of the egg-laying qualities of the fowl."

"I believe," he continued, "that the farm stock, the cross-breed stock (or, shall I say, the mongrel stock) have better vitality, are more fertile, are less preyed upon by diseases and produce more eggs than the average flock of purebreds. The way to develop the poultry industry is to stop advocating purebred or standard-bred fowls for the farmer. He should decide on the type of fowl to breed and forget the names of the breed."

It was these and similar remarks that brought upon Dryden the enmity of Big Chicken, and by extension the *Cottage Grove Leader*. Because, of course, a number of parties were making rather a lot of money putting on all those poultry shows and fancy-chicken contests and selling Certified Deluxe Blue-Ribbon Purebred Premium Extra-Fancy Chickens to farmers.

As far as I've been able to learn, the one-sided war was launched in the Jan. 3, 1910, issue of the *Leader*. On the top left-hand side of the front page in that issue, under the headline "JUDGE COLLIER AFTER DRYDEN: Shows Up Fallacy of OAC Bulletins on Poultry Raising," there appears an article that basically claims Dryden was just trying to get some cheap publicity — that the OAC bulletin was the 1910s equivalent of clickbait.

The article is presented like an interview, but the entire thing after the first paragraph is one enormous quote from "Judge Collier," a poultry breeder named Harry Collier who served as contest judge for the 1909 Eugene Poultry Show.

"Men will do almost anything in order to get their names in the papers," Collier said. "Actors have been known to 'kick' their wives in order that they might get a front-page story, and I suppose we poultrymen are sometimes guilty of the same fault."

He then goes on to say that there are so many wonderful kinds of chicken available, there's no reason to have cross-breeds or mongrel chickens, and that only a fool would take such a chance.

"Where a man has a 'dunghill' flock of birds, it would help his flock to

OAC Chicken No. C-521, a.k.a. Lady MacDuff, the world's first 300-egg hen, a white leghorn–barred rock cross. (Image: Orange Judd Co.)

cross them with a purebred male, but I cannot see the advantage of crossing purebred fowls," he scoffed. "The man who advocates crossing purebreds is a poor man to advise farmers .... The farmer has got the advantage of the chicken fancier's work. He can now buy any kind of fowl that he desires and he is very foolish to try and cross-breed the purebred when he can buy now any kind of fowl he wants."

"The Judge" then finished off with some remarkably condescending advice for the edification of those ignorant college-boy meddlers like Dr. Dryden: "If OAC wants to do something for the farmer, let them impress him with the fact that he wants to build better houses for his poultry ... Let them study the mortality in fowl life here in Oregon and teach the farmer how to prevent roup and kindred diseases. There is lots to be done. This trying to get notoriety by attacking some well-known principle is foolish in the extreme. It makes the college the laughingstock of those who know better and at the same time makes the poultrymen treat anything coming from the college with indifference or contempt."

Thus spake Big Chicken!

Most other members of Oregon's agricultural community, though, were noticeably unimpressed by these arguments. Obviously, farmers weren't keeping chickens for ornamental reasons. If OAC had taken "Judge" Collier's advice and quit telling farmers how to increase egg yields in favor of some platitudes about quality chicken coops and sanitation practices, there probably would have been a revolt.

Over the next few years, Dryden and his college moved from win to win. By 1911 it was clear that he was right about genetics and egg-laying. In December two of his chickens came within 9 percent of the world record, which at the time was 282 eggs in 12 months, held by an Ontario Agricultural College chicken. Dryden's Chicken No. A-122, a purebred barred rock, laid 259, and Chicken A-61, a barred rock-white leghorn cross, laid 257.

The next year Dryden & Co. fixed up a rail car as a mobile poultry demonstration and toured the state with it, letting everyone see the state's champion chicken alongside an apparently identical barred rock that laid only 44 eggs in the time A-122 laid 257. Dryden's point was that if farmers don't know each hen's individual output, they can't make good decisions about which chickens to continue feeding and which to turn into chicken soup, and the low-output layers will offset the high-output layers.

"Demonstration is a Revelation," the *Capital Journal* wrote in a long sub-headline about the display. "Two Hens Looking Just Alike Show Different Records — One is a Homebody and Produces 240 Eggs, While Her Flirtatious Sister Devotes Time to Lunches, Suppers, Late Dinners and Such and Gives Up 44."

"The poorer layer had a saucy, wear-your-hat-on-the-back-of-your-head sort of look and somehow reminded one of Mrs. Jack Cudahy," the reporter wrote, in a reference to a famously flirty Kansas City society woman whose millionaire husband had just attempted to murder one of her male friends in a jealous rage. "Another of the same breed, but evidently with equal-suffrage ideas about oviparity, deposited only six of the shell-covered bird seeds in 12 months."

The following year, Dryden and his team finally clinched the world record, wringing 291 two-ounce eggs out of a chicken named C-543 in the course of the year that ended on Oct. 15, 1913. In the meantime, chicken C-521 (Lady MacDuff) was at 279 eggs and counting, with 30 more days in her 12 months; barring some kind of freak incident, the college was about to break both C-543's record and the 300-egg barrier.

This, of course, happened, right on schedule in early November.

Newspapers around the state and beyond metaphorically threw their hats in the air.

Poultry professor James Dryden as he appeared in the late 1910s. (Image: Oregon State University)

"OREGON'S GREAT RECORD-MAKING HEN ONLY ONE OF FLOCK," the *Sunday Oregonian* shouted above a photo spread covering most of Page Two. And, later, "DEVELOPMENT OF BREED OF HENS WITH SPECIAL ABILITY TO PRODUCE EGGS DRAWS WORLD'S ATTENTION TO OREGON."

"HEN C-543 WORTH HER WEIGHT IN GOLD: Oregon Chicken is World Beater," the *Portland Journal* proclaimed, following up with a glowing comment on the editorial page headlined "THE CORVALLIS WONDER."

Well ... most of the newspapers did. At least one did not.

At the *Cottage Grove Leader*, the coverage of Dryden's triumph was almost whiplash-inducing. On the front page, reasonably prominently placed, was an article headlined "OREGON HEN MAKES WORLD MARK." It was a short but straightforward account of C-543's feat. But in the same issue, on the editorial page, under a headline reading "Pure Breeds vs.

Mongrels," editor W.C. Conner really cuts loose. And it's this article that led Dryden to actually complain to the *Leader* two weeks later, prompting the newspaper's call for his resignation.

The fascinating thing about this particular moment in the chicken battle is, up to this point it had not been entirely clear why the *Leader* was so intransigently opposed to Dryden's efforts to improve chickens' egg-laying qualities. It had quoted and supported poultry breeders, chicken-show judges, and other interested parties whose business models were threatened by the new attitude, and it stuck by them even when their position was obviously contrary to the best interests of most ordinary chicken keepers. Why?

Because, as it turned out, chicken C-521 was a cross-breed, and Conner was a eugenics fanatic, and — well, let's let him explain: (Bear with me here, Conner's editorial writing style was turgid and soporific even by 1910s standards.)

"The *Leader* would refrain from unjust criticism of any state educational institution or its management or the work of any department thereof," the editorial begins, "but it seems to us that the highest ideals should be fostered in these institutions and all standards of excellence upheld and maintained. And while this object may generally prevail at these educational institutions, we are unable to understand wherein the management of the poultry department at OAC expect to better or advance the great poultry industry of the country by perpetually idealizing and exploiting mongrel strains and breeds of chickens, when perfection in the various standard bred fowls is what every prominent and successful breeder in the country is striving for."

The editorial goes on to revisit "Judge" Collier's comments from three years previously, ranting tediously that chicken race-mixing is "not supported by national or international contests and the poultry records, nor by facts, figures, or Nature's laws."

"The fact is," the editorial continues, a few paragraphs later, "it would be just as reasonable to advocate the production of superior dairy herds by a conglomeration of cattle breeds, or superior horses by a mixture of Clyde, Belgian and Percheron, and so on down the line. This would mean an inevitable return in time to the razor-back hog and the inferior and mongrel breeds found a few decades ago in their native state before they were bred up to the present excellent standards by man."

And then, finally, Conner makes his true objection to cross-bred chickens plain: He sees it as a form of miscegenation:

"Of course, you might improve the characteristics and the qualifications of the Chinese or Africans by the infusion of the white race," he writes, "but it would be mighty hard on the Caucasians."

Ouch. At least he didn't use racial slurs.

Whether this exhibition of racism and enthusiasm for eugenics played as awkwardly in 1913 as it does today is very doubtful; such ideas were almost mainstream back then. But, it has to have been pretty obvious to everyone reading the *Leader* that its editor had become obsessed and was no longer talking any kind of sense. The fancy-chicken breeders and county-fair judges might have been going along with him, for business reasons; but nearly every other reader must have thought the guy had flipped his wig. The local college had set a new world record and set the entire country talking about Oregon chickens, and all that seemed to matter to the *Cottage Grove Leader* was the purity of the chickens' bloodstock? Really?

In any case, as far as I have been able to learn, the *Leader* retreated from the field after this engagement. Eighteen months later, editor Conner sold the paper to W.H. Tyrrell, a newspaperman from Iowa; and two months after that, Tyrrell, having found that Conner had misrepresented the business's balance sheets to hide the fact that it was losing money, merged the paper into the rival *Cottage Grove Sentinel*. The last issue of the *Leader* was published in August of 1915.

As for Dryden, in 1916 his book, *Poultry Breeding and Management*, was published to enormous acclaim. It became the most important chicken-farming textbook of the inter-war period. OSU's poultry building, a classic brick structure built in 1927, was named Dryden Hall to honor him.

Today, thanks largely to Dryden's work, the average egg-breed hen lays 200 to 250 eggs a year. The world record for egg laying is currently held by an Australian chicken, which in 1979 laid 371 eggs in 365 days.

Sources and works cited:
- Poultry Breeding and Management, *a book by James Dryden published in 1916 by Orange Judd Co.;*
- *"Corvallis Chicken Sets 1913 World Record," an article by Kristine Deacon posted July 1, 2021, on the Oregon State Archives Facebook page;*
- *Archives of* Cottage Grove Sentinel, Cottage Grove Leader, Portland Morning Oregonian, Portland Oregon Journal, Medford Mail Tribune, *and* Salem Capitol Journal, *1908-1915.*

PART III.

ALL OF THE ABOVE.

So far, we've met a number of Horrible People, who have run the gamut from adorably hateable to revoltingly horrific; and we've toured a pretty similar spectrum of Bad Ideas. But, so far, we've focused on one or the other.

Now, like an old Reese's Peanut Butter Cups ad, it's time to see what happens when we mix the two together. Bad Ideas and Horrible People: Are they really Two Great Tastes that Taste Great Together?

Well, um . . . no.

But they do compliment each other, as we shall soon discover.

THE STOLEN SHIPWRECK.

THE BAD IDEA:
- *Use an easily-debunked fake claim to try to swindle a town out of its number-one tourist attraction.*

THE HORRIBLE PEOPLE:
- *Cliff Hendricks, would-be shipwreck salvage operator*

A little over a dozen years ago, following the 2008 tsunami that struck Japan, a big section of a Japanese harbor dock that had drifted across the Pacific Ocean was removed at considerable expense from the beach near Newport.

The state government had gotten itself into something of a lather over the dock — as it also did several years before that with the wreckage of the freighter *New Carissa*. The government wanted that stuff off the beach immediately if not sooner, and was willing to go to great lengths and spend lots of money to get it done.

That hasn't always been Oregon's official attitude, though. There was a time when Oregon state and local governments took the opposite approach — as happened in a somewhat comical squabble in 1960 over salvage rights to the wreckage of the *Peter Iredale*.

The *Peter Iredale*, a 287-foot steel-hulled four-masted barque, had been stranded on the beach by the North Coast town of Warrenton ever since a foggy late-October morning in 1906, when the ship first ran ashore there. The freighter was running before the usual southwest wind, making for the mouth of the Columbia River, when a sudden squall roared out of the northwest, driving the ship straight up onto the beach.

What followed was, as author Don Marshall describes it, "the most singularly unexciting shipwreck scenario in maritime history." The crew members were all uneventfully evacuated with a breeches buoy (essentially a zipline with a life ring attached), but had they waited a few hours until low tide, they could have all walked ashore.

Of course, a 2,000-ton sailing ship parked on the beach like a stuck pickup truck is something you don't see every day, so there was a good bit of excitement on shore. Local schoolchildren were released early for the day so they could go check it out. A local railroad operator started making plans for a special excursion train. And photographers, both professional and amateur, started making images of the *Peter Iredale* — which has frequently been called (and may actually be) the most photographed shipwreck in the world.

It's also quite possibly the most long-lasting shipwreck in the world. In part, that's because of geology. After the ship grounded, of course, it was stuck firmly on the beach, but beaches change. Sometimes the wind and currents wear them away, and other times they grow.

In the case of Clatsop Spit, the beach was growing. Over the years, more and more sand accumulated around the wreck, until it was high and dry much of the time.

The wreck of the Peter Iredale as it appeared a few months after its stranding. (Image: Oregon Historical Society)

The wreckage of the Peter Iredale as it appeared in the summer of 2006. (Image: Matt Conwell | CC-by-SA)

This made it more popular than ever. Tourists posed on its decks and explored its depths. As time and weather and salt spray eroded away its hull, a ladder-like structure of rusty steel remained for children to climb and play on.

The *Peter Iredale* quickly became counted among the state's great treasures — a real, picturesque shipwreck that you could walk around and photograph and imagine as a setting for maritime adventures and ghost stories.

The growth of the beach sands changed other things as well, though. A ship stuck fast on a beach in three to six feet of water with West Coast surf breaking around it is a hopeless proposition for scrap salvage, but a ship stuck on a dry beach is a two-week easy-money job. Couple that with the fact that unsalvageable wrecks were frequently sold to suckers for small amounts of money in the aftermath of incidents like this, and you have a recipe for — well, for what happened next.

On June 2, 1960, a Clackamas County man named Cliff Hendricks notified the Oregon Highway Department (which was in charge of beaches at the time) that he was the owner of the wreck, having inherited it from his father, and that he intended to start salvage operations immediately.

Anyone who remembers the state government's angry determination to get every last vestige of the *New Carissa* off the Waldport and Coos Bay beaches will likely find the state's response to Hendricks's letter amusing. It started with a Clatsop County judge, who — after threatening to throw Hendricks in jail if he tried to start operations without permission — alerted the city of Warrenton; the growth of Clatsop Spit in the intervening half-century had, according to the city's maps, put the wreck inside its city limits.

Local newspapers picked up the story, and the public got very excited.

Astoria newspaper editor Fred Andrus settled everyone down by spending an afternoon at the county courthouse examining all the records for 1908, the year Hendricks said his father bought the wreck for $25. There was no trace.

But then, after everyone had settled down and breathed a sigh of relief, a county records clerk found the record. It had sold in 1917, not 1908.

Things started heating back up. An offer came in from the "Oregon Coast Ad Club," which wanted to buy the wreck and make it part of Lincoln County's "Twenty Miracle Miles" tourism project. Hendricks's attorney suggested his client might be inclined to donate it to Clackamas County, where it could be arranged in the parking lot in front of the courthouse in Oregon City. (Anyone familiar with the layout of the Clackamas County Courthouse will probably be a bit suspicious of the sincerity of this offer.)

The people of Clatsop County, of course, viewed all these schemes as attempted piracy.

Various other government agencies were taking hard lines, as well. The state parks department worried about the potential for harm to state-owned property around the wreck. The city of Warrenton asserted its jurisdiction (again) and told Hendricks to get lost. Editor Andrus wrote that if Hendricks did in fact own the ship, he owed five decades' worth of property taxes on it. (This was almost certainly an error on his part. Property taxes are assessed on real estate, not vehicles.) Attorneys for the highway department also started looking into abandoned-property laws.

By June 5, the wreck was being watched 24 hours a day by guards with machine guns.

But just as everything seemed to be building to some sort of horrible climax, the Clatsop County records clerk — the same one who'd found Hendricks's record of purchase — found something else. It seemed the elder Hendricks had, 72 hours after buying the *Peter Iredale*, sold the wreck for $325 — an annualized return of 85,166 percent on his $25 initial investment. Hendricks, it now appeared, had no claim on the wreck at all.

Then as now, it was hard to imagine how this could have all been an innocent misunderstanding. Nonetheless, nobody seems to have pursued it, apparently because it was such a relief that Oregon's only visible and visitable shipwreck was safe.

ALL *of the* ABOVE.

The barque Peter Iredale as it looked shortly after stranding on Clatsop Spit in 1906. (Image: Oregon State University Libraries)

The *Peter Iredale* remains Oregon's only visible shipwreck to this day (excluding, of course, small bits like the boiler of the *J. Marhoffer* in Boiler Bay, and occasional appearances out of the sand of buried vessels like the *Emily G. Reed* at Rockaway Beach). And, given the attitude of the state government during the *New Carissa* debacle, it doesn't seem likely that that will change anytime soon.

Sources and works cited:
- Oregon Shipwrecks, *a book by Don Marshall published in 1984 by Binford & Mort.*

THE UNLUCKY MUGGERS

THE BAD IDEAS:
- Rob a man with a cocked Colt in your hand, and your finger on the trigger
- Try to duck a murder rap by confessing to having helped commit it.
- Pick the wrong landlady to steal stuff from

THE HORRIBLE PEOPLE:
- William Dalton and Jack Wade, stickup men.

It was after 10 p.m. on a Thursday night in 1901, and Multnomah County District Attorney George Chamberlain was dressing for bed when the telephone rang.

He seized the receiver. "Who's there?" he said into it, in none too friendly a tone.

"Never mind," replied a firm matronly voice on the other end of the line. "I want you to come to 181 First Street at once. Something important has happened."

"Can't you come to my office, during business hours?"

"If you knew what I wanted you for, you'd step over here quickly. You are working on that murder, across the river, are you not? Well, it's about that. Now you understand. Ask for Mrs. Whitlock."

Mrs. Whitlock was right — now that Chamberlain knew what she wanted him for, he most certainly would step over there quickly. But she had no real idea how right she actually was.

Mostly, Mrs. Whitlock was just frustrated. She had rented a room in her boardinghouse to a trio of rough characters, one of whom had gone through her stuff and stolen $60 worth of goods. She'd been trying to get a policeman to come see her about the theft since early that afternoon, without success. She'd tried to reach Chamberlain several times earlier in the day, but his line had been busy. The police, after the usual assurances of prompt action, had never shown up. Now it was late at night, and she no doubt suspected the thieves would be gone by morning. So she'd called up the district attorney — former attorney-general of the state of Oregon, and a future governor and U.S. Senator — at his home, at 10:15 p.m., to demand instant action. And she got it.

It sort of goes without saying that stealing stuff from Mrs. Whitlock was a categorically Bad Idea.

Now, although Mrs. Whitlock suspected her lodgers of having had something to do with the murder that had happened a few days previously, she had no proof and, really, no evidence at all beyond an intuitive feeling. Mostly she was just using the reference to the murder to get the district attorney out of bed and over to her house before the thieves escaped.

It worked.

But, as an added bonus, it turned out she was right. One of her boarders really *was* one of the killers.

The murder that Mrs. Whitlock was talking about was the talk of the town just then. It was, essentially, a mugging gone horribly wrong. One of Mrs. Whitlock's boarders, William Strickland (who went by the alias William Dalton), had been leaving a saloon with a friend, Joseph Ewing (who went by the alias Jack Wade or the nickname "Kid McFadden") when they'd come upon James Barkley Morrow, a young bartender on his way home from a visit to his fiancée.

"I know him," Dalton said. "He's a gambler." And he pulled out his big-bore single-action Colt and stuck it in Morrow's face.

Now, it is possible (although very unlikely) that Morrow in fact had fleeced Dalton in a rigged card game in one of Portland's low doggeries; that sort of thing was common in 1901. Perhaps he had in mind to get his money back; if that was the case, Morrow likely would have handed over his wallet and there would have been an end to the matter; crooks don't call the cops on crooks. However, Wade and Dalton appeared to have been making a regular practice of these discreet stick-up jobs, and it's far more likely that this was just another play for drinking money. Bartenders in 1900s Portland tended to dress pretty well for the job; doubtless Morrow looked prosperous enough to be worth mugging.

But it turned out not to matter. Because out of the several Bad Ideas

ALL *of the* ABOVE.

Jack Wade and William Dalton as they appeared on the front page of the Morning Oregonian the day after they were arrested for murdering James Morrow. (Image: UO Libraries)

Dalton was responsible for that night, one in particular stands out as a life-changing "boner," the one that would send both himself and Jack Wade to the gallows: As he drew, he cocked his revolver.

And as Wade reached out to take Morrow's wallet from him, the big six-gun in Dalton's hand accidentally went off in the bartender's face, sending a .44-caliber slug crashing through his head and killing him on the spot.

The second worst decision of Dalton's life came when he arrived back at the boardinghouse the night after stealing Mrs. Whitlock's stuff (which, if not the third-worst decision of his life, was surely at least in the top five) and found District Attorney Chamberlain, reinforced with a couple of police detectives, waiting to question him about the murder (which, remember, was only a topic of conversation because the landlady had used it to get the D.A. out of bed). Mindful of the $500 reward that was being offered for information leading to the arrest, he promptly told them the whole story of the mugging, only changing one detail: He told them Jack Wade had done the actual shooting.

So basically, he confessed the whole thing, without so much as asking to see a lawyer. Which was unfortunate for him, because any lawyer would have told him that legally it didn't matter who pulled the trigger.

Not every Bad Idea in this book comes with a guaranteed death penalty. This one does, though, so it really stands out.

The police soon found Jack Wade in his room at a different boardinghouse, and arrested him as well. Wade, as it happened, had the same Bad Idea that Dalton had. Both Dalton and Wade admitted the murder had happened, but each claimed the other was holding the pistol when it went off.

No doubt the police played on their ignorance of the law in letting them do this, since clearly they did not at first realize that legally it didn't matter who did the actual shooting. Under Oregon law, if a crime goes wrong and an innocent

Defendant Jack Wade as he appeared in court pleading guilty to the charge of murder, drawn by the Morning Oregonian's courtroom sketch artist for the Dec. 11, 1901, issue. (Image: UO Libraries)

ALL *of the* ABOVE.

Defendant William Dalton as he appeared in court, along with some of the witnesses who helped convict him, all drawn by the Morning Oregonian's courtroom sketch artist for the Dec. 10, 1901, issue. (Image: UO Libraries)

person dies, every member of the criminal conspiracy is held just as culpable as if each had been the trigger man.

This is surely why the trial was so very short. Having depended on a defense that wasn't a defense, the two of them had, by the time they were assigned lawyers, essentially confessed their crime, utterly destroying all chances of acquittal.

Wade's attorney advised him to go for the Hail-Mary pass, pleading guilty and throwing himself on the court's mercy. It showed him none. Dalton, who pleaded innocent, was convicted promptly as well, and both men were sentenced to hang.

In the jailhouse waiting for their execution day, the two erstwhile partners made a very interesting pair. Dalton promptly "got religion" in the most extreme way and, painfully aware that he had to make up for an entire lifetime of wickedness and sin in the few weeks that remained to him, proceeded to make life miserable for everyone around him with his prim preachiness; Wade seemed to be playing the whole thing up for laughs.

Also during their jailhouse stay, the mayor of Portland, Henry S. Rowe, happened by and recognized Dalton as the man who had mugged him a few weeks before. Nothing could be proven, of course, and Dalton denied it — but he did so with a shaky and nervous demeanor that didn't do much to convince anyone he wasn't having a relapse from his new-found Christian enthusiasm for the Ninth Commandment.

On the Sunday before the hanging, Dalton announced plans to fast. "It is the last Sabbath I shall ever spend on Earth," he declared, "and I think too much of my Blessed Saviour to take my thoughts from him."

"I'll eat," Wade shot back. "I have a long road to travel."

And so, under the disapproving (and probably hungry) eye of his ex-partner, he tucked into his chicken dinner. Then he looked up from his repast. "What did you have for breakfast, Billy?"

"Tea," said Dalton primly.

"They must have put something in it!" Wade crowed.

On the day of the hanging, the fence around the scaffold was filled with a capacity crowd of 400, and thousands more clustered around, lining the roofs of nearby buildings and the lower limbs of trees, jockeying for a chance to watch two men die. Wade indulged in some literal gallows humor; he pulled a cigar out of his pocket and threw it into the crowd, then threw a pocket handkerchief out like a rock star with a T-shirt cannon. Then he grabbed the noose and dramatically sniffed it.

"It's tough!" he hollered, winking at the crowd.

But then, as the appointed hour grew near, he quickly grew serious, for almost the first time since his arrest.

"Don't any of you fellows follow in the tracks of Jack," he told them. "Now don't you do it. You may think I am happy here. I am not."

Sources and works cited:
- *Necktie Parties: Legal Executions in Oregon, a book by Diane Goeres-Gardner published in 2005 by Caxton Press;*
- *Archives of the* Portland Morning Oregonian, *1901-1902.*

SNAKEBITE JUNGLE JUICE

THE BAD IDEA:
- *Get drunk off alcohol that's being used to preserve shotgun-killed snake and lizard specimens.*
- *Try to murder your romantic rival by visiting him at night with a knife, without first checking to see if he sleeps James Bond-style.*

THE HORRIBLE PEOPLE:
- *Fort Williams' alcoholic tailor.*

The history of 1800s Oregon is full of the influence of good old Demon Rum — and from the "Blue Ruin" that inspired America's first prohibition law in 1844, to the "Temperance Riots" that pitted hymn-singing ladies against a saloon-owning police chief 30 years later, booze has changed the course of state history not once but many times.

And then there was that one time when it changed the course of zoology as well.

The story starts with a man named Nathaniel Wyeth, a successful entrepreneur from Boston who had made a fortune in ice production and distribution. Wyeth, in 1832, tried to parlay this fortune into empire by traveling to Oregon to set up a trading post in competition with Britain's Hudson's Bay Company. The expedition was a flat failure; but he tried again two years later.

Unlike John Jacob Astor, the other wealthy East Coaster who had tried something like this 20 years earlier, Wyeth actually accompanied his expeditions. And unlike Astor's party (and Wyeth's first expedition), Wyeth's second expedition had a relatively uneventful overland journey; in fact, the path they followed would, within the decade, become known as the Oregon Trail.

But when the party arrived in the Oregon country and set up a trading post on Sauvie Island, things got rather bad.

Wyeth's men had come with the express intention of challenging the Hudson's Bay Company trappers and traders; their new trading post, Fort William, was just eight miles from Fort Vancouver. So, help was not to be expected from the British. The HBC, which was on excellent terms with the natives, encouraged local Indian tribes not to trade with the newcomers; and, for the most part, they didn't. The year's salmon run had already come and gone, so no easy relief was to be expected from the river. Soon the supplies the party had brought from home were exhausted, and hunger became a real problem.

And, for some members of the party, thirst.

Thirst wasn't a problem for John K. Townsend, though; not at first, it wasn't. Townsend was an English naturalist whom Wyeth had brought with him on the expedition, along with Thomas Nuttall, a professor from Harvard.

For Nuttall, this was the second time out; he had accompanied the Astorian Party twenty years earlier, and the voyageurs had nicknamed him "Le Fou" (a French word meaning, essentially, "the crazy fool") for his singleminded pursuit of botanical specimens.

Now, as winter tightened its soggy grip on Fort William and people started getting really hungry, "Le Fou" lost his singlemindedness. One day, when Townsend returned to the fort with the day's collection of flora and fauna, he found Nuttall dining on one of his specimens — an owl which he had shot, intending to preserve it for further study.

Nuttall, of course, knew better; but hunger is a pitiless master.

The owl was no great loss. It was of a fairly common type, and another could be found without too much difficulty.

But in his chambers, Townsend had some other specimens that were a different story.

They were crawly things: lizards and snakes and salamanders and newts of various description, which Townsend had caught and killed and preserved in a small keg of whisky. Most likely he bled the specimens out before placing them in the alcohol, so that their blood would not dilute the potent preservative liquor. At least, we can hope he did.

Among these specimens was a particularly interesting sort of large newt, the like of which Townsend had not seen before. He was very much looking

ALL *of the* ABOVE.

Naturalist John K. Townsend as he appeared in his mid-30s. (Image: Wikimedia)

forward to getting back to his home in Philadelphia with it and doing some more careful studies upon it.

Meanwhile, Fort William's tailor (whose name I have not been able to learn) was having a very difficult time transitioning to an alcohol-free environment. The tailor, though very good at his job, liked a drink or six of an evening, and had an unfortunate habit of going into alcohol-fueled rages when he drank. No doubt all his colleagues were quite relieved when the fort ran out of liquor, and the tailor was forced to quit drinking.

All of them, that is, except Townsend, who had in his possession the last drop of booze in the fort . . . in that small keg full of snakes and lizards. All the tailor had to do was wait until the naturalist was out, slip into his room, and pour off the alcohol, leaving behind all the dead reptiles.

This he proceeded to do.

The concoction must have been pretty revolting. You know what happens to strong liquor when fruit is left to soak in it, right? Now imagine that "jungle juice" made with shotgunned snakes, drowned salamanders, and, oh yes, one large unknown species of giant newt.

But the tailor slugged it down, and it probably hit him pretty hard, being as his stomach was empty.

Townsend no doubt learned of the raid a few days later, when he caught a whiff from his specimen keg. He was furious. Months of work had been ruined; and much as he tried, he never was able to find another giant newt. Today, there is a Townsend's Chipmunk and a Townsend's Warbler, and if not every Willamette Valley resident is familiar with Townsend's Vole, every resident outdoor housecat certainly is; the Townsend's Vole is pretty much the standard-issue field mouse in those parts. But if there's a Townsend's Newt, nobody has found one yet.

As for the tailor, he made it through the hungry and thirsty winter with his taste for alcohol intact. Some time later, after the fort's supply of food and drink had been restored, he learned to his great dismay that the fort's blacksmith, Thomas Hubbard, had taken up with a Native girl whom the tailor fancied. The tailor, having taken his customary wee dram or two, worked himself into a towering jealous rage, armed himself with a knife and pistol, and went to Hubbard's room late at night to settle the matter.

And that is how the tailor learned that Thomas Hubbard, like Pierce Brosnan's James Bond character in *Tomorrow Never Dies*, slept with a loaded pistol under his pillow.

What followed was the first murder trial — and, for that matter, the first European-American criminal trial of any kind — in the Oregon territory. After hearing the evidence, the jury pronounced Hubbard's actions to be a case of justifiable homicide, and he was acquitted.

Which probably was not unwelcome news for the presiding magistrate at the trial: The Hon. John K. Townsend.

ALL *of the* ABOVE.

Fort William, like Fort Astoria before it, didn't last long. Like Fort Astoria, it was sold to the British, and everyone involved either went back home to the East or settled in the new country. By 1837, when the fort was sold, there was plenty of room in Oregon country; the diseases carried by Europeans and European-Americans had wiped out village after Native American village, leaving only empty homes and scattered bones.

Wyeth slunk back home to Boston, thousands of dollars in debt, and set himself back to work in the ice business. By the time he died, he'd remade his fortune; but he never ventured west of the Mississippi again.

Nuttall returned to Boston by sea, and some time after arriving he inherited his uncle's estate in Lancashire, England, the terms of which required him to live at least nine months of every year in the family estate. He moved there in 1842 and died in 1859.

As for Townsend, he died young, at age 41, of arsenic poisoning. It seems he had developed a special secret formula used in preparing specimens for taxidermic preparation . . . a formula, perhaps, less palatable to fellow crew members than ethyl alcohol had proved to be. The only problem was, the key ingredient in the formula was arsenic.

Sources and works cited:
- Narrative of a Journey Across the Rocky Mountains to the Columbia River, *a book by John K. Townsend written in 1836 and republished in 2001 by Oregon State University Press.;*
- *"Nathaniel Wyeth's Expeditions to Oregon," an article by Melinda Jette posted in 2004 on the Oregon Historical Society's Oregon History Project Website,* oregonhistoryproject.org.

HUCKSTERS AND KLUXSTERS.

THE BAD IDEA:
- Turn an old arson-and-murder terrorist organization into a flashy, pseudo-exclusive, faux-mystical secret society with memberships sold via a multi-level marketing scheme.

THE HORRIBLE PEOPLE:
- Luther Powell, triple-diamond-level klown-suit salesman; Fred L. Gifford, Powell's downline rep; Kaspar K. Kubli, member of Oregon House of Representatives.

In early 1921, an outgoing Louisiana salesman named Luther Powell crossed the border from California to Oregon, with business on his mind.

Powell was a "Kleagle." His job was to recruit new members for a six-year-old organization called "Knights of the Ku Klux Klan, Inc.," collecting the $10 membership fee from each new mark and selling them just as many items from the organization's catalogue of overpriced regalia as they could buy.

His commission was a whopping 40 percent. And the Oregon territory was wide open.

Powell's arrival in the Beaver State kicked off a short but interesting period that most Oregonians today would rather not think too much about. A magic combination of sour reactionary feelings against "foreign entanglements" following the First World War, the latent racism of an America in which the Civil War was still in living memory, and the opportunity for big profits from membership fees, brought the Kluxers from nothing to a position of serious political influence in just two years.

And then, even more quickly than it had risen, the Klan dropped away, fading into a cacophony of screechy internal squabbling and covering itself with the stink of hypocrisy after a few high-profile kickback scandals and, back east, by particularly terrible sexual assault and murder perpetrated by a Klan leader in Indiana. By the end of 1925 the Klan was finished as a serious political force, although it did manage to straggle on for a few more decades as an increasingly disreputable underground subculture.

In '21, though, Oregon was fresh territory and Powell was ready to work it. Acquiring the title of "King Kleagle" for the state, he settled into Medford and started gathering his army. Besides white supremacy, the doctrine the Klan preached was "One hundred percent pure Americanism," which it defined as white gentile Protestantism that put Jesus first and America a very close second. To be a member, one had to be a native-born white Protestant gentile with a good reputation. No Jews or Catholics were allowed. A subordinate order, the Royal Riders of the Red Robe, was created to accommodate naturalized Americans — that is, not native-born — but they still had to be white Protestant gentiles.

In Medford, Powell and his Kluxers stirred up some trouble here and there. A Black man was sort of demi-lynched — a rope put around his neck and used to lift him off his feet for a few terrifying moments before he was set free with a dire warning to get out of town, a practice known as a "necktie hanging" — and several others were threatened. Crosses were lit on fire on various hilltops. There are rumors that some people were branded.

But as large gangs of anonymous vigilantes go, the Klan was remarkably mild-mannered in Southern Oregon — so far as is known, nobody was actually murdered. This may have been because their King Kleagle knew if the community started to fear them, he'd have a much tougher time making sales — especially in the bigger cities to the north, which were still wide-open. There was plenty of money to be made with muscular racism in early-1920s Oregon, but the trick was finding just the right balance of dangerousness. Too much, and people would turn away — as they eventually did, but only after Powell was pushed out. He knew what he was doing.

It's important to understand that the Klan in 1922 was different from the Klan in 1866. The 1922 Klan had been launched seven years earlier, inspired by D.W. Griffith's 1915 movie, *The Birth of a Nation*, which glorified the Klan, gave the group its iconic robe-and-pointy-headpiece look, and introduced the practice of cross burning.

The new Klan was organized as a fraternal organization, like the Masons

ALL *of the* ABOVE.

King Kleagle Luther Powell, center, and Exalted Cyclops Fred Gifford pose for a picture with (left to right) H.P. Coffin of the National Safety Council; Senior Police Capt. John T. Moore; Police Chief L.V. Jenkins; District Attorney Walter H. Evans; United States Attorney Lester W. Humphries; Multnomah County Sheriff T.M. Hurlburt; U.S. Department of Justice Special Agent Russell Bryon; Portland Mayor George L. Baker; and Scottish Rite Masonic Lodge Sovereign Grand Inspector General P.S. Malcolm. (Image: UO Libraries)

or the Elks, but as a for-profit corporation rather than a charity group. It muddled along, not getting much done and not really leaving the Deep South, until 1920, when an Atlanta advertising agency called the Southern Publicity Association took the Klan on as a client and crafted its public image and its sales message with the manipulative skills honed in First World War propaganda campaigns.

The results were striking.

The original Klan of the 1860s had targeted freed former slaves and their white allies, and was quickly shut down by the U.S. Justice Department in the early 1870s after leaving a trail of bloody corpses and terrified survivors strewn about the countryside.

This new Klan would be, if you will, a kinder, gentler terrorist organization. It would last a little longer, and for a few years it would seem destined to take over, because the agency took its message down a notch and broadened it quite a bit. The new Klan appointed itself as the enforcement arm of white American Protestantism, ready and willing to undertake anonymous vigilante actions as needed to preserve white American Protestantism as the definitive American culture. Non-WASPS — Black people, Chinese and Japanese folks, Jews and Catholics — were to be kept under control as a matter of cultural self-defense. (Melting pot, schmelting pot.)

With an eye on public relations, the new Klan controlled the level of vigilantism and terrorism carefully, seeking that perfect balance between comfortable and dangerous, aiming for an attractive muscularity and avoiding becoming extreme enough to threaten mainstream society. Crosses were regularly lit afire in spots where they overlooked Catholic and Jewish neighborhoods (there were very few black people in Oregon at the time). Members sometimes barged into Catholic churches during services dressed in their sinister, anonymous outfits. They paid homage their organization's long-established tradition of lynching innocent people by conducting more "necktie lynchings," in which victims were led to believe they were about to die, lifted an inch or two off the ground by the neck for a moment, and released with a dire warning. This went badly for them on at least one occasion, when their victim (a white guy whom they suspected of having seduced a 16-year-old girl) figured out who they were and sued them.

A flyer for a Klan rally held in December of 1921 in Portland, in an attempt to boost enrollment. By the time this was published, the Klan was well established and already making plans for the next election. (Image: Georgian Press)

Much of their success was down to the sales system devised by the Southern Publicity Association. It was very sophisticated. Each recruiter ("kleagle") got a standard kit; in addition to the usual stuff like contracts and eyehole headpieces and regalia suits to sell to the new recruits, the kit included a prospect list. Kleagles were encouraged to discreetly make contact first with Protestant pastors, and then with cops and local government officials for membership. Then the ads would be placed in newspapers and the kleagle and/or an especially enthusiastic pastor would arrange a dog-and-pony show in some hotel ballroom, in which the entire community was invited to come hear all about the Klan. Since the Klan was a secret society, the promise was that you could find out what it was all about by coming to one of these things, and the people who arrived were then played masterfully by the recruiter, who would finish the evening with sometimes hundreds of new $10 memberships — $4 of which, if he was a top-level kleagle, he got to keep.

In due course the kleagle would identify and deputize sub-kleagles to go out and repeat the process at other towns. Klan membership would spread virally until anyone in the state who thought they might want to be a Kluxer had the opportunity to pay their $10 and take home their very own Klown suit.

So, this was the MLM-like system that Luther Powell was bringing to Oregon when he arrived in Medford in 1921. And everything went just the way he hoped it would, at least at first.

By June, just a few months into his tenure as Oregon King Kleagle, Powell had deputized several particularly gifted orators from his gang, appointed them Kleagles, and sent them forth to recruit members on their own in various other cities. Of course, as with any multi-level marketing operation, he'd get a piece of every membership fee they brought in. They were, in effect, his "downline."

Powell himself wanted to turn his attention to the big markets now. So he checked into the Multnomah Hotel in Portland in June and started quietly gathering his "Invisible Empire" army around him. He personally picked Fred L. Gifford, a former union electrician who'd been booted from the union for "scabbing" a few years before, as his lieutenant. Gifford was to lead "Portland Klan No. 1" as "Exalted Cyclops."

Powell spent two months getting ready for the big Klan debut. In addition to the discreet recruiting of leaders, he probably also needed the time to gauge the public mood. Remember, Powell was first and foremost a salesman. He wasn't here sowing the seeds of chaos, terror and disorder for his health — he was doing it to make money, and in order to do that, he needed to know what Oregonians wanted to hear, so that he could say it to them and cash in.

Finally, on August 1, after two months of preparations, Powell and Gifford were ready for their coming-out party. Accordingly, they started issuing invitations.

This they did, according to that evening's *Portland Evening Telegram*, with a "series of 'learn-something-to-your-advantage' telephone messages" placed to Portland Mayor George Baker, Police Chief L. V. Jenkins, district attorney Walter H. Evans, U.S. attorney Lester Humphries, and several other high-ranking city and county law-enforcement officials — as well as to newspaper reporters and photographers.

The whole event was shrouded in the kind of melodramatic cloak-and-dagger style for which the Klan had already become famous. The guests arrived at Room 376 of the Multnomah Hotel, were ushered out into waiting cars and driven to a mysterious and undisclosed "throne room" where the King Kleagle and Exalted Cyclops were waiting to receive them in their full pointy-hatty regalia.

There the visiting dignitaries (and, through the newshounds, the community at large) were introduced to the Portland Klan and reassured that the "Invisible Empire" was not a hate group — honest.

"Ours is not an anti-organization of any kind," Powell, in character as King Kleagle, said. "We are not anti-Japanese, or anti-Jew, or anti-Negro, or anti-Catholic, or anti-anything else. It is simply that the United States has not any American secret fraternal organization, and we are going to supply that need. The fact that we limit membership does not mean anything against the people we bar. They have their own organizations, membership in which is barred to us."

He went on to claim that the Klan was a powerful ally to the friends of law and order. Crime and lawlessness and moral bankruptcy were so prevalent in Portland, he said, that residents should be "afraid to let their wives and daughters appear on the streets" — so the King Kleagle had apparently learned in his two months' residency in a fancy downtown hotel.

Moral rottenness at both the city and the state level was, he added, "due for a purification process, which the Klan intends to see is accomplished."

Then the *Telegram's* reporter covering the event struck a rather ominous note:

"Respect for the law and the working of a small army of unofficial detectives who will work with the constituted authorities are the marks of the Klan character, the King Kleagle declared," the newspaper wrote. "Stories of Klan violence are largely false, [the King Kleagle] insisted. 'However,' he said, 'there are some cases of course in which we will have to take everything into our hands. Some crimes are not punishable under existing laws, but the criminals should be punished.'"

And with that naked apology for open and uncontrolled anonymous vigilantism, the new Kluxers closed the ceremony.

First, though, they posed for a photograph, which appeared in the next evening's *Telegram*, of themselves in their full Klan "eyehole suits" posing with the mayor, police chief, district attorney and other city notables.

This photo is, to understate things a bit, controversial. District Attorney

ALL *of the* ABOVE.

Members of the local Ku Klux Klan march through town during a parade in Lincoln, Maine, in the summer of 1924. Similar exhibitions were staged in many Oregon towns during this time as well. (Image: Postcard)

Evans' son later told legendary Portland historian E. Kimbark MacColl that the photo was an ambush job, that the dignitaries in the photo were arranged in front of a velvet curtain and the robed Kluxers popped out from behind the curtain just as the shutter clicked. Looking at the photograph, in which the Klan characters are in the front of the group and separated from each other, it's hard to buy this claim.

That's especially true when you consider that in 1921, the Klan wasn't considered all that much more sinister than any other secret society in Oregon, like the Masons or the Knights of Columbus. Why wouldn't the city officials be willing to be in the photograph? They didn't consider it much different from posing with a group of Shriners in their fezzes.

Within three or four years, that would have changed utterly — and membership in the Klan, or association with it, would be a substantial political liability.

But before every truly hard fall, there has to be a high rise. In the case of the Klan, that rise was almost as swift and sudden as the fall would be.

II. Kluxers on the make.

Within just a few months of Powell's Portland press conference and "photo op," the "invisible empire" had spread through Oregon society like a virus. Tens of thousands of Oregonians had paid their $10 membership fee and had expensive white regalia suits hanging in their closets, and tens of thousands more looked upon the secret society as a positive thing.

Powell, of course, did a yeoman's job of working this system. By election season in 1922, the process had completed itself and the Oregon market was saturated; the state was shot through from one side to the other with Klansmen. These local Klan groups immediately got busy packing school boards, city councils and county commissions with friendly faces.

In Salem, the Klan found a ready ally in the fortuitously named legislator Kaspar K. Kubli, who soon became a member. Because Republicans at the time dominated the state government, the Klan got involved at the party level in a campaign to "purify" its ranks. It got control of the Multnomah County Republican Party, and probably several others as well. Roman Catholic and Jewish officeholders — as well as those the Klan thought just weren't friendly enough to its aims — quickly found themselves being "primaried" by Klan-backed candidates.

The state's Republican governor, Ben Olcott, was an outspoken and intransigent opponent of the Klan. He knew the stand he was taking would probably cost him the election, but he also knew that letting a secret society of anonymous xenophobic vigilantes take over state government would be worse than losing the election, and he refused to give the state anything less than his full effort to stop it.

Finally, primary election day came, and the votes were cast.

The Republican primary was a massive dogpile of victories for the Klan. There were just two high-profile losses: Olcott had fought off his challenger, and so had Congressman Clifton Nesmith McArthur — yes, THAT Nesmith; he was the legendary pioneer's grandson. McArthur was a four-term U.S. Congressman whom the Klan had targeted for being too independent.

No problem: the Klan simply shifted its endorsement to the Democratic party's candidates in the fall, when the general election was held.

The Klan would get both Olcott and McArthur defeated in that election, replaced with men who were either Klansmen or at least friendly to the Klan's agenda. It would also get a law passed that more or less outlawed private schools in Oregon, in a direct attack on the Catholic church. And it would take over the Multnomah County Board of Commissioners. It was very nearly a clean sweep. Every race the Klan had taken an interest in had swung their way.

"There is something new under the sun," wrote Waldo Roberts of the magazine *Outlook*, at about this time. "Oregon, politically the most conservative and temperamentally the least romantic state west of the Rocky Mountains, is now under the control of the Ku Klux Klan."

But not for long.

III. KLUXERS ON THE TAKE.

After the 1922 midterm elections, the Ku Klux Klan in Oregon was riding high. It had won almost every election it had deigned to compete for. To the Klan's organizers, it looked like they'd been handed a solid mandate to remake Oregon in the image of their ethnocentric social agenda, and they lost no time in getting right to work.

There was a problem, though. Looking back now, we can plainly see that there was one key element that Oregonians found appealing about the Klan's vision and its leaders — and it wasn't what those leaders assumed it was.

That element was Klan's focus on "moral uplift." This group considered itself to be a secret quasi-vigilante society for promotion of American Protestantism, and American Protestantism had rather a lot to say about lying, cheating, stealing and tomcatting. Consequently the Klan, in public statements almost from the start, focused heavily on the corruption of government and the bad elements in society, and held itself up as an alternative to that

The 1915 movie "Birth of a Nation" sparked a Ku Klux Klan resurgence and introduced the practice of cross burnings and the pointy-topped outfits with red-cross emblems that would characterize the 1920s Klan in Oregon.

corruption and de- bauchery. In a country that had just been shaken by President Warren Harding's Teapot Dome oil scandal, that message really resonated.

As the non-Klan-related public saw it, that was the nature of the mandate they had delivered to Klan-backed politicians — to replace the corrupt Tammany Hall-type politics with a new politics of personal virtue.

And the trouble with that was, that's not what the Klan thought its mandate was at all. In their view, the victory they'd been handed demonstrated that Oregonians wanted Oregon ethnically, religiously and politically cleansed. So under the leadership of House Speaker Kaspar K. Kubli, they got right on that as soon as the session started, bright and early in 1923.

They started off in the state legislature by focusing their fire on Oregon's Catholic minority, starting with an ordinance against wearing religious outfits in public-school classrooms. This meant nuns, who at the time often served as schoolteachers in public as well as private schools, could no longer wear habits and veils. This law passed unanimously in the House and with only two dissenting votes in the Senate. (Doubtless the Klan organizers carefully noted who those two dissenters were and started making plans to "purify" them at the next election.)

Next came an initiative petition presented to the voters that would mandate compulsory public school for all Oregon children. This was a gun aimed directly at the Catholic Church, which of course had a well-developed network of parochial schools around the state. By a narrow margin, this passed, and for a while it looked like the Catholic Church was going to be out of the education business in Oregon.

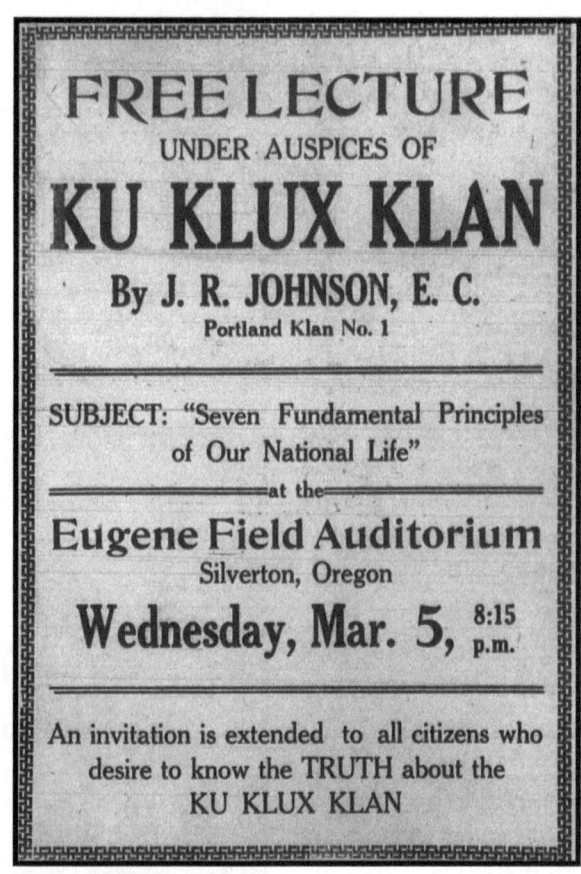

This modest display ad ran in the Silverton Appeal the week before a big Klan recruiting meeting there. Ironically, the border around this ad is made of swastikas — of course, the Nazis were still a decade away from taking power, but it's an interesting coincidence. (Image: UO Libraries)

A few other of K.K. Kubli's plans didn't fare so well. A scheme to eliminate Columbus Day from Oregon's holiday calendar (a symbolic slap at the Knights of Columbus) failed, as did a blatantly unconstitutional plan to ban sacramental wine and to start taxing Catholic church property (but not that of Protestant churches).

Still, enough legislative action did stick to keep Kubli & Co. upbeat and feeling like winners as they moved on to their next target: Japanese and Japanese-American residents.

At the time, Oregon's population of about 800,000 included roughly 5,000 Japanese people, fewer than 200 of whom owned land totaling less than 3,000 acres. In other words, Japanese nationals were about 0.6 percent of the population, controlling 0.008 percent of the land.

Never mind that, Kubli said. The Japanese were acquiring too much land, and they were "cheating" — protecting their property by having their American-born children (who were, of course, American citizens) hold the title to the land. Outrageous!

He quoted a fellow scaremonger who had estimated, apparently on the basis of absolutely nothing, that by 1950 population levels of Japanese and Japanese-American people in California would reach 50 percent.

"Why postpone action?" Kubli demanded.

Why indeed? And so the Alien Land Bill of 1923 — which banned Japanese nationals from owning land, although it couldn't touch their citizen children — rocketed through the Legislature. It passed unanimously in the Senate and was resisted by just one member of the House. It was soon followed by a bill prohibiting foreigners from operating hospitality businesses — apparently on the theory that if Japanese people couldn't run boardinghouses and hotels, it would be harder for them to find a place to stay, and they'd be more likely to leave.

And the cherry on the sundae was a literacy test to be applied to all Oregon citizens, Japanese-American and otherwise, which they would have to pass in order to claim their "right" to vote in the state.

But while the Klan-backed pols were joyfully enacting their agenda of ethnic chauvinism, it was becoming increasingly clear to large numbers of Oregonians that their talk of moral uplift didn't mean much. They were, if anything, even more corrupt than the politicians they'd replaced. Which made a certain amount of sense; after all, they were part of an anonymous secret society that considered itself at least partly above the law. It's hard to envision a more corruption-friendly environment than that.

They were also getting increasingly strident in the hotel-ballroom road shows that functioned as the Klan's primary recruiting tool — strident and, increasingly, tone-deaf. Most likely this was because the market had become so saturated that sales were getting hard to make; by 1924 or so, everyone who thought they might want to join up had had two years to think about it. The days of packing a bunch of curious locals into a hotel ballroom and signing three-quarters of them up on the spot were long gone, and the Kleagles — who were, remember, working on commission — had started getting a little desperate.

In Silverton, on March 5, 1924, J.R. Johnson, pastor of Portland's Sellwood Christian Church and "exalted cyclops" of the Klan, thundered passionately against the Roman Catholic church and its practices ... possibly unaware that the overwhelmingly Catholic town of Mt. Angel was just four miles away. There was some rivalry between the two towns, and there were some Silverton residents who agreed with Johnson that the Church was "the most dangerous power to the U.S. today," but to judge from the cautious tone of coverage in the next edition of the *Silverton Appeal-Tribune*, it's probably safe to guess Johnson didn't exactly have the town eating out of his hand.

III. KLUXERS ON THE SKIDS.

The final blows to the Klan came in 1924, when its hand-picked candidates on the Multnomah County Board of Commissioners were caught trying to hustle a padded construction bid — padded to the tune of half a million extra dollars, the equivalent of $6.8 million today. In the ensuing hubbub, the dishonesty of the Klan commissioners was exposed, and it turned out to be breathtakingly shameless. Within just a few months the entire commission was turned out of office by an angry Portland public.

About the same time, rumors started circulating that Grand Dragon Fred Gifford was using the Klan as his own personal cash kitty. Then, late that year, the Klan's newspaper editor, Lem Dever, quit the organization. Early in 1925 he published a tell-all article in a Portland journal, confirming what most Oregonians already believed — that that those rumors were true, and some others besides.

All this evidence of corruption and hypocrisy surfaced just in time for the election season, and the Klan's influence at the state level collapsed like a bad soufflé. This was shortly followed by the eviction from power of most Klan-backed politicians at the local level as well. Men who probably had been in the Klan — most notably Portland mayor George Baker (who was somewhat famous for joining every organization that would have him as a member) and possibly even governor Walter Pierce — hastened to disclaim any affiliation; Pierce lost his bid for re-election in 1926 anyway, and Baker was trounced in his bid to win a seat in Congress.

And the following year, the compulsory school bill was ruled unconstitutional before it could go into effect.

By the early 1930s, Oregon's Ku Klux Klan had faded away, and was little more than a distant and uncomfortable dream.

As for the Knights of the Ku Klux Klan, Inc., the national organization, its glory days outlasted the local Oregon chapter's, but not by much. In April 1925, D.C. Stephenson, the leader of the Indiana Klan, kidnapped a woman named Madge Oberholtzer and savagely and repeatedly assaulted, tortured, and raped her, at the same time boasting to her that he was immune from prosecution because of his position with the Klan. "I am the law in Indiana," he laughed.

Before she died (from a staph infection; he'd bitten her several times while assaulting her, and the bites got infected) Oberholtzer signed a witness statement telling the whole story. Stephenson was convicted and given a life sentence, and people nationwide quit the Klan en masse.

By the early 1940s it had basically faded away.

Sources and works cited:
- The Growth of a City, *a book by E. Kimbark MacColl published in 1979 by Georgian Press;*
- Portland: People, Politics and Power, *a book by Jewel Lansing published in 2002 by Oregon State University Press;*
- To the Promised Land, *a book by Tom Marsh published in 2012 by Oregon State University Press;*
- *"Ku Klux Klan," an article by Eckard Toy posted July 21, 2022, on* The Oregon Encyclopedia, *oregonencyclopedia.org;*
- *Archives of* Silverton Appeal-Tribune, *1924.*

SPAY AND NEUTER YOUR NEIGHBORS.

THE BAD IDEA:
- *Allow Oregon physicians to more or less arbitrarily order patients to be forcibly sterilized.*

THE HORRIBLE PEOPLE:
- *Dr. Bethenia Owens-Adair, eugenics enthusiast.*

In 1913, the Oregon state legislature passed a eugenic-sterilization law that had been written for it by one of the state's most prominent citizens.

The law's author was Bethenia Owens-Adair, the first woman M.D. in Oregon history.

Calling Dr. Owens-Adair a Horrible Person is actually rather unfair. Like all of us, she was a product of her time; and in her time, the idea of spaying or neutering "morons, imbeciles, idiots, perverts and degenerates" to stop them from reproducing was not widely regarded as Horrible.

Today, of course, it is.

But in 1913 it was a pretty mainstream idea. And it was one of the three big social-activism projects that Dr. Owens-Adair had retired from practice eight years earlier in order to devote herself to: women's suffrage, the temperance movement — and eugenics.

She was winning all three of these battles. The previous November, Oregon voters had enacted full voting rights for women in state and local elections. Prohibition, she knew (or at least strongly suspected), would follow just as soon as all those newly enfranchised ladies could get to the polls for the 1914 election.

And the sterilization law's passage that year represented victory on that third front — eugenics.

We've touched on the eugenics movement already, when discussing Cottage Grove Leader editor W.C. Conner and his lonely campaign against OSU Professor James Dryden's "miscegenated" chickens. Essentially, eugenics is an attempt to apply the techniques of dog breeding to the enhancement of the human gene pool. One could not, of course, simply kill the less desirable specimens, the way dog breeders once did. But one could, with the right kind of legislation, spay or neuter them. And that, essentially, was the solution Dr. Owens-Adair recommended.

Her victory had been a long time coming. She'd first introduced a eugenics bill in the legislature, with the help of her state representative, in 1907. It would have required that "habitual criminals, moral degenerates and sexual perverts" — including

The title page of Dr. Bethenia Owens-Adair's 1922 book advocating for eugenic sterilization. (Image: Oregon Historical Society)

people caught engaging in "the crime against nature," a euphemism for homosexual activity — "or other gross, bestial and perverted sexual habits" — should, before being released from state institutions (prison, the insane asylum, juvenile detention, etc.) be sterilized.

The bill didn't pass in 1907. Eugenics hadn't quite come into its own as a topic of popular interest yet.

Time was on its side, though. In scientific circles, the theory of hard Darwinian gene-driven evolution was becoming dominant. And it wasn't much of a leap from "our genes control our lives" to "hey, that drunk guy in the corner of the bar must have really lousy genes, let's do something to keep him from passing them on."

That sentiment didn't have enough support in 1907. Or in 1909, when Dr. Owens-Adair reintroduced it. But in 1913, it did — enough support to override the governor's veto. (Gov. West took care to explain, though, that while he agreed with the bill's sentiment, he didn't think it provided enough protection against possible abuse.)

But that's when the irresistible force that was Bethenia Owens-Adair encountered the immovable object that was Lora C. Little.

Lora Cornelia Little was born in 1856 in Minnesota. She married an engineer in the late 1880s, and settled into the life of a rural housewife. Soon the couple had a son, Kenneth.

The turning point in her life came in 1896 when her son was vaccinated for smallpox. Over the subsequent year or so, the little tyke started getting ear infections, and finally he caught diphtheria and died.

Lora Little was crushed. And angry. Very, very angry — espe-

Lora Little as she appeared in her 40s, around the time her book was published. (Image: Oregon Historical Society)

cially as well-meaning social-hygienists, many of them physicians, started pushing for the vaccination that had, she thought, killed her son to be made mandatory for all Minneapolis schoolchildren.

Little developed a cordial and enduring hatred of the mainstream medical

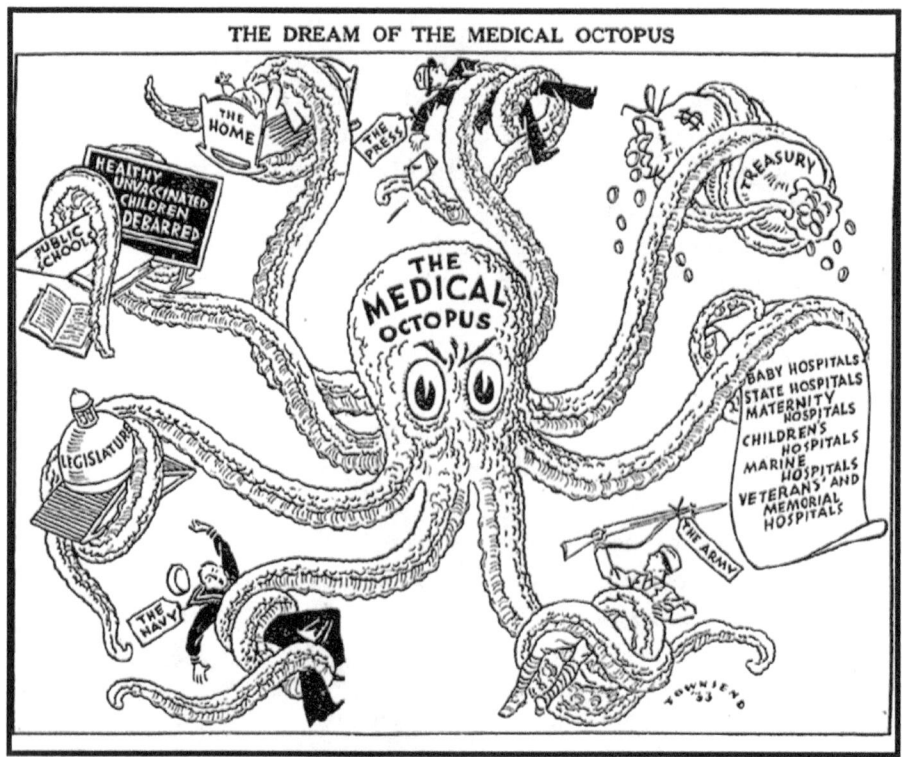

A political cartoon published by the American Medical Liberty League, Lora Little's organization, sometime in the late 1910s or early 1920s. (Image: American Medical Association)

profession, and over the subsequent decade she developed a medical philosophy of her own — one somewhat similar to that of the Battle Creek Sanitarium, or of Sylvester Graham (the inventor of the Graham Cracker). In point of fact, it wasn't too far away from the "Harmonial Brotherhood" philosophy, which you'll remember from Page 9 in this book — albeit with a less unbalanced diet and without the "free love" part.

Her theory was this: Diseases of all types were symptoms of an unbalanced life; and eating right (whole grains, lots of vegetables, very little meat) and living right (no booze or unnecessary sex, getting proper sleep, etc.) was the key to staying healthy and never getting sick. Drugs upset that balance. Vaccinations and inoculations upset that balance. Mainstream doctors (or "allopaths," as they were perjoratively called), who used those tools, were hurting people — people like little Kenneth — in their battle to establish their medical tradition as the dominant one.

In 1898 Little started publishing a magazine called "Liberator." The magazine was a big success (although it appears to have wrecked her marriage). In 1906 she built on that success to publish a book, a work in the spirit of the muckrakers titled *Crimes of the Cowpox Ring: Some Moving Pictures*

Thrown on the Dead Wall of Official Science, in which she recounted her experience in losing Kenneth. Her book, magazine, and copious letters to the editors of local newspapers made a significant contribution to anti-vaccine sentiment in Minneapolis.

And then, in 1911, she moved to Portland and settled in the Mount Scott neighborhood.

She immediately opened a health institute, the Little School of Health, and began seeing patients and teaching classes. She also began writing letters to the editor of the *Portland Morning Oregonian* — lots of letters. She started a column in the neighborhood weekly, the *Mount Scott Herald*, titled "Health in the Suburbs."

She was a force to be reckoned with in her new home. Portraits of her show a poised, confident woman in the high celluloid collar and necktie commonly worn by businessmen of the day, with steady, fearless eyes.

And it was a year or two after Little established herself in Portland that Bethenia Owens-Adair launched her successful bid to get mandatory sterilization of "undesirables" legalized.

Now, of course, eugenic sterilization was not Little's primary target. That, in memory of little Kenneth, would always be vaccination. But she saw the two issues as closely related. In both cases, mainstream physicians were asserting control over other people's bodies. And she also saw that the same spirit animated both acts — the technocratic spirit of the Progressive movement, the spirit that looked to mold and guide society in more virtuous ways by whatever means the relevant experts thought best, with scant regard for individual rights.

"A bull in a china shop is a gentle, constructive creature compared with a lot of prim and more or less pious folks when they want to clean up society and the world," she wrote in her column in the *Mount Scott Herald*. "Mr. Sudden Reformer sees something he does not like in one of his fellow citizens. Very likely it is a reprehensible thing. Plenty of evils exist in the lives and habits of all classes. This would be a thing of which Mr. Sudden Reformer is not himself guilty. Therefore he hates it with a mighty loathing. Dwelling on it, he works himself into a frenzy."

Little now worked herself into something of a frenzy as well. Reaching out to fellow "anti-allopaths" as well as civil libertarians, she joined (or possibly founded) the Anti-Sterilization League, accepted the position of vice-president, and took on the job of collecting enough signatures to refer the law to the voters in November under Oregon's then-new Initiative and Referendum system.

The *Portland Morning Oregonian*, which was a vigorous supporter of the Owens-Adair law, spluttered and fulminated against the "panicky, superstitious individuals" who were trying to block it; but this was a hard case to make in the same newspaper that had been publishing Lora Little's articulate and convincing (if frequently misguided) letters for years.

And as Governor West had pointed out, there really *were* some serious issues with the law — besides the obvious one, of course. Portland attorney C.E.S. Wood, a prominent Progressive who many doubtless thought they would find on the other side, was one of the most outspoken about the need to stop the law.

"Their chief argument was that under the proposed law the assent of only two persons was needed to authorize surgical mutilation of the most helpless members of society," historian Robert Johnson writes. "History demonstrated, the opponents asserted, that people with this kind of power tend to abuse it."

It was an argument that resonated with the public. And so, to Dr. Owens-Adair's dismay, the voters quashed the law by a substantial majority; 56 percent of them voted to throw it out.

Dr. Owens-Adair had lost the battle, but not the war. She took the criticisms of C.E.S. Wood and Oswald West to heart, and her next eugenic-sterilization bill contained more checks and balances, more processes of notification and appeal, and called for an actual state eugenics commission to provide oversight. And in 1917, it passed.

Unfortunately, by that time Lora Little was out of the picture, having left town to join the national American Medical Liberty League. In the end, perhaps she was less of a force of nature than she seemed. She left town just after the 1916 elections, in which she had thrown all her resources into a losing ballot-measure battle against her old enemy, mandatory vaccination, which she predicted would be "thrown down hard at the polls by a people who like to think they own the blood in their veins and feel it is their business what goes into it."

She had a point. But the extenuating circumstances in mandatory vaccination — herd immunity, the disruption of mass-casualty pandemics — were a lot more compelling than they were in eugenic sterilization, and her campaign fell just 374 votes short of passage.

As for Owens-Adair's sterilization act, it went into effect and over the subsequent 75 years the state of Oregon quietly sterilized more than 2,600 people — troubled youths in juvenile detention facilities, insane-asylum inmates, members of poor families selected by social workers, and penitentiary prisoners. Finally, in 1983, the state eugenics board — renamed, for public-relations reasons, the Board of Social Protection — was quietly dissolved, bringing the whole ignoble experiment to an end. And in 2002, Governor John Kitzhaber formally apologized to everyone the state had mutilated under the law.

It was bad. But had it not been for Lora Little, it likely would have been a good deal worse.

Sources and works cited:
- *"The Myth of the Harmonious City: Will Daly, Lora Little, and the Hidden Face of Progressive-Era Portland," an article by Robert D. Johnson published in the Fall 1998 issue of* Oregon Historical Quarterly;
- *" 'The Greatest Curse of the Race': Eugenic Sterilization in Oregon, 1909-1983," an article by Mark A. Largent published in the Summer 2002 issue of* Oregon Historical Quarterly;
- *"The Oregon eugenic movement : Bethenia Angelina Owens-Adair," a master's dissertation by Linda L. Currey published in 1977 and preserved in the Oregon State University Scholars' Bank.*

WORLD'S WORST TRAIN ROBBERS.

THE BAD IDEA:
- *While robbing a train, try to blast your way into a locked mail car without knowing how much dynamite to use;*
- *Murder all the witnesses when the operation goes badly.*

THE HORRIBLE PEOPLE:
- *Roy, Ray, and Hugh DeAutremont.*

Few people realize it, but modern forensic detective work — the kind showcased on the "CSI" series on television — was born in southern Oregon, back in October 1923.

Before that fateful day, there had been a few crimes solved with the help of science, including some big ones. In Portland, the evidence given by Dr. Victoria Hampton in the 1904 trial of Norman Williams for murdering his wife and mother-in-law — proving that the long silver hairs found at the crime scene were human and had been violently ripped out of the scalp before death — sent Williams to the gallows. (That story appears in Volume Two of this series, *Love, Sex and Murder in Old Oregon*.)

But stories like that were outliers. At the dawn of the twentieth century, most crimes were still solved with shoe leather and intuition (and, occasionally, with a coerced confession) — the old-fashioned way.

After 1923, though, it would be very clear to everyone that a new day had dawned in crime investigation. And the breakthroughs made in southern

Oregon that autumn would inspire, several years later, the founding of the FBI's legendary forensics division.

Of course, for forensic detective work to be pioneered, a suitably horrific crime had to be perpetrated. And on Oct. 11, 1923, one was — a crime so cold and gratuitously nasty that it shocked the whole nation.

It was a train robbery — the last big train robbery in American history, in fact. It was perpetrated by three bumbling brothers: Roy, Ray and Hugh DeAutremont, the sons of a barber in Albany.

Roy and Ray were the older brothers, and they were twins. Of the two, Roy was particularly crazy, and probably led the others in the criminal enterprise; later in his life, he was diagnosed with schizophrenia and given a lobotomy.

The brothers had been sort of trying to break into the crime business since just after the First World War, when they had been caught up in the popular backlash that had followed the "Centralia Massacre" on Armistice Day 1919. The "massacre" was a gun battle that broke out between the American Legion and members of the Industrial Workers of the World — the I.W.W., colloquially known as the "Wobblies" — after a gunman hiding in the I.W.W. hall opened fire on Legion members during a parade. The ensuing gun fight killed six people and utterly destroyed any respectability and effectiveness the "Wobblies" might have had, and was followed by a big law-enforcement dragnet operation. One of the "usual suspects" rounded up and thrown in jail during that

A Southern Pacific engine pulls out of the Oregon side of Tunnel 13, the scene of the DeAutremont Brothers' disastrous 1923 train robbery. (Image: Roger Puta | CC-by-SA)

ALL *of the* ABOVE.

Unidentified officials pose with the wreckage of the mail car blown up by the DeAutremont Brothers in a bungled attempt to rob it on Oct. 11, 1923. (Image: Smithsonian Institute)

dragnet was Ray DeAutremont — the less-crazy brother — and the experience in jail seems to have convinced him that the system was not worth saving, and that he might as well become an outlaw and grab what he could while he still could.

After his release from prison, Ray rejoined his brother and the two of them journeyed to Chicago to try to join a gang. This did not work out for them, so they returned to the Pacific Northwest, where they were joined by their younger brother, Hugh, for their second attempt to launch a career in crime — as bank robbers.

Their first and only robbery attempt was foiled by one of history's most surprising coincidences. Just as the brothers were approaching the bank they'd picked out, a car full of gangsters pulled up in front of it, and they watched in astonishment as "their" bank was robbed by someone else, right before their eyes.

So the brothers took jobs on logging crews in the woods and started biding their time, looking for other opportunities to score.

They thought they had found one in the "Number 13 Gold Special" train. Years before, when the Gold Rush was still on, the Gold Special had carried plenty of "color" over the Siskiyous and into Oregon. The California gold fields had long since petered out for commercial purposes, but the train still had the cachet; and the brothers had some reason to believe it would be carrying something particularly valuable in its mail car on Oct. 23. So they started making their plans. And on the big day, they were ready to do the job.

The heist started at the summit of the Siskiyous, as the train crossed the border into Oregon. It had to slow at the summit for a brake check just before going into a long tunnel — Tunnel 13, coincidentally enough — and when it did, Roy and Hugh jumped aboard the engine. Wasting no time, they leveled their weapons — a sawed-off shotgun for Roy and a .45 automatic for Hugh — and ordered the engineer, Sydney Bates, to stop the train right at the end of the tunnel. This was, it seems, to prevent passengers from seeing what was going on. Ironically, it was to be Bates' last day on the job; he was scheduled to start his retirement the very next day. (We'll shortly discuss the reason that was ironic. In the meantime, if you haven't figured it out, take a moment and Google "foreshadowing" and all will become clear.)

Once the train was stopped, the brothers were joined by Ray, who had been waiting at the end of the tunnel with a box of dynamite stolen from a mining operation, just in case it might be needed to open the mail car.

As it turned out, it was. The mail clerk, when he saw what was happening, barricaded himself inside the car and refused to open the door; so the brothers packed dynamite around the door and touched it off.

Unfortunately for literally everyone present, the boys had no idea what they were doing. The amount of dynamite they used completely wrecked the end of the car, filled it with smoke, and instantly killed the mail clerk, Elvyn Daugherty. And although they were now able to get in, it didn't do them much good; there was mail

This plunger-type detonator, found at the scene of the crime, was stolen from a work site for use in the robbery. (Image: Smithsonian Institute)

This front-page cartoon in the Portland Sunday Oregonian, run three days after the robbery, nicely illustrates the public's attitude toward the robbers. (Image: Oregonian)

scattered everywhere, they couldn't see through the smoke, and the fire was spreading quickly.

Plus, there was a dead body in there. The boys knew what that meant. They'd only intended to rob the train, but in the eyes of the law, they were now murderers.

Back in the train, of course, the passengers were starting to panic. The train had stopped suddenly while they were still in the tunnel; then a huge explosion had rocked the car and probably broken out some windows, and the tunnel had started to fill with smoke and fumes. They were trapped in the tunnel like rats.

One of the train's brakemen, C. Coyle Johnson, started fighting his way through the smoke and flames to the front, trying to find out what was wrong. Unfortunately for him, he made it. Emerging from the fiery tunnel

mouth, he startled the robbers, who wheeled and opened fire on him. Down he went, dead.

Double murderers.

At this point, the brothers apparently switched their plan from "salvage something from this mess" to "escape at all costs." They ordered engineer Bates and fireman Marvin Seng to uncouple the engine from the mail car, apparently planning to have the engine take them down the mountain away from the scene of the crime; but the explosion had damaged the couplers, so it could not be done.

So the brothers simply gunned the two survivors down in cold blood. Sydney Bates and Marvin Seng were simply shot in the head as they stood there with their arms in the air, because the brothers wanted no witnesses left on the scene.

And then they ran, dragging creosote-soaked sacks behind them to fool the bloodhounds.

The brothers hid out in a cabin in the woods for about a week and a half, waiting for things to settle down a bit. While they were hiding out there, they noticed an unusual amount of activity in the air. In 1923, very few airplanes were actually in operation, but it suddenly seemed like every plane on the West Coast was flying low over the Siskiyous.

But they didn't figure out what those planes were doing until Roy hopped a freight train to Ashland to pick up some supplies. Sitting in a diner with

One of the millions of "wanted" posters printed and sent out all over the country during the four years in which the DeAutremont Brothers were on the lam. (Image: Smithsonian Institution)

a cup of coffee and a newspaper, he looked down and saw a photograph of himself and his brothers there, staring back at him from the front page.

The manhunt was on. It had been on since a few days after the robbery, when authorities had turned to a university professor for help in figuring out who the robbers had been. And it was in the course of that manhunt that the modern science of forensic detective work was born.

II. THE MANHUNT.

University of California Professor Edward O. Heinrich had helped the Southern Pacific out with a few minor robbery investigations before. Now, in late autumn of 1923, SP had a big one on its hands. Four of its employees had been murdered, at least two of them in cold blood, in a train robbery gone bad at the mouth of Tunnel 13.

Posses had formed and were busily combing the countryside, bolstered by Oregon National Guard soldiers and law-enforcement officers from all around. On clear days, aviators flew airplanes low over the mountains in grid patterns looking for signs of the robbers, possibly the first time in history that a manhunt was conducted from the air.

After a week or so of this, authorities had assembled an impressive collection of physical evidence. But they had not even glimpsed the fugitives, and they'd made no progress even in figuring out who the murderers were.

That would change after they brought the 42-year-old Dr. Heinrich into the case.

The railroad and the police laid out all the evidence, like a client briefing Sherlock Holmes: Left behind at the scene, and scattered at various campsites found in the manhunt, had been a discarded .45 automatic with the serial numbers filed off; a pair of Pay Day brand bib overalls; a scorched jacket; and an assortment of other stuff — a plunger-type detonator, some blasting caps, a union suit, camp garbage, and so forth.

From the bib overalls, Heinrich learned much. In fact, they pretty muich sewed the case up for him. The pockets on the left showed more wear than on the right, and there was pitch on the right, as would be the case if a left-handed lumberjack was leaning against a tree to swing his ax. From some neatly trimmed fingernail clippings found in the pocket, he gathered that when in city clothes, the wearer was a meticulous dresser with small hands. And from some hairs found here and there, he learned that his man had brown hair and eyebrows.

But the real big score was wadded up in the bottom of the narrow pencil pocket of the overalls, which no one else had probed. It was a receipt for registered mail. And it led him directly to a name: Roy DeAutremont.

With that in hand, Heinrich was able to secure a sample of Roy's handwriting — and that's when the DeAutremont Brothers' doom was truly sealed. Because Heinrich was able to restore the serial number on the automatic and trace it back to its initial purchaser, who had signed his name "William Elliot" — in Roy's handwriting.

From there, it was as good as all over. Had they merely robbed a train, the brothers could probably have managed to disappear somewhere; but they had murdered four men — two of them in cold blood — and the entire country was outraged by their crime. The manhunt now went nationwide and even international. "WANTED" posters were printed and distributed everywhere, prominently displaying the DeAutremonts' faces; more than two million of them would be printed and distributed over the following several years while the lads were on the lam. There was nowhere the brothers could go where their faces would not be recognized.

Roy and Ray fled to Detroit, Michigan, and tried to change their hair color and personal appearance as best they could. Hugh joined the Army and was deployed to the Philippines. But all around them, pictures of themselves were staring out from those ubiquitous posters on the walls of post offices and police stations.

Eventually, one of Hugh's fellow soldiers from Manila was reassigned to Alcatraz and saw one of those posters, and the jig was up. The brothers were all arrested and extradited to Jackson County.

ALL *of the* ABOVE.

This photo spread ran in the Portland Sunday Oregonian three days after the robbery, on Oct. 14, 1923. TOP: A posse of citizens gathers at the entrance of Tunnel 13, where the robbery happened, preparatory to going forth to search. LEFT: The ruins of the mail car. RIGHT: A bundle of property left by the robbers at the scene, including shoes soaked in creosote to fool any bloodhounds. (Image: OSU Libraries)

Ironically enough, their time spent on the lam probably saved their lives. Had they been caught within a year or two of their crime, the wrath of the public would have demanded their blood. They would have been hanged for sure.

Instead, their trial and sentencing didn't take place until 1927 — four years after their crime. Time, they say, heals all wounds; and that may not be entirely true, but it certainly helps. Even as things stood, the courts came under severe criticism from newspapers and members of the public for not meting out the death penalty to the robbers.

In any case, the brothers' lives were spared, and they were sentenced to life in prison.

Hugh was paroled in 1958, but diagnosed with stomach cancer a few months later; he died the following year.

Roy was diagnosed with schizophrenia in 1949, and the prescribed cure — lobotomy — left him unable to care for himself. He died in a nursing home in Salem in 1983.

Ray was paroled in 1961 and moved to Eugene, where he worked for some years as a janitor in the Erb Memorial Union at the University of Oregon. He died in Eugene in 1984.

Now, most accounts of the DeAutremont robbery, over the years, have been drawn almost entirely from police statements and newspaper articles. But several years ago, Edgard Espinoza and Pepper Trail, two forensic scientists from the National Fish and Wildlife forensic lab in Ashland, decided to dig a little deeper into the records. They found some very interesting details.

For one thing, they found that the timeline of the robbery placed the robbers at the scene, with everyone dead and the mail car torn open and burning, for a whole hour. What would they have been doing during that time? Could they have found something in there after all? Or was this merely a flaw in the record-keeping? (Remember, the train, still behind them in the tunnel, was full of passengers, and on the face of it it seems unlikely that the brothers would risk such a delay.)

The more intriguing discovery, though, is a description of a small, dark-featured man who, three hours after the robbery, knocked at the door of a remote camping cabin in the woods nearby. He asked the man who was staying in the cabin if he could retrieve some property he'd stashed in the loft — walnuts, he said, left there to dry and forgotten when he'd camped there several months before. The man had retrieved an oblong object wrapped tightly in a mackinaw coat, which did not look at all like walnuts, and left.

The mackinaw, or one like it, was found a few months after that in a nearby creek bed within a few hundred feet of Highway 99, near a spot where a pick and shovel had been stashed. It had knife cuts in it, as if whoever was wearing it had been stabbed in the back with a sharp knife. And there was no sign of the oblong object.

So: did the DeAutremont brothers have an accomplice? Did they actually recover something from the hold-up? (Southern Pacific always refused to disclose what was in the mail car that day, if anything.) Was there a double-cross, and a fifth murder done, and a secret kept by all three brothers and taken with them to their graves?

Or is there some other explanation — perhaps the mackinaw and shovel were evidence of some other crime? Or maybe there's a completely innocent explanation?

It's almost certain that we'll never really know.

Sources and works cited:
- *"The Siskiyou Train Robbery," an article by Lawrence E.C. Joers published in* Great Moments in Oregon History, *an anthology published in 1987 by New Oregon Publishers;*
- *"Tunnel 13: How Forensic Science Helped Solve America's Last Great Train Robbery," an article by Pepper Trail and Edgard Espinoza published on the Jefferson Public Radio Website, ijpr.org, on Dec. 31, 2013.*

MONUMENT TO A MASS MURDERER.

THE BAD IDEA:
- Build a monument honoring your county's earliest pioneers, and include on it the name of the leader of a gang that gunned down more than 30 men in cold blood.

THE HORRIBLE PEOPLE:
- Bruce "Blue" Evans, horse thief and mass murderer.

Wallowa County covers the northeast corner of Oregon — a gorgeous area of rugged, remote mountain lakes, the homeland of the legendary Chief Joseph.

It's also the only county in the state whose courthouse grounds includes a monument dedicated to a known mass murderer.

That sounds worse than it actually is. There are, in fact, about 200 names on the monument, which is an archway built in 1936 through which visitors walk to approach the courthouse steps.

The archway is labeled "Wallowa County Pioneers," and the brass plaques on the inside of the arch list them by date of arrival — 1871 to 1879. And, murderer or no, Bruce "Blue" Evans did in fact settle in Wallowa County in 1879. They couldn't have just left his name off the list just because he was a notorious horse thief who'd escaped from police custody at gunpoint and led a gang that ambushed and coldly massacred more than 30 innocent people, now, could they?

Looking back on it today, it's hard to imagine why they didn't — if nothing else, they could have lopped the entire year of 1879 off the list.

But in 1936 when this plaque was commissioned, it's a good bet the people working on it didn't even know about the massacre — or if they did, thought it was a nasty rumor. Wallowa County had tried hard to forget. Records from the investigation of the incident and the court case that resulted from it had been tucked away in unlikely places to keep them from being found. People who knew about it kept their mouths shut. There was a deep sense of secret shame about the whole thing — at least in part because some of the Horrible People involved were scions of some of the county's most respected families.

Those other murderers were J. Titus Canfield, Omar LaRue, Hezekiah "Carl" Hughes, Hiram Maynard, Frank Vaughn and Robert McMillan. Evans was, beyond question, their leader, and many Wallowa County residents thought of him as having led the others astray.

One of the two bronze plaques in the pioneer archway monument, on the grounds of the Wallowa County Courthouse, which honors the first 199 settlers in the county — including mass murderer and horse thief Bruce "Blue" Evans. Evans' name (B.E. Evans) is the sixth name under the "1879" heading, in the third column. (Image: F.J.D. John)

The killings happened in the last days of May 1887, when Evans and the other gang members were moving some stolen horses around on the Oregon side of the Snake River, near Deep Creek. The area is remote and inaccessible even by Wallowa County standards, and it made a great place for a bunch of horse thieves on the run from the law to hide out.

ALL *of the* ABOVE.

The archway monument leading up to the Wallowa County Courthouse, built in 1936. The bronze plaque on the inside left of the arch includes the name of murderer and horse thief Bruce "Blue" Evans. (Image: F.J.D. John)

And they were indeed on the run; authorities had tried to serve Evans with papers a few days earlier. Trouble was coming for them, and they knew it.

Deep Creek runs into the Snake River at a spot with high rimrock all around and no cover of any kind. On this particular day, Evans and his gang came up on the rimrock and looked over the edge at the river below. They saw a group of Chinese gold miners down in the creek below, working through a gravel bar with gold pans, looking for — and apparently finding — "flour gold."

A few minutes after Evans and his gang met them, these innocent strangers were dead — and the gang had graduated from rustling to cold-blooded murder.

Stories conflict over why Evans and his gang did it. One account says they asked the miners to lend them a boat to ferry their stolen horses across into Idaho and, when turned down, became enraged; another says that, knowing the miners had been there a while, they figured they'd have lots of gold, which would be useful since they were now fugitives from justice. Greg Nokes, in his book *Massacred for Gold*, makes the case that simple racist hatred was a major factor, and he is probably right.

Whatever the motivation, the gang members coldly started shooting the terrified miners from the rimrock with high-powered rifles, taking their shots carefully and simply exterminating these inoffensive strangers as if they were prairie dogs, one by one, until they were out of bullets and only one was left — and they chased him down and clubbed him to death.

A close-up of mass murderer Bruce Evans' name on the courthouse monument (third name from the bottom). (Image: F.J.D. John)

The number of miners involved is unclear as well. Most sources agree there were ten in the first group. Most sources also say there were other Chinese miners in the area, and the gang found and massacred them in the same fashion. The total death toll was most likely 31 or 34. Of all of the murdered men, the names of only ten are known.

Of the seven gang members, one stayed at the remote cabin they were camping in — probably McMillan, who was just 15 at the time. One source quoted in Nokes' book says there was also a young orphan boy with them who, after the shooting started, took off running and was tracked down and killed by Evans to keep him from squealing.

Eventually, Vaughn turned state's evidence, and gave a confession. Evans, Canfield and LaRue fled the state before trial; the other three were arrested and given a speedy but friendly trial. After apparently blaming the missing three for the whole thing, they were acquitted.

Vaughn's confession has disappeared. The court records for the entire day in which the case was heard are likewise missing — the only blank page in the entire court journal. What documents there are were tucked away in unlikely places — the county planning records department, a dusty unused office safe — and forgotten.

Of the three fugitives, very little further is known. Canfield ended up changing his name to Charles and opening a blacksmith shop in southern Idaho — most likely with the proceeds of the massacre.

None of the men were ever arrested, charged or even really sought after. They had perpetrated the worst massacre of Chinese people in U.S. history, and gotten away with it.

But in spite of this startling lack of judicial action, it would be a mistake to suggest that the people of Wallowa County didn't think killing those Chinese people was that big a deal. The extraordinary attempts to cover the crime up and pretend it never happened testify to that.

Even today, the shame of what those seven men and boys did still haunts their families, their community — and, yes, their state.

There's one final thing that ought to be mentioned about this massacre before we move on to our next case of Applied Horribility (which will be considerably less "heavy" than this one, by the way): Of the thirty-some Chinese miners Evans' gang shot down from the rimrock, at least one was armed with a smallbore pistol, a revolver, with which he returned fire as best he could. Of course, the murderers were using high-powered rifles, so they were well out of effective pistol range. Even so, somewhat miraculously (if that's the right word) one of the bullets actually hit one of the murderers, Frank Vaughan, in the leg. He walked with a limp for the rest of his life.

Sources and works cited:
- Massacred for Gold: The Chinese in Hells Canyon, *a book by R. Gregory Nokes published in 2009 by Oregon State University Press;*
- *"Ambushed: The Hells Canyon Massacre of 1887," an article by Michael Nove published in the November 2007 issue of the* Oregon State Bar Bulletin;
- *"Massacred Chinese Gold Miners to Receive Memorial Along Snake River," an article published in the* Portland Oregonian *on Nov. 26, 2011.*

IF AT FIRST YOU DON'T SECEDE...

THE BAD IDEA:
- *Get Oregon and California to secede from the Union so that rich citizens can legally own slaves;*
- *Plan to stock the new "nation" with slaves by swindling foreigners into visiting it and enslaving them upon arrival.*

THE HORRIBLE PEOPLE:
- *Joseph Lane, U.S. Senator and candidate for Vice-President of the United States.*

(Note: This article quotes sources who use archaic terms for Black, Asian, and American Indian people which have become offensive in modern speech.)

I. The secession plot.

Sometime around early 1860, as the United States of America teetered on the brink of what would become the Civil War, a small group of legislators from Oregon and California came together secretly to make plans.

They were all Southern Democrats, members of the pro-slavery wing of the Democratic Party. In the previous year or two, they'd broken with the moderate Democrats so sharply that the two sides were barely on speaking terms. Indeed, later that year one of their number — Oregon Senator Joseph Lane — would be joining John Breckenridge to form a third-party ticket for the 1860 Presidential election, and would be the beneficiary of a plot to circumvent the Presidential election and seize power. (More on that in a minute.)

Everyone understood that the third-party Breckenridge-Lane ticket would split the Democratic vote, so it seemed at least a good possibility that the winner of the election would be an anti-slavery Republican — probably Abraham Lincoln.

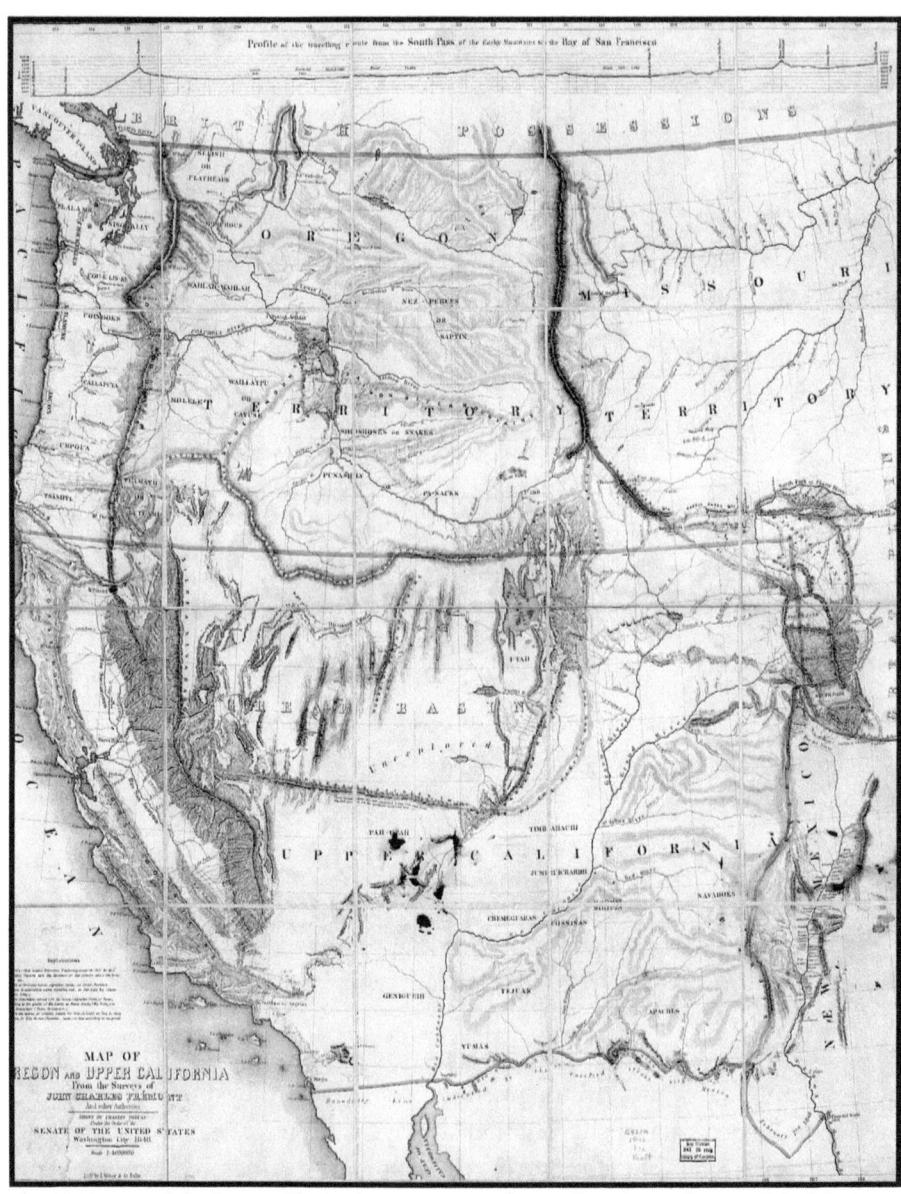

An 1848 map of the Oregon Territory, as it appeared just after the conclusion of the Mexican-American War that same year. The vaguely imagined Pacific Republic likely would have had its border along the Continental Divide atop the Rocky Mountains. (Image: sonofthesouth.net)

ALL *of the* ABOVE.

The conspirators all knew what would probably happen if Lincoln won that election.

Senator William Gwin and Governor-Elect Milton Latham of California had an idea that they wanted to propose. The idea was that when the South seceded, so would the West. The country west of the Rockies would declare itself as an independent nation, calling itself "Pacific Republic."

"The Pacific Republic was to be an aristocracy after the model of the ancient republic of Venice, all power being vested in a hereditary nobility, the chief executive being elected on a very limited suffrage," historian Dorothy Hull writes.

Joseph Lane as he appeared when he served as the Oregon Territory's delegate in Congress in the 1850s. Lane later served as Territorial Governor and as one of Oregon's first U.S. Senators. (Image: Library of Congress)

There was, alas, a subtle problem with the scheme: Very few Californians, Oregonians and residents of the Washington Territory had slaves. And you can't found a pro-slavery nation when your population of slaves is numbered in the dozens. So, Hull writes, to properly outfit the new land with the "livestock" it would need, the conspirators envisioned an international swindle of breathtaking audacity and moral repulsiveness:

"Slaves," Hull continues, "were to be procured by inviting coolies, South Sea islanders and negroes to immigrate to California, and then reducing them to slavery."

Although this proposal was by far the most audacious suggestion of West Coast independence, it wasn't a new idea. The first stirrings of a secessionist movement came twelve years earlier, in 1848.

1848 was the year the federal government finally granted Oregon territorial status, after a two-year delay while Congresscritters duked it out over whether slavery should be legal there or not. During this time, the federal government was in the hands of the Democrats, and most Oregonians were Democrats too.

Then came the elections of late 1848, in which the Whig party was voted into power behind Millard Fillmore. As was the custom of the time following an election, the Whigs immediately gave all the appointed Democratic office-holders their walking papers, and started replacing them with their friends and political cronies from the Whig party. And because these decisions were being made back east, the replacement civil servants were almost all newcomers from the Eastern Seaboard.

These officials soon found themselves up against Oregon's new but powerful Democratic Party machine, headed up by the charismatic and pugnacious editor of the *Oregon Statesman*, Asahel Bush. Tensions mounted to unbearable and business-halting levels. Something, everyone knew, had to be done.

By 1851, things were so intolerable that Democrats were whispering of secession. Whig newspaper *The Weekly Oregonian* openly accused the Democrats of "design(ing) at no distant day to throw off their allegiance to the United States Government and attempt to set up an independent republic."

But then, in 1852, Democrat Franklin Pierce won the national election; the Whig office-holders were sent packing; and Asahel Bush and his cronies simmered down and got back to work.

Eight years later, though, Bush was on the other side of this fight. The state Democratic Party he autocratically led was resolutely moderate by the standards of the day, and the relations between his "Salem clique" and Joseph Lane's pro-slavery Southern Democrats was getting worse by the day.

So when he got wind of the plot to secede, this time Bush was having none of it.

"What a ridiculous figure would the Pacific Republic cut among the nations," he jeered. "With a population of little more than half a million .... With Mexico upon one side, British Columbia on the other, a defenseless sea-coast in front, and a horde of hostile savages and marauding Mormons in the rear, and unable to protect ourselves on any side, we could only preserve our existence by forming an alliance with some powerful government which could afford us protection at the price of our liberty."

Bush's views were widely shared. Once the cat was out of the bag, word of the plot went through Salem and Portland like chain lightning, and the reaction was almost universally negative. It irreparably damaged Joseph

Oregon Senator Joseph Lane posing for a formal portrait, circa 1860. (Image: Library of Congress)

Lane's reputation and ended his career in Oregon politics. And it galvanized Asahel Bush's moderate Democrats into making an informal coalition with the new state Republicans to form a sort of fusion ticket for the state's senators, with the sole object of locking Lane and his Southern Democrats out of power.

(As a side note, the Republicans were mostly in Portland and Bush's

Democrats were mostly in Salem — and the Southern Democrats were scattered throughout the hinterlands. This may have been the first outbreak of that urban-rural divide that's still a part of Oregon politics today.)

The fusion ticket did plenty of wrangling, but they needed each other to get the job done, so finally they did, sending Democrat James Nesmith and Republican Ned Baker to the Senate to replace Joseph Lane and Delazon Smith. It was a sign of how low Lane's star had sunk that he wasn't even able to carry his home state for the Breckenridge-Lane Presidential ticket that year. Oregon went for Lincoln, and to add insult to the Southern Democrats' injury, changed its unofficial motto from "Alis Volat Propriis" ("Flies with Own Wings") to "The Union."

(And, by the way, if you've ever wondered how Oregon got stuck with such a boring state motto as "The Union," well — now you know. The motto wouldn't become official, though, until 1957, in preparation for the 1959 state centennial.)

In California, the Pacific Republic scheme still had legs well into 1862. But in Oregon, nobody in high office ever seriously considered West Coast independence again.

As for Joseph Lane, his career as an Oregon politician was over. But he did have one more part to play in national politics: He was the Southern Democratic Party's nominee for Vice-President of the United States.

As such, he was in the right place at the right time to play the central part in a plot that would have subverted the 1860 Presidential election and installed him, Joseph Lane of Oregon, as President of the United States.

Let's talk about that plot now.

II. The presidential plot.

The game of historical "what-if" is always tempting to play, but in most cases, it doesn't have much of a place in real history studies. It's like seeing a car driving south on Highway 99 and trying to guess where it's headed.

Sometimes it's useful, though — especially in cases where something terrible was avoided by the thinnest of margins.

Case in point: the almost-successful move in 1860 to prevent Abraham Lincoln from becoming President of the United States — and replace him with Oregon Senator Joseph Lane.

Here's how it (almost) happened:

The runup to the Presidential election in 1860 was unusually chaotic and messy; after all, the country was on the brink of civil war. The Republicans

ALL *of the* ABOVE.

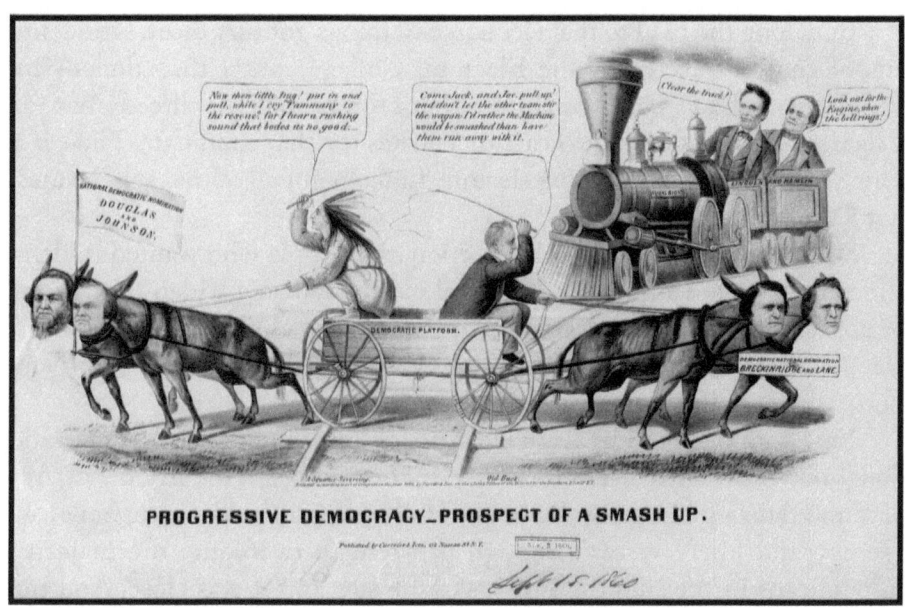

A Currier and Ives political cartoon from 1860 illustrating the expected effect of the splitting of the Democratic ticket between Stephen Douglas and John Breckenridge. Oregon Senator Joseph Lane's face is attached to the mule on the far right. (Image: Library of Congress)

nominated the relatively moderate Abraham Lincoln with no more than the usual *sturm und drang*; it was on the other side of the aisle that the real drama was happening. Democrats were deeply split over the slavery issue.

After some tussles, the Dems nominated Stephen Douglas, a moderate (by the lights of his time) whose Kansas-Nebraska Act had inspired the founding of the Republican Party by allowing new states to choose for themselves whether they wanted legal slavery or not.

But for some of the delegates, Douglas wasn't extreme enough on the slavery question. They didn't want a slavery-neutral candidate, they wanted an outright pro-slavery one, and they wanted one badly enough that they walked out of the nominating convention after it became clear that Douglas would win, and formed their own party — the Constitutional Democrats, also known as the Southern Democrats. Then they nominated their own ticket for the Big House: John Breckenridge of Kentucky for President, and Joseph Lane of Our Fair State for Vice-.

So far, so uneventful, from a Constitutional standpoint. As would happen to the Republicans 50 years later with Teddy Roosevelt's Bull Moose Party, the majority Democrats could only look on in impotent rage as their split ticket lumbered toward inevitable defeat. The final tally, when it finally came, was just about what everyone expected: 1.8 million votes for Lincoln, 1.4 million for Douglas — and 850,000 for Breckenridge-Lane.

But along the road to that election day, things got very dicey. Presidents are, of course, selected by the Electoral College, rather than directly by popular vote. Each state's voters voted not for a candidate directly, but for a slate of electors pledged to cast their votes for that candidate. Thus, if a state voted 49-51 for Lincoln's electors, Lincoln got all of that state's votes, not 51 percent of them.

So a month or so before the election, the people who wanted to deny Lincoln victory at any cost started looking for states in which they might be able to move that needle back across the 50-percent line in a big enough way to change the election's outcome. Very quickly they settled on New York.

New York was a solidly Republican doughnut with a massive Democratic doughnut-hole called "New York City" in the middle. In the city, the masses of immigrants mobilized by Tammany Hall were stridently if cacophonously Democrats. There weren't enough of them to overcome the majority Republicans in the suburbs and towns upstate; but it was close. And the state of New York swung a very big stick — the biggest in the country at 35 Electoral College votes.

Could the Democrats but swing that one state from red to blue, the Electoral College would, they hoped, be in deadlock. No president can be elected by the Electoral College without a clear majority; a plurality is not good enough. And without New York, Lincoln probably wouldn't have a clear majority. He'd have a plurality — more votes than Douglas or Breckenridge — but not enough to reach 50 percent.

So, what would happen then? According to the process laid out in the Constitution, the whole selection process would be kicked over into the U.S. House of Representatives, which would be asked to pick one of the top three Presidential candidates, ranked by Electoral College votes — in this case that would be Douglas, Breckenridge, or Lincoln.

Again, though, an actual majority would be required; a plurality would not suffice. If the House couldn't arrive at a clear majority, it would go to the Senate, which would choose between the top two vote-getting *Vice-*Presidential nominees.

Either one of those outcomes would mean the end of Lincoln's hopes. He had a plurality of support in the House — more than either Douglas or Breckenridge — but he didn't have the magical "50 percent plus one" that he needed to get a clear majority, and he wasn't going to be able to get it by any means. And in the Senate, Lincoln backers were a minority.

So in late September, Lincoln's enemies in New York hatched an eleventh-hour scheme they called "fusion." The Fusion ticket would strategically split the electoral-college votes of the state among the three non-Lincoln

ALL *of the* ABOVE.

A campaign flyer for the Breckenridge-Lane presidential ticket, showing John Breckenridge on the left and Oregon's Joseph Lane on the right. (Image: Library of Congress)

candidates with the express purpose of denying all candidates a majority. That would mean the House would be called upon to choose among Lincoln, Breckenridge and (they thought) Douglas. (As it turned out, although he was the clear runner-up in popular polling, Douglas got only 12 votes in the Electoral College, so he would have been out.)

In the House, the Republicans didn't have a majority, so they wouldn't be able to elect Lincoln without help from Dems, none of whom would give it. It was also possible that some Republicans, seeing the writing on the wall, would throw their support behind one of the Democrats. But the smart money, in both parties, was on the House being unable to pick a candidate, and having the ball kicked over to the Senate.

And the Senate, under the procedure laid out in the Twelfth Amendment, would have to pick between Hannibal Hamlin, who was Lincoln's running mate — and Joseph Lane, who was Breckenridge's.

Everyone knew Hamlin would not win that match-up. Joseph Lane of Oregon would, by default, win the pony.

So, how did it go? Well, of course, it didn't work. New York City voted for the Fusion ticket overwhelmingly, but the rest of the state voted for Lincoln almost to a man (this was, of course, before women's suffrage). The defeat was narrow but decisive.

The question is, had the parties come together just two weeks earlier, would they have had time to rally enough additional support to make it happen? Quite possibly, yes. And that almost inevitably would have put Joseph Lane — the Oregon man who may have been America's last actual slave owner — in the White House.

And what would have happened then?

Historian Si Sheppard makes a good case for the possibility that the North would have seceded from the Union, rather than the South. Even if the South let the North go, bitter strife would have broken out in states like Illinois, whose north was solidly anti-slavery and whose south was not; and, of course, New York. That strife would probably have ripened into nationwide civil war; but it would have been a different sort of civil war, and one that would probably have been won by the northern rebels, who controlled most of the industry. Far-westerners — who, remember, had actually flirted with the idea of forming an independent "Pacific Republic" just a few years before, in 1848 — might have gone ahead and done it.

We can't know the specifics, of course. But one thing is for sure: America today would be a very different place if the "fusion" plot had succeeded. And not just different in the way of politics and national borders, either. As Sheppard points out, the Lincoln Administration was responsible for the Homestead Act, the Pacific Railway Act, the system of land-grant colleges and several other key components of modern America.

Would President Lane have done anything similar? Almost certainly not.

To date, no Oregonian has ever become President. (The closest we've come is Herbert Hoover, but when he was elected, Hoover hadn't lived in the Beaver State for nearly 40 years.)

Having had a local resident become President is something of a feather in the cap of every state blessed with that honor. But all things considered, it's probably a far greater blessing, for all Americans, that Oregon didn't join that club in 1860.

Sources and works cited:
- Great and Minor Moments in Oregon History, *a book by Dick Pintarich published in 2003 by New Oregon Publishers;*
- *"Union for the Sake of the Union," an article by Si Sheppard published in the December 2014 issue of the* Oregon Historical Quarterly;
- *"The Movement in Oregon for the Establishment of a Pacific Coast Republic," an article by Dorothy Hull published in the Fall 2016 issue of the* Oregon Historical Quarterly;
- *Archives of the* Portland Weekly Oregonian, *1851, and* Salem Statesman, *1860.*

A WHALE OF A BAD IDEA.

THE BAD IDEA:
- *When an orca swims up the Columbia and gets stuck in a shallow slough in Portland, be a Mighty Hunter and kill it.*

THE HORRIBLE PEOPLE:
- *Edward and Joseph Lessard, amateur whalers.*

In August 1949, some residents in the small town of St. Helens started noticing a very unpleasant smell coming from a neighbor's orchard.

Upon investigation, police easily found the source: a large, oddly-shaped, obviously home-built galvanized steel tank, about 13 feet long and six feet wide, with great marks of rust and corrosion all over it.

Inside it, they found a dead whale.

The tank had originally been full of embalming fluid, which had preserved the whale from decomposition for nearly two decades. But the rust had eaten through the side of the tank, and the embalming fluid had leaked out, and after that a few hot summer afternoons had been sufficient to get the 1,500-pound carcass started "giving off aromas not at all like Chanel No. 5," as John Myers wrote in the *Oregonian* story about it (under the headline, "Whale of a Smell" — of course. What other headline could possibly have been written for a story like this?).

The story of this whale started several dozen miles away from St. Helens, in Portland. It's a tragic story, an infuriating miscarriage of justice that resulted in the bad guys more or less getting away with it. It also involves Portland celebrity Mel Blanc, later famous as the voice of Bugs Bunny.

It all started in mid-October of 1931, when somebody — probably a boy out fishing — saw something big swimming around in the Columbia Slough.

Soon there was a crowd there gazing out at the water, where a big black-and-white sea monster was swimming and cavorting like a Sea World exhibit — leaping out of the water, splashing around and apparently having a great time.

"It's a baby humpback whale," said one onlooker.

"No, that's a sturgeon," said another.

"It's a blackfish," proclaimed an old deepwater sailor, who was promptly contradicted by another old mariner who said it was a porpoise.

It wouldn't be until much later that the creature was identified as an orca — a killer whale. (Which means, by the way, that the old deepwater sailor was right. "Blackfish" is another term for an orca.)

Meanwhile, huge crowds of spectators — men, women and especially children — started coming to see it. *The Oregonian* tried diligently to christen it "Jimmy McCool's Whale," after the newspaper's wildlife writer, but among Portlanders the name "Ethelbert" won out.

But Ethelbert was getting another kind of interest, too. Within less than 48 hours, men were out on the slough with rifles trying to bag themselves a whale. And no one could figure out how to make them stop.

The law seemed powerless. It specified times and seasons and bag limits for all the usual things people shot rifles at — deer, elk, antelope, etc. — but anything it didn't specifically limit was considered OK to kill at any time. It forbade using firearms to take fish, but the whale was pretty clearly not a fish.

On the governor's orders, the police arrested the men anyway, more to inconvenience them than with any hope of making charges stick. But it didn't seem much to matter. The whale ignored the gunfire, and the wounds that were inflicted didn't seem to bother it much.

As the week went on, it became clear that Ethelbert was stuck. The mood of the crowd toward the men with rifles — the two in jail had been quickly replaced with others of their ilk — was also getting increasingly hostile, to the point that mob violence was starting to look like a possibility. The whale continued to play and splash in the slough, and thousands kept coming to watch.

Meanwhile, two different parties were making concrete plans to do something about the whale.

The first of these parties consisted of the management at nearby Jantzen Beach, working with the Humane Society. They were seeking permission to catch the whale with a big gill-net and transfer it to a big tank of saltwater which was being hastily prepared at the park. The management hoped the saltwater would clear up the fungal infections which were starting to be visible around the gunshot wounds on Ethelbert's back. They also hoped Ethelbert, plopped down in their park in a big glass tank, would be a fabulous attraction for Jantzen Beach.

The other party was an old ex-whaler named Edward Lessard and his son, Joseph.

The two of them seem to have taken their inspiration from a comic routine by future cartoon-voice wizard Mel Blanc, who at the time was a young comedian on "The Hoot Owls" radio show on KGW AM 620. Mel hatched the idea of getting Jimmy McCool to pretend to give him lessons in harpooning. It was played for big laughs live on the air. But it appears to have given Lessard an idea, because the very next day he commissioned a blacksmith to forge for him a pair of special barbed harpoon heads, based on the designs of the weapons he'd helped use on sperm whales back in the late 1800s, when he was a young crewman on deep-sea whaling ships.

And on October 24, at 7:30 a.m., just as the pieces were about to fall into place for the Humane Society and Jantzen Beach to effect a rescue, Lessard and his son beat them to it. In a chartered motorboat, they approached the whale — and skewered it.

"It was the quickest killing I ever made," the elder Lessard boasted to the *Oregonian's* reporter, who described his demeanor as "apparently thrilled." "Usually it takes half a day or a day to kill a whale. This one was dead as a doornail in less than five minutes."

The problem was, he couldn't find his prize. It had sunk to the bottom of the slough.

While Lessard was waiting for the men he'd hired to search for the carcass, a representative of the Portland Chemical Company offered to pay to have the whale embalmed and put on display if the proceeds would be sent to the Community Chest. Lessard "shifted uneasily on his wet perch on the dock," *The Oregonian* reports. " 'Nix,' he said glumly. 'It's my dead whale.' "

But before he could collect his prize, the cops showed up. The Humane Society had sworn out a warrant for the arrest of both Lessards. Despite Edward's protests that his cousin, an attorney, had assured him there was no law against inland whaling, the two of them were trucked off to the hoosegow. And while they were so occupied, a crew of interlopers slipped in, located the carcass, and took possession of it. They got hold of it just in time to put it on display during the Pacific Livestock Exhibition, where they charged admission to see it.

By the time the Lessards were out of jail, the exhibition was over, and all the locals who'd wanted to see the whale had done so. *The Oregonian* joined virtually the entire city in celebrating the "poetic justice" of this development: The Lessards had spent hundreds of dollars on their whale hunt, and someone else had reaped the reward they'd hoped to gain.

It was at some point after this that the Lessards apparently moved to St. Helens. It's at least possible that they did so because of how unpopular and unwelcome the whale incident had made them in Portland. But all attempts to prosecute the Lessards failed. There just weren't any laws on the books governing inland whaling, and so by engaging in it, they hadn't broken any.

But that didn't mean they could keep their prize, and the state of Oregon moved immediately to seize the whale — kicking off an eight-year legal squabble over Ethelbert's mortal remains. Finally the Oregon Supreme Court decided in favor of the state. But then, having realized what limited utility there is in a dead whale pickled in embalming fluid, the state offered to let the Lessards have it if they'd pay court costs. They did, and so for $103, the Lessards finally got clear title to Portland's whale.

And that's how the unfortunate long-dead sea creature ended up in a rusty tank full of embalming fluid at the Lessard house, where it sat forgotten for ten years before its mounting aroma brought it back to official attention.

This time, though, the proceedings were far less dramatic, and by the end of the week, the poor whale's long-suffering bones were resting peacefully six feet underground.

Sources and works cited:
- *Archives of the Portland Morning Oregonian, 1931 and 1949;*
- *Correspondence from Leofric Hylton.*

BLACK-BAG JOURNALISM.

THE BAD IDEA:
- *Commit a burglary to steal evidence to use against a politician you don't like in the pages of the newspaper you happen to own.*

THE HORRIBLE PEOPLE:
- *Henry Pittock, newspaper publisher and foiled water-service thief*

Late on the evening of June 2, 1917, the *Portland Morning Oregonian* sprang a trap — a cunning and dirty trap.
The always-formidable daily newspaper, owned and edited by Henry Pittock, had thrown its weight behind a big, boisterous City Council member named George Baker in the race for Portland city mayor. But in a fierce race with Union man and small-business owner Will Daly, Baker appeared on track to lose the race.

For Pittock, that was simply not acceptable. Daly, a former *Oregonian* employee who had gone on to become Portland's utility commissioner, had earned Pittock's lifelong hatred several years before, when he'd uncovered a secret contract between the city and Pittock — under the terms of which, in exchange for favorable press in *The Oregonian*, the city would install (at considerable expense to the taxpayers) a half-mile-long pipeline bringing unlimited quantities of complimentary Bull Run water out to Pittock's West Hills estate, which was outside city limits.

Will Daly as he appeared around the time of his campaign for mayor of Portland, in 1917. (Image: Portland Morning Oregonian)

When Daly publicly exposed this larcenous little scheme, Pittock's personal reputation was considerably sullied, and Daly instantly became his ex-boss's *bête noir*. No, Pittock would not sit idly by while his number-one enemy took over the city government.

But then, he wouldn't have to. He'd already taken the necessary steps to make sure that didn't happen.

Some time before this, Pittock had sent some of his more morally flexible staff members on what you might call an undercover investigation. You might also call it, as Watergate plotter E. Howard Hunt surely would, a "black bag job." Simply put, they'd broken into Daly's house and rifled through his papers, looking for something they could use.

They'd hit the jackpot.

What they had found was a partially-filled-out application for membership in the Socialist Party, dated 1910.

It isn't clear, even today, whether Daly ever actually joined the Socialist Party. Some sources say he did, briefly, before renouncing it and registering as a Republican; others say he never sent the paperwork in. But such niceties didn't matter to Pittock. What he cared about was not fairness or journalistic integrity, but simply denying Daly the mayorship. And now, two months after U.S. entry into the First World War, the anti-war Socialist Party was extremely unpopular. A credible claim that Daly was a registered Socialist would be some serious medicine — maybe even an election swinger if he handled it right.

And Pittock intended to handle it right. He sat on the document until the very last minute. Then, on the evening of June 2, he loaded the next day's *Oregonian* up like a cannon with the fruits of his felony and pulled the trigger. The shot hit the front porches of most homes in Portland the very next morning, the day before Election Day.

"SECURITY OF CITY HANGS ON ELECTION!" it shrieked, in heavy headline type on Page One. "Baker and Growth or Daly and Strife (is the) Issue. QUESTION IS UP TO VOTERS. Daly's Election First Number on Radical Programme. AGITATORS ALL BACK HIM!"

Such was *The Oregonian's* reputation as a voice of establishment cronyism that even this massive editorial broadside, delivered as it was the day before election (guaranteeing that Daly would have no chance to respond in any meaningful way), didn't move the election results much. But it changed enough minds to hand Baker the election, by a slim 1-percent margin.

And just like that, Daly was finished.

Show-business man and three-term Portland Mayor George Baker as he appeared during his campaign against Will Daly, in 1917. (Image: Oregon Historical Society)

Will Daly was born in Missouri and was one of those newspaper pressmen with ink in their blood. He started work at the *Springfield Leader-Democrat* at age 10 and by the time he was 31, he'd worked his way to the top — he was the press foreman there.

When his mother died, Daly and his wife, Daisy, moved to Oregon, and Will ended up taking a job working on the press at *The Morning Oregonian* a few months after arriving; a few years later, he moved on to the Portland Linotype Company. He also opened his own small printing business on the side, the Portland Monotype Company.

Meanwhile, Daly was also rising through the ranks at the Oregon State Federation of Labor. By 1908 he was the union president. As an articulate, intelligent fellow who was both a blue-collar worker and a small-business owner, he turned out to be remarkably effective at helping union workers and small-scale entrepreneurs see eye to eye. That was especially true after he was elected to the City Council in 1911.

This, of course, made him somewhat dangerous to the large-scale former entrepreneurs who formed Portland's power elite, including the fairly scurrilous one for whom Daly had once worked — that is, Henry Pittock. So it was probably inevitable that Daly and his ex-boss would stop seeing eye-to-eye pretty quickly.

Things got bad in 1914 when Daly went to bat for the drivers of "jitneys" — which were like the progenitors of taxicabs. Jitneys were privately owned automobiles that entrepreneurs would buy and then drive around town, looking for fares. This was annoying the executives of the Portland Railway, Light and Power Company, the monopoly outfit that controlled Portland streetcars, which wanted the jitneys outlawed. Pittock, who probably regularly enjoyed brandy and cigars with the PRL&P bigwigs, vigorously agreed and never lost a chance to make the case that letting these small-time businessmen continue providing service was unfair to the city's massive electricity-and-transportation monopoly. Daly just as vigorously disagreed.

Then came that incident with Pittock's attempted theft of city water, and after that there could be no smoothing things over between Daly and the Oregonian.

The Pittock Mansion as it appears today. (Image: WikiMedia/AnotherBeliever | CC-by-SA)

ALL *of the* ABOVE.

A cartoon by The Oregonian's famous Tige Reynolds illustrates the newspaper's attitude toward Will Daly. The "Single Tax" is a reference to a scheme, never endorsed by Daly, to tax real estate owners 100 percent on appreciation of their property while abolishing all other taxes. (Image: Portland Morning Oregonian)

After losing the election, Daly retired from public life and focused on his printing business. In 1920 he accepted an appointment as Oregon's federal food price commissioner, but when he learned how much red tape and scrutiny of his business was involved, he resigned. And when Mayor Baker stood for re-election that same year, Daly actually endorsed his onetime rival.

He died, mostly forgotten, in 1924, just 54 years old.

Sources and works cited:
- *"The Myth of the Harmonious City," an article by Robert D. Johnson published in the September 1998 issue of the* Oregon Historical Quarterly;
- *"Will Daly (1869-1924)," an article by Shawn Daley published on Sept. 13, 2022, on the* Oregon Encyclopedia, *oregonencyclopedia.org;*
- *Archives of the* Portland Morning Oregonian, *1917.*

THE EDITORS' GUNFIGHT.

THE BAD IDEA:
- *Escalate your feud with a rival newspaper to gunfire.*

THE HORRIBLE PEOPLE:
- *William "Bud" Thompson, newspaper owner and later vigilante gang leader*

The "Oregon Style" of newspaper journalism was already a thing in 1871, when upstart newspaper publisher William "Bud" Thompson started a gunfight in downtown Roseburg.

But until that day, the vicious personal attacks that characterized the "Oregon Style" had mostly involved the spilling of ink — not blood.

On that late Monday morning on a corner in downtown Roseburg, that changed.

The groundwork for the Roseburg Newspaper Shootout was laid when Thompson came to town in 1870, when he was just 22 years old. He'd just sold the newspaper he'd briefly co-owned in Eugene — the *Eugene City Guard*. The *Guard* had been a tough job for Thompson, because its pro-Confederate, anti-Reconstruction views were very much out of fashion in Eugene. So when he got the chance to unload it for $1,200, he had taken the offer, handed over the keys, and started looking around the state for a community in which his antebellum views would be popular enough for him to make a living printing them.

Roseburg looked as good as anyplace. It had a newspaper, of course; but the newspaper was a Republican one, the *Roseberg Ensign*. And yet, as Thompson well knew, the Roseburg area was home to a large population of Confederate refugees and sympathizers. Just four years earlier, a deadly riot between hot-blooded ex-Rebels and angry Union supporters had broken out at a Christmas party and had turned into a gun battle that left one man dead and several others badly wounded. It, and the prosecutions that followed, were reported on in newspapers all across the state and widely referred to, only half in jest, as the "last battle of the Civil War." (It was called the Champagne Riot, after the name of the farmer at whose home it broke out, and it's covered in Volume Two of the Offbeat Oregon books, *Love, Sex, and Murder in Old Oregon*.)

COL. WILLIAM THOMPSON
From a photograph at the close of the Modoc war

William "Bud" Thompson as he appeared at around age 30, during the Modoc Indian wars. (Image: Alturas Plaindealer)

So, Thompson took his even dozen C-notes and used them to set up shop in Roseburg.

He launched his paper, naming it the *Roseburg Plaindealer*, and he soon discovered he'd been right; the new paper steadily started building circulation.

This was not OK with Henry and Thomas Gale, the two brothers who owned the *Roseburg Ensign*. The Gales were the *Ensign's* founders, having launched it three years before. Like Thompson, the two of them were from the Eugene area, and like him they were in their early 20s; but, of course, unlike Thompson, they were staunch Republicans. Henry, the older of the two, was a tall and powerful man, but Thomas was tiny — under five feet tall.

Tensions between the two newspapers built as they fired salvoes at one another from their editorial pages. This was to be expected: after all, the Gales ran a Republican newspaper, and Thompson was a hardcore, unreconstructed Southern Democrat.

But there was something else happening, too, which added fuel to the brewing feud: Almost as soon as Thompson opened for business, Democrat Lafayette Grover was elected governor of Oregon, ending an eight-year run of Republican governors. The victorious Dems, in Salem, now had a choice of papers to favor with their lucrative public-notice business. That meant most of the business that had sustained the *Ensign* now started going exclusively to the upstart *Plaindealer*.

Also, looking at all the different accounts of this event, it's clear that Thompson was an unusually thin-skinned fellow. After being sarcastically called "the ripe scholar and gallant gentleman who stands — when sober enough to stand at all — behind the *Plaindealer* chair," and "a sardine among codfish" (a very-thinly-veiled reference to penis size), and various other quaint-sounding (to us) epithets, Thompson reportedly informed the Gale brothers that he would no longer tolerate this sort of editorial abuse.

Of course, the Gales kept it up. They would have been a disgrace to Oregon-style journalism if they had not.

Things came to a head one Saturday, when Thompson chanced to meet Thomas Gale in the post office. Reports on the action are varied. Thompson's memoir claims that Gale tried to draw a pistol, and he (Thompson) grabbed his hand and slapped him in the face. Contemporary newspaper accounts, including one by Thompson's own newspaper (published while he was recovering from his wounds) say Thompson spat in Gale's face and slapped him, and Gale — probably because Thompson towered over him like a giant — didn't get in a single blow. Bystanders quickly separated the two before a full-on brawl could develop, and Thomas Gale stormed off to get his gun — which he had not had in the post office, or he probably would have used it.

It was not the kind of public affront that went unanswered in a frontier town like 1870s Roseburg. Everyone knew a showdown of some kind was coming.

It arrived two days later, on Monday. When Thompson stepped out of his office to go to the post office, he found the Gale brothers waiting for him.

Again, Thompson's memoir describes the encounter with shameless mendacity. He basically claims the brothers took turns shooting him in the back as he turned from one to the other, that one pretended to surrender so he would lower his guard and then shot him, and (by implication) that he left both brothers dead. His own bravery, and the brothers' cowardice, fairly pours from the page. And again, if contemporary newspaper accounts are to be believed — including, again, one by his very own newspaper — it's almost all lies.

The newspaper accounts all say that the encounter started with Thompson apologizing to Thomas Gale for spitting in his face. The apology was not accepted, though, and Henry, the bigger brother, told him he should be ashamed of himself, and that he should pick on somebody his own size.

What happened next is very unclear. There are just too many conflicting accounts to pick a line through them, especially on the question of who shot first. The most likely scenario is that Henry Gale intended to use his cane to administer a humiliating public beating to Thompson, and had started doing so when Thompson pulled his pocket derringer out. At that point, Thomas Gale (the small brother) pulled his revolver out, and the shooting started.

First, Thomas Gale shot Thompson in the chest, but the ball was deflected by a thick sheaf of letters and inflicted only a flesh wound. Thompson turned and fired his one-shot derringer into Thomas's right side, just above the liver; he then started using his now-empty pistol to beat Henry Gale over the head. Henry then pulled a four-shooter and shot Thompson three times with it from close quarters: once in the back of the head, from the side, apparently at an angle because the skull wasn't penetrated; once in the shoulder; and once in the neck. The neck shot went behind Thompson's jaw and lodged in his tongue, filling his mouth with blood. (The four-shooter was likely carried on an empty chamber for safety.)

And with that, the drama ended. Much to the surprise of almost everyone, all three of the men survived this bloody encounter. Thomas and Henry Gale went to a nearby drugstore for treatment, and Thomas's wounds were quite serious; they may have eventually caused his death, which came eight years later. Thompson went home to have the bullets extracted.

"Although neither paper was put out of commission, both had had the stuffing knocked out of their editors," writer David Loftus remarked in his article about the incident.

ALL *of the* ABOVE.

Thompson soon left Roseburg, selling the *Plaindealer* for $4,000 and moving to Salem to take over the *Salem Mercury*. The Gales sold their paper around the same time, and, languishing with the winds of political fortune, it eventually closed.

Throughout the rest of his life, Thompson would be a dangerous fellow to have around. At the *Mercury*, he reportedly beat the editor of the Forest Grove paper with a cane after the editor wrote some disparaging things about him. Later, as a cattle rancher, he would become notorious as the head of the Prineville Vigilantes, a gang of masked outlaws responsible for at least seven lynchings and extrajudicial killings in Crook County. (The story of the Prineville Vigilantes also appears in *Love, Sex and Murder in Old Oregon*.) After that, Thompson moved to Alturas, Calif., and there were more lynchings and vigilante action there.

Thompson's enemies, of whom there were many, characterized him as that rare blackguard who had the skill to know whom he could attack and when he needed to leave town . . . and they were probably right. And few if any of the other characters we've met in this volume are more richly deserving of the title of Horrible Person.

But one thing is for sure: Bud Thompson definitely made journalism in frontier Oregon a more interesting occupation.

Sources and works cited:
- Reminiscences of a Pioneer, *a book by William "Bud" Thompson published in 1939 by the* Alturas Plaindealer;
- *"Papers' feuding editors settled dispute with gunfire," an article by David Loftus published in the Feb. 21, 1988 issue of the* Roseburg News-Review.

DRAGGING JUMPTOWN DOWN.

THE BAD IDEA:
- Shut down the hottest jazz scene on the West Coast for racist reasons.

THE HORRIBLE PEOPLE:
- Portland's City Council.

In 1945, someone had to tell Nat King Cole and Billie Holiday that they couldn't come play in Portland after all.

It seems that, in an event that has to be one of the most shortsighted bits of municipal governance in Oregon history, the Portland city authorities had ordered the flagship nightclub of North Portland's wildly popular jazz scene, The Dude Ranch, shut down. Apparently there had been a shooting nearby, and city officials pretended they thought it was related.

But it was widely known what the real problem was: White girls and black boys, and black girls and white boys, were dancing together there. And Portland, like the rest of the state, was still a pretty racist place in 1945, especially at the top.

But that was changing fast. And it had a lot to do with places like The Dude Ranch.

The Dude Ranch, for a brief shining moment at the end of the Second World War, was the epicenter of a jazz scene that put the rest of the West Coast to shame.

"There never was and there never will be anything quite like The Dude Ranch," Robert Dietsche wrote in his book, *Jumptown*. "It was the Cotton Club, the Apollo Theater, Las Vegas and the Wild West rolled into one."

Portland's jazz scene, which is now a relatively forgotten story, got its start during World War II. After the war started, thousands of people from around the country were brought into North Portland to take jobs in the shipyards that were, at the time, pumping out Liberty ships by the hundreds. The wartime shipyard scene was one of those glorious moments in which people who formerly didn't like each other are put together by forces beyond their control, united by a common goal, and more or less forced to work side by side on a winning team, until one day they realize that they actually rather like one another.

When these shipyard comrades went out on a Friday or Saturday night to have a good time, they were not going to go someplace where some of them weren't welcome. At the time, discreet signs that read "White Trade Only" were a common sight in Portland. A mixed-race group of shipyard workers was no more likely to set foot in one of these places than the Rat Pack would have been. (Can you imagine Frank, Dean and Joey going into Waddle's Diner for pie and coffee and leaving Sammy waiting by the door like a dog? Unthinkable. It was the same way with groups of buddies from the shipyards. Their attitude was, "If one of us is unwelcome, kiss all of us goodbye.")

So they often ended up hanging out together in one of at least 10 clubs in the area of Williams Avenue and what's now the Rose Quarter. These clubs were part of a thriving and booming music scene that had a particular appeal for African-American jazz legends — and in that scene, the Dude Ranch was first among equals.

A few years later, an integrated group of clean-cut entertainers at The Sands in Las Vegas would play off this scene, relaxing on stage like four old Army buddies yukking it up and having a few drinks together, regardless of skin tones. In the mid-1940s, the real thing was playing out, not only in North Portland and Vanport, but across the country.

Shipyard workers and returning soldiers may have played and socialized together regardless of race, but in the rest of Portland, attitudes were still far less cosmopolitan. It would take a humanitarian disaster in 1948 — the flooding of Vanport — to really start breaking down those walls; in 1945, most Portlanders still didn't want black people moving into their neighborhoods.

So Portland's new African-American residents mostly set up housekeeping in the Albina area, around Williams and Vancouver avenues, and in Vanport. After the war ended, hordes of returning servicemen, starved

ALL *of the* ABOVE.

The Hazlewood Building, built in 1923, was the home of The Dude Ranch for a year or two at the end of World War II. Today, it is home to The Leftbank Project, which rents flexible workspace in the building for entrepreneurs and creative professionals. (Image: F.J.D. John)

for entertainment, crowded into town, and these fellows found what they wanted on Williams Avenue. The population density was off the charts; finding a place to stay was nearly impossible. Movie theatres were turned into impromptu bunkhouses, people crashed on each other's couches. The streets were full of people with money in their pockets and no place to go, and the nightclubs were packed, 24 hours a day.

The Dude Ranch, according to professor Michael McGregor of Portland State University, rose to prominence largely because its owners, Sherman Pickett and Pat Patterson — "Pic and Pat," as they were called — "seemed capable of booking anybody."

"But though Lionel Hampton, Art Tatum and the Nat 'King' Cole Trio appeared in later days, no night ever equaled that night in December of 1945 when Norman Granz brought his touring jam session, 'Jazz at the Philharmonic,' to town," McGregor writes. " That night legendary saxophonist Coleman Hawkins led a group that included trombonist Roy Eldridge, bassist Al McKibbon and a 25-year-old pianist with 'a lightning-like right hand' who was soon to usher in the bebop age, Thelonious Monk."

And then there were the impromptu appearances, including one evening when Louis Armstrong just happened to show up, on his way from somewhere else.

Inside the Dude Ranch, the cowboy theme was played to the hilt. The waitresses wore cowgirl outfits with fake six-shooters; there were murals showing cowboys riding and roping all over the walls. And the world-class jazz was only the beginning of what you might find there: burlesque "shake dancers," ventriloquists, comics, jugglers, singers and tap dancers, according to Dietsche, were in the lineup as well.

Like all such shining moments, it couldn't last. It certainly didn't help that Pic and Pat got put out of business. They soon opened up again at a different location, but it was never the same, and the local jazz scene was starting to cool down a bit by then anyway.

Today, it's all gone — bulldozed and cleared to make room for Memorial Coliseum and the interstate freeway. That is, all but one building, the one that used to house The Dude Ranch. It's straight ahead of you as you drive across the Steel Bridge, a wedge-shaped building on the corner, just a few hundred yards north of Memorial Coliseum.

Standing there on the corner and looking back and forth between the funky, historic little brick building and the massive, impersonal Coliseum, it's funny to think about how much the world has changed since 1946. Back then, when someone like Billie Holiday came to Portland, she booked a show in that historic little brick building on your left. If someone of that caliber came today, she'd be playing in the mammoth cement hall on your right.

I'm not sure I'd call that an improvement ... would you?

Sources and works cited:
- Jump Town: The Golden Years of Portland Jazz, *a book by Robert Dietsche published in 2005 by Oregon State University Press;*
- "When the Joint was Jumpin'," *an article by Michael N. McGregor published in 2004 on Oregon Historical Society's Oregon History Project Website,* oregonhistoryproject.org.

SCHOOL POLITICS, WITH DYNAMITE

THE BAD IDEA:
- *When annoyed by the noise made by children at play, solve the problem by blowing up their school with dynamite.*

THE HORRIBLE PEOPLE:
- *"Old Joe" Huddleston, pioneer and "dynamite fisherman."*

Next time a debate over a capital levy for local schools gets ugly, count your blessings. Some Oregonians used to argue over this sort of thing with sticks of dynamite.

Back in 1895, a little one-room schoolhouse was built in an unincorporated town that today is known as Mohawk. Over the years it's also been called Donna and Ping Yang — Ping Yang having been, at the time, the popular English pronunciation of Pyongyang, then the capital of Korea (and today the capital of North Korea). Pyongyang had just made headlines as the scene of a historic battle between the colonial forces of China, which had dominated Korea for centuries, and the "liberating" armies of Japan; this fight had captured the imagination of many Oregonians, and was a regular subject in the pulps and serials of the day.

There are other theories on the origin of the name. But if the Ping Yang School was in fact named after a distant battlefield, it was an appropriate choice, because it quickly became one — in more than just a metaphorical sense. You see, a sizeable percentage of the community did not want the school built where it ended up.

Almost immediately after it was built, someone tried to torch the school by dumping coal oil on the floor inside and lighting it off. This did not work — probably because it was late winter at the time. Anyone who's tried to fire up a burn pile on a typical Willamette Valley early-spring day will not be surprised at this.

Three months later, though, a more successful attempt was made, involving dynamite. This seems to have established a tradition at Ping Yang. Over the following 15 years, three more attempts were made to blow the building up, with increasing success, until in 1909 the school had to be replaced with a bigger structure — which served the community uneventfully until it was replaced in 1963 with Mohawk Elementary School, just a few hundred yards away on the other side of Marcola Road.

So, why all the fireworks?

Historian Steve Williamson suggests it was a land-use issue. The Mohawk Valley is prime timber country. The valley floor is nice and flat; the surrounding hills are gentle, well-watered and thick with trees. Soon there was a railroad heading up the valley, carrying logs down to the mill and timber workers and their families up to live. Some of the older Mohawk Valley residents, who'd been there since before Oregon statehood, saw their wild hideaway turning into an industrial community, complete with roaring machinery, howling steam whistles and screeching

This article in the July 20, 1901, issue of the Eugene Weekly Guard gives details of the second of three dynamite attacks on Ping Yang School. (Image: UO Libraries)

buzz-saw blades. One of these, "Old Joe" Huddleston, was particularly disgusted after the railroad cut up the valley right next to his property.

To make things more complicated, Old Joe was a hard-core racist, and he was singing that song nice and loud when the school was bombed for the third time, in 1900. This blast took out most of the walls and left just a roof supported on a few surviving bits of framing. At that time, Huddleston was campaigning fiercely against the school, which — like the railroad — was annoyingly close to his home. He was using a racist, xenophobic appeal centered around opposition to the presence of Chinese and Japanese people then working on railroads and other back-breaking projects around the country. The Ping Yang School likely had never had a Chinese or Japanese student even walking into the building. But it had an east-Asian-sounding name, and Japanese workers on the railroad line had become a familiar sight.

So when the school blew up, Huddleston was widely viewed as the No. 1 suspect — especially since he was known to be an experienced "dynamite fisherman" on area waterways.

Old Joe was never charged, though. No one else was either, for that matter. But after Old Joe moved out of the valley a couple years later, the explosions stopped — well, mostly. In or shortly before 1909, there was one more, and this one finished off the building.

According to a student attending the school at the time, a group of pupils decided they needed a better building, and that the way to get one was — well, what had become the traditional Mohawk Valley way: Dynamite.

They got their new school. It lasted until 1963, when it was taken out of service in a far less dramatic fashion — with a school-board vote — and replaced with Mohawk Elementary.

Sources and works cited:
- *"The Ping Yang School Bombing," an article by Steve Williamson published at https://storiesbysteve.com, retrieved March 2023;*
- *Archives of the Eugene Register-Guard, June 1963, and Eugene Guard, July 1901.*

ENDLESS SLAVERY.

THE BAD IDEA:
- *Ignore the Emancipation Proclamation and Fourteenth Amendment, and keep your slave illegally enslaved.*

THE HORRIBLE PEOPLE:
- *John and Mary (Mulkey) Porter . . . maybe.*

In a quiet little historical cemetery in the north hills of Corvallis, there's a marble gravestone about the size of a large loaf of bread, with a simple and startling message carved upon it.

The stone reads, " 'AME,' A Slave of Mary and John Porter."

There's nothing more. The gravestone has none of the usual information. Ame's dates of birth and of death are unknown. Until not too many years ago, information like that was considered unimportant.

If Ame's date of death had been listed, though, it would have been within a year or two of 1874 — at least ten years after the President of the United States declared her a free woman, and at least five years after the Fourteenth Amendment made slavery unconstitutional. Yet she died as she had lived, as a slave, albeit now an illegal one.

But then, she'd been "illegal" ever since she first came to Oregon.

Philomath historian May Dasch told Corvallis writer Theresa Hogue that Ame was born sometime between 1808 and 1818, in Kentucky. At some point, when she was a young woman, she was sold to the Johnson and Susan Mulkey family of Missouri.

When the Mulkeys came out west on the Oregon Trail in the mid-1840s, they debated what to do about Ame. At that time, the question of whether slavery would be allowed in Oregon was still unsettled, and if it were settled with a "no," they'd lose a valuable "piece of property."

To play it safe, the Mulkeys decided they'd leave Ame behind with family members in Missouri — where, in any case, she had her own children to look after.

"When the start was made, Ame was not to be found," recalled the Mulkeys' granddaughter, Maude Cauthorn Keady, in an interview for the W.P.A. Writers Project in 1939. "Nor had she bade them goodbye. It was supposed that she was so sad or overcome with emotion that she could not watch them leave. Not so.... At the fourth camp, much to the delight of grandmother and the children, Ame appeared at the campfire, and was helping with supper when grandfather came to eat. There was nothing to do at this late hour but take her along. Her faithfulness to grandmother and the children was wonderful. She had left her own children to follow Miss Susan and the babies."

Well, that was one interpretation. Hogue, for one, seems skeptical: "Whether it was loyalty or the fear of abandonment in a place where her

The John A. Porter family of grave markers, in the Odd Fellows Cemetery in Corvallis, Ore.; Ame's is the flat marker closest to the camera. Ame's retention as a slave was a violation of federal law, all slaves having been emancipated more than 10 years before her death, as well as state law — Oregon has never allowed slave ownership. (Photo: F.J.D. John)

ALL *of the* ABOVE.

This modest marker denotes the final resting place of a "slave" woman named Ame, who died in the mid-1870s, more than 10 years after the Emancipation Proclamation. The marker is considerably newer that those of the rest of the Porter family, suggesting that the original marker was a humbler one, possibly made of wood. (Photo: F.J.D. John)

only option was to become another family's slave is impossible to tell," she writes dryly.

And indeed, Ame had been passed around the Mulkey family quite a bit, and most people she'd stayed with didn't seem to like her. Perhaps she knew that if she stayed back in Missouri with her own children, she'd just be separated from them anyway and sold on the auction block, and would end up toiling in a cotton field for the rest of her (considerably shortened) life.

Whatever the reason, Ame left her own children behind and came to Oregon with the Mulkey family. Along the way, her chief tasks were keeping the oxen in line and the children out of trouble.

Upon arrival in the Oregon territory, Ame found herself an outlaw, shielded from a hostile society only by the protection of a respected white family that was, itself, breaking the law by keeping her. Black people were simply illegal in Oregon at the time — slave or free, they were legally prohibited from coming to the territory.

Ame continued serving the family, occasionally being lent out to help with neighbors' chores. Keady said she seemed happy to be there with them — but did she really have a choice? Could she have walked away if she'd wanted to claim her freedom? Legally, she certainly could; keeping her in bondage was a crime. But as a practical matter, the community might not have allowed her to exercise that right. And, in any case, she herself was an outlaw, guilty of "being in Oregon while Black." What kind of support could she count on? A speedy repatriation to Missouri, most likely, to be handed over once again to the Mulkey family's relatives there.

She may have made the best of it, but Ame — and all other Black people in early Oregon — had been dealt a losing hand.

Time passed. Ame got older and, according to Keady, feistier — although she'd apparently been plenty feisty to start with. Young Mary Mulkey grew up and married John Porter in 1858; Ame became the newlyweds' property.

In 1859, Oregon became the only state ever admitted to the union with a law on the books excluding black people from living within its borders. So far as we know, though, this had no effect on Ame's status.

Nor did the outcome of the Civil War change her life. In the Emancipation Proclamation of 1863, President Lincoln declared her a free woman. In 1868, the Fourteenth Amendment made her continued bondage an offense against the U.S. Constitution. Still she continued to live and work as a domestic slave.

But then, by that time she was probably in her 60s, too old to go forth and start a new life in "free" society. She may have counted herself lucky that she was far enough away from Washington, D.C., to continue living as she had lived.

Ame's gravestone is a good metaphor for her life. She's buried right next to the family she served, but not among them — on the edge of the plot, closest to the path. Her loaf-shaped marker is much more modest than theirs, and is also noticeably newer — its typeface and style look like something from the 1930s, not the 1870s; it seems likely the original marker was made of wood, and had to be replaced. It was probably a little controversial to bury Ame in the family plot at all; after all, before the Civil War, black people were considered little more than livestock by their enslavers, and nobody today thinks of burying a dog or a horse in the family plot.

But perhaps that controversy is what the family intended. Perhaps the younger Porters, in this bright new world, kept Ame in violation of federal law as a favor done for an old family friend who deserved better than to be thrown away like a worn-out buggy. It's possible — remember, the people making these decisions were the "babies" she'd taken care of when she was a young woman.

John and Mary died a year or two before Ame did, in 1870 and 1872 respectively; yet nobody else seems to have taken "ownership" of Ame after their deaths. When she followed, she was buried there next to them, with that grave marker at her head, its short and disturbing message looking up at the free Oregon sky like a distant accusation.

Sources and works cited:
- Hidden History of Civil War Oregon, *a book by Randol B. Fletcher published in 2011 by The History Press;*
- *"A Grave History Lesson," an article by Theresa Hogue published in the Aug. 5, 2002 issue of the Corvallis Gazette-Times;*
- *WPA Historical Records: "Benton County, Ore./ Reminiscences of the Mulkeys."*

101 YEARS OF LAND THEFT.

THE BAD IDEA:
- *After learning a surveying error shorted a property owner 90,000 acres of land, ignore the problem and leave other parties in illegal possession for 85 years.*

THE HORRIBLE PEOPLE:
- *United States Bureau of Indian Affairs.*

If there's a category in the Guinness Book of World Records for longest-running land dispute, the 101-year struggle over the "McQuinn Strip" might be a contender.

But it might not qualify, because the land was only disputed for the first 16 of those years. The other 85 were taken up with a struggle to get the losing party to give the land back — something that didn't happen until 1972.

Oh, and did I mention — the party that wouldn't give the land back was the United States Government?

Here's the story:

In the 1850s, torrents of settlers were coming to Oregon, lured by the promise of free land. All one had to do was build a house, plant some crops — and clear the Indians off it.

These settlers were diligently doing all three of these things in 1855. General Joel Palmer, superintendent for Indian affairs, could see that this would lead to bloodshed in northern central Oregon, where the Walla Walla and Wasco tribes were strong.

To forestall this, Palmer and the tribes worked out a deal: They would give up title to some ten million acres in exchange for undisputed ownership of a 900,000-acre chunk of it, in which the government would agree not to let anyone settle.

The Indians, though quite unhappy about the whole situation, recognized that this was the best they could expect. The deal was made, and the Warm Springs Indian Reservation was formed.

Sixteen years later, in 1871, a surveyor opened up the land dispute by using the wrong mountains as a border marker — an error he certainly could have avoided had he bothered to talk to the Indians or even looked at the map Palmer had sketched out. This error resulted in the 900,000-odd acres shrinking by almost ten percent.

Although the tribes protested immediately, the government promptly gave the survey its stamp of approval and green-lighted settlers who wanted bits of the disputed part.

In 1886 Congress finally had the place re-surveyed. The work was done by John McQuinn the following year. McQuinn confirmed that the earlier survey was in error, thus bringing the "dispute" part of the story to an end.

But possession is nine-tenths of the law. By 1887, many settlers had

Directional signs at Ka-Nee-Ta Resort. (Image: F.J.D. John)

ALL *of the* ABOVE.

Ka-Nee-Ta Lodge Resort as it appears from the roadway below, during the dry season. (Image: F.J.D. John)

claimed parts of the "McQuinn Strip," and fought furiously against any suggestion that they give it up.

Congress dithered. It formed a commission to study the problem; the commission recommended sticking with the faulty survey even though it was wrong. In 1917, Congress offered a cash payment for the land — which the Indians refused; they wanted the land back. Finally, in 1930, Congress kicked the matter over to the courts, giving the tribes clearance to sue over it.

They did, and so was launched one of the more baffling legal farces in state history. In 1941, the court agreed that the Indians should have the land, but refused to give it to them. Instead, the court ruled that they were entitled to a dollar an acre in 1886 dollars — which someone decided was what the land was worth back then — plus interest. The total was just over $240,000.

But, the court added, the government had had to spend a total of $252,089 "in behalf of the tribes" over the same period.

Therefore, the court ruled, the tribes had to give up their claim on the land AND pay the government $11,005.

I haven't been able to determine whether the tribes took this as an insult. It's certainly possible that it was intended as one. In any case, it went nowhere.

Things started looking better after the war, though. In 1948, Congress passed a bill giving the tribes all the revenue from timber sales and grazing permits there. By 1970 this had brought the tribes almost $6 million, and along with compensatory payments for the loss of Celilo Falls beneath the impoundment behind The Dalles Dam in 1957, enabled them to build Kah-Nee-Ta Resort in the 1960s.

Finally, in 1972, Richard Nixon signed a bill into law — a bill sponsored by Oregon Rep. Al Ullman and senators Bob Packwood and Mark Hatfield — giving the land back.

A sign directing visitors on the highway to Ka-Nee-Tah Resort. (Image: F.J.D. John)

Ka-Nee-Ta, by the way, closed down in 2018, and an attempt to reopen it two years later had to be abandoned when the Coronavirus pandemic broke out. As of the time of this writing, however, the Ka-Nee-Ta Village Resort is slated to reopen, with some new hydrotherapy features, sometime in 2024.

Sources and works cited:

- *"101-Year Land Dispute," an article by George W. Linn published in* Little Known Tales from Oregon History, Vol. 1 *(Sun Publishing, 1988);*
- *"The Rise and Fall of Ka-Nee-Ta," an article by Juhea Kim published in the Fall 2020 issue of* Portland Monthly *magazine.*

WORLD'S DUMBEST PIRATES.

THE BAD IDEA:
- *Hijack a full-size ocean liner somewhere off the Oregon Coast, beach it, and slip away into the woods with 3 tons of gold.*

THE HORRIBLE PEOPLE:
- *French West and George Washington Wise, amateur pirates*

It was probably the last act of piracy ever carried out on a commercial ship within American territorial waters — and it was a pathetic one. In fact, "piracy" may be the wrong word — it had a lot more in common with a couple clumsy freelancers trying to hijack a 747 than anything Blackbeard would have done.

Still, piracy it was, if Webster's New World Dictionary is to be believed. And what its perpetrators lacked in brains, they certainly made up for in ambition. Their plan was for the two of them to take over a 253-foot passenger steamer, run it aground and slip off into the woods with the $2 million worth of gold that they believed it was carrying.

This was a bad plan on so many levels and for so many reasons that it's hard to know where to start. Perhaps it's best to simply tell the story.

Here we go:

In the summer of 1910, thirty-year-old U.S. Navy sailor French West had come up with a plan. All he needed was a real good friend.

It seemed he'd found that friend in 26-year-old shipmate George Washington Wise, a sailor from Boston.

The idea was, the two of them would slip away from their ship — stationed in San Francisco Bay — and travel to Seattle, where they'd take passage on one of the big steamers that hauled the gold out of Alaska and down to San Francisco via Seattle.

Off the coast of Oregon, in the middle of the night, they'd storm into the wheelhouse and take over. Then, they'd put the helm over and beach the ship, hop overboard and disappear into the woods with the loot.

Even making allowances for the benefit of hindsight, it's hard to imagine how West and Wise could possibly have thought this would work. The ship they had in mind was a huge, oceangoing passenger liner full of people who lived in Seattle. In 1910 Seattle was a frontier city awash with miners back from the gold fields in the Yukon and Alaska, many of whom carried .32 revolvers around in their pockets like we do cell phones today. Those

The Admiral Evans in dry dock, sometime in the 1920s. The colors are red below the waterline; a green hull; white cabin and decks; and a beige and black funnel. Looking at this image, it's easy to see another problem with the would-be pirates' plan: The ship draws a good 15 feet of water, so it would be a long and grueling row or swim to shore, past the breakers, if they grounded it. (Image: Superior Publishing)

ALL *of the* ABOVE.

The S.S. Buckman, later renamed the S.S. Admiral Evans, as she appeared before the aft cabin was rebuilt. The ship still looked like this in 1910, when the West-Wise piracy attempt was made. (Image: Superior Publishing)

passengers couldn't really be counted on to sit quietly by if they were to find out their ship was being jacked.

Even if West and Wise could avoid waking up the passengers, running a steamer head-on into the side of a randomly-selected piece of Oregon Coast scenery is like flipping a coin: Heads, you hit a beach and live (maybe); tails you hit rocks and die (for sure).

And if they won that coin toss, there they would be, on a strange beach in the middle of the night, trying to slip away from a couple hundred angry passengers plus whatever locals might be on hand — with $2 million worth of gold.

Two million dollars' worth. In 1910, gold was $21 an ounce, so $2 million dollars' worth was just a little shy of 6,000 pounds. Three tons of gold — a ton and a half for each of them. Of course, maybe they planned to leave most of it behind and just help themselves to as much of it as they could carry, but still ... gold is heavy stuff. It's not something you want to have a lot of in your pockets when you might have to swim for your life.

Also, most likely West and Wise thought, as many did at the time, that the Oregon Coast was a howling and uninhabited wilderness, a great place for capital criminals to go for quiet time while on the lam. They would no doubt have been astonished at the number of well-armed local residents ready to welcome them, pretty much regardless of where they landed.

And finally, it's a minor point, but — take a look at the photo of the Buckman in dry dock, on Page 422. The color change on the hull shows the waterline; notice the size of the workmen in relation to the amount of hull below that waterline. As you can see, even beached, the Buckman would be in water far too deep for the men to wade ashore. How would they get off the ship? Swim, through the surf? How would they get the gold ashore? Ingot by ingot perhaps, in a lifeboat, in the breakers?

Yes, it's probably safe to suggest that West and Wise didn't think the plan over very carefully.

Still, in the wee small hours of the morning of August 21, 1910, there the two of them were, thoroughly braced with spirits and padding along the deck to the wheelhouse of the 253-foot, 2,000-ton passenger steamer S.S. Buckman, ready to give it a good go. The ship was about 20 miles off the mouth of the Umpqua River at the time.

What exactly happened next is a bit hard to know, because every account of the attack is different. But after reading them all, giving extra credence to eyewitness accounts in contemporary newspapers, I'd say this is probably pretty close to what actually happened:

This photo postcard shows the S.S. Admiral Evans, formerly known at the S.S. Buckman, docked at the cannery in Yakutan, Alaska, in 1923. In the summer of 1910, this ship was the subject of perhaps the clumsiest attempt at an act of piracy in the history of the universe. (Image: University of Washington)

This photo postcard shows a wider view of the town of Yukutat, Alaska, with the S.S. Admiral Evans docked at the cannery. The image was most likely made on the same day as the more detailed view of the Admiral Evans, shown at left. (Image: University of Washington)

West and Wise opened the wheelhouse door. Second Mate Fred Plath and Quartermaster Otto Kohlmeister looked up in alarm, and then the guns came out: a revolver in Wise's fist, and a sawed-off double-barrel shotgun in West's hands. Plath was ordered to stretch out on the deck, and Kohlmeister remained, hands on the wheel. According to writer Stan Allyn, he was "cursing vigorously." Kohlmeister was ordered to put the helm over and head for the beach, and he complied.

Already there was a problem: The captain wasn't there. Leaving Wise to cover the two in the wheelhouse, West raced aft to the captain's cabin.

Captain Edwin B. Wood must have already known something was going on. One source suggests he was awakened by a heavy rolling of the ship, which would have told him the vessel had changed direction and was turning toward shore. Given what usually happens when a liner gets too close to the coast, it makes perfect sense that this would ring alarm bells in the skipper's head.

In any case, when West got there he found Captain Wood reaching for a pistol. The pirate raised his sawed-off and let him have both barrels. The captain died in his tracks.

Up in the wheelhouse, the gunfire startled Wise, and he poked his head out to see what had happened. One of his prisoners — most sources say it was Kohmeister — took advantage of this opportunity to yank the whistle cord. The liner's steam-powered whistle screamed a three-digit-decibel alarm. Now suddenly the whole ship was awake and wondering what was going on.

West, hustling back from the captain's cabin, arrived just in time to start collecting crew members. Like lobsters entering a trap, they would run into the wheelhouse to see what was going on and see West there with his guns on them (he had a revolver in addition to his shotgun). West would then order each newcomer to join the growing line of men standing by the bridge ropes.

West sent Wise to smash the radiotelegraph, knowing the on-board "sparky" was probably already warming the apparatus up. Wise, though, lost his nerve, and instead of doing this he ran belowdecks and hid.

This was pretty much the end of West's hopes for a profitable end to the venture. He had about eight crew members lined up in the wheelhouse facing his double-barreled shotgun and revolver, and more crew members were coming up. Then one approached from the other side of the bridge just as West was kneeling down to reload his shotgun.

"Seeing that our chance for escape was ripe, I yelled to the crew to 'run,'" Chief Mate Richard Brennan told the *San Francisco Examiner* afterward. "We all broke in different directions. For my part, I ran and jumped through the galley skylight, landing on the cook's hot stove."

Soon West was alone with Kohlmeister, who never left the ship's wheel the whole time.

Meanwhile, Brennan was running to the captain's cabin, where he got out the dead skipper's revolver. Back to the bridge he skulked with it, and from the shadows about 10 feet away he opened fire, emptying the five-shot pistol (probably a cheap .32- or .38-caliber break-frame pocket revolver) at the bandit.

"He seemed to bear a charmed life, for not a bullet struck him," Brennan told the newspaper. "By this time the lone man was thoroughly scared. He ran back to the smokestack, but as he did so he let another shot go at me. That's the last time I saw him."

Brennan, now the acting captain, ordered the engine shut off and all the lights doused, basically putting the whole show on pause until morning.

When the sun came up, Wise was found huddled in his bunk in steerage, whimpering to himself. He went insane before he could be tried, and was committed to an asylum. Nobody ever found a trace of West; most accounts say he jumped overboard, but nobody actually saw him do so . . . nor do they specify whether he had "help" in doing so.

Sources and works cited:
- Top Deck Twenty: Best West Coast Sea Stories, *a book by Stan Allyn published in 1989 by Binford and Mort;*
- *Archives of the San Francisco Examiner and Portland Morning Oregonian, Aug. 22 and 23, 1910.*

THE ROLLS-ROYCE GURU.

THE BAD IDEA:
- *Try to take over the county government by bringing in homeless people from around the country to vote for you and suppressing other voters by poisoning them.*

THE HORRIBLE PEOPLE:
- *Bhagwan Shree Rajneesh, far-out Indian guru, and "Ma Anand" Sheela Silverman, commune spokeswoman and amateur biochemist.*

I. Inception.

Once upon a time in India, a man lived. He would go on to become one of the most influential thinkers in new-age thought, but at this time — the early 1960s — he was merely a philosophy teacher, and one of thousands of gurus living and discoursing in that land of gurus. His name was Chandra Mohan Jain.

But even then, just a few years out of graduate school, Jain was different.

To call him charismatic would be a colossal understatement. By all accounts, this man could look into your eyes and speak to you for a half hour, and you would hurry home to sell all your earthly possessions to stay near him.

He was charismatic enough that, by 1966, he was drawing big enough crowds and making fat enough cash on the speaking circuit to quit his teaching job at the University of Jabalpur, seven years after taking it, to focus on his "side hustle" as an independent guru.

(It is actually possible that leaving the university wasn't his choice, by the way. Academics will be quick to recognize the significance of the seven-year mark. Someone may have slipped Jain the word that he would be denied tenure if he stayed.)

In any case, once Jain focused his full attention on the guru industry, the world seemed to fall at his feet. The field was very crowded for would-be gurus in India; but Jain — now calling himself by his boyhood nickname of Rajneesh, meaning "moon" — rose quickly through its ranks to become one of the most successful and well known.

He did this with a combination of oratorical skills, philosophical insights, personal charisma, and finely tuned instincts for how far he could go in taking controversial positions without sparking a backlash. At his conferences, lectures, and meditation camps, he criticized some of India's most revered institutions — Hinduism, Mahatma Gandhi and Mother Teresa, traditional morality, the guru system itself. People heard him, heard the certainty in his voice, looked into those hypnotic eyes, and joined his movement on the spot.

As far as religion went, Rajneesh taught that every person was a religion unto him- or herself. Rather than looking outward to some sort of external dogma or prescribed code of conduct, one should look inward, deep inside, throwing off expectations and becoming consistent only with one's own deep identity. There was, he said, a divine core inside each person, and where that core lies, there is God. Nothing outside matters; when you get right with "you-god" on a path to enlightenment, your relationship with the outside world and other people becomes far less important. Obligations? Optional. Guilt? Illegitimate. Compassion for others? Usually desirable, but not always.

It's obviously very different in most ways, but the philosophy of Chandra Mohan Jain had a few things in common with that of philosopher-novelist Ayn Rand. And like Rand, there was a lot there to like, if you were a wealthy person seeking a personal philosophy or a path to spirituality that didn't ask anything from you, require you to share your bounty, or make you feel guilty for being fortunate in life.

As with Rand, there was also a lot there to like if you were young and frustrated with the demands and constraints of society. Jain taught that the impulses and urges that most faith traditions expect young people to resist are simply part of life and should be indulged, not resisted, so as to reduce their forbidden-fruit appeal. The path to desirelessness was through indulgence, Jain taught.

And as with Rand, there was a core sense of elitism there. It was not as

Bhagwan Shree Rajneesh with a group of young disciples at his ashram in Pune, India, in 1977. (Image: Wikimedia | CC-by-SA)

blatant and offensive as Rand's "makers versus takers" paradigm, but it was there — and it would become especially obvious later on: A sense that the wise sannyasin was a special kind of human, and that the laws and morals of the ignorant rubes of the outside world had no legitimate authority over him/her.

Slowly at first, and then more and more rapidly, young and/or wealthy Westerners started to discover this startlingly different guru. His message resonated with them even better than it had with the wealthy of India.

That was especially true after 1968, when, after moving to Mumbai, he started discoursing on sex and love. Sex, he said, was a divine force, a form of worship of the god within, a step on the ladder to enlightenment.

"The primal energy of sex has the reflection of God in it," he said, in a discourse transcribed for publication later as From Sex to Superconsciousness. "It is obvious: it is the energy that creates new life. And that is the greatest, most mysterious force of all."

That sounded well, and very academic; but as a practical matter it translated into urging people to ditch all their cultural and religious norms and taboos around sex.

"Rajneesh gives you the opportunity to sin like you've never sinned before. Only he doesn't call it sin," wrote John Ephland, an ex-follower of the guru, in an article for the Spiritual Counterfeits Project, a Christian organization best known for crossing swords with the Transcendental Meditation movement in the 1970s. "The path to desirelessness is desire."

It was in Mumbai that the guru changed his name, taking the title Bhagwan ("Blessed One") Shree ("Master") Rajneesh. This would be a thing among Rajneeshees until the end — each newly added sannyasin was given a new Hindi name and new clothes colored in various shades of ocher or red.

Rajneesh continued getting more popular, and finding enough space to host his meetings and meditations became a challenge in the city. So he started looking for a place with more room, and in 1974, some of his followers found a private 4-acre enclave in Koregaon Park in the port city of Pune, on which to build the Shree Rajneesh Ashram.

This worked out really well for Rajneesh, at least at first. Now that he had an actual campus, Rajneesh was able to really put on the kind of show that took his attractiveness to Westerners to the next level.

It was at Pune that Rajneesh's movement really hit its stride, especially after 1975 when "therapy" groups were added to the meditation groups offered there. This was an attempt to court more Westerners, and it worked great. However, some of the therapies were . . . unconventional. The most notorious one was Encounter Therapy Group, which met in a windowless room with padded walls in the basement of a building called the Krishna House. Participants screamed, thrashed around, and attacked one another

The Osho International Ashram in Pune, India, as it appears today. (Image: Flyhigh Megh/ Wikimedia | CC-by-SA)

during sessions. There were rumors around Pune that they even engaged in sex acts during Encounter sessions.

In 1979 the ashram announced that violence would no longer be used as a means of emotional catharsis in therapy groups — thereby confirming that it previously had been.

Also, locals in Pune by 1979 had come to consider the ashram a public menace. They called Rajneesh "the sex guru" and resented the thousands of young well-heeled Westerners that filled their town, offending the locals with disrespectful and promiscuous behavior and engaging in drug trafficking and prostitution to raise money for extended stays. Obviously not all the Western followers were lascivious party hounds and criminals, but some of them were, and the ashram was not showing itself to be very serious about policing them.

But no amount of bad press, it seemed, could slow Rajneeshism's growth. The movement soon outgrew the Pune ashram. Four acres sounds like a lot, until you break it down: It's a square of land 417 feet on each side. Many modern supermarkets are more than four acres inside.

Followers started looking for a new place, with room to grow. But by this time word had gotten around India about this renegade guru and the gang of obnoxious young Westerners who had flocked to his banner. They could not find anyplace in India that was willing to have them as neighbors, and so things kept on as they had been, crowded into their little four-acre campus.

Moreover, there were some legal troubles on the horizon too. The Indian government, in 1974, officially revoked Rajneesh's tax-exempt status. The entire time the Pune ashram had been growing by leaps, they had been fighting with the government over this tax bill, and it was increasingly evident that they probably would lose.

Plus, the guru's health was failing him. He had developed diabetes and back troubles, and his allergies were worsening. He needed to move someplace dry anyway. Why not just skip the country entirely, keep the tax money, and never return? He just needed to find a place with wide open spaces and a tradition of leaving one's neighbors alone.

Someplace like ... central Oregon.

II. Arrival.

On June 1, 1981, Bhagwan Shree Rajneesh boarded a Boeing 747 for a flight from Mumbai to New York City.

Officially the trip was for medical treatment, and authorities were told he'd be heading back home to India afterward. But Rajneesh was not planning on returning. His movement, which had already become an international octopus with meditation centers in dozens of different countries around the world, had outgrown the Pune campus. He needed a new World Headquarters. And his new personal secretary, Ma Anand Sheela (formerly known as Sheela Patel Silverman), had found one for him.

Sheela closed the deal for the property then known as the Big Muddy Ranch the following month, paying $5.75 million for it. It was 64,229 acres of Central Oregon rangeland with only the amenities one would expect a family ranch to have. And in late August, she chartered a Learjet to fly the guru in to see, for the first time, the dry landscape that was to be his new home.

It was a bit of a shock for Rajneesh, who had loved the lush greenery and tree-screened privacy of the Pune ashram. "Where are the trees?" he asked, with obvious disappointment.

He soon got over it, though, and settled in. Sheela launched a charm offensive of sorts among the neighbors, hosting a party or two at which local cowboys whooped it up. Soon Central Oregon was feeling pretty sanguine about its new far-out neighbors, and in early November 1981 when the Rajneeshees applied to the Wasco County board of commissioners for permission to incorporate a city on the Big Muddy, they got an easy, informal country-style "yes" — and the City of Rajneeshpuram was born.

It's important to stress, at this point, that the sannyasins at Rajneeshpuram were not all rich libertines in red robes punching each other in Encounter Group. Strange and morally unmoored as Rajneesh's teachings could seem, they sounded logical and innovative and sensible to a certain kind of spiritual seeker. One could place all one's faith in that hypnotic man and, under his guidance, transcend the individuality that so much of life's pain is anchored to. No guilt for past offenses, no sorrow for lost relationships, no shame for the judgements of society, just being in the moment and striving toward Enlightenment. What was not to like? Worldwide, thousands had joined, and the vast majority of them were sincere, sensitive people. They also, as noted earlier, were disproportionately young people.

Not only that, but the sannyasins at Rajneeshpuram were acutely aware that they had the chance to make a new world for themselves and their children. Rajneesh referred to work as "worship," and while that might sound like a cheap Newspeak way to get free labor out of "worshippers," for them it was a meaningful distinction. Especially early on, Rajneeshees at the ranch "worshipped" all day with shovels, hammers, and joy. Many of them recall literally leaping out of bed and running to the workplace every morning.

ALL *of the* ABOVE.

The first "ranch crew" relaxing after a hard day of working to build Rajneeshpuram, in 1981. (Image: Sannyas Wiki | CC-by-SA)

"The work pace is totallismo," wrote a sannyasin named Michael in a letter home to New Zealand, published in a Rajneeshee newsletter; "from dawn till dusk with about 150 of us working heavy machinery, laying foundations for the new Mariam Canteen, warehouse, Bhagwan's garage, school, office block, health centre, and so on; forming the land and setting up the irrigation; putting up about 50 homes, each with space for about 14 people; gardening, cooking and on and on through each hot and dusty day till that cool shower and the queue by the keg of beer at sunset."

When the story of Rajneeshpuram is told, this is the perspective that's most often overlooked. Rajneesh catered carefully to rich people, and plenty of his followers were loaded with dough. But not all of them were, and the core of the experience — once you got beyond Sheela's avaricious crew — was not about money, or sexual freedom, or shaking down the "marks." It was about creating a new community centered on freedom from what you might call the tyranny of self. Arguably, it was a beautiful dream.

But like a lot of Utopian projects over the years, it was about to get hijacked by people who could see its potential as a personal power base.

The locals started getting to know their new far-out neighbors a little, and at first it went well. The Rajneeshees provided plenty of fodder for conversation at cafes and taverns in places like Madras and Redmond. In particular, the contrast between antimaterialist rhetoric and Rajneesh's vast and growing collection of Rolls-Royce cars (which eventually numbered 94) raised some eyebrows, and the exclusive choice of red clothing made them instantly recognizable and a little funny-looking. There may have been the occasional rumor of violence or sex in Encounter Therapy sessions, as in the Pune ashram; but if so, they didn't get much traction, and anyway most Eastern Oregonians are strongly inclined to mind their own business.

In Pune, Rajneesh had become known as "the sex guru"; in Oregon, he quickly became known as "the Rolls-Royce guru." People often saw him driving around in one of his big luxury cars; he wasn't a very good driver, but he was a fast one, and he occasionally got into crashes. Drivers who waved at him as they drove by got treated to the alarming sight of him taking both hands off the wheel and both eyes off the road to do a "namaste" salute back as his three tons of English steel careened past at well above safe highway speed. Few waved at him twice.

A flyer advertising the first World Celebration at Rajneeshpuram in 1982. (Image: Sannyas Wiki | CC-by-SA)

And at first, that was as bad as it got. All seemed to be going smoothly. But trouble was already on the horizon for the commune, and it wouldn't take long to arrive at their door.

The first big problem was centered around a mistake Sheela had made before buying the Big Muddy: she hadn't done any research into Oregon's land-use laws. These, as it turned out, were some of the most restrictive in the nation, and they were aimed at preventing exactly the kind of thing the Bhagwan's crew had in mind: the conversion of farmland into new urban and suburban spaces.

And Sheela's charm offensive hadn't won over some of the locals. A

ALL *of the* ABOVE.

Rajneeshpuram during the 1983 World Festival. (Image: Sannyas Wiki | CC-by-SA)

month after Rajneeshpuram was incorporated, three nearby ranch families got together with a land-use watchdog group, 1000 Friends of Oregon, and filed an appeal with the Land Use Board of Appeals, seeking to invalidate the county's decision to allow the city's incorporation.

Naturally, this played poorly with Sheela and Rajneesh. A clumsy attempt to bribe 1000 Friends made things worse, and from this point on, the commune was more or less in a cold war with the rest of Oregon.

While the appeals courts kicked the case up and down the line from local courts to the state supreme court and back, development continued at Rajneeshpuram. The city issued hundreds of building permits and dozens of business licenses, established a police force, and installed utilities for water and sewer service.

The land-use challenge was bad enough for the commune, but was probably survivable. Then as now, it's hard to make a case that running cattle at one head per 40 acres is a higher and better use of the land than a self-sufficient semi-urban community surrounded by an organic farming operation. If land use had been the only issue, the parties would probably have soon come to some kind of an agreement that let Rajneeshpuram continue in exchange for some mitigation work and common-sense restrictions on zoning and land use.

What really became a problem, and what made such an agreement impossible for the state or 1000 Friends to consider, was the pattern of

The town of Rajneesh, formerly and subsequently known as Antelope, as it appeared in 1985, near the end of the Rajneeshees' tenancy in Oregon. (Image: Ted Quackenbush | CC-by-SA)

dishonesty that quickly became apparent among the leaders at Rajneeshpuram.

Put simply, the top sannyasins considered state and federal laws to lack any legitimate authority over them.

So any time a law conflicted with what the Rajneeshee leaders wanted to do, the choice they made was whether to pretend to obey the law or to defy it openly. Following the law in good faith seemed to be strictly optional.

Throughout the time the Rajneeshees were in Oregon, the law would be used a lot as a weapon against those who felt themselves to be bound by it; but the commune's leaders never for a moment considered it legitimate. And that became obvious very quickly as non-sannyasin Oregonians started interacting with the group.

There was also a clear sense of contempt, a sense that the commune's authorities (and especially Sheela) considered non-Sannyasin Oregonians to be categorically a bunch of ignorant, small-minded hicks who should be easy to manipulate or dupe. This came through, loud and clear, in media appearances and interviews, and it started to change the perception of the commune from "harmless weirdos" to "offensive and probably crazy weirdos." Before long, 1000 Friends started discovering that its land-use fight with Rajneeshpuram was solid fund-raising gold. Donations poured in, reinforcing the battle lines.

The next serious source of trouble came when Oregon Attorney General

Dave Frohnmayer noticed that the city of Rajneeshpuram was operating under something similar to Sharia Law — the government of the town was the religion of the town. So in late 1983 Frohnmayer sued to get Rajneeshpuram's incorporation overturned on separation-of-church-and-state grounds.

Meanwhile, Ma Anand Sheela was talking to the media every chance she got. Oregonians were starting to get very used to seeing her on TV categorizing them all as "ignorant bigots" and worse.

By the end of 1983 or so, the Rajneeshees could see that there was a real possibility they would lose the fight to keep Rajneeshpuram incorporated as a city. Also, because the state of Oregon considered Rajneeshpuram illegitimate, the FBI had cut off the Rajneeshpuram Peace Force's access to the National Crime Information System database, which Sheela's crew had found super useful for digging up dirt on political enemies.

So they decided to take over a town that was already incorporated and transfer their energies over to that.

Their eyes turned, naturally, on the closest town to the ranch: Antelope, population 43.

III. Occupation.

In the courtyard at the Antelope Post Office today, there stands a large bronze plaque attached to the base of a flagpole. It reads, "Dedicated to those of this community who throughout the Rajneesh invasion and occupation of 1981-1985 remained, resisted and remembered."

Most visitors probably roll their eyes at this, thinking it a bit melodramatic. Invasion? Occupation? Puh-leeze, they might mutter.

But the Rajneeshee takeover of Antelope was not an anodyne bureaucratic exercise. To those who lived through it, it really did feel like a foreign military power had rolled into their town and occupied it.

It started out very stealthily. Several properties in the town were up for sale, and suddenly there were offers on all of them. Very ordinary-looking people signed the documents and took possession. Then some more very ordinary-looking people moved into the properties. Quite a few of them, actually. The population of the town nearly doubled.

They lived there in Antelope, keeping to themselves as much as possible, until just before election season, when several of them filed for election as city officials.

Then the truth came out: The new residents were Rajneeshees, and they were out to take over the town.

At the same time, the Rajneeshee leaders launched a concerted campaign to get other Antelope residents to leave town. They tried to buy people's houses, and those who would not sell were relentlessly harassed. Red-clad photographers with ostentatious cameras parked outside their houses, photographing them when they came and went, photographing their children when they left for school, following them around, staring whenever they could catch their eyes.

The Antelope residents scrambled to try and head off the invasion. They called an emergency meeting and set up a vote to disincorporate the town; but the Rajneeshees got word of it and made sure to vote in the resulting election, and there was only so much resistance the few dozen voters of Antelope could do. The vote was defeated, and, that November, so were the incumbent mayor and city officials of Antelope.

The victorious Rajneeshees promptly renamed the town Rajneesh and got busy approving variances and building permits.

By this time, nearly all executive decisions were being made by Bhagwan Shree Rajneesh's personal secretary, the ever-bellicose Ma Anand Sheela; Rajneesh himself had "entered a period of silence" and was speaking only to her and a few other Rajneeshee leaders.

Now those leaders, having tasted this cup of power, decided to expand their power base by taking over all of Wasco County using the same playbook that had worked so well in Antelope.

To do this would be trickier, though. Wasco County had about 21,000 non-Sannyasin residents, roughly 12,000 of whom were registered to vote. At least half of those voters could probably be counted on to actively oppose the takeover.

But Sheela had a plan for that: a plan called the "Share-a-Home Program."

The Share-A-Home program was launched in 1984, and cost the Rajneeshees about $1 million.

The way it worked was, sannyasins fanned out across the country driving chartered buses, recruiting homeless people to come to Rajneeshpuram to live ... and, of course, vote.

Free food, shelter, and (red) clothing: It was a compelling idea for anyone shivering under a railroad bridge in Seattle or Boston or Oakland. Thousands took them up on it.

As primary season approached in 1984, the population of the twin cities of Rajneeshpuram and Rajneesh (Antelope) swelled to over 7,000. Every newcomer to the commune was promptly registered as a Wasco County voter.

ALL *of the* ABOVE.

Air Rajneesh's fleet of passenger aircraft parked at the airport. The largest were a Douglas DC-3 and a Convair 240. (Image: Ted Quackenbush | CC-by-SA)

This was probably the point at which the Rajneeshees definitively lost the fight to stay in Oregon. Because, well, it was one thing to have a bunch of far-out mystics developing a piece of Oregon's outback; nobody really minded that. The takeover of Antelope had been bad, but Antelope was a tiny place, and the whole thing was easily understood as the commune's only option for having a municipality. The nastiness of the campaign to drive the locals out was a public-relations disaster, as was an attempt to force local farm kids to attend Rajneeshee schools; but these weren't the kinds of missteps that can't be recovered from with a quick course-correction and a little public-relations balm.

However, when Sheela and her operatives started scheming to seize power at the county level, disenfranchising thousands of Wasco County residents — and doing so in such a transparent and intelligence-insulting way, obviously thinking their plan was too clever and subtle for the local rubes to catch onto — they lost any claim they might have had on the moral high ground.

From that point on, the story of Rajneeshpuram would be a series of increasingly desperate and petulant rear-guard actions and acts of open spitefulness that quickly escalated to crime.

The state's response to Share-a-Home was a fairly obvious one: Secretary of State Norma Paulus stopped all voter registration in Wasco County and assigned a fleet of attorneys from her staff to travel to the county and interview each and every new registrant, to make sure that person actually intended to live in the county.

This, as far as the takeover plan was concerned, was checkmate. But Sheela and her lieutenants tried to play through it. If they couldn't pack the voter rolls to achieve a winning majority, maybe they could depress voter turnout enough to win . . . .

And so it was that, in the summer of 1984, Sheela and her cronies — most notably Ma Anand Puja, a.k.a. Diane Omang, the director of the commune's medical service — started poisoning people, testing formulas and seeing what might work.

First they poisoned two Wasco County Commissioners with cultured bacteria stirred into glasses of water offered to them while they were on a visit to the site. Then Sheela and Puja led a team into The Dalles to dribble cultured salmonella bacteria on the salad bars in several restaurants near the freeway.

Hundreds of people got sick — the official count is about 750, but likely there were many more, minor cases involving people who didn't bother to seek medical attention. It was the biggest biological-warfare attack in U.S. history.

Bhagwan Shree Rajneesh takes his daily drive along a road lined with his disciples. The drive was a regular daily ritual for sannyasins at the commune. (Image: Samvado Gunnar Kossatz / CC-by-SA)

The attack is still baffling today, because it was carried out a month and a half before the elections. Was it supposed to be a trial run, to test the poisons in advance to make sure they would be effective? If so, it was a really stupid move, as it put Wasco County on notice; the salad bars were shut down, and people became very serious about handwashing and other hygienic preventions. Was it supposed to actually kill people, thereby removing them from the voter rolls? If so, it was even stupider. Either way, it was not exactly a 4-D chess move.

At the time, nobody really knew the source of the food poisoning. But almost everyone suspected the Rajneeshees, and that was enough to put the stink of criminality on the commune — all of them, not just Sheela and her gang. This was a bigger deal than it has later been made out to be. Rank-and-file Rajneeshees were not the kind of nasty monsters that some of their leaders were turning out to be. They were mostly goodhearted, normal people who had found a new vision for life under the charismatic spell of Bhagwan Shree Rajneesh. They were there to bask in his wisdom, dissolve themselves into his movement, and be a part of something that was creating (as they saw it) good things in the world.

Poisoning people, stockpiling and brandishing automatic weapons, ghosting ex-members, harassing former Antelope residents with cameras — these were all very off-brand actions for them. But more and more, these were coming to characterize life in Rajneeshpuram.

A creeping demoralization started percolating into the ranks of the sannyasins, and a sort of bunker mentality — a sense similar to that of a people at war. But, remember, these were people who had sold everything to start a new life in Rajneeshpuram. This was their home now; they had burned their boats. They had little choice other than to hunker down and hope for the best.

IV. Unraveling.

After the election, the new formerly homeless residents of Rajneeshpuram were the most pressing problem for Bhagwan Shree Rajneesh and his followers. They cost a lot of money to feed and house, and they started fights and made trouble.

Rajneeshee leaders started out giving them bus tickets home, but that got very expensive very fast. After all, it had cost $1 million to bring them in by busloads; sending them home one or two at a time would be many times more than that.

So finally, the Rajneeshees gave up and, herding them all aboard buses, simply hauled them to downtown Madras and dropped them off.

Social-services agencies were forced to take on the task of getting them all home. The Salvation Army alone spent more than $100,000 taking care of them. Other Oregonians dug deep to help out as well.

By early 1985 the Rajneeshpuram experiment was a clear failure and was obviously doomed. Rajneesh's personal secretary, Ma Anand Sheela, whose natural stubbornness continued to lead her into outright stupidity, was trying to take advantage of the homelessness problem she had created by seeking a meeting with Governor Vic Atiyeh in which she hoped to use the crisis as bargaining leverage. This, of course, went nowhere. But it made it clear to anyone who might not yet have figured it out that the Rajneeshees could not be worked with, and the only solution was to get them out of Oregon.

As the investigative walls closed in, Sheela and her staff lashed out. They tried to burn down the Wasco County Planning Department office in January 1985, plotted to crash an airplane loaded with explosives into the Wasco County Courthouse, and even tried a few assassinations. None of these efforts succeeded. But an attempt to kill Rajneesh's personal physician, Swami Devaraj, nearly did. One of Sheela's lieutenants jabbed him with a syringe during a Rajneeshee festival, injecting him with what she thought would be a lethal dose of adrenaline. She was nearly right.

A Buddhafield Transportation bus brings sannyasins to Rajneeshpuram past the marble welcome sign. (Image: Sannyas Wiki | CC-by-SA)

> ### "Shut Up, Sheela": The hit single
>
> One particularly memorable contribution to Oregon's effort to get the homeless people taken care of came from Portland disc jockeys Dan Clark and Dave Kanner at radio station KZOO, who made a parody version of the 1962 Tommy Roe classic "Sheila," which they called "Shut Up Sheela" and released on the B side of a 45-rpm record made of red vinyl. Proceeds of the record sale went to help the homeless, and plenty of copies were sold.
> The lyrics ran like this:
>
> *Sweet little Sheela, Ma Anand Sheela,*
> *You're the Bhagwan's right-hand gal*
> *Big-mouthed Sheela, Ma Anand Sheela,*
> *You should take a silence vow.*
>
> *Shut up Sheela, on the news we see ya,*
> *Sayin' words you should not say,*
> *She's a red disaster, that is why we ask her*
> *To dry up and blow away.*
>
> *Me and Sheela go for a ride, oh oh oh oh feelin' funny inside.*
> *Then little Sheela screams in my ear, ow! Ow! Ow! Shut up Sheela dear.*
>
> *Sheela said she'd feed me, she said she'd never leave me,*
> *But the bus won't come around*
> *I'm so doggone angry, stuck in Wasco County,*
> *Man this little girl is loud.*
>
> *Never knew a girl like a little Sheela,*
> *Her name drives me insane,*
> *And everyone in Madras Sheela calls a fascist*
> *Says man this little girl's a pain.*

(By the way, the motive for wanting to kill Devaraj was a rumor Sheela had heard, that Rajneesh had asked him to prepare a suicide pill for him to use if things got really bad. It's not clear if the rumor was true and it's super unlikely Devaraj would have complied with this request if it was made; but apparently Sheela took it seriously.)

By now the hostile energy was really affecting the rank-and-file

Rajneeshees, and it was causing the group's income to collapse. Remember, these were spiritual seekers who were actually paying to be there and working all day on a volunteer basis. Being surrounded by hard-eyed men with Uzis all the time, and being forbidden to run to Madras to shop, made the experience of living at Rajneeshpuram a lot less appealing. And Rajneesh's continuing penchant for buying Rolls-Royces — by the end he had 94 of them — added insult to injury. It seems pretty clear that Rajneesh didn't yet understand how bad things had gotten. Sheela would come back from battling with state officials and insulting Oregon residents on TV and have to deal with the oblivious Rajneesh demanding another Rolls — he really wanted to get into the Guinness Book of World Records as the man who owned the largest collection of them.

Finally, at long last realizing the case was hopeless, Sheela and her cabal fled the country, leaving Rajneesh behind to salvage what he might.

Rajneesh did so by basically throwing Sheela under the bus, blaming her alone for all the stupid and illegal activities and inviting law enforcement to come to Rajneeshpuram to gather the evidence they'd need against her.

And yes, they found plenty.

They found two laboratories set up to produce biological and chemical agents that could certainly be used as weapons. They also found some books detailing how that might be done. "Deadly Substances," "Handbook for Poisoning," "The Perfect Crime and How to Commit It" and "Let Me Die Before I Wake" were some of the titles.

Investigators for state and federal agencies and police departments, invited to come to Rajneeshpuram and build a case, got a real earful. Rajneesh told his followers to be completely frank and open, and they were. The depth and breadth of the criminal misconduct they learned about astonished them.

Perhaps the investigations went a little too well, though, because a few days later Rajneesh started getting less cooperative. Doubtless he was eager to help get Sheela prosecuted — he clearly felt betrayed by her — but the investigators were asking other questions as well, and some of them were landing very close to the guru himself. This was especially true with questions of his immigration status.

At the same time, some of the law enforcement officers were getting very nervous about what they were seeing at Rajneeshpuram. By now — summer of 1985 — the Rajneesh "Peace Force" was bristling with Colt AR-15 rifles and other military-style firearms, including the semi-automatic civilian variant of the Uzi submachine gun. Most investigators saw it as mostly theater, to make the group look like a harder target; but there

ALL *of the* ABOVE.

Rajneeshpuram as seen from an aerial shot up the canyon circa 1984. (Image: Sannyas Wiki | CC-by-SA)

were a lot of guns, and a lot of ammunition, and the whole compound was arranged very effectively for urban defense.

To make matters even more nerve-wracking, Rajneesh had, after Sheela's departure, lifted the red-clothing requirement for the group. This meant if something went horribly wrong, it would be very hard for outsiders to tell friend from foe.

Police in the compound — both investigators invited in by Rajneesh and undercover agents posing as followers — started warning darkly that any attempt to arrest Rajneesh would be likely to turn messy and bloody. The worst-case scenario still fresh in everyone's mind was Jonestown, which had happened just a few years earlier.

Bhagwan Shree Rajneesh's booking photo from 1985. (Image: Multnomah County)

Then came the spark that could have blown the whole thing up: The warrant came through. It was a sealed indictment from a court in Portland charging Rajneesh with immigration violations.

This presented law enforcement officers with a serious problem. It was now their duty to go and get him. But they would have to be very careful. It was not hard to imagine what the Peace Patrol could potentially do: they had hundreds of innocent noncombatants in their direct control and a huge arsenal at their disposal. They could surround themselves with a human shield of women and children. They could take hostages. Would they? What would they do?

Luckily, no one ever found out. Because a few days later, Rajneesh boarded a chartered Learjet and flew to North Carolina with a small entourage of his people. This flight has been characterized as an attempt to flee to Bermuda, and it may have been so; but the complete absence of any kind of secrecy, along with the fact that he filed a detailed flight plan with the Federal Aviation Administration and followed it to the letter, suggests that Rajneesh was at least half expecting to be intercepted. Most likely his departure was motivated by Rajneesh's growing worries that his presence could bring trouble upon his people.

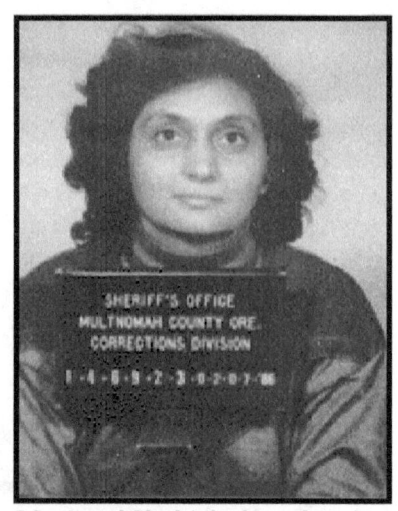

Ma Anand Sheela's booking photo from 1985. (Image: Multnomah County)

In any case, Rajneesh's flight meant that instead of having to invade a

ALL *of the* ABOVE.

The only evidence of Rajneeshees in Antelope today is this plaque, mounted to a flagpole base at the Antelope Post Office. It reads, "Dedicated to those of this community who throughout the Rajneesh invasion and occupation of 1981-1985 remained, resisted and remembered." (Image: F.J.D. John)

heavily armed compound with a huge SWAT team, authorities simply had to dispatch two U.S. Marshals Service officers to the North Carolina airport and pick him up there.

V. Aftermath.

And that was the end of it. Germany extradited Sheela to the U.S. for trial on various charges including arson, poisoning, and assault. She worked out a deal that included a few years in federal prison, from which she was released in 1988, after which she immediately married a Swiss sannyasin named Urs Birnstiel and left for Switzerland with him.

Rajneesh was simply deported after receiving a prison sentence for immigration violations, suspended on condition that he leave immediately and not return. By this time, he was happy to comply.

Several other members of Rajneeshpuram's leadership also drew prison time for their various escapades. And the rank-and-file sannyasins were left to piece their lives back together as best they could. This was no small thing for most of them; many had actually sold everything they had and contributed all the proceeds to Rajneeshpuram.

And they probably wouldn't be getting any of it back. The organization had more than $57 million on its books at the start of 1985; by the time of Sheela's flight, nearly all of it had disappeared somewhere. Sheela claimed to be unable to pay $270,000 of her fine to the state of Oregon. Where had the money gone? Nobody ever figured that out.

As of the time of this writing, Sheela is still alive and living in Switzerland. Her marriage to Urs Birnstiel came about in the nick of time for her, as it made her eligible for Swiss residency and subsequently citizenship. Fresh from the slammer, she skipped out two steps ahead of the law, which wanted her to face trial for attempted murder in some of the assassination schemes she'd participated in.

Birnstiel died of AIDS in 1992, leaving Sheela a widow and a Swiss citizen by marriage. Switzerland does not extradite its citizens to face charges in foreign courts, so she is quite safe so long as she stays there in country. The Rajneeshees were well known for having members marry each other for citizenship reasons, going back to the Pune ashram days; chances are pretty good Sheela's marriage was at least partly motivated by desire to get her safely out of the U.S. and beyond the reach of extradition.

And as for Rajneesh, after moving back to India and changing his name to Osho, he died in 1990 of a sudden heart attack at age 58. He left behind more than 650 books — transcriptions of his lectures and discourses — which have since been translated into more than four dozen languages. His stock as a guru has never been higher, and hundreds of thousands of people come to his "Osho International Meditation Resort" in Pune every year.

In Oregon, though, his name is still mud — after all these years.

ALL *of the* ABOVE.

Sources and works cited:
- A Roadside History of Oregon, *a book by Bill Gulick published in 1991 by Mountain Press;*
- *"The Rajneesh Story," an article by Win McCormack from* Great Moments in Oregon History: A Collection of Articles from Oregon Magazine, *an anthology published in 1987 by New Oregon Publishers;*
- *"Osho? Oh no!," an article by Rachel Graham published in the Feb. 2, 2000, issue of* Willamette Week;
- *"Osho-Bhagwan, The Movie," a movie directed by Robert Hillman released in 1978.*

www.ingramcontent.com/pod-product-compliance
Lightning Source LLC
Chambersburg PA
CBHW020728220426
43209CB00095B/1967/J